HOPE DEFERRED

This book is dedicated to all the people who spent many hours—and in some cases days—sharing their stories with us.

And to the writer Charles Mungoshi

HOPE DEFERRED
NARRATIVES OF ZIMBABWEAN LIVES

EDITED BY

PETER ORNER AND ANNIE HOLMES

WITH A FOREWORD BY

BRIAN CHIKWAVA

Associate editors

AURORA BRACKETT, JOSEPH CHIKOWERO,
DOUG FORD, BEAUTIE MASVAURE

Assistant editors

NATALIE BASZILE, THEMBA BUTAO, GIYANI DUBE,
ALEX GORDON, KATE RUTLEDGE JAFFE, JOHN KNIGHT,
BECCA LEAPHART, M.H., THEODORE MCDERMOTT, SARA
MARINELLI, DYLAN MOHR, BRIAN NGWENYA, KATE REELER,
ONNESHA ROYCHOUDHURI, LAURA LAMPTON SCOTT,
JANE SHEPHERD, TUCKER SLOSBURG

Research editor

ALEX CARP

VOICE OF WITNESS

VOICE OF WITNESS

M^CSWEENEY'S BOOKS
SAN FRANCISCO

For more information about McSweeney's, see *mcsweeneys.net*
For more information about Voice of Witness, see *voiceofwitness.org*

ISBN (Hardcover): 978-1-934781-94-4
ISBN (Paperback): 978-1-934781-93-7

VOICE OF WITNESS

The books in the Voice of Witness series seek to illuminate human rights crises by humanizing the victims. Using oral history as a foundation, the series explores social justice issues through the stories of the men and women who experience them. These books are designed for readers of all levels—from high school and college students to policymakers—interested in a reality-based understanding of ongoing injustices in the United States and around the world. Visit *voiceofwitness.org* for more information.

VOICE OF WITNESS BOARD OF DIRECTORS

VOICE OF WITNESS BOARD OF ADVISORS

CONTENTS

FOREWORD: *History by Ordinary People* 11
INTRODUCTION: *Nzara* 15
NOTES FROM THE ROAD: *Rusape, July 2009* 25

SECTION 1: *Exile* 27
   VIOLET 29
   AARON 41
   ELIZABETH 55
   ZENZELE 73

SECTION 2: *Matabeleland* 99
   JOHN 103
   NOKUTHULA 127
   BONIFACE 145

SECTION 3: *Farms* 165
   TSITSI 169
   GEORGE 187

SECTION 4: *Rurals* 213
   ALICE 215
   LOVEMORE 229

SECTION 5: *Mountains* 249
   SAMUEL 253
   BRIAN 259
   NICOLA 267
   EDMORE 283

SECTION 6: *The Capital* 301
   FATHER JOHN 305
   PAMELA AND THEMBA 323
   BRIGGS 329

SECTION 7: *Border* 361
   OSCAR 363
   BERNARD 379
   AMOS 395
   MATTHEW 399
   RUDO 405

SECTION 8: *Sankoh Chari Is Still Alive* 427
   SANKOH 429

APPENDICES 459

HISTORY BY ORDINARY PEOPLE

by Brian Chikwava, author of Harare North

It may be apposite to start in the tradition of the authorities of Zimbabwe by declaring that over the past decade this little country has been a land of milk and honey. Of course one way of reconciling this with the hard reality—as the ordinary Zimbabwean always must in jaunty township bars—would be to further the story and suggest that Zimbabweans are flies. For a fly that lands on honey is doomed, as is one that finds itself floating in a pail of milk. Only when it lands on dung does it truly strike bliss. Curious then how, given what has gone on in Zimbabwe over the past decade, bliss has been elusive, except for a few. Again, in the township bar, such discrepancy may be resolved by suggesting that it is not Zimbabweans that are flies per se, but their political elite who thrive on dung.

The disconnect between the stories told by a state and those told by its citizens at best obscures the moral choices that must be made, and some states may well prefer it that way. It is probably for this reason that the novelist Louis De Bernières once said that "history ought to be made up of the stories of ordinary people only." Indeed, no matter how long one stares at the darker patches of a nation's history, it is only from the low, street-level vantage point of the ordinary person that one is able to point a torch at the cost of the choices that nation is making or has already made. From the lofty heights of men of power the torchlight vanishes into the vast night long before it hits the ground. For that reason, yes, one can understand why political history must be read alongside social history; on its own the former becomes a vulgar abstraction of the truth if not a clanging lie, in which case it deservedly becomes the subject of ridicule in the local bar.

The histories, or stories that we tell ourselves, like the songs we sing, make us who we are. On the personal level, our stories are the tools by which we recall events of import in our own lives, how we interpret those events and ultimately how we hold our sense of self together when times are such that we could easily lose ourselves and our way. Once, I was told of a young and restless writer-woman living in exile in the capitals of Europe. Her family was a closely knit unit with whom she had lived for nearly all of her life, until she had to come to London. But exile is a hard place even for the toughest; one has to find a place in a new environment, wrestle loneliness, sometimes suffer a temporary loss of social language and be plunged into expansive silences in life. As is often said, you can be at your most lonely right in the middle of a throbbing crowd. In the crowd that is London, this young woman felt herself slipping through her own fingers. And so started a compulsion to call her family every evening and unfailingly relate her day to them and describe how her plans worked out. Asked why she felt that compulsion, her answer was that if she failed to talk over what had happened during her day, sometimes it felt as if it had not happened at all; what had happened and what had been imagined became impossible to tell apart. Probably a rare case, hers, but what can not be underplayed is what it says about the psychological significance of storytelling and holding onto one's self.

One reads this collection with heartbreak, at times laughter, but ultimately a sense of triumph against all odds. In some way a good number of the people behind these stories have, no doubt, been alone in the crowd of humanity heaving across our globe and known exile on so many levels, physically and in their minds. As the poet Gwyneth Lewis once shrewdly observed: exile, with its attendant loss of language, mimics depression, and vice versa. Yet perhaps the greatest achievement of this collection of stories is how it has enabled each of these individuals to emerge out of their blue depths clutching their experiences and to reclaim themselves in a manner at once irrepressible and life affirming.

There are indomitable spirits like Elizabeth, whose fearlessly free-thinking instincts could not be accommodated within her family; quietly resilient individuals like Samuel, who have known what it's like to have your innocence rudely yanked from your hands; the wild and unaffected George, who has witnessed brutality and prejudice by both the Rhodesian and Zimbabwean states; Aaron, who knows why the devil's household has an appetite for its servants' heads; and Zenzele, whose noble determination to serve the people saw him unwittingly step on the devil's tail.

If victim and perpetrator are sometimes hard to tell apart, it is perhaps only because things, in the manner of things, sometimes make it such that the ordinary person can only maintain a particular moral or political posture for so long without the survival instinct kicking in. At the end of the day the ordinary person becomes a mere conduit through which larger power struggles operate. In that way, a torturer can easily become victim, or vice versa, depending on your vantage point. But the stories that make any nation what it is and the moral choices it has made are always better understood from the level of the ordinary citizen than from the high-placed seat of the weaver of the overarching national narrative. For that reason this collection is an invaluable addition not only to our sense of what it means to be Zimbabwean, but also to the record of what it means to be human.

Brian Chikwava is a London-based Zimbabwean writer and author of the novel Harare North, *which will be published in the U.S. by Random House in 2011. He is a winner of the Caine Prize for African Writing and a former Charles Pick fellow at the University of East Anglia. He is currently working on his second novel.*

NZARA

by Annie Holmes and Peter Orner

The Shona word for drought is *nzara*, which literally means "hunger" or "suffering."[1] Nzara is an apt metaphor for the crisis in Zimbabwe, which over the last decade has devastated thousands, even millions of lives, while leaving a tiny minority not only unscathed but enriched. The drought of human rights and accountability in Zimbabwe began in the late 1990s, although its roots can be traced back to more than a hundred years of colonial and white-minority rule.[2] But on March 29, 2008, election day in Zimbabwe, there was hope for a break in the metaphorical drought. A well-mobilized opposition seemed set to carry the vote after the least violent election build-up in a decade.

This collection examines Zimbabwe's recent history through that window of expectation, a historical moment from which individual Zimbabweans trace their experiences before and since.

---

[1] Shona is the dominant African language in Zimbabwe. The three principal languages spoken in the country are Shona, Ndebele, and English, Zimbabwe's official language. The equivalent Ndebele word to *nzara* is *indlala*.

[2] Zimbabwe was originally colonized by the British in 1893, and later became known as Southern Rhodesia. In 1965, a white-minority Rhodesian government repudiated British rule, and issued the Unilateral Declaration of Independence (UDI). For an outline of the struggles against colonial and white-minority rule in Zimbabwe, see the appendix.

* * *

In 1980, Zimbabwe was considered a jewel of Southern Africa.[3] The country had emerged from decades of colonialism and a brutal liberation struggle against the Rhodesian military to become a unified nation, one committed to democracy, reconciliation, human and civil rights for all, universal education, and economic development. Hope was in the air, and people throughout Southern Africa (and in apartheid South Africa in particular) were looking toward Zimbabwe as a beacon. Robert Mugabe, leader of the Zimbabwean African National Union (Zanu) party, and a renowned freedom fighter turned statesman, had been swept into office after a landslide victory in the nation's first free elections, and was considered by many to be the ideal man to oversee Zimbabwe's emergence.

Soon, however, in spite of significant economic and social reform, cracks began to show in the façade of Zimbabwe's great promise. Mugabe's ruling party—now called Zanu-PF[4]—moved to consolidate power and crush opposition. In the early 1980s, the army was sent into the Matabeleland and Midlands provinces in the south, the traditional home of the Ndebele minority. Ostensibly, the goal was to root out supposed traitors among the former soldiers of the Zipra, the former liberation army of the Zapu,[5] but the operation soon became a larger campaign of intimidation. About 20,000 people are believed to have been killed in the prolonged violence.

The campaign, known as Gukurahundi, lasted from 1982 to 1987. To this day, it remains an event not openly discussed in many quarters of Zimbabwe. It went without public acknowledgment until the Catholic Justice and Peace Commission finally released a long-suppressed report in

---

[3] For a more detailed account of Zimbabwe's history—including key issues and a glossary of key figures and organizations—please see the appendices. Briggs's and John's narratives provide compelling historical overviews as well.

[4] Zimbabwe African National Union–Patriotic Front. See the appendices for more on the evolution of Zimbabwe's political parties.

[5] Zimbabwean African People's Union, a liberation movement led by Joshua Nkomo.

2008.[6] But a number of narratives in this book suggest that the success of Gukurahundi set the stage for future, similar violent actions on the part of the government.

Even after the violence in the south lessened, things continued to get worse. A severe (actual) drought in the early 1990s, together with disastrous International Monetary Fund economic restructuring, weakened the economy considerably. Growing political corruption did little to help matters. Zimbabwe, once a proudly self-reliant agricultural powerhouse, was forced to import food for the first time.

In the late 1990s, occupation of mostly white-owned commercial farms accelerated. At the 1979 Lancaster House conference that led to independence from foreign rule, Mugabe had pledged to introduce major land redistribution. In return, Western countries, particularly Britain, Zimbabwe's former colonial power, promised substantial funding to ensure a willing-buyer, willing-seller basis for the new government's acquisition of land.[7] Yet the Zimbabwean government resettled under 40 percent of the targeted peasant families, and Britain cut short the funding, citing corruption and cronyism in the land-redistribution process.

In 1999, the government was confronted by angry war veterans of the liberation struggle demanding recompense for their sacrifices. Government payouts triggered a dive in international confidence, a crash in the value of the Zimbabwean currency, and, eventually, ruling-party support for the war veterans' occupation of commercial farms—a move generally seen as politically motivated. Occupations and land seizures turned violent. The international media focused on the white landowners, fuelling support for Mugabe, among some, as an African nationalist.

---

[6] *Gukurahundi* is a Shona word that means "the early rain that washes away the chaff before the spring rains." See: *Gukurahundi in Zimbabwe: A Report on the Disturbances in Matabeleland and the Midlands, 1980–1988* (Columbia University Press) prepared by the Catholic Commission for Justice and Peace and the Legal Resources Foundation.

[7] See the introduction to Section 3, "Farms," for more on land, as well as the narratives of Briggs, Tsitsi, and George.

In 2000, the government proposed amendments to Zimbabwe's constitution that included the further expansion of Mugabe's presidential powers. The new constitution was defeated in a national referendum, in large part due to organizing by a new political party, the Movement for Democratic Change (MDC), led by a trade unionist named Morgan Tsvangirai. The defeat came as a great shock to the government, and a wake-up call to civil-society groups across Zimbabwe. Change, it turned out, was possible.

Soon after the referendum defeat, the government accelerated the forced takeover of commercial farms. The fiery narrative of race and ethnicity that accompanied "Fast Track Land Reform," said many observers, served to smokescreen government failures and corruption. Land reform, it seemed, was less about restoring racial and economic justice, and more about entrenching power and enriching loyal elites.

Soon the industrial sector, like the agricultural sector, began to decline seriously. Most of the population experienced growing food shortages. Meanwhile, the MDC and other opposition groups built increased support across the nation.

By 2008, Zimbabwe was an economic disaster. Inflation topped 11 million percent. In March of that year, one U.S. dollar traded for twenty-five million Zimbabwean dollars; two months later, it traded for a billion. Food prices often tripled overnight, and the salaries of the few who still earned them (unemployment exceeded 80 percent) became virtually worthless. While a small group of elites continued to reap outrageous profits, many Zimbabweans did their best to survive on one meal a day.

The education system had been a great success story—for decades Zimbabwe could boast of one of the highest rates of literacy in Africa—but now it too began to collapse. By early 2009, many of the country's more than seven thousand schools were closed, and school attendance plunged from 85 percent in 2007 to just 20 percent in 2009.[8] An estimated 20,000

---

[8] See "School Attendance Plummets to just 20%," by Lisa Schlien, (January 8–14, 2009) in *The Zimbabwean*, an independent newspaper published in the U.K., quoting a statistic released by the United Nations Children's Fund.

teachers left their jobs because they were being paid in virtually worthless Zimbabwean dollars or harassed as supporters of the opposition.

Holding fast to the rhetoric of law and order, the government passed draconian legislation to justify the repression of opposing voices. State and party groups—often supported by the police and the army—were given free reign to terrorize the populace and intimidate the opposition. People began leaving Zimbabwe in ever greater numbers. Some estimates say that possibly up to a third of the population has crossed international borders in recent years, some fleeing the violence, others desperately seeking work.[9] Countless others have been internally displaced.

Many of these problems can be linked to the March 2008 presidential and parliamentary elections. Intimidation and violence actually eased up considerably in the weeks preceding the vote, and the MDC was poised to take advantage and gain ground.[10] On election day, on-site monitors photographed local election results posted outside the halls, tents, and classrooms that served as polling stations in villages and towns around the country. The math showed the opposition MDC headed for certain victory over Mugabe and his ruling party.

You didn't have to be an MDC supporter to want the violence to end and the shattered economy to revive. Perhaps—many allowed themselves to anticipate—this relatively peaceful election might begin to reverse a decade's despair. At home and in the diaspora, people waited—and waited—for the results.

The buoyancy was short-lived. Release of the results was delayed

---

[9] Estimates vary widely as to the size of the Zimbabwean diaspora. Human Rights Watch puts the figure at 1.5 million out of a population of 11.6 million (according to the 2002 Zimbabwean census). Richard Dowden in *Africa: Altered States, Ordinary Miracles* (Public Affairs, 2009) writes that as of early 2008 as many as 4 million Zimbabweans had left the country. See also: Andrew Meldrum, *Guardian* U.K., July 1, 2007, "Refugees Flood From Zimbabwe," which puts the figure at 3.7 million. The South African government, where a significant majority of the diaspora is now living, has to date released no official numbers.

[10] Simba Makoni, a former Zanu-PF finance minister, ran as an independent, making it a three-way race for the presidency, with Tsvangirai running as the MDC candidate.

and then delayed again. After five tense weeks, the government finally announced that in the presidential election, Tsvangirai led by 47.9 percent to Mugabe's 43.2 percent, a close enough margin to require a run-off election under Zimbabwe law.

After the run-off announcement, a wave of well-planned violence, reminiscent of Gukurahundi, ensued. In what one narrator in this book describes as a reign of terror,[11] opposition supporters were arrested, abducted, tortured, raped, and beaten. At least 163 MDC members were murdered, and upwards of five thousand beaten, while tens of thousands more were displaced from their homes.[12] In an attempt to stave off even more death, Tsvangirai withdrew from the run-off. In the face of international condemnation, Mugabe declared victory. He and his government remained in power, and the economy plunged.

A year later, at an emergency summit of the regional body, the Southern African Development Community (SADC), mediation between Zanu-PF and the MDC led by former South African President Thabo Mbeki resulted in a power-sharing agreement. Tsvangirai accepted the position of prime minister in a government still headed by President Mugabe.

Yet even with power sharing, by mid-2010, most Zimbabweans were still struggling. Mugabe and Zanu-PF still controlled the army and the police, and opposing voices were still being imprisoned, censored, or harassed. Refugees were still fleeing to South Africa and other neighboring countries. Dollarization increased the amount of goods available in the stores (for those who could afford them), but the economy continued to stagger.

It bears stating that, unlike other some other oppressive contemporary regimes, even in the worst of times, Zimbabwe has always retained the institutions of a functioning democracy. For example, when mem-

---

[11] See Father John's narrative for a vivid description of the post-election violence.

[12] Human Rights Watch, World Report 2009 (Seven Stories Press, 2009).

bers of the judiciary aren't being harassed (in some cases, judges have been physically attacked), many have been able to do their jobs quasi-independently. In one celebrated case, the Zimbabwean Supreme Court ruled that a well-known human rights activist standing trial for terrorism against the state[13] had herself been terrorized and kidnapped and beaten by government agents—not the other way around.[14]

Likewise, a number of independent newspapers—notably the *Daily News*, firebombed in 2001 and shut down in 2003—have kept functioning on paper or virtually, while a few independent literary book publishers continue to release high-quality (and at times politically critical) books.[15]

All face perhaps the most unsettling aspect of rule of law in Zimbabwe: the capricious nature of its enforcement. One day you are safe to speak out or publish; the next you are breaking the law. In this unpredictable environment, the narrators in this book, like so many other Zimbabweans who have dared to speak out, are taking a significant risk by sharing their stories with the public. For this reason, many of the names in this book have been changed.

Nigerian fiction writer Chimamanda Ngozie Adichie[16] has said:

You can't tell a single story of any place, person, or people. There are many stories that create us. The single story creates stereotypes. There are other stories that are just as important to tell. The problem with stereotypes is not that they are untrue, but that they are incomplete.

With this collection, we hope to complicate any single or simplistic narrative about Zimbabwe's recent history. We've gathered a range of

---

[13] Jestina Mukoko, director of the Zimbabwe Peace Project.

[14] The *New York Times*, September 28, 2009, "Court Ends Terrorism Case Against Zimbabwe Activist" by Barry Bearak. See also: The *New York Times*, January 15, 2009, "Opponents of Mugabe tell Court of Torture" by Celia W. Dugger.

[15] See Weaver Press: *weaverpresszimbabwe.com*.

[16] See Adichie's TED talk, entitled "The Danger of a Single Story" (July 2009), *TED.com*.

vastly different voices from inside the country, and from Zimbabwe's ever-growing diaspora. We spoke to survivors, as well as those who might be considered perpetrators. We spoke with a banker as well as a farm worker, a policeman as well as a trade unionist, a farm owner as well as a miner. Some but by no means all of the narrators here have been involved in politics, either by choice, necessity, or, in some cases, force. Political involvement in a nation like Zimbabwe is not at all unusual. It is sometimes difficult, in an environment where people are forced to take sides within families, in the workplace, and on the street, *not* to become politically involved.

Hope Deferred is the result of hundreds of hours of interviews with more than fifty Zimbabweans, conducted over the course of two and a half years. The two of us, along with our team of Zimbabwean, South African, American, and British interviewers, spoke with people in various parts of Zimbabwe, South Africa, and other neighboring countries, the U.K., the U.S., and Canada. Not all of those interviews are collected here—some will be made available on the Voice of Witness website.[17]

The crisis in Zimbabwe is well documented. As one veteran human-rights worker remarked to us in Harare, *What's been happening in this country over the course of many years is among the best-documented human rights crises in the world. My question is: has it helped?*

A difficult and unsettling question. In some ways this book is meant as one response.

Too often, the people who are most affected by a human-rights crises become, at least in most media accounts, abstractions or three lines of evidence. But what if we dig deeper, spend more time, get to know the complicated person beyond the human-rights violation they have suffered? We want readers to get to know Violet, Lovemore, Rudo, George, Tsitsi, Sankoh Chari, and the rest in just that way, as complicated—and

---

[17] *voiceofwitness.org.*

imperfect—individuals. *Hope Deferred* is not intended to be a comprehensive look at Zimbabwe, nor do the narrators collected here represent anybody but themselves. This is a gathering of unique lives. The stories have been fact-checked to the best of our ability, and many narrators produced documentation to support their stories. You'll read about a man named Zenzele, a former police officer who endured an almost unspeakable form of torture to his genitals known as "degloving." To authenticate his account, Zenzele supplied medical records, doctors' testimony, and photographs. In general, however, it is important to note that memory, especially traumatic memory, is often subjective. Oral history, even more than other kinds of history, is subject to the perspective of the teller. As Joan Didion puts it, we tell our stories—the ones we tell ourselves, the ones we tell other people—in order to live.

The reader is invited to be aware of silences and omissions. To take responsibility for a bombing, to endure the shame of being raped, to admit that you weren't able to support your family—sometimes these things are too difficult to speak about directly. Zimbabwean English makes greater use of a general "you" than, for instance, American English does. *You take money for sex*, for example, can be a way to discuss something "I" can't quite own up to. And for this book, it's a highly appropriate form, inviting you, the reader, into each narrator's own story.

The book is structured as a journey through Zimbabwe and its diaspora, loosely tracing the two long trips we took to gather the narratives. It begins in exile, where so many Zimbabweans now find themselves. Then, crossing the Limpopo River and heading north to Bulawayo, it seeks to understand the roots of Zimbabwe's ongoing and politically fueled ethnic conflict. Next, we proceed into the rural areas, again the sites of much brutality, to get a sense of life in the villages, on the farms, and in small towns. Traveling east toward the mountains, we pause in a smaller city, Mutare, close to the border with Mozambique and buffeted by its own set of historical currents. Finally, we make our way to Harare, Zimbabwe's once vibrant but now subdued capital city. We end the book, appropriately, in the South African border town of Musina, makeshift home to so many thousands of Zimbabweans.

In some instances we didn't conduct these interviews in the chapter location. The book's structure is intended to connect each story to its most significant place, whether this be inside the country, or outside of it, in exile.

It should go without saying that there are so many more places in Zimbabwe, and so many more people whose stories need to be heard. Collected here are only a vital few. One stark warning emerges from the individual histories: the need to remember, to recount, to tell and tell again. Keeping silent about injustice has never been in the best interest of the Zimbabwean people. Whatever direction the country takes going forward, we hope that this book will stand as a call against forgetting.

—*Annie Holmes and Peter Orner*

RUSAPE, JULY 2009

On the road back from Rusape yesterday we saw something beautiful. We were driving to the capital from a farm about 170 kilometers east of Harare. In Rusape, we'd spent the night in the house of a white tobacco farmer who'd been chased off his farm during the land invasions, but who is now managing a farm for a black farmer. We spent a day talking with this former owner, now manager, George. George acknowledged that the old ways had become unsustainable—that no longer could there be any white kings in Zimbabwe. That Robert Mugabe may be completely ruthless, but that commercial farmers like himself in fact had it coming. After years away, after the loss of his land, he'd come back to the country to work once again farming tobacco. Only this time the land wasn't his anymore. This was fine with George so long as he could continue to live and farm in the country of his birth.

So maybe we had the right, for a little while, to feel optimistic. On the potholed—no, cratered—road to Harare, we were thinking of the possibilities. Maybe things are going to get better here. How much worse can it get? Millions of Zimbabweans are still living outside the country. Starvation is on the rise. Political violence continues unchecked. Pick your statistic, Zimbabwe will be way down on the list. Life expectancy is among the lowest of any nation in the world.[1] And we talked to many people who are lucky to be alive at all. We did one interview with a man who'd done organizing for the MDC[2] during the March 2008 elections. He told us that on the night he was arrested, the police stuffed him in a coffin and drove him around for hours. Apparently this is not an uncommon torture technique employed in Zimbabwe—more than one person described this method to us. The man said that when they let him out, he was ready to confess to any crime they could invent, so long as he didn't have to go back in that coffin. *Call me a terrorist*, he said. *Call me anything you want.*

But there must be some point when things turn, when violence finally gives way to exhaustion, when people have no choice but to rebuild. The farm in Rusape was, possibly, a small step. These were some of the things on our minds when we were driving to Harare yesterday. It was late afternoon. We'd just passed the town of Marondera when we saw, by the side of the road, what looked like a wooden cross sticking up out of the ground. The horizontal piece was lined with a row of what seemed at first like little fists of fire. We pulled over and walked back down the road to see what it was. Honey. A row of old mason jars packed with brown-yellow honey. The little fires set by the glass catching the fading sunlight. A guy emerged from out of the thick bush. An American dollar apiece, he said. Cheap. He was right. It was cheap. We ate that honey this morning on bread, fresh bread—because this week the stores are selling bread, but only for those who have the dollars to buy it.

---

[1] In 2006, it was actually the lowest in the world, according to the World Health Organization. Female life expectancy stood at thirty-four, while male life expectancy was at thirty-seven.

[2] Movement for Democratic Change. Led by Morgan Tsvangirai, the MDC is the leading opposition party in Zimbabwe, and formed a coalition government with Zanu-PF in 2009, with Tsvangirai as prime minister and Mugabe as president.

EXILE

Anyone who is familiar with exile has gained many insights into life but has discovered that it holds even more questions. Among the answers there is the realization, which at first seems trivial, that there is no return, because the re-entrance into a place is never also a recovery of lost time.

—Jean Améry, "How Much Home Does a Person Need?"[1]

Millions of Zimbabweans are now living elsewhere.[2] People have fled Zimbabwe because of political violence, lack of jobs and livelihood options, and the almost complete breakdown of the education and health-care systems. Most of the exiled Zimbabweans live in South Africa; others live in the neighboring countries of Botswana, Mozambique, and Namibia, and still others live further afield—primarily in the U.K., but also, the U.S., Canada, Kenya, Nigeria, and pretty much anywhere that English is spoken. Every day the Zimbabwean diaspora grows larger.

---

[1] *At the Mind's Limits*, Jean Améry, (Indiana University Press, 1998).

[2] See footnote 9, page 19.

Migration out of Zimbabwe may be seen as one sort of measure of the country's internal problems; since 2000, migration has reached unprecedented numbers.[3] Resilience and ingenuity take many forms, and people leave in different ways: John[4] flew first class to Canada; Elizabeth traded sex for a ride across the Limpopo River into South Africa; Zenzele crossed the same border but on foot across the dry riverbed, by night and in excruciating pain. Once they arrive in new countries, many factors shape Zimbabweans' choices. Bernard,[5] for example, was a banker at home but now labors on building sites in a small South African town. By contrast, Zimbabwean academics are staffing and leading university departments from Cape Town to Canterbury, and you can hear Shona conversations on Oxford Street in London, the city known to Zimbabweans as "Harare North."

The narrators in this section (and for that matter, those other members of the Zimbabwean diaspora who are scattered throughout this book as they are across the world) are all attempting to move forward with their lives far away from their homes. Even so, going home is always on their minds, even or perhaps especially because return seems so impossible. Yet, as Jean Améry emphasizes above, even if it was safe, returning never makes up for lost time in one's own home place. For now, all these narrators can do is wait. Some have waited years, others, decades. As Zenzele, the former police officer put it in a recent email, "It's very lonely here by myself and every day and night I think and dream of my family in Zimbabwe."

---

[3] See the appendix section on Zimbabweans in South Africa.

[4] See Section 2, "Matabeleland."

[5] See Section 7, "The Border."

VIOLET

AGE: *19*
OCCUPATION: *Domestic worker*
INTERVIEWED IN: *Johannesburg, South Africa*

Seated on a couch in Father John's[1] apartment in central Johannesburg, Violet speaks haltingly in Shona, her fatigue and shyness exacerbated by flu that makes her voice scratchy and harsh. Often she pauses to catch her breath. Uncountable numbers of Zimbabwean children have been orphaned by political violence, by preventable and treatable diseases such as cholera, and by HIV/AIDS. Many of them have been left, like Violet, to head households. In her case, her father was beaten to death for his political involvement. Her mother subsequently fled, without her children, back to her family home in Mozambique. Left alone to raise her much younger sister, Violet eventually decided to make the dangerous crossing into South Africa to search for work. There she was tricked into working in Internet pornography. The line between political rights and economic survival is a porous one, as Violet's experience shows. Now, wrenched from one kind of life in a rural area, Violet has landed in a tough, violent city she is not equipped to navigate.

---

[1] See Father John's narrative on page 305.

We were a poor family, but we had fields so we could farm. However, we were really disadvantaged people, so we used our hands to cultivate while others used oxen. Even though we were poor, my daddy was a person who took really good care of his children. When my father was still here, we never went to bed hungry. He was a farmer, and we would go to the fields to help him. He also built houses for other people, and they would give him goats. Goats or money.

And then, around 2000, when I was ten, he got involved with the MDC.[2] He used to go around the streets putting up posters. He was one of the few people involved with the MDC in our neighborhood, so the local MDC—Lovemore Madhuku's group[3]—gave him money for doing that. He had an MDC card. He had a T-shirt. He used to go to MDC meetings in Harare. And Tsvangirai sent our family food and stuff. At times, he would send a senior leader with money. I would say my father was a person who loved politics. When he was drunk, my father would start shouting in the street: *Chinja maitiro* or *Mugabe mudenga*.[4] Other people would be listening.

During that time, Zanu-PF youths would come from other places. They would have been told the names of all the MDC troublemakers and they would head to their houses. They'd come and knock and tell you to come out. A lot of people just disappeared.

They came to take my father at night while we were sleeping. My father was asked to go out, and he went out. Because of what was going on—the disappearances and stuff—it was not safe to walk around at night. So, when my father was taken from the house, my mum didn't go looking for him because she was scared herself. We just waited in the hope that he would come back.

---

[2] Movement for Democratic Change, the leading opposition party in Zimbabwe.

[3] Madhuku was among the leaders of the National Constitutional Assembly (NCA) and the MDC.

[4] MDC slogans: "Change the way you do things," "Mugabe up" (in order to drop him down).

Very early the next morning, my father's friend came to our house and told my mother what had happened. The night before, he'd found my father lying on the side of the road crying, unable to walk. My father had been beaten up by the Zanu-PF people on the street. He was wearing a Tsvangirai T-shirt, one of the white ones that had just come out. The friend recognized my father and lifted him up and took him to the clinic. He told my mother that he had left my father at the hospital in Chipinge, and that my mother should take some food to him.

My father stayed at the hospital for one week and never recovered. He came back home in the morning, in a donkey cart. His legs were covered in wounds and he couldn't even walk anymore. He was coughing up blood. He was carried out of the cart and into the house. He died in the afternoon on the day that he was discharged, after eating *sadza*[5] at around two p.m. He didn't even live at home for a day.

My sister was three or four years old. I was ten. That's when life began to get really difficult in our home.

I CARRIED HER ON MY BACK

About two months after my dad died, the Zanu-PF youth came one morning while Mum was at the borehole fetching water. They were carrying sticks and asked me where my mother was. I told them that I didn't know. They said okay and left. I told my mum about it when she returned.

Some other people came at night while she was sleeping and knocked on the door. I opened the door and they said to me, *Where is your mother?* I had been told to say that she wasn't around, so I said that she wasn't in. They slapped me twice, saying that I should tell them the truth. I told them that my mum was really not in the house. They asked me where she had gone, and I lied and told them that she had gone to visit the chief. They said they would return the following morning.

---

[5] Stiff, maize-meal porridge, the Zimbabwean staple food, eaten all over southern Africa and also called "mealie-meal," or "pap" in South Africa.

My mum said that she was going to leave and go back to her own home,[6] in Mozambique, and that she would come back for us. Then she started crying. She thought of taking my sister with her but she ended up leaving her. She said that she was going to go and look for a place to live and then she would come back and get us.

Mum left the very same night that the Zanu-PF people were there. She did not even pack any things. She left with two sets of clothing—one that she was wearing at the time and another in her bag. She boarded a bus and went home to Mozambique. I wanted to go with mum, but I didn't tell her that.

She didn't tell me anything about what we were supposed to do. She was the kind of person who would just stop caring about something when she ran out of ideas. But my mum used to leave my sister with me when she went to the fields, so I knew how to take care of her.

My sister didn't see her leave. She was sleeping. She was about three years old. She was talking, and she was just starting to walk. At first, I didn't tell her that Mum had left. She used to go to sleep thinking that Mum was outside on the street and would be coming back. She used to cry every time she saw an adult outside on the street.

My mother left on a Saturday. On Sunday I was at home, and on Monday I went to school with my sister. I carried her on my back. I told everyone there that my mum was not around. After three days, I told my sister that Mum had traveled far away.

THE CYCLONE CAME

After our mother left, it was just the two of us. But some of our neighbors looked after us and gave us food. Then some of the teachers from the school came and told us to come and live at the school for the time being.

---

[6] Shona speakers distinguish between your *musha*, the rural home of your family, and your *kumba*, a house you live in elsewhere. Here, Violet's mother means she's returning to her parents' home area.

But we stayed at home. Most people thought that our mum would return after a really short time.

People only started to worry about us after five months. A woman who lived close to us fetched water and cooked sadza for us. She would wake us up each morning in time for school. She would wash the baby, I would bathe, and then we would go to school. After school, she would do our laundry. Sometimes, the teachers at school gave us soap. The person who helped us the most was the headmaster, who was our uncle by marriage. He would give us money for sugar every time we ran out. He also gave us money for salt, and he always asked me if we had maize meal. When we ran out, he would give us maize to grind.

Except for the headmaster, our relatives never really helped us. Our other uncles never came because they thought that they would be asked about where our mother was and that they might be killed like my father was.

Once two relatives came. They said they were our father's younger brothers, but they were not at the funeral when our father died. They came three months after Mum left, and they offered to take us to go and live with them. I said to them, *Who is going to look after my mum's property?* They said that we should just leave everything there. But I was worried about my mother's things because I thought she would return one day, so we did not go with them.

Our neighbors felt pity for us when it started raining and when the cyclone came.[7] It rained for three weeks without stopping. Our little house was made of thatch. There were two rooms: the kitchen and the bedroom we slept in. The thatching was already rotting and the house started collapsing, so they moved us from our home and we went to live with the woman who cooked sadza for us. Mum had been gone for almost a year by then.

Then a donor came. They wanted to build houses for ten children in

---

[7] Eastern Zimbabwe has frequently experienced cyclones, usually in February (as with Cyclone Eline, in 2000) or March (as with Cyclone Japhet, in 2003). Cyclone Japhet is probably the one Violet describes.

the neighborhood in Chipinge.[8] The donor built our house first and it was done in two weeks. It had two rooms. The donor was very good to us. They found someone to take care of us and also gave us food every month.

SHE THOUGHT WE HAD DIED

Our mum came back from Mozambique in 2005 because someone lied to her that her children had died in the cyclone. She wanted to see before she believed.

I wasn't there when she arrived, but my sister was, playing with other kids. My sister was called to come and greet her mother, but she did not believe that the woman was our mum because she did not remember her. She had been gone about two years. My sister started telling her that our mother had gone and left us, and that we thought she had died. My mum started crying and saying that she thought *we* had died.

When I came to the house and saw her, she said to me, *You are so devoted. I thought you would leave your baby sister.* I kept quiet. I thought it was fine. We had lived without our mother for a very long time. I was really happy that my sister got to know Mum.

When my mother came back in 2005, my sister was already going to school. I was now fourteen and my sister was seven or eight. We started farming cotton and bought two cows and things improved at home. Then our mum fell ill with cholera. She died in March of 2006. The cows and everything that the donor had given us were taken away by our uncles. They said that their father's child[9] had worked to provide all these things.

---

[8] A number of agencies provided such assistance, although many had begun to freeze development assistance to Zimbabwe in protest against the political situation.

[9] The uncles are speaking of their brother, Violet's father. Inheritance is a highly contested field in Zimbabwe. By custom, everything a man leaves when he dies—including his wife and children—now belong to his family. Until Independence, two sets of laws applied: civil and traditional. Despite new laws passed in the late 1980s barring the custom, many people still follow tradition, leaving widows destitute and homeless or forcibly "inherited" by their brothers-in-law.

They took everything we had and went back to their homes, leaving us there. There was a bit of cotton left, enough for one bale. We sold it, but we didn't spend the money on food or other things. Instead, we bought goats. Two goats. The goats started having kids.

I left school at the time of the August holiday. I was in Grade 6. When the schools reopened, I didn't go. Instead, I sent my little sister to school, and I started going to the fields. My sister would go to the fields in the morning before going to school. After school, she knew that she would have to eat her sadza at the fields and then we would cultivate the crops together. Then a woman showed up claiming to be our aunt. She said she was our mum's younger sister and started living with us. She took very good care of us. She already had her own children, but we lived with her all the same.

When the MDC rose up again, people already knew that we were MDC because our father had been killed because of his involvement. They came and started teaching us how to campaign in the neighborhood and to go to political rallies. We were forced—all the youth were forced—to go to MDC political meetings.

In Zimbabwe, things had become really difficult, and I decided that if I came here to South Africa I could support my sister better than if I stayed at home. I bought everything my sister would need and took some of our money and came across the border.

TEA AND SIX PIECES OF BREAD

I left in August 2008, on the second. I didn't have a passport so I paid the *malayitsha* one thousand rand to help me cross the border.[10] Some man gave me an ID. We were really crowded in the car on the way here.

I arrived at the Methodist church[11] in Johannesburg. I stayed for two

---

[10] Approximately US$100 at the time.

[11] Bishop Paul Verryn's Central Methodist Church in Johannesburg has provided a base for Zimbabweans and others with no resources for several years.

days, and then I went to the Home Affairs office in Mayfair.[12] I wanted asylum, but I was told that I was too young and that I should go back to Zimbabwe and go to school. I went back to the Methodist church and a lady said to me, *Just look for a job. You'll get one.* I stayed at the church for maybe a month without going to work. Every morning I would go to Munenzva.[13] They gave us food—tea and six pieces of bread. We would go to shower at Hillbrow[14] and come back.

I looked for a job. A certain boy and I started liking each other like friends. He had grown up like we had, an orphan. He started hunting for a job for me, and then I got one sometime in October 2008. It was house-work. I worked for an Indian man. He said he would give me a hundred and fifty rand per week. Because I was struggling and needed a lot of money I just said okay and started working.

The thing that bothered me with the Indian place is that they eat food that has chilies. I wouldn't eat it. Their food bothered me, so when he gave me my salary, I would buy maize meal and cook sadza for myself. With the rest of my salary, I bought food to send to my sister in Zimbabwe.[15]

THEY WANTED GIRLS WITH GOOD BODIES

There is something else that bothered and angered me. A woman named Tulu came to the church in her car with a Zimbabwean boy called Bless-

---

[12] A suburb near the inner city of Johannesburg, where most Somali asylees and immigrants live. The Home Affairs Office is where migrants apply for asylum.

[13] A depot of a Zimbabwean bus company that shares basic facilities with those who need them. For many Zimbabweans in exile, it is an important piece in the diaspora chain.

[14] Many Zimbabweans have congregated in certain parts of Hillbrow, an inner-city residential area of Johannesburg. Some cross-border traders pool resources to share rooms, sometimes with ten or more women to one room. Many Zimbabwean sex workers are based in Hillbrow.

[15] Zimbabweans have devised a number of systems to send money and food home, from sending bags with *malayitshas* (see Nokuthula's story, on page 127), to online services based in South Africa, the U.K. and U.S.

ing. And this Blessing boy said something to the security guards; he did not even tell the guards the truth. He told us that there was a job and they needed girls who had computing skills. He said, *This will be good for you. It's nice work.*

He chose six of us—me, Grace, Coletta, Beyonce, Patricia, Lee, and Beauty—and Tulu came to pick us up in her car and we all went to a place called Westgate.[16] When we arrived she gave us panties. They had lied to us that there was a job available working with computers. They wanted to make us do porno. They said that they wanted girls with good bodies and they didn't want anyone who was too slender.

Blessing spent two days trying to convince me, telling me that it was artificial porn and I would only appear on the Internet. He said that I would have to talk to someone who would be maybe in the U.K. and the person would tell me what style they wanted me to do. He had also lied to us that they would give us R2,500 per fortnight.[17]

On the first day, I told Blessing, *Take me back!* But he sweet-talked me. *Don't go. Just see the job first.* So I stayed.

I said that I didn't know what to do because I had never done it before. I've always been really shy about my body. I just told them the truth. Tulu said that there was no problem. We were given a room. They gave us everything, even clothes so that we could change, but most of the time we were naked and didn't have time to wear clothes. We just wore bras and panties. It bothered me because at home I never used to walk around naked and then here in South Africa someone wants to teach me to walk around without my clothes on.

Tulu was South African, and she had a husband who was white, from London. He would come in even when we were naked, without towels wrapped around ourselves. He would just come and sit at the computer, do whatever he wanted to do, and then leave.

---

[16] A suburb and mall in Roodepoort, near Johannesburg.

[17] About US$250 at the time.

They would give me a computer and a private customer would come on, on the Internet. He would appear on the screen and say, *Hi, baby*, and then you would answer him. After, he would say, *Make doggy style*, and then you would bend over and pose in the the doggy style. Or he would say, *Do it for me*, and then you would take those artificial things and put them inside yourself and start doing it alone. One private customer wanted me to take everything off and remain naked with my legs open. I told him that in Zimbabwe that made people sick because too much air would come in. I refused to do it. He started yelling at me that I was trying to be a know-it-all.

Sometimes, the people who came on spoke in English, and other times the person would be a Zimbabwean, living somewhere else, maybe Botswana. You could see that the person was Zimbabwean and he would use Shona. They could give you a phone number over the Internet and tell you to call, using the phone in the house. You always had to have a pen and book at hand in order to take down the phone numbers you were given. They would say, *Give me your phone number*, and you would give them the phone number at that house and they would call you. They would say to you, *Hi baby*, and start *kupfimba*[18] over the phone.

I told Tulu that I no longer wanted that job. And then I said to her, *I'm really angry. Give me twenty rand for transport right now so that I can go back to town.* Selling my naked body on the Internet really bothered me. I left, and I wasn't ashamed to tell people at the church the truth. On the day that I came back, I went to a girl called Shelter who worked at the hospital. I told her the truth and explained it to her.

Some of my friends stayed there for a week. Some of the girls liked it and some of them, like me, didn't like it. Seven of us had gone and most of us came back pretty soon. But one didn't give up and spent about a month there. Of the seven of us, two got married here in South Africa. Another is selling her body on the streets. One other person went to Cape Town and another went to Pretoria.

---

[18] In Shona: To propose love to, to come on to.

I SHOULD BE AT SCHOOL

When I returned to the church, I stayed for about two weeks without going to work. I was being given food by other people. At first, I was afraid of working for anyone else, because of my experiences and what I had been made to do. But Shelter started lecturing me, saying, *Don't worry. Look for another job. You'll get one.*

Someone got me a job in Thembisa[19] in January, and that's where I work now. I earn eight hundred rand[20] per month, taking care of a South African person's children. It is better than staying at the church, but what I want is a job that pays at least R1,500. If I get another job I'll leave this one, but I don't want to work for another white person like Tulu's husband.

Right now, my sister is still living in Chipinge, in the house the donor built for us, with the woman who claims to be our mum's younger sister. I send her money. From the eight hundred I'm paid, I spend maybe two hundred and send the rest to my sister. She is now in Form 1.[21] She is still in school. I might think about getting married. I don't have a brother at home, so there is no man to help us.

At times, when I think of what I've been through, I cry. Life is painful. I sometimes think that Zanu-PF was responsible. If the Zanu-PF people had not beaten up my father, he wouldn't have died then, and if my father was alive I would never have come here. But maybe he would have died anyway, from illness like my mum. She's the one who was supposed to be taking care of the baby. I should be in school with my family taking care of me. But instead I have to take care of another child by working here for money.

---

[19] One of the black townships outside Johannesburg.

[20] About US$80. As with undocumented workers elsewhere, "illegal" immigrants like Violet cannot fight for minimum wages and are vulnerable to exploitation.

[21] The equivalent of seventh grade in the U.S.

AARON

AGE: *30*

OCCUPATION: *Former soldier in the Zimbabwe National Army*
INTERVIEWED IN: *Musina, Zimbabwe*

Aaron agrees to be interviewed in a motel room in Musina, the dusty border town on the South African side of the Limpopo River.[1] This town is a sort of funnel: desperation forces Zimbabweans with limited means, or no means at all, through Musina into a new and often brutal life. Thousands of Zimbabweans here are fleeing the fallout from violence perpetrated by people like Aaron himself, violence directly ordered or condoned by the state. As a former soldier, Aaron is especially concerned for his safety, worried about who might come to know his whereabouts. He knows that the CIO (the Zimbabwean Central Intelligence Agency) has a long reach, and that agents operate in South Africa. By speaking out, Aaron was clearly breaking a kind of code of military silence. The interview began in the early afternoon in a motel room on the outskirts of town. At first, Aaron was hesitant to be very specific. Yet, hours later, toward evening, he began to unburden himself of ugly memories, and revisit other times in his life as well.

Okay, fine, I'll tell you.

---

[1] See Section 7, "The Border," for more on Musina.

Let's say it's a Friday night, around ten p.m. You're soldiering. You get to this bar. Usually when you go for such missions you prepare yourself—maybe you use a barbed-wire belt. Some guys, they use the butt of a rifle. The moment we kick open the door, the patrons are terrified. First, they're scared even of the uniform, and secondly, we are the army. And so let's say one of you goes to talk with the owner of the bar. The rest of you, you pick from the patrons, you ask all the patrons to bring out their belongings, especially their money, cell phones, everything. You say: *Put it aside, put it here, your cell phone is your property and we do not want it damaged so put your cell phone here.* So they take their cell phones, they take their money, and they put it aside. Then from there you say: *Single ladies move to this side, married ladies move to that side, same applies to the men.* And then they fall into their groups. Then you ask from the married women, *Where is your husband? Is your husband in the bar?* Sometimes, if she says yes, that her husband is in the bar, she'll pick out her husband. You stand both of them there. Then you check on their ages. For myself especially, I respect people who are old. With the old ones, I always tried to persuade the others to let them go.

Then the rest, you make them dance.

They're crawling on the chairs and cupboards, singing, dancing, jumping. Remember: when people are scared and terrified, they can't dance even though they know how to dance. It is very impossible for them to dance, so you want them to dance. So you sit there and drink their beer and yeah, you make them do it.

Then maybe you say... you've all had enough? *Okay*, you say. *If I count to three, you all disappear from this bar.* So you say *one... two...* and the moment you get to *three*, one of you closes the door and you say, *No no no, you are too slow.* So you make them do it again, the same exercises as before: repeat left, right, center, dance. Then after the second time, the owner might come to you. He might come and ask for forgiveness. He might beg you to let his patrons go.

So, you say, *No, we cannot let you all go because this was an MDC*[2] *rally that was taking place. Next time, don't make rallies within your bar.*

And then, let's say, you find out there is a member of MDC there, and he has a cell phone and he has been recording what we've been doing. Maybe he wants to use the video against us. So this one has to suffer double. Like he has to receive some beatings for everything he's recorded. He has to be beaten. We beat him, we beat him, we beat him, we beat him.

We make some of them get naked. Usually, we're more interested in the women, so mostly the women undress. Then we mop the floor with their clothes.

It is dark outside by then. The whole process lasts about an hour and a half. Let's say there are almost forty or fifty people at the bar. Time to let them go. So, you say, *When we count to three, we want you out.* You open a very small door for them all to go out at the same time. It always happens. Some people get stuck, others injure themselves during the process of trying to run away.

STANDBY

In the army, there is a process you undergo. When you are in the army, you are supposed to be given some leave to go home and live a normal life with people—but this leave is never given. Instead you are confined—the army calls it *standby*, but the truth is you are 100 percent confined. When you are confined, you are just looking to do anything, anything at all. It's like—let's say you have a dog, and you know that this dog is bad and you put it in a cage for a long time, and then you just let it out.

ALL THE BEAUTIFUL SOLDIERS

When you are growing up, you have a dream that you want to fulfill, and

---

[2] This accusation creates the pretext that the soldiers' reason for entering the bar was to disrupt a political rally of the MDC. For more on the MDC, see the appendix.

you know you will be so in control the moment you fulfill it. My dream was to become a soldier. I did not know what I was going to come across. As far as I knew when I was growing up, a soldier was a servant for the nation, not for a certain political party. There's this American video game I used to play: *Call of Duty*. I just played too much *Call of Duty* when I was growing up. All the beautiful soldiers. Judging from what those guys were doing— they were rescuing people, saving people's lives, you know, doing all those good things for the community—I wanted to be a soldier.

My father had been in the Zimbabwean army during Gukurahundi,[3] but he never discussed it. He said it was rather best not to talk about it because the moment he starts to talk about it, the stories, the memories get so bad. He never thought I would join the same army that did those things.

And for a couple of years after I got out of school, I didn't join. I got a job as a private nurse in a hospital. This was when I was seventeen. I worked for a white patient, Mark Peterson. He had something called Huntington's Disease. It's known especially in the U.K. and the States. As far as I know, it's a rare disease in Africa. They say it is inherited, generation after generation. So I was Mark Peterson's private nurse. I have to say that it was the most interesting job that I have ever done. Because when I worked with him, Mark Peterson taught me so many things and the family was so appreciative of me that they didn't even want me to leave for the army. When I told them my plans, they offered to double my salary.

My family also wanted me to keep working in the hospital. But I thought, *To be honest I still want to be a soldier.* I told my father. I knew his position. He told me the reason why he hated the army is because it didn't do its duty, which is protecting the nation. At that time I didn't even tell my mother. I knew that she was going to be cross. But if you have a dream to fulfill then sometimes you have to go and do it. I think

---

[3] This Shona word translates to "the early rain that washes away the chaff before the spring rains come," and refers to the 1982–87 military campaign launched ostensibly against dissidents from the former Zimbabwe Independent People's Revolutionary Army, ZIPRA. See the appendix for more on Gukurahundi.

that's when I made a big blunder. This happens especially when you are young—you end up doing the wrong things. I think the problem was that my family was making me feel like a coward. I don't ever want to look like a coward.

WE ARE CARRYING THE GUN

I started serving in the Zimbabwe national army around 1998 when I was nineteen, and I served up till last year. From 1998 to 2002 I was busy in Congo, fighting. There were the Congolese, the Rwandans, and the Ugandans, all fighting there.[4] The Ugandans had their army, and we were also fighting the Congolese rebel fighters. That's when I finally told my mother I was in the army. After four months in the DRC, I knew death might knock you at any time so I had to write to my brother, "Please tell her because anything can happen."

It was definitely a war in the Congo. But at the beginning I enjoyed it. It was almost like watching a movie. But when I saw its implications, the casualties and everything, I started to think—no, this is bad. They say in life you've got a choice, why can't you take the other choice? The question I was always asking was, *Why are we here? Is this Zimbabwean soil?* And my commander would say, *We are helping our African brother.* Fine, helping an African brother, but what damage were we also doing to them? You find children affected, gunfire, hunger, you feel pity for them. These children in the Congo were dying.

And as a soldier, the more you are into war the more you lose; you lose so many things and you end up causing some unnecessary conflicts, so to speak, because you overstayed in the battlefield. You lose your mind if you overstay in the battlefield. You lose your mind and you end up do-ing stupid things. Like girls. Girls. Once, in the Congo, another soldier

[4] The long-running conflict in the Democratic Republic of Congo, or DRC, is fueled by diamonds and fought by military from many different African countries. Zimbabwean soldiers were deployed there from 1998 to 2002.

in the unit took someone else's wife right in front of the husband. I saw that. Ah, there was nothing this woman could do; she thought that we have money, food. Besides that, there is the fact that we are carrying the gun. You know, when you have a gun, you wonder, *Is she cooperating because she wants to or is she cooperating because she is a slave to you?*

This one we took, we used to pay her. We had money. She and her husband, the family, they were hungry. I won't say it was prostitution. The first day, we took her the first day, but the second day she came on her own.

The problem with the army is that it has all types of characters, the good, the bad, you can name any. Some people pay for their badness, some don't. I remember another case of a guy who slept with a twelve-year-old girl. The guy was sent back home and charged and he was sentenced, I think, to twenty-five years in jail.

YOU DISAPPEAR

I became a corporal in 2007. I was a noncommissioned officer. In the army, there are non-commissioned and commissioned ranks. Commissioned ranks are called political ranks. In order for you to get to that rank, you have be political. And like in the whole of Zim, the problem in the army is with the tribes. There is the Ndebele tribe and the Shona tribe. The army is dominated by the Shona tribe. In most cases, in order for you to pull up into the higher ranks, you need to be part of the Shona tribe. Or, if you are Ndebele like me, in order to fall into a higher rank you have to be highly active in politics, in Zanu-PF. But for myself, I have always hated politics. People have been suffering just because of these politics.

In March 2008, around the political elections, the police were never there—it was always the army and the riot squad. Crowd control was a big problem, a very big problem. I think the system that we had is to only scare people with the army. But so many people ended up being hurt. As a soldier you soon learn that if you don't kill, you will be killed, so it just became a circus. That was the other thing that was keeping me going: if I don't, they will. So the only way to defend yourself is to attack.

One day, we had the demonstrators surrounded. I can't tell you exactly where this happened but some tried their luck. Unfortunately, you try your luck on us and you will get yourself into more trouble than you are already in. We started hitting them with our barbed-wire belts. There was blood oozing all over, people crying, this and that, begging for mercy. But we continued hitting them. The hitting only stops when the commander says to stop. If he doesn't tell you to stop and you stop, you're in trouble again. So, you've got to recognize orders. That day, what the commander actually said to us was, *You want to make sure they don't do this again, so you hit them to the fullest.*

So the people gave up. They knew they couldn't fight with us so they turned themselves in. A truck came and collected them, took them to a police station.

You see, in the army, there's too much stress, too little money. The stress of missing your family, the stress of trying to control the crowds. At the end of the day, you lose your senses. And what happens next?

I saw that my father was right. The army was serving Zanu-PF more than it was serving the people. Now we weren't fighting a foreign war, we were fighting our own people at home.

But the thing is, as a soldier, when people start throwing stones, you have to react. The problem now comes: if you fire, you kill somebody, an innocent person maybe. Then it's possible that you are going to be the one sent to trial and taken to prison. Soldiers are expendable, something that you can use and dispose. So they put you on trial, and you don't matter to them. They have used you, you have killed the people, done what they wanted. Now they take you to court, you go to prison. All is done for you.

I didn't want that to happen to me.

WHICH BULLET WILL BE FRIENDLIER

During the campaign of the last elections, people were told that if they don't vote for Robert Mugabe, Zanu-PF was going to find out and war was going to erupt. There was going to be gunfire. So, before they vote the people must decide: which vote will help us? Meaning to say, if you vote for MDC there is going to be war, and if the war erupts there are going to be victims.

In the army vote, we vote in the barracks. The system in the barracks is we are told that the army belongs to Zanu-PF. The counting is done in our polling stations. So I voted for Zanu because I knew what would happen if I voted for MDC.

What finally made me make up my mind to leave was that I was worried what would happen if they discovered my family's involvement in the MDC. The MDC changed everything drastically, because there is this process in the army. What they usually do is they send someone to try to investigate how you live your life with your family. Through those investigations, they get a clear picture of what your family's activities are. You won't know that they are doing it, and if they get that information fast before you can make a move, then you're in for it. You disappear. Or you get taken to prison. And in prison, you know by the time you get out you'll be done. There are punishments that you get inside, like torture; they know how to shut you up for life. So if you get out, you won't live for very long, you'll just live for a while and then you'll pass away.

Unfortunately for me, my family is strongly MDC, especially my mother. She's one hundred percent MDC. At that time, around the elections, my mother even went on television. So it became a threat to me because I thought some of my friends might know her. I was now afraid that anything might happen once it was discovered whose son I was.

So I resigned from the army in December 2008 and came to South Africa. The resigning process was frustrating because it wasn't moving the way it was supposed to. Like, normally, a resigning should take three months, but then they changed it to six months, then to nine months. Then they check on the courses that you have done while you were in the army and they ask you to pay money for those courses. And they don't pay your benefits. In my case, when I followed up on my resignation, they said they couldn't find my application, so I had to write it again. It was very hard because some people were saying, *You are going to join MDC, that's why you are leaving.* I told them it had nothing to do with politics; I just wanted to go back to school.

Eventually, I got out. But not everyone is so lucky. I had a friend—he said something about Mugabe, and he was taken to prison. In prison, he was tortured, physically and psychologically. When he came out, he had deteriorated. He was not in good health. He didn't want to talk about what happened. When I asked him, he'd start crying.

THE SON WHO WAS LOST

After I left the army, I got home and informed my family and they were so very happy. They had celebrations. They bought meat. We drank beer. Everyone called me the Prodigal Son, the son who was lost. When I got out, I just wanted to see my daughter. She was with her mom— we had separated before she was born. Actually, we were never really together, because in the military, like I said, you spend almost 95 percent of your time at work and 5 percent at home, so I hardly ever saw her or my daughter.

So I was back with my family. In our tradition, we have two homes: one in the city and one in the rural area. In the rural area, there is peace and quiet. So I went back there, to my father's homestead. I wanted to lay quiet there for a while.

But after I was home for a couple of days, I called some friends who were within the military just to check how the situation was. And they told me that many things had been discovered. See, even after you have resigned, if the army feels like investigating you, they can. They still own you. It was just two days, and my friends were saying, *If possible, get out of there because they might find you. They were asking questions about you.*

So that is why I thought of leaving the country as quickly as possible.

ONE HELL OF A STINKING PLACE

Crossing the border into South Africa was the biggest problem. I paid the guy who was helping us cross one hundred rand.[5] There were eleven people crossing with me: three men and the rest were women, and one of the women had an infant, a small child. But before we crossed, we saw those guys they call *amagumaguma*—they are the working hand of the *malayitshas*:[6] they rape people in the bush. So seeing that we were only four guys and the rest women, I was a bit scared. But then I thought, I'm a soldier, I have the power to protect these people. Because, you know, often the *amagumaguma* rape women. They steal everything you've got, they even kill you in the bush.

When we were in the middle of the bush, I looked in the face of this *amagumaguma* and he looked so puzzled. *Where do you think you are going?* he asked. *Listen my friend*, I said. *I want to be honest with you: you see this jersey? I am from the military. I'm aware of what you do in the bush and I am here to protect all these women and children we are crossing with, so if ever you are planning to do anything to harm these people, you will be warned because I've got a gun.* I didn't have a gun, I just wanted to scare him a bit. After that he was civil with us.

There are two routes into South Africa. The shortest isn't safe because it goes to where the South African soldiers are waiting; the longest is safer but there is a group of *amagumaguma* waiting to rob people there. The guy helping us cross took us to the shortest route. Then he ran away—we were about five meters from the road when he just ran away.

I had no option but to take over. I told the people not to panic, but soon after we'd crossed the border we ran into the army. One of the soldiers said to me, *Your face looks familiar. Were you in the army?* I told him yes. I had once come to do some exercises with the South African army. We recognized each other and we talked. *My friend*, he said, *you know how*

---

[5] Approximately US$10 at the time.

[6] *Amagumaguma* are gangs of thieves, most of them Zimbabweans, preying on border-jumpers along the Limpopo River between South Africa and Zimbabwe. *Malayitshas* offer to help Zimbabweans illegally cross the border into South Africa in exchange for payment, a relationship which is often exploitative.

*good everything was. The system has changed; now Zim soldiers are meant to harm
their own people. I can understand your situation. But you are now putting me in
a bad position: my job is to arrest you and deport you back, but I feel pity for you
guys.* I said, *You do what you're supposed to do.* And so he phoned them and
they came and collected us and took us to a station by the border. They
did documentation and everything. After that documentation we were
taken to SMG.[7]

That was one hell of a place, one hell of a stinking place. I knew that if
I was a Zimbabwean inside there, life was going to be a mess. Because even
the police are sick and tired of the Zimbabweans. So I knew I had to change
my status. I said I was a Congolese. I knew all the problems of that country.
I thought being Congolese would give me a chance in South Africa. So
when they asked me, *Where were you born?* I told them that I was born in
Kappi. An officer said, *Where is your birth certificate?* I laughed at him. He
said, *Why are you laughing?* and I said, *It's a war-torn place. In Kappi we don't
have birth certificates, it's only known that you are born on such and such date and
that's all, there is no documentation.* I explained to him the situation of the war
and everything, the efforts of the war, the homeless who are left because of
war, the people who are tired because of war, everything. They accepted my
story and said, *Okay, he's Congolese.* Then I thought of my Zimbabwe status.
I thought, *Even if politics and violence are killing my country, I cannot denounce
my Zimbabwean citizenship.* So I ran away from the asylum queue. Soon they
caught me and I got deported, along with many other people, back to Zim.
The next day I tried again to return to South Africa.

---

[7] Soutpansberg Military Gebied (SMG), a disused military base outside Musina, served
as an immigration detention facility for several years. Conditions were notoriously abys-
mal. People were detained in an old basketball court divided in half by zinc sheeting
with barbed wire at the top, men on one side, women on the other, with no toilet facilities or water. Sustained pressure from human rights organizations, along with a cholera
outbreak, finally resulted in the closing of SMG in 2009. In addition, the South African
government began issuing ninety-day work-seeker permits to Zimbabweans who crossed
the border legally. Ironically, SMG has subsequently become a transit facility for undocumented Zimbabweans awaiting asylum, who may otherwise be vulnerable to mugging
and attacks.

I found another *malayitsha* and he said, *Since you know the bush as a soldier, what I can simply do is give you a hint of the easiest route that you can use to get to South Africa.* So he gave me the route to use, and I took a group of people and we crossed the border. But that area of the river was too wide, meaning the distance from one end of the river to the other was something like three hundred meters, and on the other side there was a South African military vehicle monitoring. So I had to tell the group to be patient and just relax. Then we had luck. Another group was coming up behind us. That group crossed, and they were arrested by the soldiers while we were just lying there by the bush, so that was our luck. So when the soldiers were busy with the others, we crossed.

But getting to Johannesburg wasn't easy. I remember we were eleven, twelve people crowded into a small van for many hours. There wasn't even sufficient space to raise your head up. We were too crammed together to even talk.

In Johannesburg, I also had a big problem. I phoned my stepbrother, who had promised that he would wait for me, but he tells me that he's somewhere else out of the city and there's no one at home so they cannot let me in. I wandered up and down the streets for two days. Finally, he took me home. I sought asylum there.

You know, you can try to put a certain message about Zim out to people through the TV. *Oh, my gosh*, the people think. *Woooo*. And the next morning they have forgotten about it. It's like a book—they just close it and forget about everything. I really don't know how to talk about the situation in Zim—it is so bad. I feel responsibility for the suffering of my people. But now I want to do something to help them.

Does anybody listen? The cries of Zimbabwe are being sent day in and day out. *Oh my god, oh sorry*, people say, the world says—and the next day they have forgotten about it.

I don't even blame South Africans for the way they treat us. You know why? If you visit a house where the parents begin paying too much attention to the visitors—what happens to the children? That is what's happening here. South Africa has its own problems. We Zimbabweans, how many are we? Close to 3 million here? How can South Africa handle this? We failed to look after our own country, and now we are here. But can we blame others for what we have done to ourselves?

ELIZABETH

AGE: *Late twenties*
OCCUPATION: *Former youth leader*
INTERVIEWED IN: *Johannesburg, South Africa*

An energetic woman in her late twenties, Elizabeth speaks as she lives: fast and impetuously. She left Zimbabwe in 2006 for South Africa. As a small-town teenage activist in the early 2000s, Elizabeth was threatened, abducted, and tortured on several occasions. She has a scar on her stomach from being burned with flaming plastic. Still passionate about the principles she fought for, Elizabeth is open about her role as a youth leader in the opposition, and even describes an attack on the ruling party headquarters. But, looking back, she admits to mixed feelings about the political path she chose: a combination of pride and bitterness. Having thrown herself into the opposition cause, she now feels cast aside. Among her regrets is the fact that political differences divided her and her mother.

I am Elizabeth. I wish I could use my real name, because the situation in Zimbabwe is real. It would be better for those back home to know it was me.

This is not a story that I heard about anyone else—this happened to me. I don't know how other Zimbabweans feel about it, but anything that happens in Zimbabwe, I take it personally. If I'm told right now that people are dying in Zimbabwe, it is as if I have been told that my own mother is dying.

The Zanu-PF thugs used to ask, *Do you want long sleeves?* That meant they were going to cut your hands. *Do you want short sleeves?* That meant they would cut you at the elbow. People laugh at that. I don't laugh at such things. They are not jokes. It is someone's limbs that are being cut, and I have seen people who lost their limbs. I have experienced how it feels to be tortured. I take it personally because I know it has happened.

THE VERY WATER SHE DRINKS

I grew up with my mother. My father passed away when I was quite young. My mother took good care of me. She wanted the best for me. I have nothing against her as a mother. We lived in a high-density suburb,[1] the oldest high-density in Marondera. My mother wanted me to go to school, get a profession, and be somebody. Before the politics, our relationship was good. We were six in our family. One brother was in the army, one is a doctor with the government, one was in the CIO.[2] The one in Marondera does nothing, he's the lazy sheep of the family. He just does his own thing.

After I got involved in politics, we would fight, my mother and me. She would tell me to stop my political activities, but I wouldn't. Sometimes I think, *If only I had listened to her.* I passed my Ordinary Level exams but I didn't go any further with school. So, when I look back, I am not happy. I could have carried on with school at the same time as politics, but instead I chose something that I got nothing out of.

---

[1] Also known as a township. Before Independence in 1980, the "suburbs" were restricted to whites only, while black residents lived in townships or "locations." Since Independence, this urban division has effectively continued, with "low-density suburbs" home to the middle classes (and their domestic workers), and working class "high-density suburbs" the de facto home for black Zimbabweans.

[2] The Central Intelligence Organization, the much-feared state intelligence unit. Its agents, known as "CIOs," are believed to be responsible for the surveillance, harassment, abduction, and torture of government critics, opposition politicians, and their supporters.

But instead I had wanted to go to a local day school, with boys and girls together, but by the time I got my Grade 7 results, my mother had already signed for me to go to Nagle House, even though she had to pay fees there. It's a private Catholic girls' school, a very small school. There were about six hundred students from Form 1 to Form 6,[3] so you would know everyone by name, where they come from, their background, everything. I was into drama from a young age and I was also an athlete at school. I used to run in the four hundred meters, the eight hundred meters, the relays. One time, at a competition with a white school called Watershed, I thought, These people, they only sprint the last quarter of the race. So I started the four-hundred-meter race sprinting like mad. When the gun went *boom*, I ran like it was a one-hundred-meter race, and I kept on with the same energy. People were cheering me on, you know, but everyone thought I was going to get tired, because I was going full speed. This white girl thought she'd catch up with me. Her cheeks were red, she couldn't believe it that I didn't slow down. But she never caught me. I got the trophy there.

I was fifteen years old and the junior headgirl at my boarding school when people from an organization called the National Constitutional Assembly[4] came to our school. They said that the constitution of Zimbabwe was going to be rewritten and the youth should be involved because the constitution would affect us for the next twenty years. Only a few students were interested in the constitution-writing thing, so adults also used to attend our NCA workshops. First we had to get to know what was in the constitution, because most people did not know. Then we would get into an agenda and spend the whole day giving ideas. It was a discussion. The NCA people were not telling us what to do: we asked questions and gave our own suggestions. At those workshops, we learned how to go and mobilize other people, how to teach people that the constitution

---

[3] The equivalent of eighth to thirteenth grade in the U.S.

[4] Formed in 1996, the National Constitutional Assembly is a group of civil society organizations that began a campaign for a new constitution for Zimbabwe. The NCA's founding chairperson was Morgan Tsvangirai, who later became founding president of the MDC.

needed to be changed. In those days, working with NCA on the constitution and our rights, we used to have banners and we would sing songs based on the message. The reason they chose the youth was because they knew we had the most energy. They wanted us for the long term.

They didn't reveal it in the beginning, but I started to realize that behind the NCA a political party was being formed by people like Learnmore Jongwe.[5] I stayed involved. I don't know what pushed me, but probably it was the nights of working together or the people that I used to meet. I was beginning to understand the need for change, not just at the constitutional level.

I was a member of the first youth movement of the MDC—the Movement for Democratic Change.[6] We used to travel to Harare, to the University of Zimbabwe, where we had meetings about how we were going to change the minds of the people, to show them why they needed a new government.

The school authorities knew about my political activities because I sometimes missed school. And you know what the Catholics are like—there would be a hearing, a procedure every time. At first I was a boarder, then I was expelled from the hostel and became a day scholar, living with my mother.

It became very difficult for me at home, because my mother was from a rural background and strongly believed in the Zanu-PF government.[7] Zanu was the only party that my mother's generation knew, besides the whites. They had lived through the Rhodesian era; she had grown up with the apartheid of the white regime. Most people who lived through the liberation struggle believed that Zanu-PF was the only way.

One day when I was sixteen, my mother beat me. By this time my dad had passed away. She told me that even the water she drank came

---

[5] Learnmore Jongwe was the first spokesperson for the MDC. See Briggs's story.

[6] Then the opposition political party led by Morgan Tsvangirai.

[7] Opposition to Zanu-PF grew in urban areas, with support for the ruling party remaining strong in rural areas into the 1990s. See Briggs's story for more.

from a tap given to her by Zanu-PF. She said she wouldn't let me live with her if I was going to be involved in an opposition political party, but I didn't listen to her. I am the only girl in my family. As I told you, all my brothers worked in jobs that were connected to the government. So they were not ready for the youngest, the girl, to be different. My brother tried to speak to me about it—the one who was in the CIO. But I would speak my mind. I was just the opposite of other members of my family. My brothers didn't open up and discuss their opinions with me—they never do—but they did tell me to stop what I was doing. I told them, *You're protecting your jobs, I'm protecting the nation.*

Finally I had to leave school altogether. You know how it is with public exams: one day you are writing and then next week you are not and then the week after you are writing again. So I wrote one paper and then went to Harare because I had no exam. The next day I had an exam at two p.m. but I was late. I got into the exam room at seventeen minutes past two. My literature teacher begged the teacher in charge to wait for me. But the headmistress heard about it. When I was writing my accounts exam she came and said, *Even if you get ten As, I don't want you back in my school, Elizabeth. I want to train nuns, people who want to preach—I don't want politicians here.* The Catholic sisters really want you to pay attention and show you are listening, so everything you say must have *sister* at the end. When she had spoken I said, *Sorry, sister*, and she said, *Don't sorry me, Elizabeth.*

I was happy when my accounts results came. I had a B. Yes, I passed my O-Levels.[8] That's why my mother was so mad at me when my life got messed up with all this rallying and dancing. I didn't even go for my Advanced Levels. No school would want me. I think it all changed my character. Am I a difficult person? I don't know, but I do make things difficult for myself.

---

[8] Public exams taken in the equivalent of eleventh grade. You need good O-Level results to be accepted to study A-levels, and then good A-levels to be admitted to university.

I WON'T WALK BACKWARD

At seventeen, after I passed my O-Level exams, I got deeper involved in politics, mobilizing people in the area where I lived. In Marondera I was known, I was popular. At the rallies they used to say, *Where is she? Where is she?* I wasn't the only one, but what made me different from the few other women was that I didn't wait for something to happen, I would just speak my mind.

When I look back at those times, I feel this anger, and I don't know how I'm going to get it out. I've been a ladder to some other people. Some just used me to get to the top. *Voom!* they are *at* the top. But I am also proud that I've done my best, the best that I could have done. I'm proud that I was tortured for information and that I was able to endure it. I didn't reveal any secrets.

The Zanu-PF people offered me jobs in their party, but I never regretted that I didn't take them. As a human being I will never accept Robert Mugabe. I could have done what others like Jonathan Moyo[9] did, sitting in some office ordering people around if I wanted to, but I didn't want that. I wanted change. I still want change.

Marondera was one of the strongholds of Zanu-PF. In 2002, they came personally to ask me to mobilize people to go to a Zanu-PF rally— even though these Zanu-PF youths knew I was an MDC member. Robert Mugabe himself was coming to Marondera to address the people because we were getting toward the presidential elections that year. MDC had won some seats in Marondera two years back in the parliamentary elections, and now Zanu-PF were coming in force.

They came and said to me, *Elizabeth, we know you are MDC, but you are*

---

[9] Jonathan Moyo is widely known as a political scientist who penned articles criticizing the Mugabe government until he joined that government as Zanu-PF information minister and government spokesman. From that position, he designed a series of censorship and public-order laws that consolidated police and government power. He fell out of favor with Mugabe after registering as an independent candidate for a 2005 parliamentary election, which he won, but has since rejoined the Zanu-PF fold when it suits his political interest.

going to do this work for us, this dirty work. They even called it dirty work. *You are going to call your friends to come to the rally*, they said. *And we want you to be there.* And I said, *What if I don't? Would you kill me?* They said they would not but they would teach me a lesson. But I said, *If you can't mobilize your own people, I can't do it for you. I will mobilize my own people for Tsvangirai. If I walk backward, I will fall. I won't do that.*

So they went away. They had threatened me and thought, because I was only seventeen, that that would make me do it. Actually, I went to my people and told them not to go to that rally. And I have scars from the beating I endured as a result. They beat me that Saturday. They just came to my house not long after the meeting where Robert Mugabe was busy addressing people. I didn't go to the rally or close my door. I just sat at home. They came and kidnapped me. I don't remember how many people. We drove for almost an hour, then we stopped at a place near Rufaro Dam—you know that place where they found eighteen bodies in the dam?[10] Those were their areas. They beat you there, and if they wanted to kill you they just tied a rock to you and threw you in the water.

When we got to that place it was almost dark. The torture wasn't planned. These people were drunk. I was kicked and beaten. I was lying there and one of them set a piece of plastic alight and was using it to burn me, again and again on the same spot. See here on my stomach? This was a deep scar. I wasn't the only one who was taken there and tortured. The beating and torture only stopped because the Zanu-PF guys had to go to Harare. One of them dropped me off. I refused to go to the hospital. Later, MDC people managed to bring medical people to my house to help me. It was a deep burn on the stomach. You can imagine. If it was somewhere else it would have been less painful.

I was left with injuries to my ribs and my chest. I can't carry anything. Sometimes, at the Methodist Church here in Joburg, I walk up to

---

[10] Elizabeth says that, according to local accounts, someone fell into the dam while fishing and drowned. Trying to recover his body, his friends discovered eighteen unidentified bodies.

the third-floor office,[11] and when I get there, I can't breathe. I feel like something is pressing me down. I can't run or stand for a long time.

After that beating, as the June elections of 2002 were getting close, my mother was abducted for twenty-one days. I don't know where they took her or what they did to her. All she would say after was it was because of me. There was some information that the Zanu-PF people wanted from me. I am sorry I can't disclose that information. That was exactly what they wanted from me. All I can say is I was involved with Learnmore Jongwe, Job Sikhala,[12] and other top MDC guys. So the Zanu-PF knew I knew something. They knew I knew something that would help them.

They hadn't taken my mother to torture her, but they wanted me to believe they would. They knew she had a son who was in the army. That stopped them from harming her. She didn't say anything to those who were holding her. When she came back after those twenty-one days she wasn't in very bad shape, but she had deteriorated. My mother was old. You can imagine: she gave birth to me when she was forty-one, so when I was seventeen she was in her fifties, late fifties. She said to me, *Why don't you surrender and join them as others are doing? When the elections come, you can just vote MDC.* I said, *No, I have to act and vote MDC. I can't be MDC and act Zanu-PF.*

We continued to do workshops to learn how to teach the electorate, what to do when you are voting, things like that. Projects would come and go, and sometimes I didn't have time to be in those projects because I was always on the run. I would be told, *Be careful, they are looking for you.* We would stage a rally, and for two weeks I would be told I had to go underground, because that's when the Zanu-PF thugs would come after you. When I heard there had been a demonstration or rally in Marondera, I would run away to Mutare or somewhere else.

I couldn't stay easily in the same place as my mother either. I don't know why my mother feared my face. I said, *Let's not talk about politics*, but

---

[11] See footnote 11, page 35.

[12] Another MDC leader, a member of parliament, and a torture survivor.

it didn't work. We couldn't even speak about cooking. Either she would start the political arguments or I would. Even when we listened to music, everything would turn to politics. Maybe wherever she is today she is wondering what she could have done differently. But she tried to force me to stop politics, and that did not work.

I went to live in Chinhoyi with a friend. I was still seventeen when I went to Chinhoyi.

WE COULD HIT BACK BUT WITHOUT KILLING PEOPLE

In Chinhoyi, you know, things were happening. Remember, Tsvangirai had lost the election in 2002. So it was now more difficult, because we felt we had lost. You know when you have lost, you feel inferior? Just that feeling: you can't put up a fight; they are on top of us; there's killing and abducting everywhere in Zimbabwe. I have seen people who have been broken but are still alive. You ask them, *Who did this to you?* and they can't speak because they think their tormentors will come back for them.

We petrol-bombed the Zanu-PF headquarters in Chinhoyi in 2004. We were doing it for the people who had really won those elections. The people had voted MDC, but Zanu-PF rigged the election. All the rigged papers had been put in that building in Chinhoyi, the Zanu-PF headquarters. Also there were names of people recorded there, people they were going to go after, people who they knew voted MDC or who had mobilized people to vote MDC. People who had survived so far, but now they wanted to go after them. So it was like when they bombed the *Daily News*[13]—we also wanted to destroy information.

Other people were driving us. We went in the evening and we bombed the place and came back. It could have been done by one person,

---

[13] The *Daily News* was perhaps the most critical of Zimbabwe's independent newspapers. Between its founding in 1999 and its banning in 2003, the offices and printing press of the independent *Daily News* were bombed twice, while its issues were publicly burned and its journalists threatened and beaten up.

the driver, but who wants to do this alone? We did this because we were tired of being attacked. We wanted to show them we could fight back. We didn't want to kill people like they do. This was our demonstration to show that we could hit back but without killing people. Even the security guards, we told them to leave so they would not be harmed.

In the days following the bombing, the Zanu-PF guys took about seven of the guys I was working with. They took them to one of those Border Gezi camps and beat them.[14] Some died. They didn't do it to me, because they couldn't find me. I was in hiding. They also took innocent people and blamed them for the bombing, like an old man of seventy-five from Murehwa. They killed him. That's what they do: if something happens in Masvingo East that they don't like, they don't take revenge in Masvingo East—they do it in another area. You see, my family comes from Murehwa and that old man was kind of related to me, he had the same surname as me. They drove him all the way from Mutoko and they took his eyes out. Maybe they were cutting him while he was still alive. I don't know. What did he have to do with our actions?

When I was in Chinhoyi, they also abducted my brother's son. They wanted my brother to say where I was hiding. I think they took him when he was playing in the street. You know how kids do. My brother's wife phoned him to say she couldn't find the child. And my brother was being interrogated about my whereabouts by other CIOs. They told him, to his face, that they had his son and they wanted information. They didn't want to do it, because he was their workmate, but they had to follow orders. My brother knew where I was, but they didn't get any information from him. They gave the child back to him two days later.

Where was I hiding? In a village in the rural areas with the granny

---

[14] Border Gezi, after being named Minister of Gender, Youth and Employment in 2000, was involved in recruiting and training youth for Zanu-PF militias that went on to attack opposition organizers. A youth militia training camp—also rumored to be a torture camp, where many women were raped—was named after him. He died in a car accident in 2001. Zimbabweans tend to take a skeptical view of politicians' car "accidents"—see John's narrative.

of someone I knew. I stayed there for some months, trying to hide my identity, pretending to be a rural girl. I ate what they ate and dressed like them, because at that point Zanu-PF really wanted my head.

DYING IS A PROCESS

Time passed and I finally felt safe to come out of hiding. I thought they weren't looking for me anymore. You know Philip Chiyangwa[15] is from Chinhoyi? I spoke to him directly at his rally. That was in 2006. They had asked if anybody wanted to speak, expecting a thank you, and I stood up in front of him. I told him, *You are rich and I am poor, so there is a big difference between us.* I told him, *You are speaking from a full stomach, I am speaking from poverty, so you are telling me nothing about helping the poor. You need to come from the poor to understand them.* I told him that coming here and giving people blankets was not going to help them. I shamed him. I told him, *Don't even think people will vote for you because you gave them blankets after five years. Things have to change, and they will change one day.*

You know what happened? I didn't make it out of that place! Those people are so professional. A woman came up to me from the crowd and said, *Sisi, that was a really good speech.* Like, *Haa mwanangu wagona kutaura haa ndiwe chete.*[16] And then, *Imbouya pano tione.*[17] And that was it for me and the people I was with. When they take you, you are just surrounded. Their eyes tell you not to scream.

I was beaten again. I don't know where they took me, but I think it took an hour to drive there at a speed of about one hundred kilometers an hour, which means it was a hundred kilometers from Chinhoyi. They beat me. I was not beaten by men. I was beaten by women, maybe seven

---

[15] Philip Chiyangwa is Robert Mugabe's nephew, a Zanu-PF politician and one of the richest black men in Zimbabwe. He became known as one of the leaders of the "indigenization" program.

[16] My daughter, you spoke very well. You are the best.

[17] Kindly come over here.

or eight of them. They told me to remove my clothes and I didn't want to. I told them, *Dying is a process. I can either die here today or I can die some other day, so if you want, kill me. I am not going to take off my clothes.* They hit me.

These were women of my age. Zanu-PF has a lot of money because they are so corrupt, and that money is their power to make people do things like this. The women hit me until I blacked out. I couldn't even feel them. Then they tied my hands and legs so the only thing I could do was roll. They hit me with a pole and I started bleeding. Then, later, they left me under a tree. I was not dressed. The next morning, someone found me who knew me and helped me. It took me two weeks to recover. I couldn't speak well because my jaw hurt. I could hardly eat.

All that time my mother was sick. Then she passed away. When I went for her funeral, that was my last time home. My mother died a member of Zanu-PF. She never changed. Zanu-PF supplied everything for the funeral. I called my friends and told them not to attend.

The people in Mashonaland East heard I was back in Mashonaland West,[18] so when I went for the funeral, who do I see? Aah! The same people who had tortured me! They whispered, *After the burial*, so I knew they were ready to come after me again.

The Zanu-PF people told me they wanted all the information I knew about the opposition, from the beginning. They wanted to know how we communicate, what kind of tactics we used. I told them, *I am only in the youth and I don't know anything. We don't really know how the seniors do their things.* I said, *Let me go, let me leave the country.* Then they let me go. I had a passport.

People knew I had certain information, and I left because I didn't want to give away that information. It was not about the demonstrations or anything. It was not something I was involved in myself, but I had the information.

I was working with the youth activists. I had done some things. We

---

[18] Marondera is in Mashonaland East. Chinhoyi is in Mashonaland West.

would see Mugabe posters and then spend the whole night pulling them down. That kind of thing. But the way they talked about everything, it would be *Elizabeth did this*, not *Elizabeth and friends*. I would be blamed. I asked questions like, *Kana wandirova uchawanei?*[19] I was the same person who had spoken with Chiyangwa, and I was there at the petrol-bombing. My name always came up on top. I knew there would be trouble if I got caught again. That's why I wanted to leave.

So I said, *I am going*. The night of my mother's funeral, I left for South Africa.

TRAINED TO ASSASSINATE

On April 26, 2006, I left from Chinhoyi. I didn't want to go to Roadport[20] because I didn't want to run into someone who would recognize me. So I went to Mbare[21] and got on a bus to Beitbridge.[22] I suspected I was being followed. Every roadblock was terrifying. I suspected the soldiers at the border post would recognize me. I had told no one I was crossing the border, because I was afraid that I would be followed.

While I was in Beitbridge, I learned that my brother had died, the brother who was working in the CIO. That's why I am still alive—he wouldn't let the CIO kill me. The family love was still there even if we had our differences. My brother had told me, *We are trained to assassinate*, but then he himself died a painful death.

That brother was involved in politics, and so was my brother the soldier. Do you remember that time when some brigadiers died? That time when Mugabe was in Malaysia? There was a suspicion that some guys in the army wanted to assassinate the president. This was when the president

---

[19] What will you get after beating me?

[20] The terminus in Harare for informal transport heading south.

[21] Harare's oldest township.

[22] A town on the Zimbabwean side of the South African border, before the Limpopo River.

was out of the country, when the March 29 election results were delayed.[23] They really wanted to assassinate Mugabe. I know it, not from a personal source but from what was being said in political circles. They wanted to do it, but then what happened? One of the soldiers went and told the CIO. He wanted to sell the information for money, but he was the first to be killed. He was stupid enough to think Mugabe does those sorts of deals. They said, *How did you know? You must have been involved.* And they killed him. It was the same with my brother. They said my brother died in a car accident, but he wasn't in that car. He was taken from home. What we heard was he went away with friends. The next thing we heard was he had died, but there were no scratches on his body, no injuries.

When I heard this news, I ran away from the border post. I asked somebody for help and he said he had a truck. The truck driver was from the Congo. I stayed with him the whole night. It was around seven p.m. when I got into that truck. Unfortunately, I slept with him. I slept with him—otherwise he was going to say, *Get out.* I don't want to think about it.

THAT'S ALL SHE GETS

I got to Musina[24] but I didn't stay. I took a taxi to Joburg. The first two nights I was at Park Station, but you can't sleep there—it's a waiting area for people who have bought tickets, for people who have missed their train. So at night they ask to see your tickets, and if you don't have one then you must leave. During the day, I just sat in Joubert Park. Blank. I felt empty. Then this guy showed me the Methodist Church, the Johannesburg Central Methodist Church. People notice you have nowhere to go and they tell you about it, that there's a place where Zimbabweans can stay.

---

[23] During the tense period between the election and the delayed release of the results, with the future of Zimbabwe's government largely unknown, rumors of behind-the-scenes political machinations circulated freely, fueled by political violence on both sides. See the appendix on the 2008 elections.

[24] A town on the South African side of the Limpopo River.

It's very difficult to live at the Methodist Church. People come there with a lot of hope. People back home think there are jobs here, they think everything flows easily, but at the Methodist Church, you live according to the situation. You act according to the situation. It's not what people are but what the situation forces them to be. Life in Johannesburg is tough. People stab each other, people die. Maybe they just want your phone. There are Zimbabweans killing Zimbabweans.

I started sleeping in the church. It's a big place, from the ground floor to the fifth floor. The main sanctuary is on the second floor. Only the women sleep there, under the benches or on top of benches. The church was very full when I first came. Men were even sleeping in the streets because there was no space inside. There is no order, really, at the Methodist Church, except when the bishop tells us to shut up. That's when we have silence. There is a smell, because there are a lot of people, but it's cleaned every day. I appreciate that. I slept there in the sanctuary for quite a while, and then I got a space in the storeroom.

Some people don't think there is life outside that church, you know what I mean? They don't even leave that church. They just wipe their faces and sit again in the building, eat, bathe, and then it's night and they sleep again. People arrive with projects and plans, but nothing really happens. I don't know. There are a lot of job offers. Anybody who wants some cheap labor comes there. Every day. But the money they pay? Hey! It's so little that people would rather sit.

I stayed there for a month. It was quite weird for me. The only way women like me live there is by prostitution. Even those who have other kinds of jobs do it because they want extra money. You see women sitting there. Some guy comes with an offer, the woman can't say no because she has nothing. The men know what to say and how to offer. Imagine: she's hungry and somebody offers her a plate of *sadza*.[25] Tomorrow he comes again with another plate of sadza. That's all she gets.

---

[25] See footnote 5, page 31.

When you are a woman, you want to have your own kids, your own husband. So women think they are doing the right thing for themselves when they get a boyfriend. It's not like they are stupid; they are doing the right thing but in the wrong place. They want to have a family, but they are doing it with the wrong people. They want to fulfill their womanhood, but the guy they are dating does not even have a job.

GIVE ME BACK MY LIFE

In 2009, I decided to go back home. I thought people had forgotten, I thought we had buried the past. I met a friend of my father's. The only thing that he asked me was, *Wadzoka? Don't ever think kuti uchagara kuno.*[26] I couldn't stay in Harare because of my past. I felt that if they knew I was back, they would kill me. Even though I had gone home with the idea of starting afresh, I decided to go back to South Africa.

I was in Zimbabwe for only twelve days. After the violence in 2008, my relatives were not comfortable with me. People have had enough trouble. They didn't want to have anything to do with me. They would say, *If you are still the same Elizabeth, I can't have you in my house.*

I saw my CIO brother's son in those twelve days before I came back to South Africa. He was four at the time he was abducted. You know kids have vivid memories, so I didn't want to ask him about it, because it was almost three years later and he was going to school now. But the people there had influenced him, telling him the kidnappers had taken him because of his aunt, myself. The boy was scared. He wouldn't come near me. I tried giving him chips, I tried giving him chocolate, but nothing worked. When I was in the kitchen he stayed close to his mum, and when I made a move you could see he was afraid. Probably he thinks I am the same as the people who took him, I don't know. But I just pray that by the time he's ten or eleven, he will have forgotten.

---

[26] You have come back? Don't ever think you will live here.

My other brother doesn't talk much about politics. He tells me that I am the only one he has left, and if I do something silly, I will be gone. But me being me, I keep coming back to politics.

My plan is, if Morgan[27] wins the presidential election, I will confront him and tell him to give me back my life. I know that right now he can't, but it will happen one day. I will, I'll confront him. It will be face to face.

DEMOCRACY THAT I CAN FEEL

These days, we get the impression that the MDC can't do anything for us. I talk with the MDC here in South Africa, but all they do is promise and promise. All they say is, *We see some potential in you, Elizabeth.* That's all. They should give me something to do. I really regret the past. All I can do here is work for no pay. Even if you can do a certain job, if you can't list it as your experience on paper, it's useless. I have gone through a lot, I have been beaten up and burned. I have no profession. I gave up all my opportunities. It makes me angry, but I have no one to blame.

Others who were with the MDC in Zimbabwe are still there. They say, *We are still in the struggle.* There are people who have lost their eyes and lips, people who have lost their loved ones, people who have been paralyzed. I don't want to talk about compensation, I don't want to be paid, but for Zimbabwe to have democracy, it must be something I can feel.

I will find something to do here. I will build a career here, but only God knows where I will start. I just hope one day things are going to change. Probably I will not be in the books of history, but I know I have gone through a lot.

---

[27] Tsvangirai, MDC leader.

ZENZELE

AGE: 46

OCCUPATION: *Former police officer and teacher*

INTERVIEWED IN: *Vancouver, Canada*

Zenzele lives in a cramped, government-subsidized studio apartment in a high-rise overlooking downtown Vancouver. He says he doesn't like living so far above the ground, and that when he finishes school and is working again, he will find his own place, street level, something with a porch, maybe even a yard. A thin man, dressed in running pants and a T-shirt, Zenzele tells his story calmly, lying in his bed, staring at the ceiling. He smiles often. He closes his eyes and sings. But as he begins to talk about the events that led him to flee Zimbabwe, he stands and paces the room. He riffles through a dresser drawer, pulling out hospital records and other evidence, pointing at the pages, reading names and dates and diagnoses. As a teenager and then as a teacher in his native Matabeleland, Zenzele experienced the campaign called Gukurahundi during the 1980s. Joining the police in the late 1980s did not, as he had intended, prevent the government from harassing him. Instead, it launched him on a collision course with the authorities, leading to an appalling case of torture. He has been in Canada for a year and a half, and spends his days in school, his nights studying. When asked about the family he left behind in Zimbabwe, he became silent. He tapped his head with the flat of his hand and stared out the window at the city far below. I don't like to talk about that, *he said.*

I've got a passport here. It's called a refugee passport. It says, *This guy can travel to all the countries of the world except to Zimbabwe.* This is my first passport. I got it one week ago. On the first page it says, *This refugee travel document is valid for travel to all countries except to Zimbabwe.*

I read the news from Zimbabwe every day. I just want to know whether or not it is safe to go back home. As soon as Zimbabwe is free, I'll try to find an air ticket and then go, because I can't die here. Of course, I am grateful for Canada for giving me a home as a refugee. But how can you make your life here by yourself? You need to go where there are people you know, where you are free, where you are happy. Here you are always depressed. You come into this room. You stay here the whole day. The food is a strange type of food. This apartment is too high and it's too lonely.

I miss the wide-open spaces, the bush, the forest. I miss the sounds of barking dogs, and of crowing chickens. In the morning there, you hear the chickens *cocoricorico*, and you know it's time to wake up. There's so many things... I miss the children playing in the streets. There are so many different types of games that they play during the evenings, the afternoons. I miss the noise—the noise of people singing, playing music. People there open up their radios so loud.

I grew up in Bulawayo, in what we called the western suburbs, where only blacks used to live. The government of Ian Smith was in power. So all white people used to live in the eastern suburbs, and the blacks used to be separated into the western suburbs. But my childhood was okay. There were no shortages of food, no shortages of jobs. There was bush, outside of the city, a forest—big, tall, green trees. We used to go hunting with our dogs, for rabbits and deer, what we call bushbuck, for guinea fowls and birds. We used to shoot birds with catapults.[1] We would leave in the morning and come back later in the afternoon from the forest. Bulawayo has got these very nice wide streets. And it's not hilly. There are a few hills here and there.

---

[1] Slingshots.

We used to enjoy life in what was called Rhodesia. No one was starving like what is happening in Zimbabwe now. My mother used to work at a factory called Voyagers House, where they made shirts and suits. And after she quit that job, she worked as a housemaid for a white couple. My father was a policeman in the British South Africa Police. He used to ride on a motorbike, or sometimes a bicycle, patrolling or arresting miscreants. Normal police duties.

Maybe because I was young, I wasn't too aware of racism. I didn't experience much of it. But I remember one time, I went with my grandmother to the trade fair in the white suburbs, and I bumped into this white man. I was very young, about eight or nine years old. We were having a look, walking on the streets because black people weren't allowed to walk on the sidewalk. There are so many nice things to see at the trade fair, all the people showing their wares, so I was distracted, not watching where I was going, and I collided with this big white guy. He gave me such a beating! He slapped me and kicked me and I fell down. And his girlfriend was standing there, smiling and clapping. She was clapping her hands. My grandmother was crying. There was nothing she could do.

I'll never forget that. But at the time, I didn't think much about it. I was a kid. My grandmother held me by my arm and we moved on. There were some other things to enjoy at that trade fair.

LIBERATION WAR

When I was young, the soldiers used to patrol in the townships in big heavy vehicles, called Puma vehicles. There were so many kinds of security forces patrolling the townships. There was BSAP.[2] And then there was PATU, the Police Terrorist Unit. These were the security forces of the old regime. The guerillas used to infiltrate into the townships and place bombs. I remember one time, Smith's security forces were looking for

---

[2] The British South Africa Police.

these guys, and they surrounded a house and there was heavy shooting. And you know what happens in the townships when there's an incident like that—people come and try to have a look. They tried to chase people away, but in townships people like to have a good look at things. I was eight or nine. I saw the soldiers carrying dead bodies into their truck. They were guerillas from ZIPRA, the Zimbabwe People's Revolutionary Army, Joshua Nkomo's men. I think they were using that as a safe house. But they got discovered by the soldiers, and then there was fighting. Some of them got killed and the others escaped.

I got involved in Zapu,[3] the Zimbabwean African People's Union, when I was fifteen, in 1979. My mother had a Zapu membership card; my grandmother had a Zapu card. Bulawayo was a Zapu stronghold. My father didn't like that we were involved in such political activities, because he was a member of the police. He didn't get involved. But everyone was involved in politics in those days. And people thought the guerillas were good and smart, and that they had some medicine which made them disappear. They would smear themselves with this medicine and vanish, and then the soldiers and police would find no guerillas. People used to believe that sort of thing.

We used to hold marches during the night. We would go all around the streets of Bulawayo, singing and clapping hands, marching and dancing. The western suburbs have so many streets, those nice wide streets, and when we would pass, dancing, other people would join us until in the end the streets would be blocked. There were so many people there— children, elderly people, adults. We used to travel very far away, right up to the next township. Singing until twelve midnight, or one. Then the police and the soldiers would come and spray tear gas on us and we would disappear into some houses on the street. We would put water on a handkerchief and put that over our noses, so that the tear gas wouldn't affect us.

---

[3] Zapu was one of the two main nationalist political organizations fighting for Zimbabwean independence; ZIPRA was its military wing. For more details, see the appendix.

We used to sing about Joshua Nkomo, the leader of Zapu, a song that says, *They won't kill him, they won't kill Joshua Nkomo.* Everyone loved Nkomo. He was a charismatic character. Everyone loved him all over the country.

RECONCILIATION

When Mugabe came to power, in 1980, things were pretty good. The Zimbabwean dollar was still strong. There was food. But he ran down the country, bit by bit. I didn't like him from the start. One thing is that most people from Bulawayo don't like Mugabe. I had been taught to be anti-Mugabe. But the other thing is that he was just an impostor. During those first days he said, *Reconciliation, reconciliation. The people in Zimbabwe must reconcile.* And then he turned on the people. First he turned on the Ndebele people, and then he turned on the white people.

In 1982, soldiers surrounded the whole city of Bulawayo and herded people into beer gardens. They were saying they were screening for dissidents. And they searched house by house. These four men came into our yard. There was a big rock outside our house and I was sitting on that rock. I was seventeen, still in high school. They said, *Everyone, let's go into the house.* They herded us into the house and said, *Open this trunk* to my grandmother. *Open this* and *Open that.* Grandmother opened everything. They couldn't find anything. They didn't care about me because I was wearing my school uniform. If I was older, maybe I was going to vanish like other people. Many people were taken away, some we never saw again.

THE WIND THAT CARRIES AWAY ALL THE CHAFF

Gukurahundi means "the wind that carries away all the chaff" or "the trash." They were saying that all these people in Matabeleland are trash. In the first election, everyone in Matabeleland voted for Joshua Nkomo. All twenty seats went to Nkomo. And Mugabe was very angry about that. He called Nkomo "the self-appointed Ndebele king." The Ndebele are the people who live in Matabeleland, a Zulu offshoot. Mugabe said that there were ex-ZIPRA soldiers, from Zapu's armed wing, working for the South African government, which was crazy. He didn't have any support in the south of the country, so he wanted to beat up people so they would be more compliant. It was a sort of revenge measure, starting from as early as 1982, because no one had voted for him. Mugabe is a very vengeful person.

Of course, the ex-ZIPRA were there, but from what I knew, these guys went back to the bush because they were being victimized in the new, integrated army of Zimbabwe for being ZIPRA. They deserted the army and went back to the bush. Some of them took up arms. Some were fighting Mugabe's government. But Mugabe was saying that all Ndebele people were dissidents. He was trying to play the tribal card, to get the Shona to hate the Ndebele people. He was trying to find an excuse to eliminate the people in Matabeleland.

The government created the Fifth Brigade in 1982. In Zimbabwe, they have many brigades. There is one brigade, two brigade, three brigade. But this Fifth Brigade was specially trained by North Koreans. The Koreans came to the country and trained these people for the purpose of sending them to Matabeleland. They took them from other army units. It was sort of a tribal army, made up of Shona people only. They'd been indoctrinated to be hostile to Ndebele people. And that was their mission, to eliminate. They didn't want any conversation with you. They would look you in the eye because they were powerful. They carried the guns, so they could do whatever they wanted.

YOU MUST SING PRAISES TO ROBERT MUGABE

After secondary education, I became a teacher. During those days, there was a shortage of teachers because Zimbabwe had just got independence. So the government recruited many teachers, untrained teachers, to fill in those vacant positions. They were called temporary teachers. I finished high school in 1983, and then I started teaching. I was teaching in Tsholotsho, in the rural areas, and I was given a beating during Gukurahundi.

These soldiers used to make us sing during the night. They called them *pungwes*. It's Shona for "an all-night party." If you didn't go, they would identify you as someone who didn't come to the meeting. At their meetings, they would denounce Joshua Nkomo and the dissidents, and say, *You must sing praises to Robert Mugabe.* These parties were out in the forest, in the bush, under the trees. There would be a big fire and they'd be holding their rifles and dancing and jumping up and down. And you were expected to dance too. Sometimes I danced because I knew that if I didn't, they would kill me, these guys.

Even children had to go to these *pungwes*. After the meeting was over, the soldiers would take all the girls who were old enough to have sex, and they would say, *Remain behind.* Then they would sleep with them, rape them. The girls were thirteen, fourteen, twelve years old. Some of them were my students. I was teaching Grade 7 at the time. They would come into the class and fall asleep because they'd been sexually abused the whole night.

These parties were happening every night, and we were expected to teach in the morning. You couldn't talk about it with your students. If you did that, you'd get killed. The kids didn't talk about what was happening. They knew. Even the parents of these raped kids could do nothing about it. There were no police to make a report to. The students, headmaster, the parents, the whole village was terrorized. Sometimes the students didn't come to school. And you never asked why they're not coming to school. But even though we were terrorized, we were still teaching, because if we stopped, the soldiers were going to say, *Why did you stop teaching?* They wanted things to look normal when they were not.

IT SHOCKED ME

Once we went to the store in Tsholotsho, three teachers from my school. This may have been in 1983. Coming out of the store, we saw soldiers talking to these young men. They were boys, about my age, eighteen years old. They were driving a Scotch cart, pulled by donkeys. The soldiers said, *Run!* And the boys ran. And then, when they were some meters away, the soldiers started aiming. They said to us, *You teachers, get away from here!* And we had to run for our lives. I thought they were going to shoot us too.

All the time we ran, we were looking back. They used the boys as target practice. They aimed like that, then, *Pah!* They shot one. And then, *Pah!* They shot the other one. These soldiers. Just like that. And the worst thing was that one of those boys didn't die there. People told us that boy died at five o'clock. He was shot in the morning, around eleven. He bled to death. And they didn't care. They were not accountable to anyone. They were just village boys. It shocked me. And no one could do anything about it.

One other time, a village man was cutting thorn bushes to make a fence of thorns to protect his fields from cows, donkeys, and elephants. When the soldiers saw him dragging those bushes, they said, *You are hiding dissidents' tracks.* Then they shot him. I saw that. There were so many such instances. In Tsholotsho, they made people dig their own graves. And then after they dug the grave, they used to shoot them, and they would fall into that grave. Some of them, they herded them into their houses and lit a match and burned the whole thing down.

They knew that no journalist was going to go there to document these mass killings. Journalists were banned from going to the countryside during those days.

YOU ARE A VERY LUCKY MAN

The first time the Gukurahundi soldiers beat me, I was in a bus traveling to my school. I was drinking with some friends in the bus. Tsholotsho is about 180 kilometers from Bulawayo, and most buses coming from Bulawayo are heading to rural areas out of the city. They used to do these roadblocks regularly, saying they were searching for dissidents. They would ask everyone to get out with their bags and they would search you. The bus came to a roadblock and the soldiers ordered us all out. There were ten soldiers. I was drunk. I started to yell at them, *You have killed all our people.* I was yelling and swearing, and then they grabbed me. I said, *You have killed so many of our people. You are dogs and bastards.* I said, *Your hands are full of blood.*

They said, *Okay, everyone get back into the bus except for you. We are going to deal with you.* We were in the bush, right in the middle of nowhere in Tsholotsho. They gave me a beating, a real beating. I was rolling on the ground. And the bus left. But when the bus was a few meters away, they shot some rounds into the air from their AK rifles. *Pop, pop, pop!* Then the bus stopped. They said, *Run and get on the bus.* I thought I was going to get shot. I ran.

There were other teachers from my school on that bus, and everyone was saying, *This young man has got so much courage, but they will kill him.* When I got to school, I was bruised all over. My headmaster said, *You are a very lucky man.* Because so many people in Tsholotsho were getting killed.

I was always running afoul of these soldiers. Another time, we were having a nice weekend of drinking in a place called Jimila in Tsholotsho. We were drinking under a tree and these youth brigades—Mugabe's militias—ordered us to go to their meeting. Youth brigades were a sort of militia that Zanu-PF was training to intimidate people or to beat them up during election time, so that they would vote for Zanu. Mugabe used to bus in these youth brigades from other provinces. That weekend, they drove in on two buses to Jimila and they told us, *We are holding a meeting here and you must all attend.* They didn't talk to us. They gave us an order.

We said, *No, we're not going.* They gave us all a beating. They used sticks and boots, screaming and cursing and shouting, *You refuse to go to the people's meeting! You will get what you deserve.* No, we didn't go to their meeting. Instead, we went to the small clinic nearby. My arm was broken and they put it in a sling. My friends' faces were bleeding.

It was getting too bad. These nightly meetings were driving us mad. The children were falling asleep in class. The teachers were falling asleep in class. And at the meetings, sometimes we would get abused. They'd say, *Hey, you teachers are not singing. You're not singing loudly enough.* They would say, *If you don't sing we are going to punish you.* There was never a beating at the meetings, but there were threats. So many threats. At one time, they made me secretary and gave me a book and said I must write down all the villagers who were supposed to come to the meeting who didn't show up. That was the last straw. Documenting people and giving their names to the Gukurahundi soldiers? That was as good as killing them, because they would be hunted down and killed. It was either do that or leave. When I left, I threw that book away.

There were seven of us who ran away. This was late 1983. But we didn't plan for the seven of us, because if you plan like that, people will sell you out. We planned for a few, but others joined because they knew they couldn't remain. We left at about two in the morning. There was a *pungwe*, and when it was over, we took our suitcases and started walking to a place about sixty kilometers away, to catch the train to Bulawayo. We were scared all the time that maybe they would come after us. The bushroad we were using was sandy. There is lots of sand in Tsholotsho, fine, deep sand, so it took us hours to walk there. There were soldiers at the railway station when we got there, asking questions: *Where are you coming from? Where are you going?* We said, *We are going to the city for payday*, because on paydays we used to go to the city and get our money and then come back to school. This time we were going for good.

I stayed with my grandmother in Bulawayo for around seven months, until the Fifth Brigade was replaced.[4] Then all the teachers started going back. The school was in ruins. It was overrun with goats and donkeys and chickens. Our huts had fallen down, so we had to sleep in the classroom for the first days while the villagers repaired the houses.

---

[4] It was only in December 1987 that Joshua Nkomo and Robert Mugabe signed a peace accord and amalgamated Zanu and Zapu as Zanu-PF. Dissidents were granted amnesty if they gave themselves up by May 1988. The Fifth Brigade withdrew from Matabeleland South in late 1984.

NO ONE WAS GOING TO HARASS ME

I went back to teaching in 1984 and taught until 1986. I joined the police in 1987. Even though the Fifth Brigade had been replaced by another brigade, they were still harassing and terrorizing the people. I was sick and tired of being at the mercy of these so-called security forces. In the police, no one was going to harass me. Being a policeman, I was secure because I was in a position to defend myself. The fact of my father being an ex–police officer also had a big influence on my decision to join the police.

I spent one year in training, six months at law school studying what is called "law and police," and then another six months in counterinsurgence, COIN training. I was a regular police officer, but my branch of the police was called the Zimbabwe Republic Police Support unit. It was sort of a fighting wing of the police. It has been in existence since the days of the Rhodesian government. People don't like it, because it's notorious in Zimbabwe for beating people up. We were trained for counterinsurgency and riot control, special operations, VIP protection. We also had anti-poaching duties. We went out into the bush to fight poachers who were killing elephants and rhinos. The whole time I was a police officer, I lived in a police camp. First I lived in Harare, then in Rusape, and then in Fairbridge Camp, in Bulawayo. We lived together in police camps because we were supposed to work as a unit, not on our own.

I worked in Rusape from 1988 to 1998. I met my wife there. She lived in one of the villages. Rusape is a very big farming area. I was there about the time they were starting the farm takeovers. I knew some of these white farmers, because we used to go to those farms to buy goats or cattle to slaughter for meat in our police camp. Their land was given away to Mugabe's supporters. They would just tell these farm invaders to go and settle on that land. If the farmer tried to throw them out, they would beat up that farmer or arrest him, or even murder him. Some of these farmers were making reports to us that there were people settling illegally on their farms, but we were told to do nothing about it. There was nothing that I could do. It was sad to see these hordes of misinformed Mugabe supporters, cutting down trees, killing wild animals, and generally laying all the land to waste.

It gave me so much pain to see all those things. Someone has been working on that farm for many years, and from nowhere they just say, *Leave the farm.* He leaves his tractors, all the farm equipment, his house, his cattle. He goes away with nothing. I saw a farm that was burned down at Nyazura by these so-called war veterans.[5] They were above the law. Most of them were ex-combatants from ZANLA, the armed wing of Zanu. Of course, you felt your hands were tied, that you had to do your duty partially. Because one of the moral principles of working in the police is that you must not show any fear or favor when you deal with people. But if you are scared of war veterans, then you are not executing your duties in the correct manner.

GREEN BOMBERS

There were other instances in which I needed to do something that I didn't want to do. They'd say, *Go and break up NCA meetings.*[6] I did that some number of times in Rusape and I didn't like it. There are these rallies all the time. I had to give them tear gas so that they would scatter to all corners of the earth.

In 1998 I left Rusape and went to Fairbridge Police Camp in Bulawayo. Those were the days when a newspaper called the *Daily News* was still publishing.[7] Members of the police were prohibited from reading that paper. They said, *You can't read this paper, because it speaks badly about Mugabe.* They meant that it was anti-government. I used to buy it in the city, hide it in my underpants, tuck my shirt in, and go into my housing

---

[5] Those who fought in the liberation war (also called the Rhodesian civil war) against Rhodesian forces, roughly between 1964 and 1979 with 1971–1979 seeing the most intense fighting.

[6] The National Constitutional Assembly. See the timeline in the appendices.

[7] The independent *Daily News* was founded in 1999, bombed twice, and banned in 2003.

camp and read it. After I read it, I would give it to some friends.

Morgan Tsvangirai started to appear on the political scene around the time of the constitutional referendum, before the constitutional referendum in 2000. Mugabe wanted to turn Zimbabwe into a one-party state using the constitution, but people said no. The Movement for Democratic Change, the MDC, was newly formed. People said Mugabe lost in that election, and he was very angry. I was working at a place called Binga, a very small town on Lake Kariba, near the border with Zambia. Mugabe sent youth militias called the Green Bombers there because he had lost the election in the Binga constituency. They are called the Green Bombers because of their green uniforms. At every constituency where Mugabe lost, a reign of terror, including murders, tortures, and maimings, would follow. The Green Bombers are very destructive. They are young people—some as young as sixteen, seventeen, some are school dropouts—trained to beat up those who are opposed to Zanu-PF during election times.

These youth militia were beating people in Binga, and I was called to go there and restore order. I had six men under me, and we teamed up with police from Binga. They were destroying buildings, beating people up, burning shops. There were about fifteen of us and over fifty of them. They were drinking alcohol that they had looted from the bottle store. When we got there and the Green Bombers saw us, they said, *You are Zanu-PF police. We are members of the same party. We will continue with our looting because the police belong to Mugabe.*

And I said, *No, that's not the case.* I was the leader of that section. I said, *You are committing a crime. You must stop. You are all under arrest.* Oh, they were very angry. They started insulting us, threatening us. And I said to my guys, *Boys, tear gas them.* We sprayed them with tear gas and broke up their ranks with rubber batons. We were carrying AK rifles too, but we did not have to use those. They screamed and shouted. They were surprised. They didn't know that was the reaction they would get. They were used to doing whatever they wanted and getting away with it because they belonged to Zanu-PF. We gave them a beating and they ran away in all directions in the bush.

We arrested thirty-three of them, loaded them into trucks. We gave them a taste of their own medicine: what it felt like to feel tear gas on your eyes and get a beating and be thrown into the cells. At least we gained the trust of the people, that these cops are doing their duty. I talked to one guy as we were leaving, the owner of the bottle store which had been looted and burned. I said, *Don't worry. We've got those people and we will take them to jail. They won't bother you anymore.* But he had lost his property and his store was burnt down—there was no way he was going to recover his money.

We drove them to the police station in Binga and locked them in the cells. It was late in the afternoon, around four or five. I said, *Let's go home. We'll come back tomorrow and document the evidence for the prosecution in court.* But the following day, when we drove back to Binga, there was no one in the cells. They had been released. I was angry. I thought, *Where are these people, these criminals, these arsonists?* The member in charge of that police station said to me, *I'm sorry, Zenzele. The order came from Harare that these people must be released.* He said, *This is a political matter, my hands are tied.*

After that, I took time off. We used to take ten days after every tour of duty. A tour of duty could last one and a half to two months. When I returned, we were deployed to the Beitbridge border post. There, I heard a radio signal that I was under arrest myself. It said I must come to Binga to face a prosecutor on charges of assault GBH—grievous bodily harm—because we had beaten up these Zanu-PF youth militia. Later, another signal, this one from the commander of the police in Harare, declared that everyone who had been involved in recent violent acts had been pardoned. This was a blanket pardon issued to protect the Green Bombers. But one of my bosses said that the pardon applied to me, too.

I said, *But there is nothing to forgive. I was doing my duty. I want to go there and say so in court.*

He said, *You can't go there.*

I HAD NEVER VOTED

I started to feel the country was ruined. Before 2000, it was already sliding into ruins. But then the war veterans went on strike and Mugabe said he was going to pay them pensions from the national coffers. That money was not budgeted for. They gave these war veterans money that wasn't in the bank. And that was the second time those people were being paid. They were paid immediately after 1980, when they came in from the bush. They gave them lump sums, thousands of dollars. And they were given monthly payments for a certain period of time. Then, after they squandered it, they wanted some more. And Mugabe gave it to them from nowhere.

Things started getting very expensive and inflation grew. We used to get paid about two hundred dollars, and it was enough for a person and his family. As time went on, we were being paid three, four, five thousand dollars, but it was not enough to live on. All the people in Zanu-PF were being given big positions in the army and police, while we, who had never been war veterans, were living on nothing. To be promoted in rank in the police, we had to write a test, five papers. You pass those papers, and you went to the board and they didn't give you any rank. They gave priority to these war veterans. Most of them were illiterate. We used to joke that we would give one of them a resignation form and he would sign it without even looking, and the next thing you would hear is that he's out of a job. Most of the work was done by us. We used to write operational orders and give them to them to sign. Those guys got all the promotions because they were ex-guerillas of Mugabe's ZANLA. They were our bosses, but we did all the work.

By this time, our money was mostly useless. But somehow we survived. Just like people are surviving right now on nothing in Zimbabwe, on one meal a day. Or no meal a day.

In 2002, there was a vote. In Zimbabwe, on the day of elections, every policeman must vote in his senior officer's office. They would say, *Put your X here, on Zanu-PF*. You were forced to vote for Zanu-PF whether you liked it or not.[8] The police, the prison services, the army. Everyone comes in and they tick off all your names, that so and so has voted for the proper party. But on this day, with voting in the senior officer's office, I said to myself, *No, I'm not going to go there.*

I had never voted in my life. This was the first and only time I would do it. I had never been politically active before. Even when I was a Zapu member as a kid, I was just enjoying myself, singing with other people. I had never had time to go to the voting station, killing the whole morning in a long queue until I got to vote. I just wasn't interested. I got interested in politics when the MDC was formed, and when I could see that Mugabe was ruining the country. That's when I got really interested in politics.

So on that election day, I said I was sick. And I went out the back door of my house, and through a side gate. I snuck away and went to vote with the civilian population, at a school called Fairbridge Primary School. There were lots of people there. This was the first time for the MDC to be in an election, and everyone wanted to vote. I joined the queue and waited two hours. At the police station, you had to put your X down under the watchful eye of the commander. But at the civilian polling station, you went by yourself into the polling booth and put your X on your ballot paper. When you left, someone else registered your ballot paper so it was anonymous. I voted for the MDC. When I marked that paper, I felt like I was getting my revenge on Mugabe. It felt good.

But unfortunately, I was seen there by members of the CIO or PISI. PISI is a branch in the police, called Police Internal Security Intelligence. Their prime duty is to spy on other policemen.

The following day our commanding officer called me into his office. He was a war veteran, the officer commanding the whole district. He

---

[8] Shepherd Yuda, an employee of the prison service, filmed this process of forced voting with a hidden camera after originally setting out to document life inside Zimbabwe's jails. His film, made for the *Guardian* U.K., captures these instructions being given to prison officials and voter meddling at Zanu-PF rallies. Yuda has since fled Zimbabwe with his family.

said, *All the others voted here in this office, but you did not come. You said you were ill, but you were seen voting with the civilian population and we know you voted for MDC.*

I was standing at ease, with my hands behind my back. *We have been watching you for a long time*, he said. *Look at all these things.* He took a thick file out of his drawer. He said, *You are disloyal. In Binga you arrested members of the government. You have been bringing subversive newspapers here and distributing them to other members of the force. You want to cause mutiny here.*

I was speechless. That was the first time I'd seen that file. He told me, *You are always doing these things against the government that pays you.*

I told him, *I'm not going to beg or anything. In Binga, I was doing my job, and I've got a right to read any paper that I want.* I told him, *Look, my vote is my secret. That's what the constitution says. We're always writing tests about the Zimbabwe constitution. The constitution says I can vote for whomever I want.*

He said, *Here, the only vote is Zanu-PF. If you work, you are getting paid Zanu-PF money, so that's the party you should vote for.*

Excuse me sir, I said, *but the party is not paying me. The taxpayers of Zimbabwe are paying me. I work for the people of Zimbabwe. I don't work for Zanu-PF.*

Then he got up out of his chair and started pointing and swearing at me, saying, *People like you won't last in this police organization. You are a traitor, a reactionary.* Whatever that means. He said so many things. I can't remember. What I knew was that he was furious. He said to me, *Get out of here.* And I banged the door and left.

From that time on, I was never involved in active duty. They made me work in camp. At the main gate, there is a guardroom. That's where I was working, opening and closing the gate for cars that come into the police camp, writing down license plates and asking, *Who are you going to see inside the camp?* That type of job. It was nothing, in fact. I was a sergeant. Sometimes you would be sitting all day, for eight hours, doing nothing. There were so many things going on in my mind at that time. Those first days I wanted to resign.

They started searching my house in camp. When I was out, they would come into my house looking for what they considered to be subversive material. My kids were at school. My wife was scared all the time. She wanted me to resign or to desert, but she didn't want to leave the country. I don't know if the men were CIO or PISI. I have no idea who they were. They didn't talk to me, but I saw them all the time. They used to hang around on corners. Sometimes, they would sit in a car. They were different people every day, coming to my house, following me around. I could see them changing shifts. And I could detect when someone had been inside. I knew how to do that. You tie a thread on the door and if someone pulls that door, the thread will break. I did that every time I went out. When I wanted to go out to the city of Bulawayo, I had to ask for permission so I could leave camp. My father was sick during those days. He was sick in hospital. I had to find time to go and visit him, but sometimes they didn't give me permission.

Don't think it was only me. There were so many of us who were in trouble. Those were the days when they said they were getting rid of undesirables in the police force. This PISI was busy. The MDC was becoming a political force, and they thought some of the police were members of MDC. They were right to fear, because some people didn't like the government anymore. They could see that things were going downhill. There were so many senior officers who were taken out of active service and put into what is called the police commissioner's pool. They used to sit outside under a tree all day doing nothing, playing checkers and dice because they were withdrawn from duty. Very, very, senior officers. They used to put on their uniform and go there. It was mental torture.

When I saw things like that, I decided to quit. All that time, the pressure was mounting. I signed my resignation form and I went to my commanding officer, this war veteran. But he refused to sign it. He said, *No, you are not going anywhere. We want to keep an eye on you.* I didn't talk much that time. I just took my resignation form and left. I knew many guys who deserted with their guns and left for South Africa, but I wanted to resign in the proper manner. So I decided to fill in the form myself. I forged it and posted it to Harare. And after three months, it came back saying, *Your resignation, 28th February 2003, has been approved.* My commanding officer was so angry.

I couldn't wait for my last working day to come to leave the police camp. We went to stay in a house near my parents' place in the Western suburbs of Bulawayo. And these guys continued following me. They continued following me.

WE WANT TO KNOW WHAT YOU WERE DISCUSSING

One day, I had visitors, some white friends from a farm in Nyamandhlovu. We were just drinking tea and talking. When they left, these CIO guys came into my house. I was at home alone. There were two of them, wearing those nice suits that members of the CIO and PISI usually wear. They knocked and before I said, *Come in,* they walked into the house as if it was theirs and said, *You had some white visitors here. What were you discussing? We want to know what you were discussing with those white people here.*

I said, *You can't do this. This is not your house. I quit the police and left the police camp. I don't live there anymore, so why are you here?* Then I said, *Okay, I will show you what I've been doing.* I went into the bedroom. They waited there. I had this rubber baton that I took with me from the police when I resigned, and I brought it out. The room was so small, that they had no room to maneuver or move around. I hit the first guy behind the neck. As he tried to lift up his hand, his pistol fell from his shoulder holster. The beating I gave this guy was so painful. I don't think he was thinking of fighting back. They just ran away. Before they got to the gate, I picked up the pistol and pulled out the magazine and threw it into the street after him. They were so angry. They were shouting, *We will fix you!* and calling me all sorts of names. Then they got into their car and drove away.

I didn't stay too long after that. I put my baton stick away and left in the other direction. I went to see a friend of mine. I was worried because I thought this time I had gone too far. I was so angry. When you are angry, you do things before you think.

The following night, I was walking home. I had taken a combi taxi to see a good friend, an ex-policeman who was undergoing the same sort of trouble. It was very late, past midnight, and it was very quiet in the streets. It was hot. October is very hot in Zimbabwe. When I was near my door, I could see two Land Rover Defenders parked a few meters away from my gate. I knew it was those guys. I wasn't scared at first, because I was used to seeing them there. But when I was opening the gate, four of them jumped out of the car and stuffed a piece of cloth into my mouth so I wouldn't scream. They knew I could fight, so there were plenty of them. They were using sticks, rubber batons, everything. I should have died, they gave me such a very hard beating. Then they took off my trousers and they cut me up. They cut me up. They cut my genitals to pieces. I tried—I tried to fight back. But I lost consciousness.

My family was asleep inside the house. They heard nothing. The only guy who saw me was a taxi driver who lives next door. He was parking his car at his house. It was about two or three in the morning. I had been unconscious for a long time. I was lying in a ditch, in front of my house. So he parked and opened the door and then he shook me up. There was blood all over. I could feel blood in my mouth, blood between my legs, on my clothes. I didn't know what they had done to my genitals because I had passed out. The taxi driver called my wife. My kids saw me like that. They didn't run away. They were shocked. They were surprised to see me in a bloody mess. They just looked at me and cried and cried and cried. The taxi driver took me and my wife to the hospital, to Mpilo hospital, where I was born.

The skin of my penis was hanging by a small piece, hanging down to my knees. These guys had cut off all the skin from my penis. The doctors called it "de-gloving." They took a knife and sliced it open and cut it off. There was no skin left. The whole thing was red. There was a hole on the side of my penis made by a knife or sharp instrument. And when I used to go to the toilet, the urine would come out of the side of my penis when I would go to the toilet, from that hole. It was so painful, I've never felt such a pain in my life.

I don't know how these guys came to know that I was still alive. But they came to the hospital and they told the doctors and nurses not to treat me. The nurses only gave me painkillers and left me there in a bed. I was bleeding. It was very hot in that hospital. You know when something hasn't been treated, it starts to smell. I started smelling. My skin was rotting. The nurses told me they were scared to touch me. They said they've got orders. And when I was in hospital, these guys came back. I was in a big ward full of beds, sort of an emergency ward for people who are very sick. They came to me and said, *This time we will finish you off.* After two days I discharged myself.

A taxi took me home. From there on, I had to live with many people in my house all the time, my friends and family. They were protecting me. I spent those days in my bed. I could not sit. If I tried to sit up, the pain would shoot up, and I used to cry. When it was time to eat I had to kneel on my hands and knees like a dog. I could stand but I couldn't walk. I used to put rock salt in hot water and sit in that. There was no other way. There was no disinfectant. I only had painkillers. It wasn't a nice thing. It wasn't nice to me or to anyone. It wasn't nice for my mother. She was worried to death. And my kids were always crying. It was hard for them to see me like that. They were eighteen and twelve at the time. There was nothing they could do to help me. They just cried. I was always worried about their safety. I worried about everyone: my mother and kids, I was always worried.

This happened on the 10th of October, 2004, and I left for South Africa on December 29th. For three months I had no medical treatment. I was just sitting in this bath of hot water. Even the painkillers did not work in those days. When I took painkillers, I ended up taking nine at one time. I was going to commit an overdose and die, so I drank alcohol. Alcohol is the best painkiller in the world. When I drank, I could sleep. I used to wonder, where is all this pain coming from? When is it going to end? I can't describe for you how bad the pain was. I prayed all the time. God heard my prayers.

SOUTH AFRICA

I stayed so long because there was nothing I could do. I was being watched all the time. I couldn't walk. I couldn't do anything. I was treating myself. And I had no means of getting out of Zimbabwe. We planned the escape with our friends. I left during the night through a window. My children were watching. They had come to see me off. My friends lifted me and carried me out the window and put me in the back of a pickup truck. I couldn't sit, so I was lying on my back all the way to Beitbridge. I had to cross the border on foot because I didn't have a passport. My friends dropped me at the gate and waited for me on the South African side. When I crossed the border I was drunk. I had bought a liter of vodka in Gwanda and was drinking the whole time, so that when I got to Beitbridge I would be drunk enough to be able to walk. I was in so much pain. Without that I wasn't going to get across.

Getting across the border was easy because I used to work there. When these guards saw me there, they didn't know that I was going away. I was wearing shorts and some sandals and carrying a small bag with only two pairs of pants, and a T-shirt and a sweater. I said I was going to the duty-free shop across the border.

It wasn't registering with me that I was leaving Zimbabwe. When you are in pain, you don't feel many things. You only wish the pain would go away so that you could start thinking like a person.

My friends, who had passports and papers, were waiting for me on the other side with the pickup. When we got to Johannesburg, we stayed in a township called Orange Farm.[9] In Johannesburg they arrest people who have no passports. They will throw you into a jail called Lindela for deportation. One day, the police raided Orange Farm. They were going to arrest me and put me into jail for deportation back to Zimbabwe, so I showed them everything. I showed them my mutilated testicles. There was a female

---

[9] An extensive, originally informal settlement in South Africa, about twenty miles outside Johannesburg, known for unemployment and hardship.

policewoman with them. She screamed. I told them my story. They were horrified. They said, *Let him go.* I had no documents. I had no nothing. The police went away. Two days later they were back with food and blankets.

It took me some time to get treatment, because I had never been to South Africa before and I didn't know how to go about things. I was taking life as it came every day. One day I went to the Roman Catholic Church in Orange Farm, and a priest gave me some money and referred me to a place called the Centre for the Study of Violence and Reconciliation in Johannesburg. When I got there, things started going better. They gave me money and they took me to the hospital. My first surgery cost a lot of money— R32,000,[10] South African currency. Some people teamed up and paid for it. Geoff Hill was a friend I met there at CSVR, a journalist. He paid some money and the CSVR contributed. The doctor who saw me was horrified. He said, *I've never seen anything like that in my life.* Then he said he was going to do what is called reconstructive surgery. He told me, *Of course, you will never be the same again. I will do what I can, but you'll never be the same again.*

In April and June of 2005 I was interviewed in some newspapers in South Africa. After that, the CIO phoned. They left messages, saying, *You're tarnishing the image of the government of Zimbabwe.* They said, *We know where you stay. There's no security there. We'll come after you.* I was angry: I'd run away from Zimbabwe and they were following me again. I tried to track them down. I even went to Vodacom, a South African cell phone company. It was a South African number, but it was an automated number. There was no trace of it. I wanted to trick that person. I was going to call him and tell him, *You've won a cell phone, you've won a lucky prize because you're a customer of Vodacom.* Then I would ask for his number and address. I was going to track him down and then I was going to go there and kill him. I tried and tried. I was so angry. While I was in South Africa, they used to threaten my mother, these guys, ask her all sorts of questions.

In late 2005, I registered for asylum with the United Nations High

---

[10] Approximately US$3,200.

Commission for Refugees. I left South Africa in 2008. In between, I worked for a short time in hospitals in South Africa, counseling people who are HIV-positive.

I've had two surgeries since I came here to Canada. In the first surgery, they took some skin from another part of my thigh and patched up the penis. But that first surgery didn't make everything okay. Since I've been here, I've been in and out of the hospital. The last surgery made it a little bit better. It functions normally. It doesn't hurt anymore. But the sadness never goes away.

I MISS THEM TOO MUCH

My wife came with me to South Africa. But when I started treatment, when I was okay, she went back to Zimbabwe. She left during the days when I was preparing for my surgery. We arrived in Johannesburg in January 2005, and she left in May. That was the last time I saw her.

I don't like mentioning my family. I don't like talking about that. Some of my friends here don't even know I have a family. Why should we talk about it? There's nothing they can do to help. They will start asking questions but they can't do anything to help. Even if I am thinking about them, it's useless to talk to anyone about it.

They say you can't live in the past. Even the Bible says so. If you try to live in the past you get into trouble with yourself. You get depressed, end up committing suicide. So you think about what you should do every day. Go to school, do your homework, watch television, check emails, exercise. Church is good. When you go to church you get uplifted spiritually, meeting other people and singing.

I have a picture of my daughter here. I was twenty-three when she was born. She's got a baby now. He was born while I was in South Africa. I was hoping to talk to him on the phone sometime, but he's still very young.

I don't know what my son does. During the days when I last saw him he played soccer. I don't know what he does now.

I miss them. I miss them too much. Sometimes we talk, but in Zimbabwe the phones are always down for one reason or another. The postal service doesn't work. All the services in Zimbabwe broke down long ago. My mother always needs money. If I have it, I send it. I had to send my student loan to them one time. That's not allowed. It's supposed to be for your living expenses and to pay your rent, but I sent it anyway.

2008 ELECTION

I was in South Africa when I heard the election results. At first I was glad because I thought maybe this time Mugabe would go. I was thinking that maybe I could go back home. It was so good to feel that. Most people living in South Africa had high hopes that at last we would go home. But those hopes were dashed very fast.

What makes me sad is that people in Zimbabwe have come to think that suffering is normal. Those who were kids in the '80s have known of no other life other than poverty, disease, hunger, death, and misery. In Zimbabwe children never enjoy their childhood. They are busy going hungry, foraging for food, and learning the tricks of survival.

Mugabe is very old now, and when he dies his party will disintegrate or start fighting among themselves. Even the army and the police will desert Zanu-PF—they will quit, or they will actively support another leader. And when Mugabe finally goes, it will be a lesson for all members of all security branches of the country never to become partisan. Right now, they can't resign because of fear. They are riding a tiger. When they try to get off, the tiger will eat them. The riders are Mugabe and his henchmen. The tiger is the long-suffering people of Zimbabwe. You cannot hold a nation in bondage for such a long time.

Meanwhile, we watch and wait and pray. There is nothing as painful as knowing you can't show your face to loved ones in the land of your birth, and the sad thing is that even if Mugabe were to go tomorrow, Zimbabwe will never fully recover in my lifetime. The only good thing is that when it does happen, Mugabe's death, I might get to see my mother and my children.

MATABELELAND

BULAWAYO

Moving north into Zimbabwe from the South African border, the country's second city comes first. Baobab trees dot the plains, their bark tough as elephant hide, their branches like roots reaching in the air. This was the direction taken by a breakaway group of Zulus nearly two hundred years ago: over the Limpopo River, through the dry, flat scrubland. The Ndebele leader, Mzilikazi, set up his base in Bulawayo. The ruins of his court, Khami, stand on the outskirts of present-day Bulawayo.

Another group of settlers followed this same route in 1890—a column of British soldiers put together by Cecil John Rhodes. Later, the colony would be named for him. Rhodes's British South Africa Company hoped to find a second gold reef to rival that in South Africa. Failing that, they settled for—and on—the land. Rhodes, who had great expectations for the city, is said to have demanded that the streets of Bulawayo should be wide enough for a fully inspanned wagon to turn around. Myth or truth, the city's streets are certainly wide, but no wagons turn there these days. Nor too much other traffic either.

People in Bulawayo can be sarcastic about researchers and interviewers. *Always Harare first, and Bulawayo as a footnote*, they say. The capital is known here as Bamba Zonke—*Take Everything*. And second place is where Bulawayo was relegated in the years directly after Independence.

This was largely because the Ndebele people, rightly or wrongly, were associated with Zapu, the Zimbabwe Africa People's Union, led by veteran nationalist Joshua Nkomo. In the elections that followed Independence, Zanu and Mugabe triumphed in the north and the east (to win control of the government), while Zapu and Nkomo won in the south. Mugabe perceived Nkomo and the Ndebele to be a threat to his hold on power. Thus, under the new Zanu-led government, the south of the country saw much less funding for development than the north and east.

Ethnic tensions exploded into violence in the early 1980s, when a special unit of the army, the Fifth Brigade, was deployed in Matabeleland. Ex-fighters from Zapu's army, ZIPRA, were working with apartheid South Africa to destabilize the newly independent country—so went the official explanation. The narrators in this collection have other explanations and experiences of the campaign known as Gukurahundi. As described in the introduction to this book, the sustained government-sponsored violence resulted in tens of thousands dead and many more homeless and traumatized.

The political violence of the late 1990s and 2000s, culminating in the bloody aftermath of the first round of the 2008 elections, struck many as reminiscent of the Gukurahundi. Once again, the government, backed by the army as well as private militia groups, was targeting those members of the population who were perceived as not supporting Zanu-PF.

As the respected political scientist Bhekinkosi Moyo wrote in the South African *Mail and Guardian*:

> *There is no doubt that the situation in most rural areas now reflects the Gukurahundi period. The nights are the worst times in the lives of the rural folks. People are assembled, usually in a school or headman's place. They are made to sing liberation songs the whole night under the watch of soldiers. People are given logs to "beat themselves." People who have lived together for a long time now become enemies simply because one is an*

MDC member and the other is a Zanu-PF supporter. Life is supposed to be bigger than these two entities... Let us go a few years back and imagine the war against Smith's regime. It is clear that the violence script was written during that period.

Yet even with this history of oppression, the people of Bulawayo and Matabeleland have never feared speaking out. It was on the wide streets of Bulawayo that the women of WOZA (Women of Zimbabwe Arise)[1] began their series of peaceful protests. That first day they handed out roses on Valentine's Day. Subsequently, they were beaten.

These days things are a bit quieter in Bulawayo and the rest of Matabeleland. Yet the scars, both decades old and newer, remain prominent.

---

[1] A grassroots movement of over 60,000 Zimbabweans throughout the country, empowering women to take non-violent action against injustice. WOZA was the 2009 winner of the Robert Kennedy Human Rights Awards.

JOHN

AGE: 63

OCCUPATION: *Teacher, editor, journalist, former press secretary*
INTERVIEWED IN: *Vancouver, Canada*

*Even though John Ndhlovu had successful careers in Zimbabwe as a teacher, edi-
tor, and journalist, it is clear when he talks that his passion has always been politics. John's story takes us further back in time, and provides an insider's account
of Zimbabwe's independence and the pivotal events of the early 1980s. He started
working for the Zimbabwe African People's Union, Zapu, when he was in college, organizing meetings and recruiting guerillas to fight at the front, and when
the war ended, he managed publicity for the elections. A man who has found
himself on the wrong side of two successive regimes, John was harassed by police
and agents from Ian Smith's government during the liberation war, and then arrested and imprisoned thirteen years later by Robert Mugabe's regime. When asked
why he'd been put in prison the second time, he laughed and said,* I married the
wrong woman. *The woman was Zapu president Joshua Nkomo's daughter. In
1983, two months after his wedding, John was arrested for helping Nkomo flee
the country. John was in prison for a year, and after his release moved with his
wife and young son to Vancouver, BC, where he has lived for twenty-five years.
John laughs easily. He laughs about the mysterious accidents that have killed his
colleagues, about his treatment during interrogation, a laughter weighted with*

many other emotions. This is ever so funny, *he says at one point. Then he opens his shirt to reveal a network of scars, like worm trails in wood, across his chest.* Cigarette burns, *he says, this time only half-laughing.*

I grew up in a boarding school in Mzingwane, outside Bulawayo. My father was a teacher. I had a privileged childhood because my father made as much money as his white counterparts. We had everything. We had a car. We even had running water in the house, whereas some kids had a collar around their necks because they didn't take a bath for days. Teachers' kids had shoes. The rest of the class went barefoot. When we went out playing, I would take my shoes off. Even after we moved to town, I would leave my shoes home and go to school barefoot, because the whole school, almost one thousand kids, didn't have shoes. I took mine off to fit in.

At that time Mzingwane was a breeding ground for nationalists. Most of the people who went to that school ended up in the nationalist movement. The students used to come to the teachers' houses to do chores. One of them was Jason Moyo.[1] He used to come and chop wood for my mother.

My mother became politically active just by talking to the students who came into our house, and looking after them. My mother was their favorite because she was young and beautiful. She would make scones and serve tea—much better than what they ate in the dining hall.

The leaders of the nationalist movement were trying to get blacks to wake up. My mother got sucked into it all. She used to go to all the sit-ins when blacks decided to go in places where they were not allowed because of their color. You know, at that time, blacks couldn't go into a restaurant and eat, couldn't go to a store. Most stores had a small window where blacks would buy from.

I remember in 1957, my mother almost got my father fired from

---

[1] Jason Moyo was a pre-Independence Zapu leader, under Joshua Nkomo. He died in 1977.

work. She went to a department store to buy a dress. She was standing there with the dress she had picked, waiting to pay, and the saleslady by-passed her several times serving white ladies. Finally, when all the white ladies had been served, my mother told the woman, *You know, one of these days we are going to take over, and you're going to be out of here.* The saleslady was furious. When she found out that my mother was the wife of the headmaster of the school, she got in touch with the education department. The school inspector called my father into his office. *You've got to control your wife*, he said.

LAND OF THE ELEPHANTS

In the early '60s, things heated up with the riots, and some of those leaders like Jason Moyo would come and spend the night when the police were looking for them. They would use our place in the school as a hideout, because my father was a civil servant and was supposed to be apolitical, though he was sympathetic. So we had all these nationalists coming to our house. They called my mother *Sisi*—Sister. But I have to say I hated those guys, because each time they came, I had to give up my bed and sleep on the floor.

The first time I met Nkomo[2] was in the '50s. Nkomo was maybe thirty-five or forty years old then. He was a big guy, a very passionate, affable man.

In 1960 and '61, there were riots in several towns. The initial cause was general disgruntlement with the system. People wanted to burn down the downtown business area, but troops were sent to cordon off the whole area. So they started looting grocery stores in the townships, which were all owned by blacks. There was general pandemonium for three days. We called it *Zhiiiii*. *Zhiiiii* is a war cry of the Matabele, the warrior tribe, an offshoot of the Zulus in South Africa. I don't know what

---

[2] Joshua Nkomo was the leader of Zapu and of its armed wing, the Zimbabwe Independent People's Liberation Army, ZIPRA. See the appendices for more on Nkomo.

they called it in Salisbury (now Harare). But we had riots the same week-end all over Zimbabwe. That's when they banned the nationalist parties and sent the leaders into detention.

Smith put them all—all the leaders—into these so-called restriction camps. Nkomo and a whole bunch of them, including Mugabe —the whole nationalist movement was detained in various parts of the country for eleven years. They were banned in 1964 and didn't come out until the mid-1970s.

Zapu leaders were sent to Gonakudzingwa, in the southeastern part of Zimbabwe, close to the border with Mozambique and South Africa. Gonakudzingwa is a game reserve. The name means "land of the elephants," because only elephants live there. They put up a detention camp made of corrugated iron huts and detained the Zapu leaders there. They couldn't go anywhere, and they lived off canned food provided by the government.

Guys like Jason Moyo, or Lazarus Nkala, the Secretary General of Zapu, would go to the hospital for treatment after being tortured in Gonakudzingwa, and as a boy I would go visit them and help them pass messages. I'd bring a letter and slip it under the mattress. The following day I would go back, pick up another message. That's how I started in politics.

THEY'D SEND THE DETAILS BY BICYCLE

Eventually, like my father, I became a teacher, too. That's the only way any black person in Southern Rhodesia could get work. If you were a law-yer or an economist, nobody would give you a position. You pretty much had to be a teacher. Every scholarship available, every course of study led you into teaching. There were scholarships in medicine, but the first doc-tors graduated in '67. That's when the University of Rhodesia and Nyasa-land produced the first doctor. And doctors worked in the black hospitals only; they couldn't treat white patients. Similarly, as teachers, we could work only in black schools.

In 1971, I went to teach biology and general science in a black school, a Salvation Army boarding school, in Mazowe, thirty miles outside Harare.

And it so happened that this school produced most of the guerillas that are in Zanu now. Many senior officers in Mugabe's army were in that school. I knew them as kids. They were in my class.

At that time, in 1971, the Smith government passed a law that gave white teachers more money than us. We all went through the same classes in university, and in some cases we taught at the same schools, but he was white and I was black, and now he was going to make twice as much. That raised a big stink. I was actually kicked out of a Teachers' Association meeting because I wanted to look into this thing. I was young, I was twenty-three. The other teachers were twice my age, and they didn't want to go on strike. When I said, *Let's go on strike*, they said, *You're being rowdy*. They kicked me out.

One day we wake up and there are no kids in the school. The kids went ahead with their own protest. They walked through the night to go demonstrate in town. That happened in a lot of schools around Harare and Bulawayo. There was a spate of demonstrations, specifically demonstrating against this law on teachers' pay. In the case of our school, I got the blame. Because I had spoken up, the authorities thought I had planned it. I got visits from the Central Intelligence Organization (CIO), a kind of secret police, which Mugabe has turned into his own party thing now. Just about every other day, I got a visit from those guys. The poor bastards would come on bicycles, biking for thirty miles. When I'd get home at lunchtime, there was a guy on a bicycle waiting for me. They called them "details." They'd send these details by bicycle to come and harass people.

I left the school because the police wouldn't stop hounding me. They'd quiz me, and they'd be there all night outside the window while I was sleeping. So I went to teach outside Bulawayo for two years. Back in Matabeleland, I became very active with Zapu. I organized meetings. Almost every weekend we would meet to recruit people to go out of the country to join the guerillas, to fight. But I never went myself. No, I'm not a foot soldier. We recruited older, working people, people who were independent and willing to make the sacrifice. We didn't target school kids. We would send people through Botswana and then to Zambia, where there were training camps.

THEN MARGARET THATCHER CAME IN

The truth is I never liked teaching, and I finally stopped in '75. I went into the newspaper business in '76, first as a sports reporter. I did that for six months at the *Chronicle*. Then I quit and started my own paper, the *Zimbabwe Times*, with Herbert Munangatire, in '77. We were weekly for about a year. It was just him and me; then, after a year, we expanded and went daily. The point of starting the paper was to make people look at the black nationalists in a better light. The two daily papers, the *Chronicle* and the *Herald*, called the black nationalists terrorists: *Terrorist leader Mugabe. Terrorist leader Nkomo.* We sold every copy among the blacks. Our paper was popular until Muzorewa[3] banned it in '79.

1979 was when the Lancaster House Conference was held. I was there covering it as a freelance journalist. At the time, Zapu and Zanu still went as the Patriotic Front. They were like two pieces of one unit. PF-Zapu and Zanu-PF. They had joined forces to fight Smith. Lancaster House was initiated by the British and the Americans. Andrew Young, the American UN Ambassador, came down with the British Secretary of State, and they held talks in Harare with Smith and Muzorewa. But nothing came out of it.

Then Margaret Thatcher came in. She muscled the Lancaster House agreement. She called a conference and pushed everybody into agreeing to a settlement, because Smith and Muzorewa were really down on their knees. The war was too much to handle. It was costly, and they were losing too many people. I saw a lot of horse-trading there. The British and the Americans made a lot of promises. And the British had already designed a constitution for Zimbabwe. They literally forced it on us. The conference took a

---

[3] Bishop Abel Muzorewa's UANC party (United African National Congress) was drawn into the compromised Zimbabwe–Rhodesia partnership with Ian Smith in the late 1970s, losing his credibility as a former nationalist leader. Lovemore's narrative explains this further.

lot longer than it should have—three months. What finally made the deal was that the British and the Americans promised to finance land resettlement, buy off the land from the white farmers and give it to the blacks.

Zapu was being pushed aside because of our connection with the Soviet Union, and Zanu was favored in the negotiations because Mugabe kept threatening to go back to war. So they were really pandering to him. But Mugabe just opposed everything and never came up with a solution. General Josiah Tongogara is the one that forced him to sign that agreement—and he got killed before he got back to Zimbabwe. He told Mugabe, *If we don't sign an agreement now, if you keep on saying you're going back to war, when we get back to Mozambique, you are going to the front too.* The guy knew what he wanted. So Mugabe gave in.

After Lancaster House, Mugabe went to Mozambique and decided he was going to run in the 1980 election on his own as Zanu, and he opted out of the partnership with Zapu. His general, Tongogara, wanted to run a joint election campaign. And what happened to him? He was killed in a mysterious car accident in Mozambique two days before he was supposed to come back to Zimbabwe. There is a long history of car accidents in Zimbabwe. Often they have involved a collision with an army truck that is never found—those big mine-proof army trucks made out of steel, which Smith used during the war. In a collision with one of those, you're gone.

I was in charge of the publicity for Zapu during the 1980 elections. I prepared and printed campaign material, posters, flyers, T-shirts, and sent them out all over the country. On the second day of voting, Mugabe went to Maputo, in Mozambique. He had a meeting with General Peter Walls and the South African general, Magnus Malan. When he left Maputo that day, Zanu announced they had won fifty-seven seats. And that was only on the second day of voting!

A COBRA IN THE HOUSE

What Mugabe really wanted was a one-party state. But when Mugabe won, he had to give Nkomo something substantial, because of his contribution to the armed struggle. Mugabe became the Prime Minister and Minister of Defense, and Nkomo was Minister of Home Affairs. Mugabe kept the armies, and Nkomo kept the police. Nkomo wasn't at all bitter about losing the election. He was comfortable being Minister of Home Affairs, which is one of the most powerful ministries because it controls police and security. He was working very hard. I think he kind of believed that Mugabe would turn over a new leaf, but he also knew the guy was a loose cannon. He did his best to try and make things work out.

Then Mugabe fired him. Suddenly, one night, Mugabe says he has found arms on Nkomo's properties. Actually, he knew those arms were there. Because he had arms on his farms too. The arms had been declared at the time of the partnerships between Zapu, ZIPRA, and ZANLA, in case the agreement with Smith didn't work out and they would have to go back to war. So he knew exactly where to look for those arms. He said Nkomo was planning to conduct a military coup against him. *Nkomo is a cobra in the house. And the only way to get rid of a cobra is to hit its head.* That's what Mugabe said.

But Nkomo was smart, he knew how to hide. He had his survival instincts. He would show up at home in Bulawayo, and then disappear. That guy could go anywhere in Zimbabwe. People loved him so much. In Mashonaland, he had such a big following. He could go into the countryside there and live with the peasantry and the government couldn't find him, big as he was. He would spend weeks in the countryside, in the bush, sleeping in tents and huts, with no running water, nothing. He really hid from Mugabe, who could never catch him.

WILD BERRIES

In '82, when they had supposedly found the arms, what they did was declare a curfew in the whole of Matebeleland, north and south, which is a huge area, about half of Texas, let's say. People were given a curfew: dusk to dawn. And during the day, you could not be found a thousand meters away from your dwelling. That's how painful it was. It went on for almost six months. Some people's fields were too far from their house, so they couldn't go and get vegetables. You couldn't look after your cows and goats or take them to the pastures. People were surviving on wild berries.

A lot of people went through a very difficult period of starvation, because if you lived too far from a store or a trading post and you didn't have food at home, you were in real trouble.

They also banned vehicular traffic in the area. Most husbands work downtown during the week and travel back into the countryside, to the village, on Friday night, on rural buses, and carry groceries and stuff to their wives and kids. They come back to the city Sunday night. So the men stayed in the city. They couldn't go and see their wives on the weekend. This went on for more than six months.

You had thousands and thousands of traders, store owners, business people who owned stores out in the country who couldn't access their stores; they couldn't restock their supplies. So there was no food coming in and out of the area.

That's how tenacious that curfew was, the curfew that preceded Gukurahundi. That was the beginning of all the troubles out there.

MY WEDDING

But life does go on, doesn't it? Thandi, Nkomo's daughter, was ten years younger than me. We grew up knowing each other. It's a small world in politics. Thandi left in '73, she went to the U.S. I was already teaching then. She went to Stonybrook and she did her master's in urban planning at Columbia. She came back home in '81 or '82, and we reconnected and became engaged. In January of '83 we were married—in the middle of everything.

Now, to say the least, this was a tough time to get married. Joshua had this farm out in the country, a big place. It's called Magwe. And he wanted his daughter's wedding to be out there. The problem was Mugabe had confiscated the farm; it now belonged to the government. But Nkomo's wife still lived there.

Everything was tense. Mugabe used our wedding against Nkomo. Mugabe called Nkomo and said, *The wedding cannot happen at Magwe unless you denounce the dissidents.* But there were no such people as far as Nkomo was concerned. So Nkomo said, *No. How can I denounce people that do not exist?*

In the end we had the wedding not at the farm but in downtown Bulawayo, at our big, beautiful City Hall. And as a gesture of friendship Nkomo even invited all the high-ranking Zanu people, including Mugabe. Mugabe didn't show up, but he did send three senior ministers.

The wedding went for three days. And of course Nkomo had slaughtered twenty cows. For two days people came and ate all the cows. And then Sunday we had a private reception at my father's place, just family.

We had fun, like all weddings. You see, weddings and funerals in Zimbabwe are big. And they're all open, everybody comes, especially when it is the wedding of the daughter of such a big man. We had an army band and they played and sang. The singer was a man named Freedom Sengwyo. He got killed in South Africa sometime in 2000. I don't know exactly what happened to him, but he sang very well.

I was disappointed that the wedding wasn't on the farm. Because while there was no curfew in downtown Bulawayo, they were enforcing it out in the bush, in the rural areas. So people from the countryside couldn't come to town. A lot of our relatives didn't make it. For example, my father's immediate older sister—my father comes after her—she couldn't come. She lives out in the bush there. That was terrible for us.

This was at the beginning. We got married on the 9th of January. The killing in the countryside hadn't quite started yet. The true Gukurahundi hadn't begun. It was just quiet. Two months later, in the beginning of March, that's when the shit broke loose.

MADE TO DIG THEIR OWN GRAVE

By the end of 1982, in order to pursue his one-party state, Mugabe started the Gukurahundi, using the vicious Fifth Brigade, trained by Northern

Koreans. It was a kind of ethnic cleansing, because they wanted to subdue all the Ndebele people, destroy Nkomo and Zapu.

During Gukurahundi, even the people who did not support Zanu-PF at all were cowed into supporting it through fear. They were very violent. Extremely violent. I would like to see them face justice at one time or the other. Some of them deserve to go to The Hague, because they have perpetrated serious human rights violations and serious atrocities. They killed almost twenty thousand people from 1982 to 1987. And the world just turned a blind eye. They were killing people left, right, and center.

I saw a lot of victims. My brother's father-in-law got killed. He was with a group of about twenty men. They were made to dig their own grave. They dug this great big hole, and were told to jump in. They shot them in there. And then they ordered their wives and kids to bury them, shovel the dirt over them.

They would come into every house and search everything. One morning they came to the house of a guy I knew, Victor, and asked for his daughter, who was in the bedroom getting dressed to go to school. We have a derogatory word for a Shona, it's *Swina*, and Victor said, *I will not have a Swina look at my daughter's nakedness.* They beat him up so much that he died two weeks later.

Then there was another girl I knew. She was in her house, sitting on the couch, on a Sunday morning. A bullet came through the door and took part of her vagina out. And they wouldn't let her go to the hospital.

It was so bad. There was a father to a friend of mine who was a businessman and owned a local store. They got to his place and gathered all the people from the villages around. They sat him down, tied him to a chair, and put bales of straw around him. They poured gasoline on the bales and lit them on fire. He burned to death in between those bales of straw, and the villagers were made to watch him. He got punished just for being an elder and not being in Zanu-PF. Horrific things happened to people.

The Fifth Brigade would throw them into mineshafts. Alive. When the Antelope Mine, which had closed operations during the war, reopened in the '90s, they found piles and piles of bones in the mines.

They made all this nonsense about dissidents. *Dissidents*, they said, *are trying to overthrow the government.* They would even bayonet a pregnant woman open and say they were looking for dissidents. *You're carrying the child of a dissident.* Many women died that way. And the rape. There are so many kids born out of rape. And to make things worse, most of those kids born of rape were called *Pasi*, which means "down," from their slogan *Pasi na Nkomo—Down with Nkomo.*

IT WAS MAYHEM

We were at our little country home, just outside of Bulawayo. One morning, I look out through the window, and there are all these Support Unit trucks, the Black Boots, paramilitary police. Hundreds of huge mine-proof trucks, stretching for over two miles. Their leader comes to our house asking for water around seven in the morning, and I say, *What the hell is going on?* He says, *Oh, we're going into town to do a cordon and search.*

So I thought, *Big trouble*, because Joshua Nkomo lived in the township in a big house. We phoned Joshua and told him, *Get out right away.* His wife, Thandi's mother, was there, too. So they fled, and stayed with friends while Thandi and I looked for a house for them. We found one in a white suburb, in the eastern part of the city, and they moved there in just one afternoon. Thandi and I went to live in a motel way outside of town. We were preparing to leave the country.

That same evening, some men went to Joshua's house and emptied a whole magazine into his whatchamacallit, his La-Z-Boy. And they shot his driver, Lot Ncube. Lucky enough, there was a woman who was a nurse nearby, and she came and bandaged Lot's wounds. The bullet went right through Lot's rib cage, just missed the lungs, and he had a big hole at the back.

When I went over to the house, they had turned everything upside-down, kicked the doors with their boots and fired bullets through the windscreens of the cars outside. It was mayhem. They say these guys looked like they were crazed or on some drug or something.

I organized a press conference so Nkomo could speak directly to the press. I took a group of journalists from AP and UPI and BBC and the TV crew from ITN. There must have been about twenty journalists. At the press conference, Nkomo told them that Mugabe was hunting him like an animal. That they had shot up his La-Z-Boy and killed one man and injured another one seriously. Nkomo left the country the day after that press conference.

Later, when Nkomo came back, I went to Harare to meet him, and he had a press conference at his house in Highfield. The journalists were quizzing him about this shooting at his house, asking, *Where is the evidence?* I knew most of the foreign correspondents, so I pulled three or four of them aside and said, *You come here.* I brought Ncube, and made him take off his shirt.

CELL THREE WAS READY FOR ME

A friend of Nkomo's, Tiny Rowland, was Chairman of Lonhro, a big multinational company. He told me, *Go to Harare and meet this guy Nick. Nick will give you money so you can buy tickets for Nkomo's family to get out of the country.*

So when I got to Harare, I met with this Nick at the Meikles Hotel. It's a big five-star hotel. He gave me the money and I got on the plane to go back to Bulawayo that same day. The plane was full of businessmen. I remember the mayor of Bulawayo was on the plane, too, and the town clerk and several businessmen, black and white. Soon after we landed, just as I entered the terminal in Bulawayo, I was surrounded by armed police, twenty or thirty of them, plainclothes but making sure to show their guns. They put me in the back of a truck while somebody was driving my Mercedes behind and took me to Stops Camp. Thandi, her mother (Nkomo's wife), and her brother were already there when I arrived.

What happened was they had caught up with Thandi. She spilled the beans. Thandi would never say if they tortured her that day, but she tried to commit suicide after that. When they got hold of me, they beat the shit out of me. They almost killed me. And then a few days later, somebody told her that I was so badly beaten up that I would never be the same. They said, *He's crippled.* I don't know where she got the Valium from, but she took an overdose of it. It must have been March 12, 1983. I was arrested on the 9th.

Stops Camp was in the middle of a big police station, right inside town. They had converted mule stables into a detention area, surrounded the place with a wire fence. When I got there, there were about two thousand people in the yard, packed in tight like sardines.

There was a guy that I knew. His only crime was that when they caught him, he had napalm scars from when the Rhodesians bombed the camps, and so they said, *How come you have scars? With these scars, you must be a dissident.* There were lots of people like that. There was a member of Parliament, Sydney Malunga, who had been in a cell for three months. He was a very vocal Zapu guy. Mugabe didn't like him at all. They picked him up in his pajamas, and he was still in his pajamas. After he was released, he died in '86 in one of those mysterious car accidents.

There were babies there, whole families. It was a terrible tactic. They would go to a residence looking for the man of the house, and if he was not there, they would take the wife and the kids and put them in Stops Camp, hoping the husband was going to come looking for them. In our case, though, Thandi and her mother got released after a week. Thandi's brother and I were there for a month.

There were five cells. They took me straight to cell three, which was ready for me. It was a ten-by-ten cell with a little hole in the ground for a toilet. The chief of police, the chief of the CIO, and the Gukurahundi commander, Perence Shiri, were in there. Three or four other CIO guys immediately pounced on me and attacked me. Fists, boots, everything. Shiri was kicking me. He was the architect behind the killing of twenty thousand people. Now he is commander of the Air Force. He's a guy that everybody says should go on trial at The Hague. And he was in my cell with three or four other policemen, beating the shit out of me.

They were yelling and screaming insults: *Dog. Motherfucker. Puppet.*

Sellout. A puppet of the Americans. Funnily enough, they liked Americans at that time, but that didn't stop them from the insults.

You see, they were pissed off that Nkomo left right under their eyes. They wanted to know how he got out. They were asking, *Where is Nkomo? How did he get out?* But they were so silly. They said he had gone out across the border dressed as a woman, and when they were beating me up, they wanted to know where I bought a dress to fit him.

Nkomo actually drove across in a truck. At the border, there's a railroad crossing at Plumtree, and there were policemen sleeping with their rifles, resting on the sides of the crossing. And Nkomo just drove past and went through.

I fought back. But they'd handcuffed my arms were behind me. My arms are very long, and I managed to get my hands from my back over my knees, and I stood up and started fighting. It was ever so funny, because the big chiefs all ran out. But then when they subdued me, Shiri and the chief of the CIO cocked their pistols, and they stuck one in my left ear and the other in my right ear. I swear I peed my pants. Because I knew that when a gun is cocked like that, *click click*, any hairline movement, if he panicked and moved his finger, that would be it.

The beating went on until sunrise. Fists, rubber truncheons. I've got lots of scars from being kicked, and broken ribs that didn't heal properly. I think I passed out at one point. Then they left me for dead. They didn't come back for about two weeks, and I didn't eat for a week.

I slept for about two and a half days. There was one thin blanket and a wooden door for a bed. The door is made of two-by-sixes held together by some cross-planks. But between the two-by-sixes, there is an inch or two gap. So however you lie on them, part of your body goes into that gap so you can never be really comfortable. And when you wake up, it's so painful where the body has been in that gap. You have to lay the blanket on the door, and with whatever remains of the blanket you try and cover yourself, because it gets cold at night.

Nkomo's driver and bodyguard were in the next cell. There were about twenty of them in one cell. I was on my own. And this guy, Thomas, kept on calling me: *Come out, come out.* I couldn't even move myself. I was hurting so much. My whole body was aching. And I didn't really want to be seen looking that bad. My eyes were swollen, and my wrists were swollen from the handcuffs, which were so tight they left scars. The swelling didn't go down for days. My back was bloody. I only saw that when I took off my shirt and it was full of blood. I wore those same clothes for about three weeks. I lay there in those bloody clothes, and I couldn't bring myself to look at other people the way I was looking.

WE'RE GOING ONE STEP FURTHER

A new lot came back two weeks later and they took me to an interrogation room. A room with two or three chairs and a table. They have these cheap old wooden chairs. No curtains, no nothing. There was one window there. It looked back into a yard with broken police cars.

They were all CIO, four, five of them. Waterboarding? I had that a long time ago. It was very crude. You're handcuffed. They tied a rope around your ankles and drag you up on this pulley to the ceiling. Then they put a big bucket of water underneath you and lower you into the water. They keep you there until they think you've taken enough water. And then they pull you out and they say, *Taura*, which means "talk." If you don't talk, they put you back in there. They lower you back in.

The water thing went on the whole afternoon. And when they finished with the water, they started the generator thing. They took me, sat me on a chair, tied my ankles onto the legs of the chair, and tied my hands behind the chair. Then they brought this hand-wound generator. They used to use them in the First World War or something. I look at this and I think, *Oh shit*. They tied the wires from the generator on my toes. They wound that thing and I would jump. When the high voltage goes through you, you just kind of jump. They do that, and then stop and ask questions, and do it again, maybe ten shocks. They were trying to get me to implicate other people in the escape plot. They were asking about party functionaries whom I didn't even know.

I said, *But I don't even know the people you're talking about.*

They said, *Now we're going for your genitals.* When they put it on my genitals, I peed. You scream. Oh, I've never screamed so loud in my life.

They'd say, *Talk, or we're going to do it again.*

I never did, I never talked.

KHAMI PRISON

I stayed there for a month. Then, one afternoon, they take me in their Land Rover and drive me twenty miles to a maximum-security prison, Khami Prison. When I get there, they take my clothes, a dirty suit I'd been wearing for a month, and tell me to walk fifty meters in a big open courtyard to get to the maximum-security door. Naked. I say, *No way I'm walking naked.* And they start beating me up, and I'm thinking, Oh God not again. Fists and open palms. But this wasn't too bad. I managed to grab one of them by the throat, and they let me go and gave me some prison clothes.

Khami Prison is a huge complex, probably as big as five or six soccer fields. The outside walls are four-foot-wide concrete. And then there's a perimeter wall that's about twenty feet high with broken bottles at the top. I think there were about three thousand people in there.

It wasn't really bad in there, because the prison guards didn't bother you. I wasn't tortured except for the first day. You woke up in the morning and had your big slice of bread and coffee. And then you went back to clean your cells, polish the floor. Then around eleven, you'd go and have lunch: thick porridge and beans. And then the dinner was thick porridge and a big chunk of pork or beef or a quarter of a chicken because the minimum-security prisoners looked after pigs, chickens, and cows. So there was lots of good food. There were vegetables, but every now and then there would be a wasp cooked with the vegetables.

The worst part was inspection. You had to take off your clothes. You gave them to the guard and he searched and he saw nothing, no weapons, and then you had to lift your legs so he saw you didn't have anything between the crack of your buttocks. You did that three times a day in front of a hundred men.

At night when you went to sleep, they took your clothes. You had to roll them into a bundle and leave them in the bathroom and go into your cell naked. No bedsheets. They have those blankets that feel like they're made of horsehair. There were no windows, just an opening and no glass, just with the bars. When it's cold and windy, that wind is coming straight through your cell and out through the little hole on the door.

But I managed to keep myself busy at Khami. I took books from the library. Weird books. There's one that I kind of enjoyed by this British guy called George MacDonald Fraser. The book was about his adventures as a colonial in India, when he was in the army and the police there. It was one of the *Flashman* books. I think I must have read that one again and again. There weren't too many books in the library. There were lots of bibles. I knew all the good parts and the bad parts. I wasn't really keen on reading the bible.

There were some interesting people inside. For instance, there was a young German guy who used to work for the railways in Botswana. He had immigrated to Zimbabwe after Independence and immediately got into trouble. He got loose with his tongue and said to the guy he worked with that Mugabe had been castrated. This guy reported him to the general manager of the railways, and they brought him from Botswana. He gets to the general manager's office and finds the chief of police in there. And he's taken straight to Khami Prison. He got detained there and lost so much weight. I didn't smoke, but he smoked. I was allowed visitors and they could bring smokes for me. So I used to get a brick of cigarettes a week, about four of five cartons, and I would give them to this guy, because he was just chain-smoking. I shared some of my food with him, and he had started to gain weight by the time I left. He was eating, but he was just devastated.

We were also with the real bad criminals, the murderers and the lifers, the common criminals. We were not sentenced to anything. And we wore different uniforms from them. They wore shorts and we wore long pants. But they kind of had respect for us. And they came to us for wisdom and stuff like that.

Now, my father was still in good books with Mugabe at that time. The year I was imprisoned, he was the ambassador to Senegal. He would get in touch with the Foreign Affairs office in Harare. They'd tell him, *Oh, no, your son has been released.* Meanwhile, I was still inside. My wife knew I was inside, but she was under house arrest, so she couldn't communicate with anybody. Amnesty International wanted to know why I was in prison. My father was good friends with the American ambassador in Senegal at that time, and he pushed my case with the State Department, and then they were making inquiries. And Mugabe kept on denying and saying, *Oh, no, he's out.*

The new Minister of Home Affairs was a nasty guy. Very tribalistic. And at one point, Mugabe sent him and two other ministers to come and see me. So on this day, I get new clothes: new shoes, new jacket, new pants, new shirt. And I go and sit in the superintendent's office. The two ministers come in, and the Minister of Home Affairs doesn't show up. They phone him. He keeps on saying he's on his way. And the two ministers said to me, *We don't really understand why you're in here. It's becoming an embarrassment.*

Eventually, I was released on the condition I didn't sue the government because they had no reason for holding me. I spent nine months in detention without trial.

Nkomo was in London then. He didn't come back until after I had been released.

I WAS TOO HOT A POTATO TO GET INVOLVED

I was released in September of 1983, and then I spent a few weeks in Zimbabwe. Then my wife and I spent a month in Dakar. I had been beaten up so much in prison, and I wanted to get checked out at the U.S. Embassy clinic in Dakar. I also wanted to see my mother and father.

After Dakar, we flew to New York. We needed fresh air. We stayed for about a month with Arthur and Mathilda Krim, who had looked after

Thandi while she was in school. Arthur owned Orion Pictures and his wife was one of the scientists who had identified the AIDS virus in the earl '80s. We stayed with them in their place on East 69th. They told us that the bedroom we were using was once used by John F. Kennedy!

After that, I went and spent another month in Birmingham, Alabama, with a cousin of mine who's a doctor there. We came back to New York from Alabama the Monday after Thanksgiving. We spent the rest of November in New York, I think, then went back home to Zimbabwe for Christmas.

I didn't have to work at that time, but there was a shortage of science teachers, and a man I had gone to university with was headmaster of a secondary school. He asked me to come and teach high school biology, so I went back to teaching for half of '84 and part of '85.

I wasn't involved in politics anymore. I didn't want to be. I was clandestine. I was too hot a potato to get involved, even though I still had contacts with my journalist friends. I would put them together with people who came out of the countryside where the people were being killed during Gukurahundi.

The '85 election was approaching, and things were hot. It was the first election after Independence. Nkomo had come back in '83, just after I was released from detention, and he entered the election. But he was muted. Zanu had started deploying their troops again in the countryside and forcing people to vote for Zanu and not for anyone else. It was a big intimidation campaign. Things were getting bad again.

By that time there were tens of thousands of people killed, mostly civilians, always with the excuse of looking for dissidents. But there was no insurrection or organized rebellion—even though the *Zimbabwe News* kept reporting that there was.

I tried to fly out on British Airways. My wife and I were supposed to leave separately. And so I drove to Harare, got on the plane—and when the plane was about to leave, these state agents came in and demanded that I get off the plane. I was reluctant to go, and the captain said, *You stay there, I'll take you to London. And if they want to come along, they can come for a free ride.*

Then I thought, *If I go, my wife and child won't be able to leave.* There would have been trouble for them. So I got off the plane and they took me to the police station and interviewed me. I was at the police station until about three in the morning, and then I drove back to Bulawayo. They had asked me to come back to the police station in the morning. Instead, I drove back home.

For two weeks, there was a lot of negotiation over our fate. It went all the way to Mugabe himself. My father was, by that time, back home. He had just retired from the diplomatic service. He phoned Mugabe and Joshua phoned Mugabe, too, and they negotiated and asked him to let us leave, as we were no longer part of his fight with Nkomo. Finally Mugabe agreed to let us go. I left two weeks later with my wife and child, who was a small baby then. He had just started crawling. He was born in August and we left in May.

We decided to come here, to Vancouver. My brother-in-law had left Zimbabwe earlier and had settled here. Canada was willing to take refugees from Zimbabwe. And Vancouver had a good climate. It's not as cold as Toronto and Montreal. In Zimbabwe it's dry sunshine, here we get wet sunshine.

WE GAVE IN TO THE DEVIL

So I was already here in Vancouver by the time the election happened in 1985. A lot of people died during that year, but Nkomo still won twenty seats in Matabeleland. And the killings escalated. Gukurahundi wasn't letting up. The whole point of all the murdering was to subdue Nkomo's following so Mugabe and Zanu could form their one-party state. They were squeezing him. They followed him everywhere he went. Most of the time he didn't sleep at home. If he went to the supermarket, the CIO was there, these secret police.

In '87, Nkomo was finally subdued; he capitulated and signed that Unity Agreement in order to stop the killings. But he was broken-hearted about it. He was a good man, but he had no control over the Gukurahundi, the Fifth Brigade. All he could do to stop it was capitulate. He had no power to stop it any other way, because he didn't have any insurgents and people were just being butchered. He tried to resist, but he was getting old too. In the end he gave up.

But I admit when the Unity Accord happened, I was pretty disgusted. We gave in to the devil.

In the truce we, Zapu, were swallowed and became part of Zanu. That was the whole agreement, that Zapu becomes part of Zanu and gives up the name Zapu.

Mugabe was still prime minister then, and he wielded all the power. Nkomo was named vice president, second vice president because there was already a first vice president. He didn't have any official duties and couldn't do anything. It was just a title, a house, and a few bodyguards. Nkomo was seventy then. He stayed vice president probably ten years, but he developed dementia and prostate cancer, so he wasn't really with it. But Mugabe wouldn't let him retire. I think he's afraid of change.

ZAPU

We have revived Zapu and are recruiting people to become members so we can win a majority of seats in the next election. What we in Zapu are advocating for is a devolution of power to the provinces, because right now everything is controlled from Harare, and the faraway provinces don't get anything. Roads are neglected, schools are neglected, hospitals are neglected. Zanu has put all of their resources into pet projects like Borrowdale and Helensvale where the elite live. That's where the power doesn't go off. That's where the roads have no potholes.

So what we want is for each province to have a say and control over certain aspects, like we have here in Canada. Here, the provinces have education and roads, and the cities have control over their infrastructure.

IT HURTS TO THINK WHAT'S GOING ON THERE

I think Tsvangirai masturbated his power by going into the agreement with Mugabe. He has lost credibility. People are holding on to him as a last hope, but Mugabe has blocked him every way he can. That old bastard is obstinate. He won't let Tsvangirai do anything to change the situation. He's still in charge, and people are beginning to see that.

I pray that Mugabe dies. But when he dies there is going to be big, big trouble, because the tribal stuff is only going to get worse. The tribal split started with him. He used it for his purposes. The Shona–Ndebele split wasn't much of a problem when we grew up. It was like they were there and we were here. Whenever we came together, there was no friction. But then when Mugabe came in, when they formed Zanu, that's where tribalism started to flourish. They actually started the tribal hatred when they split from Nkomo. And it has deepened between different Shona groups—Karanga, Zezuru, Manyika.

The man has ruined the country. The economy is down the tubes. Now Zimbabwe doesn't have its own currency, so we're relying on these U.S. dollars and we don't have enough. People in the rural area don't have access to U.S. dollars, so how do they become a part of the economy? How do they go to the store to buy? They are forced to go in and barter with chickens and goats. It's a catch-22 situation for the poor, unless they have relatives outside of the country who send them foreign currency. It hurts to think of what's going on there.

Tsvangirai keeps on calling himself a peaceful democrat. How can you be peaceful when people are killing you left, right, and center? I would be willing to go to war, if it comes to that. What else can we do?

A friend of mine who was in the MDC—the smaller one that split from Tsvangirai—was killed in a car accident recently. Renson Gasela was his name. He was in a little twelve-seater bus coming from a meeting in the southeast of Zimbabwe, and they rounded a corner and there was a front-end loader in the middle of the road, coming their way with a shovel aimed at their windscreen. Gasela was sitting in the front seat of the bus. He and two other people were decapitated.

He was an MP in the previous parliament and was the agriculture critic for the smaller MDC, and we'd been talking about him coming back to Zapu. I just spoke to him in February when he was in London. He was a bright fellow. Very confrontational, but peaceful. He spelled things out the way they were. And all of a sudden he is decapitated. Everybody knows that's an arranged accident. Mugabe has gotten rid of so many people using these funny accidents.

Zanu needs to be confronted. We have to get rid of them before anything can go right in that country. They're not going to walk away from all the stuff they have stolen. They have their fingers in everything. And the army is complicit in all the theft and plunder. It's everywhere. They need to be confronted for all of the evil they have done. They need confrontation in parliament, confrontation in government, confrontation in the economic sector. They need confrontation on the farms. Otherwise we will not be able to produce food for ourselves. Right now we don't even have enough milk for the country because they've slaughtered and eaten all of the dairy cows.

NOKUTHULA

AGE: *31*

OCCUPATION: *Domestic worker, former hairdresser*

INTERVIEWED IN: *Cape Town, South Africa*

The Cape Town suburb where Nokuthula works—cleaning and doing laundry—is over a thousand miles from her home in Bulawayo, Zimbabwe, where her young son stays with his grandmother, and about thirty miles from the township where Nokuthula lives now. Before being interviewed, Nokuthula changes out of her work clothes and into a stylish skirt and blouse and sits down at the kitchen table. A strikingly beautiful woman with a straight back and a quiet air of self-confidence, Nokuthula pauses before each piece of the story, and then perfect sentences flow. Her son's father, an opposition activist, left Zimbabwe in the early 2000s, fearing for his safety, and has not been heard from since. Unable to support her son and her mother as Zimbabwe's economy failed, Nokuthula set off for Cape Town. Here, along with earning a living and sending money home, she managed to survive the wave of xenophobic violence that spread across South Africa in 2008. She never names those who continue to threaten her precarious Cape Town existence, speaking only of "them" and what "they" do. Now, with every choice that she faces, Nokuthula turns over her options carefully, weighing each by its impact on her child.

In March last year, 2008, I was here in Cape Town, watching the elections in Zimbabwe on TV. We were hoping for the best. Most people wanted Tsvangirai to win, so that things could change for the better and people could stop starving. Because back home it's very bad. I used to call my family every week during the elections, to hear from them if they were okay. I was mainly worried about my son. He's nine years old and he lives with my mother in Bulawayo, in the location.[1] He used to go to a school in the suburbs, but once the elections started, I asked my mother to change him to a nearby school, there in the location, because when elections happen, many people are beaten.

Back home, my mother is a domestic worker, like I am now. She's still working, so she travels every day, leaving home at around five a.m. and coming back late. So I was worried about her safety, too, because you can meet some Zanu-PF guys, and they ask you, *Which party do you belong to?*

I miss my son a lot. I last saw him in December 2008. I went home, after being here in South Africa for more than three years. I do not have the correct papers, so to get back I did this thing we call *dabulaphu*, a Ndebele word that means "long-distance crossing," crossing the river. It's risky, but it was a long time since I'd been with my son. In the river, some people disappear, get eaten by crocodiles. But I had to do it. I had to. I missed him. He's nine years old and I have to be there for him, because his father has gone. He was a member of MDC, the father, and he used to take part in political events. Before the elections in 2000, members of Zanu-PF threatened him. He felt very unsafe. We had to sell some of our belongings so that he could go and hide somewhere. He managed to get to the U.K., so he's in London now. Since then, we haven't heard from him. He doesn't contact us. My baby no longer has a father, so as the mother I have to make sure that he doesn't feel left out by his parents.

---

[1] Another word for the formerly blacks-only townships. Since Independence in 1980, they have been replaced—in their official classification, at least—by "high-density suburbs," which are the de facto home for working-class black Zimbabweans. The formerly whites-only "suburbs," now called low-density suburbs, are now home to middle-class Zimbabweans (and their domestic workers). Bulawayo is the second-largest city in Zimbabwe, situated in Matabeleland in the south of the country.

At the time when the father left, we were living with his family, with my mother-in-law, also in Bulawayo. But then, as time moved on, I decided that I should come and look for a job here in Cape Town so that I can take care of my son, because there are no other ways to support him. I'm thirty-one now—I was twenty-six when I left Zimbabwe in 2005, and my son was five years old. At that time, he had not yet started school. He used to go to preschool. At first he stayed with my mother-in-law, but after about two years I decided he must live with my own mother because I couldn't afford to support both families. That was the only way that I could manage, by supporting my mother and my son at the same time.

EGGS

We are four children in my family, three girls and one boy. The oldest is my sister. She's also here in Cape Town—she just arrived this month and she doesn't yet have a job. In December 2008, when I went home, I had to struggle to collect money so that she could also come here and start looking after herself and her family. My elder brother works for Dunlop[2] in Zimbabwe, but he's struggling there. They're not paid well. So I think as time goes on he'll also come and look for a job so that he can support himself. Then comes me, and then my younger sister, who is twenty-four and married, living with her husband in Bulawayo. She was one of those people who used to change foreign currency to survive.[3] Her husband is a mechanic, and she sometimes goes to Botswana to buy fuel to resell back home, to support the family.

When we were growing up, my mother couldn't afford to look after us. She had to take us to live at our aunt's. My auntie and her husband were teachers. They had a big house and we had everything we needed growing up. Their house is near where my mother lives now, but then my

---

[2] A tire company.

[3] For more on currency trading, see the appendix section on economic decline and also Bernard's story.

mother had no house. She used to rent. My father is still alive. He has his own house in another location. When they got divorced, my mother got nothing. That's why we had to go and live with my aunt.

I did my secondary school and passed three subjects at O-level[4]— English, Food and Nutrition, and Ndebele. But my mother couldn't afford for me to continue at school, so I had to make a plan. I love hair, so I started doing people's hair to make a living. I went to college to do hair-dressing and after that, I started working in a salon. That's where I met my child's father.

I had a baby after that, and the father paid *lobola*.[5] We were living very well, no problems. I told him not to get involved in politics, because we were still young. He never listened. He went to rallies and meetings. Once, coming home from work, he met these other guys. They knew that he was from MDC and they pretended that they were also from MDC. He told them, *No, I've never seen you before.* Then they said, *You are a pimp,* and they started beating him up. They took his clothes. When he arrived home, he had only his shorts left. He was beaten badly. This was before the 2000 elections, in 1999. So after that, we decided that we should start saving money and selling some of our things. First we planned that he should go to Botswana, but he said he was afraid. Botswana is a nearby country; there might be people from Zanu-PF there too.

Before that everything was okay, because we could afford to buy things, everything was there in the shops. As for my baby, when he was young, when he was about a year old, I could afford to take him to a pre-school, because I worked in the salon. The schools were affordable, the teachers were there, the hospitals were there, medication was okay, everything was okay. Then it just changed. Back then, it was easy. But not now. Now, at home, I can't buy my son a small thing like a fruit. Now, people are dying. A neighbor of ours died and was bitten by rats. When his

---

[4] See footnote 8, page 59.

[5] Bride price, paid by the groom or his family to the parents of the woman he marries.

family went to bury him, he had no toes. He had to be buried like that. It's bad at home, very bad. You know, when I got home in December, I had bought eggs and put them in a container. They arrived home safely without breaking. And my child was like, *Sithabile akaze sidle amaqanda!* He was saying, *For such a long time we have never eaten eggs.*

YOU PAY THEM WHAT YOU HAVE

To get into South Africa from Zimbabwe, the way I did in 2005, you pay an *umalayitsha*. The translation means a man who'll take anything home. It used to be derogatory at first, but now they are used to it. It's expensive. From Bulawayo, some charge R3,000, some charge R2,000.[6] As for the people in rural areas, some give the *omalayitsha*[7] cows and some give them goats and donkeys, anything of value. The omalayitsha are everywhere. They're all Zimbabweans, with papers to cross the border—some have Zimbabwean papers, some have fake South African papers. These people, they meet with the police every day. So they're not afraid of them. They just give the police money to allow them to pass. That's how they survive. Some are businessmen with big houses back home, driving expensive cars through being an *umalayitsha*.

When you get to Beitbridge, you pay people called *impisi* to help you to cross the river. The *impisi* tell you if you get stuck in the river, it's your fault. They leave you. If you get bitten by a crocodile, it's your fault. They leave you. If you can't cross the river, it's your fault. They leave you.

What happens is the *impisi* look for a big, big, strong stick. Then everybody has to remove their clothes, whether you're an adult or a kid. You have to go bare there, not wearing anything. Clothes weigh you down. All that you can do is concentrate and make sure that you hold tight to the stick. It's scary, it's very scary. Like most others, I can't swim. My first time

---

[6] US$500 and US$300, respectively.

[7] Plural of *umalayitsha*.

coming to South Africa, the water was very, very high. At times I could see myself underneath, up and down, up and down. But I managed, and this second time, coming back after Christmas, I also managed.

If you've got bad luck, you can meet some of those criminal guys from our country who want to rob you. So you're told not to carry any money, no cell phones, just wear rags, because they can also take your clothes, *takkies*,[8] everything. After crossing the river you put your clothes back on. You're told to go and sit somewhere in those wet clothes and wait for the omalayitsha while they first check if there are any soldiers around. Usually they patrol, the soldiers; they know that people cross at night. On our way to Musina, after the car picked us up, we met some soldiers. Some of them want money. They don't care about the law or anything. You pay them what you have, and they let you move on.

KIDS DISAPPEAR

My mother has been working for the same family in Bulawayo for almost twenty-five years. They have been very good to us. I got this job where I'm working now through a contact from their daughter, who is also here in Cape Town. It was much easier for me to get work because she helped me when I first got here.

Some days I work at this house and other days I work at another family's house. I work from Monday to Saturday, full days, and on Sundays we go to church from nine in the morning up till four. So we spend most of the day in church. It's just work and church. I knock off from work late, at four, and I get home at around six at the earliest, depending on the transport. So I just cook, sleep, do my laundry early the next morning. On Sunday you also have to wake up early in the morning, do the washing, clean the house, get water for bathing, and prepare for church.

For us to get refugee papers, it's very, very difficult. You have to go

---

[8] Tennis shoes, sneakers, trainers.

in the morning and stay there the whole day, without being attended to. Sometimes you are told, *We only take ten people*, and maybe you are at the back of the line. So you have to be patient. Some pregnant women faint there, some because of hunger. Then, if you get a permit, it's difficult to get the ID. Some people say that we Zimbabweans are not given permits and IDs, for I don't know what reason. Those people working there, at times they harass people. So you just have to be patient to get what you want. You have to keep on going there for your papers to be stamped. My application for permanent residence was passed there. Once your paper has been stamped for two years, then you can apply for permanent residence and for a study or work permit. Then if you pass, you are told to apply for an ID I applied but the ID has not yet come.

Even with the ID, you can't go home. You can only go home after five years, once you've been given a passport. Before that, you are not allowed to go home. At times a relative or a close friend dies, but even then you can't go home. A cousin of mine had TB. In December last year she went home, and in January she passed away. I couldn't go home to bury her because I was scared. If you get deported and you don't have enough cash to pay an *umalayitsha* to bring you back, you might stay home for the rest of your life.

Most of my money is to support my son and my mother. Those *omalayitsha* people, you give them your money and the address in Zimbabwe, and they take your money or groceries home for you. To send one hundred rand in money or groceries with them you must pay them twenty rand.[9] When I buy groceries, I buy mealie-meal,[10] rice, cooking oil, porridge for my son to eat when he goes to school, plus soap and washing powder. If I have money, I spoil him with sweets and toys, whatever I can afford.

At the end of last year I met this other man who goes to our church. In December, he paid *lobola* for me. So for now I'm married to this other

---

[9] Approximately US$10 and US$2 respectively.

[10] See footnote 5, page 31.

man from our country and I'm living with him. My cousin is staying in the house I rent in the location, with my sister who came in January. I put up a Wendy house[11] there for two thousand rand, and we pay three hundred rand per month rent.[12] My sister is not working—she's still looking for a job—so I have to support her, buy her food, make sure she gets everything she needs.

The man I am now married to has a job. He's been here in South Africa for a long time. He was married before and his wife passed away, so all of his kids are here in South Africa, and we live with them. I think it suits him to live with his kids. But as for me, huh-uh, no. Back in Zimbabwe we are taught to have respect, while here, children have too much freedom. My mother is my mother—wherever I go, wherever she lives, I call her "Mama." But here, kids call their mothers *uSisi*, sisters. One of our neighbor's daughters, she's about fifteen, if she doesn't want to cook, she doesn't cook. If she wants to go drinking, she does that. She sleeps out. You see?

Some people have already brought their kids from Zimbabwe to join them here in South Africa. I wish I could do it, but I'm not sure whether that would be the right thing. It's not good for my son to grow up a naughty kid, somebody who has no respect. I want him to grow up in a family where he knows that he must always go to church and respect the elders, go to school, all the things that I was taught. Because in Zimbabwe, education used to be the best. I'm a proud Zimbabwean woman. It's only that things are not good back home.

Kids here in South Africa get involved in bad things, like drinking, drugs, killing people. So I'm afraid I might bring my son and he might grow up in the wrong place. If ever I do that, I have to make sure that he goes to school in the suburbs, not in the locations. And the other thing: kids disappear. They go to school one day, they don't return. What if

---

[11] A small, prefabricated timber shed.

[12] Approximately US$200 and US$30, respectively.

I make a big mistake and he comes to this side and gets lost, or a bad thing happens to him?

My mother doesn't want me to bring him here. She always says, *No, we look after him. Even if we starve, we'll make sure that he gets whatever we have.* I don't want to oppose my mother, because if I bring him and anything bad happens, my mother won't help me. She'll just say, *I told you so.*

So I'm confused. I wish that he could come and have fun like other kids and eat whatever I can afford to buy him. I wish that. But I can't do it. What if this xenophobic thing[13] starts again? Where will I run with him? What if it starts when I'm at work and he's alone at home?

IS ANYONE IN THAT TAXI A FOREIGNER?

We heard about the attacks in Joburg last year before they started to happen in Cape Town. Some of my friends and relatives live in Joburg so as soon as we started seeing this xenophobia thing on TV, we contacted each other. Some were in Hillbrow,[14] some are working as domestic workers in Roodeport,[15] so they're staying there. I used to contact them, to hear how they are. At first, people said it wasn't going to come to Cape Town, the police were going to take care of it. So at first we weren't afraid. But as soon as I heard that it was starting, that's when I became scared. First,

---

[13] Resentment of foreigners, in particular against poor, black foreigners is an ongoing problem in South Africa. Here, Nokuthula is talking about an outbreak of xenophobic violence that began in Johannesburg in May 2008 and spread to many other areas, especially urban townships. For more, see the appendix section on Zimbabweans in South Africa.

[14] Hillbrow is an urban residential area of Johannesburg, now known for unemployment, poverty, and crime. Made up of high-rise apartment blocks, Hillbrow has Africa's highest population density after Cairo. In the 1970s it was an apartheid-designated whites only area but soon became a "grey area," where people of different ethnicities lived together. It acquired a cosmopolitan and politically progressive feel, but most middle-class residents left in the 1980s and buildings decayed, leaving an urban slum by the 1990s, populated primarily by migrants from the townships, rural areas, and the rest of Africa, many living in abject poverty.

[15] A fast-growing residential area on the edge of Johannesburg.

I heard that in Du Noon,[16] they were putting small pieces of paper under the door, saying, *Can you please go back where you come from before we start?* As soon as I heard that, I became scared. Because I knew it was coming to Cape Town. And it came.

The day it started, I woke up in the morning, I went to work. People were starting to talk about it in the taxis[17] in the morning. *This thing is going to come*, they were saying, the Xhosa people. Xhosa only differs a little from Ndebele, so I understand it. Even so, the people from here, they can see that you're not a Xhosa. And when these people start talking, you have to join them so that they don't suspect that you're not local. Some of the people know me in the taxis—I go to work with them every day—and I told them that I'm a Zulu, I come from Durban. They were asking a lot of questions, like, *Are Zulu people not allowed to have sex unless you are married? Are you checked every month if you are still a virgin or not?* So I tell them whatever I have learned from the TV.

It's an advantage for us, Zimbabweans from Matabeleland who speak Ndebele, because we can speak Xhosa. It's easier for us. But it's a disadvantage for the Shona people, because once you speak Shona, they say you are *ikwirikwiri*.[18] That's why most of us from Matabeleland can stay in the locations where rent is cheap. Most of the Nigerians and other people from other countries have to stay in places around town, because they can't speak the language. And if you speak your own language, they notice that you're *ikwirikwiri*. Then they make your life a hell.

On that day, when the people started talking, I joined in. I said, *These ikwirikwiris must go back to their country*. Yet, deep down in my heart, I knew I was one of the *ikwirikwiris*, and I did not want them to go back to their countries. We all came here for a reason. Some of the people here think that we from other countries are what they call *isikoli, isikebengu*—

---

[16] An informal settlement on the outskirts of Cape Town.

[17] Minibuses, the main form of transport in South Africa.

[18] Derogatory term for a foreigner in South Africa.

thieves, murders, criminals. But we're not. When it started in Du Noon, people from Somalia were beaten. I heard Xhosa people saying they were beating these criminals. But they're not criminals.

Then, when I was coming back from work that afternoon in the taxi, they had blocked the road and told the driver to stop. They were carrying batons, some were carrying stones. They told the driver to ask in the taxi if there was anybody who was a foreigner. *Akhona lapha amakwirikwiri emotweni?* If there was, they asked the driver to drop him out. And the driver told them, *Awekho lapha amakwirikwiri. No, there's nobody here who is a foreigner. You can see for yourself.* At that time I was shaking, really shaking. Then they let us pass.

After that, we drove past a police station. A lot of foreign people had managed to carry only their clothes with them to the police station to get help. And there were already buses there, taking people to churches for safety.

By the time I got back to the location where I was living, people were all over, out of their houses. I was scared because I knew that some people in nearby houses suspected us. My cousin speaks Ndebele. Another time, one woman had said to me, *Your cousin speaks like a Zimbabwean I saw on TV.* I told her, *No, that woman was speaking Zulu, and we also speak Zulu, but we're from Durban.* My landlord had even asked for my ID. I told her that I left my ID at work for safety because so many of the shacks burn down. I always sent food home at month's end, and I think that's why they got suspicious. You wouldn't send food to people in Durban, because what I can buy here is also available in Durban. So you would just send money if you were going to send something. I told the landlord that groceries are cheaper here in Cape Town.

What happened in our location during that time was that, if they knew that you were a foreigner, they would come to your house and either they'd beat you up or they'd tell you to go. They come into our houses, they take anything they want, anything, and the people who live there are just told to go without anything. Some people were burned. They would put tires on them and set them on fire. Others were beaten. They didn't care whether it was a child or not. The other thing I heard that scared me was about a woman who was pregnant, and the baby was taken out of her stomach. I was really scared. My tummy was running all the time.

Some people from other countries own a lot of property. We were staying next door to a tuck shop[19] that belonged to some Somali guys. They broke into the Somalis' shop, pushing those large rubbish bins, and they stuffed food in them. They took everything, even the fridge. The next morning, we heard that those people were selling the fridge for only two hundred rand.[20] Maybe they wanted to go and buy beer, I don't know. Small kids also came to the house selling stolen chocolates. At the shops, those chocolates are five rand, but they were selling them for one rand.

When I got home from work that day, the landlady wasn't there. So I told my cousin-sister[21] to pack only a few clothes in a handbag. A man whom we go to church with owns a house in another location where there are mostly colored[22] people. He's one of the Zimbabweans who managed to buy houses here. They have been here for a long time, and they speak Xhosa well now. So the locals don't suspect anything about them. There wasn't any violence in that colored location, so we phoned him to ask if we could come over, and he agreed. We stayed there for about three days. It was quiet there. It wasn't like other locations.

But I heard that more Zimbabweans were being killed in Du Noon. When these people were asked why they had killed them, they claimed

---

[19] A very small neighborhood shop, run from someone's house, where you can buy bread, milk, paraffin—daily necessities. The Somalis are known for offering "packs," which include mealie-meal, cooking oil, rice, samp, flour, sugar, and toilet paper for less than you can buy "one-one" at Shoprite in town. Tuck shops, also known as "spazas," are usually more expensive than the chains in town, hence the conflict between South African spaza owners and Somalis.

[20] Around US$20.

[21] Cousin in English, *udadawethu* or "sister" in Ndebele or Shona. "Cousin-brother" and "cousin-sister" have become common expressions in Zimbabwean English.

[22] "Colored" is still often used to refer to people of mixed race in South Africa, though the term originated as a way to classify South Africans under apartheid.

they were criminals. But residents were saying it was the xenophobia thing again.

We talk about this, about why it happens. The thing I know is that people here in South Africa are given everything. Women are given rights, unlike us from our country. Young women who have got children are given grants. So I think they expect everything just to come to their hands without working. When we come here to their country to look for jobs, they say we are taking their jobs. But there are chances for them to look for those jobs, they don't take the chance. All that they do is smoke and drink; they do some of the dirty things which they say we do, but we don't. I think maybe that's the reason. Some people say we are like the Nigerian guys who own clothes shops—they say those people do drugs and use their own children, get their children pregnant. But I disagree with them. Not everyone who does drugs is a Nigerian or a Zimbabwean. There are some people who do drugs, I agree, but not all of them.

It hurts a lot. It hurts a lot when people say that word—*amakwirikwiri.* At times, even if I'm just walking along, I can feel that I don't belong here, as if I'm lost, I came to the wrong place, I was going somewhere and just got lost. It's a revolting word. We don't like it. But we have to just accept it.

When they were attacked, people who had no other place to go ended up going to camps. Tents were put up for those people running away from the South Africans, located out of the city. I chose not to go to the camps because I knew a place where I was going to be safe. Most of those who beat people up and chase people from their houses are Xhosa people, not the colored people. The colored people only took food from the shops, they did not beat people. So I knew that if we looked for a place where there were colored people, we were going to be safer. Some Zimbabweans stayed in town or in the suburbs. But we couldn't come to town because here people rent out only one room, and you are not allowed to bring more than five people into your room. So it was better in that man's house, because it's his own house, so he can bring as many people as he wants to.

We know that man from church. I go to Zion church, the Zimbab-wean church. We have five branches in Cape Town, and from all of these branches, I did not hear about anybody going to the camps. People just looked for safe places. Some asked their bosses if they could come and stay over; some came to town; some looked for places like where I stayed. We knew that if you went to these camps, people were going to be taken back to their countries. That was going to be the wrong choice for me—to be taken back to my country, to lose my jobs and my belongings. If I went to the camp, I would have lost a lot of things. Although I lost some of my stuff anyway. When I went back to my house after this thing had quieted down, I saw that they had come through the house and taken some of my stuff. That was three days later. After three days, we were told that police were everywhere so nothing was going to happen. We could see police cars moving around everywhere, so we were not scared.

At first I told my cousin-sister to go back to our shack in the loca-tion. When the landlady asked her where I was, she told her that I was at work. When I used to work in St. James,[23] I would stay over for weekends when there were visitors. But the landlady was suspicious, so I moved to another location. After the attacks, a lot of us decided to move from there, to go and look for places somewhere else, so that these people don't notice things like the *omalayitsha* who come to carry things home to Zimbabwe for us every month. The guy might come to collect things from your house in the afternoon, with these big *tshangani*[24] bags, and everybody will be watching, wondering, *Why is he carrying food all the time?*

On the Sunday of that week, some people did go to church for prayers, but as for me, I was scared so I did not go. I decided to stay home with my cousin and the other people whom we were staying with. Some people in the area know that ours is a Zimbabwean church, but not everybody. In the location where I stay now, people looked for a piece of

---

[23] A suburb of Cape Town, some distance from the city center and even farther from the township where Nokuthula had been living.

[24] Inexpensive, large, striped, zippered canvas, or plastic bags.

land and built their own shack there. And that's where we go to church. Only a few residents, the closest ones, know now that the people at that church are Zimbabweans. Because these neighbors need help from our people and from the prophets[25] who have got the spirit. Other neighbors might ask questions, because we have a burial society and if someone dies, only Zimbabweans are selected to go and bury the person. We have never chosen a Xhosa to go and bury someone from our country. Some Zimbabwean guys are now married to Xhosa women, so they also know about us. When the xenophobia thing happened, they were safe. I heard some of the women were fighting for their husbands, telling people that their husbands are going nowhere. If they were told, *Your husband is an* ikwirikwiri, *he must go away*, some managed to fight for their husbands. So I think we are safe. For church, there were no problems.

I think it's a good thing for you to join a church. I don't know for other countries, but as for Zimbabweans, you can go and be buried at home if you die, because the members of the burial society will collect money and buy you a coffin, and you go and get buried at home. A few people are selected, and they go home with you.

HOME FOR CHRISTMAS

To get home—like I did at Christmastime to see my son for the first time in three years—you first take a bus to Joburg. From here in Cape Town to Joburg, there are no roadblocks, no police asking any questions, so it's safer. When you get to Joburg, you go with omalayitsha, either in a private car or a bus. In a private car, when you get to the roadblocks, you are going to be asked for a passport. I told them I had no passport. Then you are told to get out, and they form a group of people. You know that you are going to get deported—that is the plan, so there's no problem about that when going home. The problem is coming back.

---

[25] Leaders of the Zionist church in Zimbabwe are called prophets.

What happens is, they put you on one side, and you are told to produce your papers. If you don't have any proper papers, then you will sit and wait for them to take you to the detention camp in Musina.[26] If it's going to be a public holiday, you stay in detention until the public holiday is over, but otherwise you are deported after two days. You are given food there. It's okay. It's only that jail is not a nice place. In the morning, you are deported, driven across the border and into Beitbridge.[27] Those omalayitsha are waiting on that side, and they drive you to Bulawayo.

I had called my mom and told them that I was coming, so they kept on phoning the day I was coming to make sure that I was on my way, and I called them when I crossed the bridge—*I am now in Zimbabwe!* I arrived home late in the evening. When I got to my mother's house, the gate was already locked. I just touched the gate, and my son heard me. He came running out, shouting, *Mama, Mama!* Then he jumped onto me. He's so tall now. I was tired and hungry, so I nearly fell over. He was very happy, yes, he was very happy.

The things that I bought them for Christmas had already arrived with the *omalayitsha* people. So then we did not sleep that day, because they wanted to see everything. I bought them DVDs, clothes, food. Sometimes I didn't eat—just fruits for supper—to save enough money to send them things. But I managed, and it makes him happy.

On TV, we see people who are HIV-positive. And when I got home, my son looked very thin. It crossed my mind, *Hey! my son just looks like those people that have HIV.* But he's okay. It's only that he has got very much thinner. That worries me. They survive on vegetables because they're easy to grow, you just water them. My mother told me they can't afford to buy red meat, and this year at Christmas we did not even have any chicken.

But he's fine. He's doing well. He was doing Grade 4, but since the previous year in October, he hadn't been going to school because schools

---

[26] The town on the South African side of the border with Zimbabwe, south of the Limpopo River. See Section 7, "The Border."

[27] The town on the Zimbabwean side of the border.

were closed. We were paying one hundred rand per week for private teachers to teach him—from the money I earn as a domestic worker in Cape Town.

MY MOTHER KNOWS HIM BETTER THAN I DO

At first I thought things were going to change, as Tsvangirai had managed to make an agreement with Mugabe.[28] But I don't see any changes. A lot of teachers have quit their jobs and come this side, and some have gone to other countries. Some of my friends who were teachers and nurses, they're now domestic workers. A graduate is now a domestic worker. So I think it will take a long time, if it's ever going to change in Zimbabwe.

But when I called home this week, I heard costs were going down, and things were available at the shops. A taxi to town from my location was five rand in December, but now it has gone down to three rand. A loaf of bread was twenty rand, and now it has gone down to ten.[29] People can buy things at the shops now, like mealie-meal. There wasn't any mealie-meal in December.

I wish things could really change and I could go home. That would be best for me. Here it's okay, but there are times when you need your family around, like when you get sick and there's no one to look after you, when you miss your family, and when you need somebody close to talk to. Yes, there are church elders, but at times you need somebody very close.

When I call, my son asks me, *Mom, can you please buy me clothes?* Some of his friends, their mothers are also here in South Africa, so he also likes asking for the same things they get from their parents: *Can you please buy me such and such a thing?* Every time, I make sure I buy it for him, so that he doesn't feel that he is a lonely child without a mother.

---

[28] In January 2009, President Robert Mugabe and opposition leader Morgan Tsvangirai formed a coalition government under an externally mediated Global Political Agreement. See the appendix section on the 2008 election.

[29] US50¢, 30¢, US$2, and US$1, respectively.

BONIFACE

AGE: *28*

OCCUPATION: *Former clerk, current day-laborer and preacher*
INTERVIEWED IN: *Musina, South Africa*

Boniface is a fervent believer and aspiring preacher. In Musina, he stays at the men's shelter run by I Believe in Jesus Church. Speaking in a combination of English and "Zinglish," Boniface gives a frequent and resounding clap of his hands as he warms to his story. Born into a trade-unionist family, he describes the buildup of his own political fervor with a preacher's cadence, finishing each anecdote by calling, in a resigned tone, on the Lord. His faith is pretty much all that Boniface has left at this point. But he remembers Abel fondly ("my friend from a tender age"), and Arthur, his Ndebele friend in Bulawayo. Not yet thirty, Boniface's experience covers many of the worst moments in this recent era of Zimbabwe's history. His friendship across tribal lines encouraged him, in the early 2000s, to research what happened in the 1980s during Gukurahundi, the semi-secret war waged by the government in the South of the country. Then, in 2005, as Operation Murambatsvina made many thousands of people homeless in urban centers all over Zimbabwe, Boniface was forced by the authorities to tear down the small house belonging to his Harare landlord. His political activities later landed him in the thick of the violence of the 2008 elections. At the end of that year, he left, and crossed the Limpopo. To keep out of the way of the South African authorities while he waited for papers, Boniface and his brother settled in a remote part of the country, near Thohoyandou, doing piecework and living rough until they were robbed at knife-point. (Large numbers of Zimbabwean men live in the bush like Boniface did, camped in dry riverbeds, laboring for farmers who may or may not pay them what little they promised.) While a huge improvement, the church shelter he stays in now can provide only buckets of cold water to wash with, Boniface reports, and the men's sleeping tent is open at the top and bottom to the icy air and dust of the Limpopo Valley winter.

On the 27th of March, 2008, when the election results started to come out,[1] I was an election agent for the Movement for Democratic Change, the MDC. I was in Ward 8, Masvingo, in the central part of the town. When the elections were counted I was optimistic that Tsvangirai was going to win. I knew that Zanu-PF was capable of anything, so I was a bit worried, but at the same time, I was happy because of the vote counting: Tsvangirai, Tsvangirai, Tsvangirai, Tsvangirai, Tsvangirai, Tsvangirai, Mugabe—maybe one, Tsvangirai, Tsvangirai… We were counting out of the ballot box. As an election agent, I was representing MDC, so we were counting together in a hall in the showgrounds where the polls were done: two of us representing MDC, two for Zanu-PF, and two for Simba Makoni, the independent candidate. Mutambara didn't qualify that time.[2]

We were counting for the presidential elections first, then for the

---

[1] The elections in March 2008 were marked, first, by a relatively calm lead-up period, by projected MDC wins based on individual polling-station tallies, and by long delays in the release of results, along with accusations of rigging. Finally, when the results of the presidential election were announced (as Boniface explains in detail), the government called for a runoff between President Mugabe and Morgan Tsvangirai. Because of the vicious intimidation and attacks that followed this announcement, Tsvangirai withdrew from the run-off, leaving Mugabe in power.

[2] By the 2008 elections, the Movement for Democratic Change (MDC) had split into two factions, one led by founder Morgan Tsvangirai and the other by former student activist Arthur Mutambara. The other significant contestant, besides Mugabe was Simba Makoni, the former head of the regional body SADC (the Southern African Development Community), but he did not make much of a dent in the votes overall. For more, see the appendix section on the 2008 election.

MP, that is, the member of Parliament, then for the senator, and then for the councillor. After counting, we collected the results from other centers and we added them together, and in Masvingo, MDC won everything. From the look of things, it was obvious that the MDC was going to win. Obvious!

When we finished the counting, we were phoning our relatives in other areas, and there was joy all over Zimbabwe, there was celebration, because in the past Zanu-PF used to get all the seats in rural areas, but we could hear from the people that we were winning. It was our first time as MDC to win rural areas, especially in Mashonaland, in Masvingo Province, and Manicaland and Midlands. These were Zanu-PF strongholds in the past, so we were happy to win there.

But come the time when the results should be announced on the television, they were delayed. We started to ask, *What is happening now?* When MDC won a seat, they would not announce it, they would wait for another seat to be announced for Zanu-PF so that the people would think that the parties were neck and neck. They were playing games. We knew we were in trouble. Because in Zimbabwe, when you are in the opposition, you feel you are constantly in danger.

We waited. Finally, for the MPs, we won. For senators, we lost by four seats. And as the opposition, MDC Tsvangirai and MDC Mutabambara, when we came together, we won outright. And considering that Mutabambara wasn't contesting the presidential race, it was obvious that Tsvangirai was going to win the presidential election.

I think you know what happened. For the whole month, we didn't know who won the election between Tsvangirai and Mugabe. We heard the Minister of Defense saying, *We will not salute Tsvangirai. Even if he wins the election, he is not going to be our leader. We are going to war if Tsvangirai wins.* It wasn't good.

Twenty-seventh March? It was the people's verdict: Tsvangirai. Zimbabwe spoke with one voice, even though the government rejected our decision. We just say, *God, the people have spoken. But what we want as the people of Zimbabwe is not forthcoming, so our hope now is in You.*

IN THE BLOOD

When Tsvangirai was the leader of the Zimbabwe Congress of Trade Unions, ZCTU, I liked him. My father was a unionist, and MDC was formed by unionists. It's a labor party, a party for workers. My uncle, my father's young brother, is also a unionist. (That one is known around Zimbabwe!) So MDC is not something I just *wanted* to join—it's in our blood as a family. When Tsvangirai formed the MDC in 1999, I said, *I want to join this party.* I'm twenty-eight now and I was seventeen then.

My father's name is also Boniface, and my mother is Mary. I'm the first-born in a family of five children. My father was a driver for Cane Haulage, the trucks which carry sugarcane. He started working there when I was very young, about 1982. Then he was promoted to become a transport manager. He was a unionist, and sometimes he led strikes when the working conditions or the salaries were not good. Back then, he was a Zanu-PF supporter, even the district treasurer for Zanu-PF.

My mother is a housewife, she didn't work, she just stayed at home. And now that my father is retired, he is also at our rural home in Masvingo. The second-born, the brother after me, was born in 1983. By now he was supposed to be finishing his degree at the University of Zimbabwe in metallurgical engineering, but he won't finish because of the problems that the country is facing. The third one fled the country in 2007. I don't even know where he is now, and I don't feel right: Is he still alive or not? I don't know. Then the fourth one is in Zimbabwe. He finished his A-levels last year. For now, he is applying for a place at the university or maybe another institution of higher learning, but I wonder if he is going to make it because of financial constraints, since my father is no longer working. And the last one is a girl, born 1995. She is disabled; she is deaf and dumb and partly blind. You cannot control her because she cannot see, she cannot talk, she cannot hear, but if she is sitting there and you give her food, she eats. And when it's time to go to the toilet, it's a problem. I feel a heavy burden when I think of her, and I just pray that God will do something, because I believe that God can do all things.

In 1988, when I was seven years old, I had a friend named Abel. We grew up together and we are still friends. When we wrote our examinations in Grade 1, the first stage of primary education, I got higher marks than him. He was crying! When we walked home from school, we would be together. But my friend's parents were poor compared to my parents. Sometimes I gave him my shoes. And my parents would say, *Where are your shoes?* In Grade 4, Abel became number one in class, and I was number five. He loved that! But when we finished primary level, Abel and I got the same points, nine points, the highest at the school. This was in rural Masvingo, where I was staying with my mother while my father was working in Chiredzi. But then came the time that we had to separate, because I went to Gweru for my secondary education and my friend had to stay in the rural areas.

We had a good life then. My father had a car and when he came home to Masvingo, he would buy clothes for us, drive us to Chiredzi and to see other relatives in other areas. It's hard to imagine that now.

For my secondary education, I studied at Makoba Secondary in Gweru, 1995 up to 1998. After finishing Form 4, the O or Ordinary level, I wanted to go on to A-level (Advanced), but by then my parents could see how Zimbabwe's economy was declining. From 1998, I started to see for myself that things were getting tough economically. When I was in secondary school, you could buy Freezits—frozen juice in a plastic tube— for fifty cents each. From Form 1 up to Form 4, the price didn't change, showing that the economy was strong. But when I finished school in 1998, the prices of Freezits suddenly increased, from fifty cents to two dollars.

TURNING POINT

In 1999, the MDC was formed. Then in 2000, there was a referendum. Everyone could vote yes or vote no to change the constitution of Zimbabwe, to give more room to Mugabe so he could do what he wanted. By then I was supporting MDC, so we were motivating people to vote no in my rural areas. As MDC we used to say, *No, guys, this thing has gone too far. This man is trying to suppress you, so you have to vote NO.* And people understood it, and they voted no. Our party won, and Zanu-PF lost, so it was a wake-up call for Zanu-PF. They started to realize, *Oh, people don't like us, we are no longer the people's party, MDC is now taking our position.* That's when they started to be brutal, to be cruel, to beat people. If you said, *I support the MDC,* or if you were found wearing an MDC T-shirt, you would be in trouble.

So that was the year 2000. It was a turning point for Zimbabwean people in the sense that that's when the land invasions started.[3] That was the sword that was used to destroy to the economy of Zimbabwe. As you know, Zimbabwe's is an agri-based economy. Remember, Zimbabwe used to be the breadbasket not only for Southern Africa, but for Africa as a whole. What happened in 2000 when the land was taken from the white farmers is that our economy started to decline. Sometimes you hear people say, *MDC members like white people.* But I'm not being a racist by saying when they invaded the farms, chasing away the white people, it was a mistake. Not taking anything away from us blacks—when it comes to farming, we know how to farm—but those white farmers mean business.

Even our President Mugabe knows that that was a very big mistake. He gave the so-called war veterans the farms. Maybe because they fought for liberation, they have that spirit of war in them. Whatever they do involves violence. When they took the farms, the irrigation equipment was destroyed. They chased away the white farmers, took the property, and sold it cheap. It was just vandalism. They were not building anything, they were not constructing anything, they were just destroying what was there already.

---

[3] See timeline and other appendices for more details on this. Like many others in this collection, Boniface goes on to give his own perspective on what came to be known as Fast Track Land Reform. Building from instances of spontaneous occupation of absentee-owned farms by land-hungry peasants, at a time of both economic downturn and increasing opposition to the ruling party, the state backed the widespread and often violent takeover of commercial farms—most but not all owned by white farmers—by groups of so-called war vets (ex-combatants from the former liberation movements).

The workers on the farms were left jobless. They had to move from the farms. Some of them came from Malawi, but they had became Zimbabwean citizens by virtue of staying for a long time. Zimbabwe was their home. They have suffered a lot.

BULAWAYO

As for me, after O-level, I went to Bulawayo to start work there as an accounts clerk at a company called T.O.P. Agencies. I worked for them from 1999 up to 2004.

My ambition, my aspiration was to be trained as an accountant. From a tender age I wanted to be an accountant. I was inspired by my uncle, who was an accountant. When I finished my exams, my uncle spoke to some colleagues in Bulawayo. They had a vacancy, and so that's how I got that job. I wanted to join the Association for Chartered Accountants, ACA. But they wanted something like two hundred pounds for me to register as a student, and I couldn't raise that.

When I moved to Bulawayo, I lived in North End suburb, in my aunt's house. She built another house in Shelbourne Park and left me living in North End with some Tswana girls who were going to school in Bulawayo. Botswana people prefer Zimbabwean education. I used to work with a Russian lady and she became my friend. She used to come every day in her car to pick me up for work. She had met a Zimbabwean guy, a black Zimbabwean, in Russia when he went to pursue agricultural studies there. They had married there in Russia, but when they came to Zimbabwe, the guy fled. He left that lady desperate in Zimbabwe, with nowhere to go.

My friend Arthur was very important in my life in Bulawayo. He was Ndebele. I used to visit his rural home where everyone speaks Ndebele. His parents were surprised: *Arthur, your friend can't even speak one Ndebele word!* But I believe that it was God who caused Arthur and me to meet. Because being friends, Ndebele and Shona, is something! You know what happened during the early 1980s to Ndebele people? There were atrocities, Mugabe attacking the Ndebele people, Zanu-PF massacring Ndebele people.[4]

I liked the Ndebele leader, Joshua Nkomo. That was Father Zimbabwe, I tell you. He had a heart for the people, but because of this tribalism, people voted for Mugabe in 1980. I think if Joshua Nkomo had a chance to rule Zimbabwe, we could've been in a better position now. Now he is late,[5] but I liked him.

All of that is history now. I wasn't born yet, or I was still a baby, when this was happening. But according to my father and according to my own research (because I wanted to know more about what happened), in the Independence elections in 1980, in which Mugabe was elected the prime minister of Zimbabwe, Mugabe won fifty-seven seats in Zimbabwe, and Joshua Nkomo won twenty. The twenty seats for Father Zimbabwe came from Matabeleland, and the fifty-seven seats Mugabe got were from Mashonaland—the Shona people voted for Mugabe. Maybe Mugabe was still worried about the Ndebele. Maybe he thought, *These people want to rise against me, they may plan a revolt*— I don't know what he thought. But what happened is that a wing of the national army, called the Fifth Brigade, led by Perence Shiri, who is still there, and Emmerson Mnangagwa, who is now Minister of Defense, attacked Midlands Province and Matabeleland Province, South and North. (That's where you find Ndebele people in Zimbabwe, in Matabeleland and Midlands Provinces.) And they killed people for no reason, innocent people, civilians.

When I was in Bulawayo, I used to ask the old people what really happened during that time. You could see tears running down their cheeks, because what happened was so cruel. There were some cases, they said, in which people were thrown into pits. They put grass down there,

---

[4] Boniface is talking about *Gukurahundi*, the 1982–87 military campaign ostensibly against dissidents from the former Zimbabwe People's Revolutionary Army, ZIPRA. See the timeline for more.

[5] A common and polite way to refer to someone who has died.

and while people were sleeping there in the pits, they lit a fire. I think their idea was to kill the whole tribe. If the world was just, if life was fair, Mugabe would be punished for that.

I am trying to explain that the evil that Mugabe is doing now didn't start now, it started long back. If you look into history, it took a lot of cruelty for him to be the Zanu-PF leader.

So a sort of hatred has grown between Ndebele people and Shona people. But I learned a lot because of my friendship with Arthur. He wanted to come to Masvingo, to see where I stay, but it was too far. So when I went home from Bulawayo for the Christmas holiday, I took Arthur's jacket. My parents asked me, *Where did you get this jacket?* I said, *It's my friend's jacket.* They said, *Why didn't you bring your friend? We wanted to meet him.* It meant something to me that my parents accepted my friend, that Ndebele. It showed me that we as Zimbabweans have to be together, irrespective of our tribes, Ndebele or Shona. Even up to now, we are committed friends, Arthur and me. He is still in Bulawayo.

HARARE

In 2004, the company transferred me from Bulawayo to Harare. I went to live in Glenview 7 in what we call the high-density suburbs. But Glenview 7 looks different from other high-density areas. It looks like the houses that you find in the city, with tile roofs, and each house having its own style different from the next. I was staying with Abel, my friend from a tender age, sharing a room. Abel is also a Christian now. We go to the same church, the Apostolic Faith Mission in Zimbabwe. Harare is where I grew spiritually. It shaped my life in Christianity.

There are two things that I like very much: the gospel of Jesus Christ and politics. Nowadays, the gospel is taking me by storm, I'm in gospel full-time now. Now, by God's grace, I want to be a pastor.

I'm now twenty-eight, but I'm not yet married. I said to God, *God, when I marry, I want someone like me, because I think I'm honest and I'm faithful.* I had a girlfriend when I was very young, and that girlfriend had another man, and I was disappointed. I never wanted another love affair in my life. Up to now, I'm eleven years without a girlfriend, because I don't trust those ladies. Because of Christianity, I'm still a pure young man, a virgin. I pray for a wife: *God, I'm twenty-eight and my parents need a daughter-in-law, because they are advancing in years and I'm their first-born.*

You know, in Shona culture, when you start working, you are expected to buy something, maybe a cow to keep at our rural home. While I work in town, no problem, my parents rear and keep the cattle. If I am retrenched, or fired, then at least I have a cow at home to plough the land. That's what our parents teach us.

I did manage to buy a cow while I was working in Bulawayo, but when I moved to Harare, it was hard to buy another one. In 2003, our currency, the Zimdollar, lost its value dramatically. In 2004, I moved to Harare, and it looked like there was some improvement. But then 2005 came.

Zimbabwe should be one of the greatest economies in Africa, so what is happening now, you can't explain. In 2005, life was difficult, I tell you! I could not afford to travel from Harare to Masvingo to see my parents. I couldn't even make ends meet in terms of buying groceries for the whole month. My salary and my friend Abel's salary put together wasn't sustaining us for the whole month, so we were struggling, struggling, struggling.

Also in 2005, we had Operation Murambatsvina, destroying people's homes for no obvious reason. Murambatsvina is a Shona word. *Tsvina* means dirt, *muramba* is like "we don't want"—so together it means "we don't want rubbish." By calling it Operation Murambatsvina, they were saying that the places where people were living were like rubbish. They destroyed people's homes, saying they were not built according to plans passed by the local government authorities. They called them "informal settlements." This happened in the winter season, when it was very cold. You could see people left out in the open winter air. It happened wherever ordinary black people live, the low-class people. They used bulldozers to push those houses over. Day after day. In the morning, you could hear the bulldozers moving and destroying.

Urban areas are MDC stongholds. So, maybe Murambatsvina was to give a message: *You people have to go and live in rural areas, because if you live in towns, you are a problem for us.* I think Mugabe was trying to frustrate MDC supporters, because the operation was done only in urban areas, where MDC is supported. Because in Zimbabwe, in every town, in every urban area, there is no chance for Mugabe, no chance at all, he knows that he cannot win in urban areas. So he wanted to show us: *Even if you vote for Morgan Tsvangirai, I have the power to destroy you.* Murambatsvina was all about destroying the hopes of MDC people. Because we voted for Tsvangirai, and Tsvangirai was not defending us.

I was affected indirectly by Murambatsvina. Where I was staying, we had a main house and a small house, what we call a boys' *kaia*. I was living with my friend Abel, renting a room in the main house. With the house owner and his family, there were about eleven people in the big house, and two guys renting the small house. And then you know what happens in Zimbabwe: Zanu-PF people come in a group, singing, chanting slogans, moving around the whole area. They came to our place early in the morning on the weekend and said, *We have to destroy this house. It's Operation Murambatsvina.* What could we do? We could only comply with orders.

Because there was a durawall and some houses in the way, it was impossible for their bulldozer to reach the small house, so they made us destroy it. It was made of bricks. Fortunately, we managed to save some of the materials—asbestos roof sheets, windows, doorframes, doors. Our landlord was a friend to us, he was like a father. So we were glad that at least we managed to salvage something. Nothing was destroyed completely; we broke it down carefully, at our own pace. They were not forcing us—*do this, do that*—they were just standing there, to see the house destroyed. The two people who had rented the small house now had to move, find somewhere else to live. They had to take their property to their rural homes because they had nowhere to put it.

In Zimbabwe in general, Murambatsvina affected millions of people. Some were left homeless, and up to now, they cannot recover what they had. Up to now, it's still a problem.[6] And the worst part of it is they just destroyed people's homes without building anything else. If it was a real plan, they were supposed to build first, not just destroy people's homes so they have nowhere to go. To us, as MDC members, it was clear that it was meant for the party, to thwart the hope of the people of Zimbabwe, to say, *You cannot do anything without Zanu-PF.*

MASVINGO

In 2007, I had to move from Harare, because my salary wasn't enough to live on. My uncle in Masvingo found me another job, so I left the company where I had been working for a long time, the T.O.P. Agencies, and went to work as a records clerk at Masvingo City Council. It was cheaper to travel from where I was staying to work, but it still wasn't possible to live. Once I paid rent, the water bill, and the electricity bill, my salary was finished. Nothing left for food for the whole month.

Then it was elections—March 28th, 2008, election day, as I told you before. Now, for Zanu-PF supporters to know you were an election agent for MDC—that was dangerous. My parents were saying, *You have to leave Masvingo and go somewhere to hide, or else you will be killed.*

After that it was the time of campaigning for the run-off election. After the March election, when they announced the results, they said Tsvangirai had won only 48 percent, and Mugabe 42 percent. They said, for someone to be declared the winner, the law requires that they have to get above 50 percent of the vote. So they said Tsvangirai and Mugabe must contest again. Zanu-PF called that election campaign *100 percent Black Empowerment* and *Total Independence.* But it was total independence only for the Zanu-PF people. They had no one to control them, they were independent to kill. Not 100 percent total independence for other Zimbabweans. Zanu-PF were saying, *29 June, Mugabe chete, chete!* meaning

---

[6] Political violence targeting urban areas, similar to Operation Murambatsvina, has recurred at intervals.

Mugabe only, only. I remember being forced to go to Zanu-PF rallies. When Mugabe came to Masvingo, everybody was forced to attend the rally in Mucheke Stadium. Soldiers and police went around the streets, armed, telling people, *Everybody to the stadium, the president is coming. We have only one president in Zimbabwe, that is Robert Mugabe. This is Zimbabwe, no one is going to rule Zimbabwe without war credentials.* They were referring to Tsvangirai: just because he didn't go to the liberation struggle, they said he had no credentials to rule Zimbabwe.

At the stadium, one of the army commanders made a speech. *We know that you people of Masvingo want Tsvangirai to be your leader. But as an army commander I have left my office to come here, not to beg you, not to persuade you, but to force you to vote for Mugabe.* That was the speech. *You see that man?* There was a certain soldier holding a gun. *If you want to rule Zimbabwe, go to that man and take the gun out of his hand.* He was saying, without a gun, you cannot rule Zimbabwe. This is the reality of Zimbabwe, right? They were showing their true colors, declaring that, *We took this country from the white regime by using guns. Now if you MDC people want to rule Zimbabwe, you have to take it with guns, not by voting, not by Xs. You can't take this country by a ballpoint, it's impossible. Compare how big a gun is and how small a pen is.* That was the speech of the army commander.

For me personally, there was a lot of pressure and threats. When I was in my room, they could come and knock around twelve o'clock, one o'clock in the night. *Boniface, where are you?*

I'm here.

We know that you are a Christian, so we don't want to do bad things to you, but if you continue this political action, definitely you will be killed.

Some people came to me, Nicodemusly,[7] telling me, *They want to teach you a lesson. You have to surrender your MDC T-shirts, your MDC card, your membership card, and your posters* (because I used to put my Tsvangirai posters up in my room). These people told me quietly, *You have to sur-*

---

[7] In the New Testament, Nicodemus is a Pharisee who shows favor to Jesus.

render your caps and red cards. Because I kept the caps for the party. And we had red cards, we used to flash them, saying, *Mugabe off the pitch!* In a football match, when you are penalized, you are supposed to leave the stadium, get off the pitch, you can no longer play football. So, when we flash the red cards, we are saying we are the referees and Mugabe had gone against the regulations, so he has to get off the pitch. That's the meaning of the red card.

By then, killing you wasn't something they would even count; it was like killing a fly. So, I said, *Guys, this is the thing. Tell your bosses that now I'm no longer an MDC supporter, I'm now a Zanu-PF supporter. I've repented, I'm now behind Mugabe.*

People were living in fear. You could think about committing suicide because you had no right to choose, no right to freedom, no right even to express what you wanted. Right now in Zimbabwe, if I said anything bad about Mugabe, I would be in trouble.[8] The Central Intelligence Organization is always running around Zimbabwe, picking up people who say anything bad about the president. In a democratic country, you don't expect such things. You cannot call Zimbabwe a democratic country. We had hoped the international community would chip in to help Zimbabwe, but their hands are soft, they cannot grip Mugabe hard. So our hope now is only in God, it's not in this world.

Everybody can see what is happening in Zimbabwe. That old man doesn't want to go, under any circumstances. Whatever he is doing now, he is doing it in bad faith. He is just pretending to be together with Tsvangirai, trying to get international recognition by using Tsvangirai.[9] You will not be surprised to hear that Tsvangirai is dead. Zanu-PF can

---

[8] Mugabe's government has put in place a number of laws restricting speech and writing that opposes that government, the enforcement of which have often served as a pretext for political violence. Since the formation of the unity government, there has been renewed hope and indications that these laws would be repealed, and that policies encouraging freedoms of speech, assembly, and the press would be codified.

[9] In January 2009, the two MDC factions joined Zanu-PF in a coalition or "unity" government, under the Global Political Agreement. See the appendix section on the 2008 election.

do anything, they are unpredictable, they are dubious characters. So I feel pity for my president, Tsvangirai, because anything can happen. I think you heard of his wife's death: it was something which was plotted by Zanu-PF.[10] Even if Tsvangirai himself denied it—*Ah, it's just an accident*—he knows it wasn't an accident. He knows. I remember Zanu-PF threatening Tsvangirai. When Elliot Manyika was the National Political Commissar for Zanu-PF, he was involved in an accident and he died. They said to Tsvangirai at the time, *If we did it to our own child, if we did it to our own Elliot Manyika, we can do it to you as well.*

THOHOYANDOU

In 2008, I told God, *I'm now going to South Africa. I want peace of mind. I don't feel comfortable in my home country, I don't feel secure.* How painful that is.

I traveled with my cousin-brother, and it wasn't easy, because we did not have enough money to take us to where we wanted to go. We had to walk more than one hundred kilometers altogether. First we traveled by bus to near Beitbridge. Then from Luthumba, that's the township of Beitbridge, we walked about thirty kilometers to the Limpopo River. We kept on walking until it was dark, about eleven p.m. We were hungry, we were thirsty, we didn't know anyone in the area, but we were seeing homes here and there, so sometimes we would approach people and ask for some water to drink. But we slept far away from people's homes, to be safe. At about two a.m., we started to walk again. We reached Limpopo at about eight a.m. the next day. I thank God that we didn't meet the *magumaguma*, the robbers, because near Limpopo River, it's dangerous. And I thank God that at that time the river was not flowing, so we just walked across the dry riverbed.

We were now in South Africa. At one point, I could not walk any

---

[10] Susan Tsvangirai died in a car crash in March 2009, when a haulage truck sideswiped the car she and her husband were traveling in. Many have suspected that this was another targeted attempt to assassinate Morgan Tsvangirai.

farther. But my brother said we were not even halfway to our destination. He said, *We have to be man enough.* So we went on.

We arrived at a place where there were some shops. I had around eleven rand in my pocket, my cousin-brother had about twenty rand in his pocket.[11] Should we board a taxi or should we find something to eat? I said, *I cannot walk now, let's take a taxi.* Unfortunately, the people operating the taxi that we boarded were *tsotsis*, robbers. They took our money, *Ten rand each and we leave you in Thohoyandou.* After about twenty kilometers, they said, *Guys, the money you gave us is too little, can you add some more?* My brother had ten rand left and he gave it to them. They drove about five more kilometers, then they said, *If you don't have more money, we are leaving you here.* They took advantage of us because they knew that we had no documents, we were illegal migrants, so we could not report them to the police. We had to soldier on, we had to walk.

We walked the whole night in the bushes, because if we walked along the road we would be caught by the police. It took us almost three days to reach where we were going. We were getting food from people along the way. Venda people are kind, especially the mothers. They see you and they say, *Oh, my children, come and get food. We have to help, we know that situation in Zimbabwe is not good.* But the men were not good to us. If we met young guys, they would see that we were suffering, we were hungry, but they demanded money.

When we arrived where we were going, I was surprised. This is the place? Thohoyandou, that's where I was.[12] It was just bush. Zimbabweans living in the riverbed and by the riverbanks. It was terrible. We had to make a shack out of plastic. Just take some sticks and make them dome-shaped, put some plastic sheets on them, and that was our room.

Now, how do we survive? That was my question. It was time for cultivating, people were preparing for the rainy season, so we had to go

---

[11] Approximately US$1.10 and US$2.

[12] Thohoyandou is about 125 miles from Musina and surrounded by farms and empty bush.

around the people there, looking for piece jobs, work in the fields, digging, preparing the soil, and so forth. But it wasn't paying—we would work the whole day and get only about twenty rand! September, October, November. Life was tough, living like that.

Then I met a certain Zimbabwean who said, *My brother, are you aware that in Musina you can get asylum and you can start living in South Africa? You will be documented.* That's when I came to Musina. I tried to get asylum then, but it was tough, so I had to travel back to Thohoyandou. In December, I returned to Musina to apply again for asylum. There were many people at the showgrounds. I can't even estimate how many. I stayed there for almost two weeks, no food, no blanket, nowhere to sleep, nowhere to take a bath. I don't want to think about that. It was something like hell. I was just saying, *God, I want this paper.*

People in the South African Home Affairs office were corrupt. Some people were paying money to get asylum. It's not formal, it was done secretly. And some people were caught by the police and arrested for that. It's known, and it was in the media. After these people were caught, the situation improved. And that's when I got my asylum. It was the 19th of December 2008.

I went back to Thohoyandou with my paper. Now it was better, because I could move freely, finding piece jobs here and there. I managed to raise some money, but unfortunately we were attacked, and all the things that I worked for were taken by robbers. They came to our shack in the night and attacked us. They were about eleven guys armed with those big knives that look like swords—*pangas*. In Zimbabwe, they are used to cut sugarcane. I was staying with my cousin-brother, and my new friend Godfrey, and my brother's friend Kennedy. There were four of us in that shack and they took everything that we had. We had to start again from zero.

I had bought two pairs of jeans, some T-shirts, and some *takkies*, and I had put my asylum card in the pocket of my new jeans. They took all of that. I had to come back to Musina to get another asylum card. On our way to Musina, my friend Godfrey was caught by the police and deported to Zimbabwe, but I ran away and they did not catch me.

MUSINA

It was March when I came back to Musina. It took me four days to get another asylum card. That's when I came to know about the church where we are living now, I Believe in Jesus Church, and about the pastor. He used to come to the showgrounds, preaching the word of God there. When he noticed me and saw that I have zeal, we went to his church, and from then on I began to preach, even at the showgrounds, sharing the word of God, encouraging people.

At the church, the pastor treats us well, the conditions are okay, we cannot complain. Organizations are helping here and there—the NGOs and organizations like the UN, Red Cross, IOM—International Organization for Migration—Doctors Without Borders, UNICEF, and some churches. Médicins sans Frontièrs built a toilet at our shelter. We appreciate that. They are promising now to make showers for us. But we are facing problems at the church. We don't have a real shelter for the people. We have only one tent with sides. When it's cold like this, it's terrible in the other tents.

What bothers me so much is that when I came to South Africa I was expecting to help myself, maybe further my education. But I'm a Christian. I don't doubt my God. I just pray that God is going to open doors for me. My dream and my vision is bible college. This bible college should be non-denominational. I don't believe in denominations, but I believe in Jesus Christ.

We say, *God, we want help. God, these are your people, you know what is happening in Zimbabwe, we are here because we've been compelled, we've been forced to be here.*

Last night, I was preaching about three friends who were taken captive in Babylon—Meshak, Shadrak, and Abednego. They were thrown into a furnace blazing with fire, but they were not feeling the pain. When the King looked, he asked the officials, *Didn't we throw three men in the fire? Because I can see a fourth man there and he looks like an angel.* God had intervened. God was with them in the fire and they could not be burned.

But the fire they were in was real fire—fire that can hurt people, that can burn people, right? But because of the presence of the Lord, they couldn't feel the pain. So I was telling them, *Guys, we have to put our trust in God. If God is with us, even though there is a problem, we are not going to feel the pain of the problem.*

Look, we are in poverty, but we are not poor. Just like those people were in the fire, but they were not burned. Even in this state, we are hard pressed, but we are not crushed; we are down, but we are not destroyed.

FARMS

LAND

In Zimbabwe, the term "farms" refers to a different category of land from wide swaths of land known as "rural areas." The 1930 Land Apportionment Act firmed up the division of landholding in the country into roughly two main categories: commercial farms and what were then called "native reserves" or "Tribal Trustlands." In 1930, only white farmers held title deeds to commercial farms (as Briggs explains in his narrative). These farms amounted to many thousands of acres in regions with the best soils and rainfall.

By contrast, except when employed on these commercial farms, the black population was pretty much confined to the reserves known since Independence as "the rural areas." In these areas, land was (and continues to be) held in trust under the authority of traditional leaders—chiefs, *sabukus*, and headmen—who allocate parcels of land to families. To actually buy land to own and farm on individual basis, black farmers had to meet stringent conditions of education and wealth.

The early years of independence saw huge changes in the rural areas. Small farmers gained access to credit for the first time. As roads and transport to these areas improved, peasant cash-crop production rose by more than 100 percent. But drought, World Bank conditions, and overcrowding all placed severe limits on how far that kind of expansion could go.

Driving round the country as recently as the mid-2000s, it was impossible to mistake one land category for another. Along most paved roads through the country, commercial farms would spread to the horizon—vast fields, fenced and plowed, filled with maize, cotton, citrus, and tobacco, or endless miles of thick bush and forest, an occasional farmhouse visible at the end of a long drive. Driving past commercial farms, you might go many miles without, from the road, seeing anyone at all.

Yet in the communally owned rural areas, where the roads were more likely to be dirt or narrow tar, you'd see people everywhere. You'd have to drive more slowly on the bumpy roads, slowing for cattle and the herd boys chasing them, for crowds of uniformed school children heading to class or home, for rural buses kicking up dust. Every arable acre would usually be cultivated, while trees would be far fewer because people had cut them down for fuel.

Driving along a rural road during our research, we stopped for a man hitching a ride. He lifted a sack of maize into the back seat and introduced himself as Mr. Shiri. After about fifty kilometers of silence, Mr. Shiri began to speak about his situation. His wife could not grind the maize she grew because there was no fuel to run the local grinding mill. Mr. Shiri was on his way to Harare to sell the cobs. He would return to their rural home with maize meal for his wife and his ailing father. Mr. Shiri himself used to work as a security guard, but as the economy disintegrated, his wages no longer covered the cost of transport to get to work. He was reduced to trading small amounts of maize and groundnuts back and forth between the rurals and the capital.

We turned onto the main road that runs north-south up the spine of the country, past a stretch of commercial farms. Even here, traffic was thin. Vendors hoping to sell their wares to the occasional motorist or passing bus sat by the roadside behind neat pyramids of avocados or stacks of firewood. Others were selling wild mushrooms or eggs or honey or armfuls of wild St. Joseph's lilies. Mr. Shiri pointed out the wide swaths of farmland lying fallow. *These areas used to produce food for the whole country, but now…* He sucked his teeth.

We had heard about this before from narrators in this book such as Boniface, Nicola, George, and from others. About the terrible failure of the government's Fast Track Land Reform, about the majority of Zimbabwe's 4,500 commercial farms being "designated"—occupied by war veterans (or people claiming to be ex-fighters) and handed over to new black owners—and about how this has been catastrophic for the food production of the country. But, however cynical and political (and violent) the implementation of land reform, we also found counter evidence: many small farmers around the country have benefited from access to new land for cultivation and grazing.[1] As Briggs emphasizes in his narrative, not every farm has gone to political cronies.

Aware of the irony in this exchange, we tried to introduce this additional complication into the discussion. After all, even if land reform is carried out in a seriously flawed way, didn't the land need to be distributed after more than a hundred years of all the good land going to whites? But Mr. Shiri was having none of it. *These ones are not farming,* he said angrily. *They are just selling off the equipment and the produce that they found here.* He dismissed the idea that the new occupants needed more support to get established.

Just then, we passed a scene that Mr. Shiri might as well have conjured up to make his point. Grass waved in a tree-cleared field on a former commercial farm. The only cultivation now in evidence was a small stand of uneven maize plants. In front of a group of newly built huts, a new tractor was parked at an extreme angle on a hillock. *No fuel,* Mr. Shiri said. *They sold it.* And it is true that grass was growing thick around the unused tractor tires. It was only one farm, on one stretch of road, but the image left an impact.

---

[1] See papers in the series, "Livelihoods After Land Reform," *lalr.org.za*.

TSITSI

AGE: *41*

OCCUPATION: *Former commercial farmer, now a trade-union organizer*
INTERVIEWED IN: *Harare, Zimbabwe*

A soft-spoken woman, Tsitsi nonetheless holds strong, passionate views. She was interested in telling her story in order to correct the common assumption that all the commercial farmers who lost their land were white. An atypical commercial farmer, Tsitsi found herself, in 1996, leasing land and learning to grow onions in her late twenties, and grew to love her new way of life. When war vets began occupying farms around her, she assumed she and her two neighbors, being black, would be left alone. "I thought I was black enough," she says. But events proved her wrong. Tsitsi learned that "Zimbabwe's problems were bigger than my farm."

I'm from a Christian family. I was basically raised on church premises. My parents were Salvation Army leaders, with my father being a minister of that church, so we moved around quite a lot. I lived in Chinhoyi, Chiweshe, Masvingo, and so forth. But I grew up mostly in Harare and went to school there, starting at Houghton Park Primary.

When I was born, we were living in Chinhoyi in the so-called "big-yards," suburbs where white people lived. I played with the Harpers, the Bates, and other white families' children. There were even Indians there. I never felt that I was different from non-black children, because I played with them all the time. Sometimes the Harpers' boys used to stay at our house when their parents were traveling out of town, and sometimes I stayed at their place when my own parents were traveling. But we also had black friends and family living in rural areas, so I never used to discriminate against anyone based on color.

You could say I was raised on Christian values, such as love, respect for others, fear of God, and fellowship with the people you live with. Our parents are spiritually strong, and as a family we believe in listening to the inner voice, the conscience. We are part of the Moral Rearmament movement, which believes in absolute love, absolute purity, and absolute unselfishness. Even when I was a child, the movement was involved in efforts at racial reconciliation in this country and elsewhere.

My mother is a very prayerful woman. She ran the women's ministry and she used to drive out to do her work while my father went about his own church activities. At the time of their retirements, both my parents were lieutenant-colonels, which is fairly high in the Salvation Army hierarchy. I am the last born in the family—we used to be five children but now we are four. My parents have taken care of so many children that my mother couldn't even keep track of what diseases I had as a child. She had to ask my father, *Baba, did this one have measles?*

At first my parents were completely loyal to the Zanu-PF government but when their worship and church activities began to be disturbed, they had some doubts. One of the activities we do in the Salvation Army is to dress up and march in the streets, singing church songs with the band playing and the women beating tambourines. This marching was stopped by the police, nothing to do with the formation of opposition parties—it happened while I was still going to school. So these things—the suppression of rights such as free movement—started long ago. At that time, though, we didn't even realize these things were serious, but they did begin to affect my parents' views.

Even after retirement, my parents have remained busy, so busy that if I want to visit, I have to check that they are home first. When he retired, my father became an HIV/AIDS activist. He still distributes donated food to people affected by HIV/AIDS, makes the rounds in the villages to see that patients are taking their medication regularly, and checks on orphaned children. My mother went on to take a diploma in agriculture at the Chinhoyi University of Technology after retiring.

After secondary school, I worked for Barclays Bank for ten years. Then my elder sister, the oldest girl in my family, died suddenly in an accident. She was an icon to me and to the whole family and even beyond. She had gone to the UK to study for a master's in economics. When she came back she worked for Stanbic Bank and then helped form the Indigenous Business Development Centre. She drafted the original IBDC formation bill and presented it to the Zanu-PF Politburo. She used to work on these documents at home, in her spare time, and she used to tell me about what she was doing even though I was still in high school.

When she died, my sister was involved in starting an NGO, the Indigenous Businesswomen's Organization (IBWO). The members felt like orphans without her, and the funding partner wanted someone to rely on to see the project come to fruition. Because I used to assist my sister, the other women in the project approached me, and I became the organization's founding national coordinator.

At the time of her death, my sister was buying the flat that she and I were staying in. Two bonds still needed to be paid. There were also other debts because she had bought furniture and appliances on credit. We decided to hold on to the flat as family property, but we had to find money to do that.

The IBWO collaborated with the CZI, the Confederation of Zimbabwe Industries, of which the Commercial Farmers Union was also a member. On the Pricing and Commodities Committee where I represented the IBWO, I met a white farmer named Roy Peterson. It wasn't common for white farmers—or any white Zimbabweans, for that matter—to befriend black Zimbabweans, but perhaps because of my upbringing, I found it easy to relate to white people. Mr. Peterson told me that he was leasing out sections of his farm. He said that I could live off the land and also use it to raise enough to pay off some of these debts. That's how I got involved in farming.

FARMING IS A WAY OF LIFE

Mr. Peterson was a regular white farmer, wearing khakis. His wife wasn't very well at that time, and I knew he missed his sons. One of them farmed farther off in Beatrice, and the other settled in the U.K., well before the land invasions. Mr. Peterson's farm was part of Mupfurudzi Estate, situated near Bindura. The estate originally had twelve farms but part of the land was taken in the early to mid-1980s to resettle ex-combatants.[1] That's what I learned from Mr. Peterson. He was leasing part of the estate to individuals and he leased me a portion, about twenty hectares, beginning in 1996. This was well before the second phase of land reform, even before the war veterans began getting paid for their role in the liberation war.[2] The other two farmers leasing land from Mr. Peterson were also black. One was growing maize while the other was experimenting with tobacco. This second guy had probably seen his parents grow tobacco elsewhere, but Mr. Peterson advised him that the soil in this area was not the rich black soil that is good for tobacco.

The whole farm Mr. Peterson was leasing was about 150 hectares, but only 50 were arable, so I used 20 hectares, another guy had 20, and the third one 10. The land that was not arable was meant for cattle grazing, and we used the forest for firewood. For me, the lease also included a farmhouse—not the main one—and the tractors and trailers that we used. The main farmhouse was elsewhere on the estate. The three of us had a combined lease agreement with Mupfurudzi Estate, an agreement between the three of us and the owner.

I was between twenty-seven and twenty-eight years old when I started

---

[1] Veterans of armies that won the liberation war, ZANLA and ZIPRA, refer to themselves as "ex-combatants" or "war veterans." See the appendices for more information.

[2] Growing pressure on the government to allocate payment to ex-combatants culminated in a demonstration outside a meeting of international heads of state in Harare. Attendees, including President Mugabe, were trapped inside the building by the demonstrators. Soon after, the government made cash payments to all registered war veterans. See the appendix section on war veterans and farm invasions.

in 1996. I was single and had no children. I grew onions mostly. Later on, I also raised chickens and experimented with bananas. I didn't try difficult crops such as cotton. I didn't have any formal training in farming but the farmers' union sometimes organized courses, say on mushroom growing, and I would attend those. But most of my training came from neighboring farmers who knew the rain patterns and how to grow the crop itself. The farmer's main job is to plan the farming, guard the crop, and plan for any eventualities.

As a new farmer, I did not benefit in any way from government funding. At that time, and considering my age and sex, it was difficult for bank managers to take me seriously. I would be seen as too risky to qualify for a loan.

But with the teaching and the mentoring, I realized I could farm and earn enough to pay the lease. When you are living on the farm, you don't spend too much on petty purchases. However, farming is not an activity that generates money on a monthly basis. You have to wait for the right reaping time even when you have a cycle. The way this works is you start with one portion of land where you plant your crop, and when that crop has two months to go before harvesting time, you then start planting the next field or portion, and then the next after that, and so forth. The plan is for the supermarkets to come to rely on you for a constant supply of produce. You have to arrange for constant labor to work in the various fields, while you manage the cashflow, concentrate on the quality of the produce, and to figure out what do in the event of a drought.

I hired a student from the university who helped me with the technical elements of farming: how much water this crop needs, the quality of the soil, things like that. When I wanted to go and stay in Harare, she would say, *You are not yet serious about farming. If you are serious, you will stay at the farm full-time.* When you recruit workers you need to take care of the administrative side of things, and all this required that I be involved full-time at the farm. I began to enjoy farming and was making good progress. I learned to sell onions on the local market, in the supermarkets in Bindura.

When my sister died, I became very lonely. She had always taken care of me, and now I had to shoulder many solid responsibilities. When I went into commercial farming, I was still lonely. Farming is more than a profession; it's a way of life. Other farmers treated me very well. In fact, I was in charge of ensuring the smooth movement of farm produce to the market for the whole farming community. I used to ensure there was enough diesel for the road people to maintain good roads and so forth. Mr. Peterson was a people-person and was well liked in the community, including the black community. I'm not saying no one stirred racial tension, but they were usually overridden by older people, community leaders who had seen life. Mr. Peterson was also good friends with the local *sabhukus* (village heads), so that also helped.

In the beginning, another farmer helped me to recruit my first five workers. Farmers know which workers have the capacity to work. Farmworkers share information about a new farmer and how he or she is doing. Then you get people coming to you saying, *This is my brother and he also wants a job*, or *Here is a sister who wants to come and work here*. And as you grow, it becomes easy to recruit as your conditions of service improve. When you are going into a period that requires many workers, the word spreads and workers come. When they are done, they move on to the next farm and so on. Among the workers a good number were of foreign origin, with Malawian, Zambian, and Mozambican parents.

Each farmer only kept a small core group as permanent workers. Toward the end, I had eighteen workers, although the number sometimes fluctuated. I needed a lot of workers for the chicken project, and also for the onion crop, which was my cash cow. We had a netball[3] court and a soccer pitch. Workers from the different farms would play against each other on the weekends. As neighboring farmers, we shared the trailers that took our products to the market or carried inputs to our farms. We cooperated on implements and even security issues, and we shared the engine that pumped water onto the fields.

---

[3] A game similar to basketball.

In the early years, things were tough, because whatever I made had to go toward paying my debts. But after 1997 and '98, you could say I was on my feet.

I THOUGHT I WAS BLACK ENOUGH

The political situation around this time—toward 1999, leading up to the elections of June 2000—was deteriorating. This is the time when the farm invasions began, and when Zanu-PF began to set up the Border Gezi camps. These were training camps for youth militia who then supported and protected the Zanu-PF regime. The way it works is that the camps are usually resuscitated at around election time to terrorize people. They were named after the then Minister of Youth, who was good at motivating the militias, and at singing, dancing, and so forth. They wanted to establish a camp near us but I think they had problems recruiting from our farming area. Even though where we were farming, the Bindura and Madziwa area, was supposed to be a Zanu-PF stronghold. At that time, Border Gezi even claimed a farm not so far from our place. That was the first stage. We didn't think it would get to us.

I remember hearing shocking stories emerging from the youth training camps. The gender ministry was exerting pressure to have the camps closed. In one case, one of the youth trainees, a girl, had her hair shaved to discipline her. Youth trainees were made to run in rough terrain, and if you are sickly, you are beaten up. Hospitals reported cases of sexually transmitted diseases at these camps.

Meanwhile, those ex-combatants who had been resettled on the other eight farms from the original estate, back in the 1980s, were not producing anything at all. They were running the farms like villages. And yet the authorities said they wanted to establish Border Gezi camps on our farms. We sent back word that yes, there was plenty of land on these other eight farms which were being underutilized. However, they sent word back that they wanted to establish the camp on the farms we were using. The war veterans wanted our land.

Other farmers in the area harvested their tobacco and maize and then left. They were not sure if they were safe from having their land invaded, with violence. A while after I harvested, I was left alone there, still thinking that I was safe. I thought this pressure to give up our land was short-term and would not last. I also had some crops in the ground, so I had to stay longer than everybody else. If you go into farming, you put all your money in the soil, and then it's only when it grows that you can see it. There was no way I would just uproot and quit.

I tried to appeal through Zanu-PF structures. Blacks were supposed to benefit from this land invasion—that's what I heard. I thought I was black enough! All I needed was to make a claim and I would keep this piece of land. I tried to organize with others to prepare a position paper so our issue could be heard by the government.

When I got back to the farm from meetings in Harare, the workers had been chased away and there were even some people cooking inside my house. These people said they had been sent by those who gave them orders, and told to stay there. Some were youths whom I had hired as seasonal workers. These ones were nice and tried to explain why I had to leave. I told them, *I live here*, but they said, *No, you don't live here anymore*. I tried to explain that I had to stay until I harvested my crop, but they wouldn't listen. Even the police wouldn't help. In those days the police used to say land was a political issue which was best left to the government. It was all very sad to find myself helpless like that.

When they first tried to use the local people to make me leave, it did not work because I was on good terms with them—we attended the same church services and funerals, plus I knew the *sabhuku* of the area. But those who did the actual eviction, I have no clue where they came from. They said, *How much do you want for your crop?* and I said, *What do you mean? You will have to wait until I harvest*. They said, *If you want to survive, you have to go*. They said, *We have been told by* mashefu[4] *that you have to leave*.

---

[4] Party and government bigwigs. From the Portuguese *chefe*, adopted by Zanu and ZANLA when based out of Mozambique from 1975 to 1980. The *ma* prefix makes a plural in Shona.

These people taking over the farm were not local, not from the villages, and my impression was they were not even doing it for themselves. They must have been doing it for someone else. The place was targeted because it had a nice farmhouse.

By this time, most of the workers had left. The takeover did not cater for farm workers. It wasn't well planned. If you are coming into such a place, surely you need to have a job plan for all eighteen workers and sufficient funds to see the project through. That's my assumption, but I don't think the plan was to resume the farming activities or boost farming, but just to remove us and then decide what to do with the farm later.

A lot happened to farmworkers who were of foreign origin and had no other homes to go back to. Some of them moved to neighboring villages and settled there. Others crossed into Malawi, Zambia, and other countries, and started cross-border trade. Also now, the flea market craze hit Zimbabwe. So these people began to buy and sell their wares since there was no employment being created in the cities.

Mr. Peterson left at the same time the farm was taken. I haven't heard from him in recent years.

Strangely, in those days I didn't feel afraid, but what I couldn't imagine was how my parents would take it if something happened to me so in the end, I just left the farm.

I did try to go back. The invaders did not physically harass me, but they wouldn't allow me to set foot in the house or even on the farm. So I had no choice but to turn back, given that the police were refusing to intervene. I left and went to Bulawayo and stayed with my sister there.

TOO LOGICAL

Why was I treated this way? I have tried to work it out.

My name is Tsitsi Murimi. I was born in Zimbabwe and I am very black—using that logic, I thought I would hold on to that piece of land, my only source of livelihood. Unfortunately, our identity was not the point. They just wanted me to leave the farm for whoever was the intended beneficiary. Empowering blacks wasn't the main purpose.

In our area, you can't say we were chased off our land because we were politically active in MDC or Zanu-PF. MDC was only formed that same year, in 1999. At that time, most people in Madziwa did not know much about it. There were no meetings being held at our farms. And if anyone was to trace my background, my parents were loyal supporters of Zanu-PF in Chinhoyi. More than loyal, in fact. My father would be asked to lead the prayer at Heroes' Day events. Sometimes campaign materials for Zanu-PF in Mashonaland West would be distributed from our house.

My workers were organized under GAPWUZ, the General Agricultural Plantation Workers Union of Zimbabwe. The unions used to come and hold workshops, and we agreed because we respect the rights of workers. But why would you target a farm owner because she lets her workers attend workshops?

I can't say that my sex has anything to do with it either, because men farmers lost their farms. Since 2000 I have been wondering why we were targeted, and I fail to come up with a reason. I feel that if you are not powerful within Zanu-PF or linked with someone who is powerful in that party, then you are vulnerable. It happened to me not because I am a woman but because I was not recognized, not politically powerful.

The powerful people are the ones who can issue commands and terrorize people, suppress people, beat people up, and so forth. And because these people are then saluted, they create fiefdoms within their party and government, and you find that you can't report violations by these people to the police. Even in cases of land invasions, the police will simply say, *You will be allocated another piece of land*, and you are supposed to be satisfied with that. You cannot make claims because there is no one to make claims to, and if you keep asking questions, you are exposing yourself, you are exposing your family. I kept saying to myself, *I don't want my mother to lose another daughter.*

So the whole situation was not whether you are MDC or Zanu-PF or you are supporting whites or not. It was more about someone recognizing, *I am in a powerful position in Zanu-PF and so let me grab as much as I can and become even more politically influential while I'm at it.*

I did not try to take the matter to court on my own, but I did try to persuade the other two. I said, *We have a lease agreement and we must take this up with the courts*, but farmers were hesitant. They sent their children away and then followed them as soon as they harvested their crops. I submitted the position paper, saying that we are blacks and that if the policy is to empower blacks then we should keep the farm, even if it meant paying for the lease. I got no response. Perhaps the letter offended someone. The government barred people from approaching the courts with such matters, the police were barred from taking any police reports on these issues, and you could not even claim that you had left a single spoon behind.

I have not gone back to farming again. Let's say I'm still waiting. I was aware of the violence that went on at these farms from 2000 onward. In the end that's what forced me to quit my battle. At first, I felt, If I am clean, then nothing can happen to me. But I guess I was too logical.

WALK NAKED

When I left the farm for good August of 1999, I went to live with my sister in Bulawayo. I was totally unprepared for the change from farming onions to something else. I didn't collect my things from the farmhouse because I kept thinking that I would be resettled.[5] I traveled to Chinhoyi and registered for land, traveled to Bulawayo and did the same. I was still hoping I might get back the land and resume my farming. For two years I was in this back-and-forth situation, wondering, Will I get it back? You know, when you are farming you develop certain relationships with your workers, so you want that to continue and grow.

When I started looking for a job, I would be asked, *What is your current occupation?* and I would say, *Growing onions.* In Bulawayo where I was

---

[5] This is a common term in Zimbabwe, meaning "to be allocated land." From 1980 onward, the government made efforts to resettle small farmers on former commercial farms.

now living, there would be all these people familiar with IT, so my sister encouraged me to learn new skills. In the end I applied for a job advertised by the Zimbabwe Congress of Trade Unions.

By this time, the shops started running out of mealie-meal because agriculture suffered. Thereafter, life became harder and harder. Even industry began to collapse, jobs were not being created, young people were graduating but they had nowhere to practice their skills. So you now had this rush of people saying, *Let's go to South Africa, let's go to the U.K.* Almost everyone I knew wanted to go to the U.K.

Honestly, I had expected the 2000 elections to change the government so that I could go back to my farm. But then I was employed to work on a project with informal traders, and I began to realize that Zimbabwe's problems are bigger than my farm.

The goal of the project was to organize informal traders to support their activities and to strengthen the voice of vulnerable groups. I began to understand how poor governance trickled down to affect me as a person. The bigger picture is that you have someone at the top who must be protected. In Bulawayo I learned about the killings that took place there, the elimination of Zapu so as to protect Zanu-PF, the attacks on the civil society, the attacks on ordinary citizens.[6] I could now understand the meaninglessness of saying *We are empowering black people* when the farmworkers are black people but there is no plan to help them. You can see that a whole government is organizing the violence, the money printing, the money to hire thugs to kill people even though there are hospitals that are not working, and no money to pay teachers so that our schools can function. I could see that it is not the person who came to drive me out of my farm who counts, but the person who controls him and is benefiting from the system.

I think the key moment for me was when I asked myself what I could contribute to the lives of others. The workers needed to be organized.

---

[6] For more about Gukurahundi, see the stories of Zenzele, John, and Boniface.

I helped to organize informal traders after Operation Murambatsvina in 2005.[7] It felt like me losing my farm all over again.

You can imagine the suffering of informal traders as a result of Murambatsvina. Afterward, the Harare City Council had a housing waiting list of more than 1 million people needing housing. People moved in with relatives, whole families had to share very little sleeping space. Children had to quit school because the parents had had their accommodations smashed by the government. Even social and other services suffered, because it was the informal traders living in the cities who had been paying the rates. These informal traders had lost everything except hope, but they were not giving up.

They forced me to be stronger. The informal traders said, *Let's write a letter to ask the UN to intervene.* And the UN Secretary General responded. The UN envoy, Anna Kajumulo Tibaijuka,[8] may not have come with a lot of money, but just by coming she raised the spirits of the informal traders. They were ready to talk to her, to share experiences. When Ms. Tibaijuka came, she said she would not talk to us technical people, but rather with those who had directly experienced Murambatsvina. She said, *I know people from Zimbabwe can converse in English, and I want to talk with them myself.*

Around the 2000 land invasions, I could see that the Zanu-PF politicians were trying to convince us, the youths, that it's better for us to walk naked for the sake of our economy. I mean that they were trying to limit people's thinking, saying, *There is no need for you to demand better conditions as long as you have your land.* But in truth, they were taking away people's civil liberties. In reality, we used to have a strong economy, ready to compete with those of first-world countries. And yet these politicians would always stave off expectations of development and force us to be content with maladministration and poor quality of life in the name

---

[7] In Operation Murambatsvina, many urban homes were razed with little notice, and livelihoods destroyed, by Mugabe's forces, under the pretext of reforming illegal housing and the parallel markets that had risen to combat Zimbabwe's economic decline.

[8] Tibaijuka is also mentioned in Father John's story.

of patriotism. This is the force that the trade-union movement was up against, this backward movement perpetrated by Zanu-PF. Our expectation in 2008, with the elections, was to stop that trend.

INDEPENDENCE HAS COME

On the 28th of March 2008, I was observing the parliamentary elections in Harare in the Kuwadzana[9] constituency. I was there as part of the observer team of the Zimbabwe Congress of Trade Unions (ZCTU). I used public transport to get to Kuwadzana, the *combis* that most workers use to get around. In the *combi*, people were saying openly, *We want to change this*. On the way to Kuwadzana, schoolchildren were singing, *Independence has come!* The song went like this:

> *Independence baba*
> *Yazouya baba*
> *Independence baba*
> *Yazouya baba!*
> (Independence, Father. It has come, Father!)

It's an old song, but they were adding the "independence" part. In a country which was already free from colonialism, these children were implying that after 1980, we went into another kind of bondage. People could see that even in poor communities, you would get some people suddenly getting very rich. Unexplained riches. Even children felt that there was a lot wrong.

Voter turnout was great. People were happy, they were expecting a new government that would bring about a new environment. They were expecting change—better services, not having to scrounge for food—and, more importantly, they were hoping to live in a more secure and stable environment without fear. We were in a situation where people were not

---

[9] A high-density suburb/township on the outskirts of Harare.

free to express their dissatisfaction. Even at family level or talking to a friend, it was becoming difficult to just comment that *This is not nice*, or to wear a T-shirt carrying a political message or women- or youth-oriented views. You couldn't wear such a T-shirt because that would invite violent action against you. Expressing your views as a member of a school development association or inviting certain speakers to conferences—such things had become taboo. Activists who championed various rights became open targets. Such activists would get beaten or detained, so what chances did ordinary people without protection? These are some of the abuses that people thought would vanish after the 2008 elections. Everyone came out to make their statement, to make their contribution.

Kuwadzana being an urban working-class suburb, these people had been involved in forming the Movement for Democratic Change, the MDC. This was an opportunity for us to express our views in peace and bring about peaceful change, by the will of the people. People wanted to participate.

I was one of the ZCTU observation team for this constituency, but other organizations were also observing the elections in Kuwadzana. There were observers from Zimbabwe Election Support Network and the Catholic Justice and Peace Commission. The international observers would come and go, but we, the local observers, stayed in the constituency. ZESN had trained us in how to conduct ourselves, so even when someone wanted to use the bathroom, we would plan so observation went on all the time. As accredited observers, we were not allowed to talk to voters unless there was a problem. Our statements could have been misconstrued as campaigning for a particular political party because we were wearing our ZCTU T-shirts. International observers were observing us as well as the process. The people that we managed to speak with were those who were turned away, not allowed to vote. Most were Zimbabwean citizens by birth, but because their parents had migrated to Zimbabwe some two generations ago, new laws stopped them from voting.

There are groups of people whose forefathers moved here from Malawi, Mozambique, or Zambia a long time ago to help build railway lines and roads. Some crossed over to work in the mines of South Africa and others stayed on here in Zimbabwe and worked on mines and farms, living in mine and farm compounds.[10] Even those whose families moved here way back are no longer allowed to vote. As observers, we were questioning this, asking why these people were being turned away. But there was nothing that we could do because of that new law. These people contribute to government—they pay their taxes—and some of them have never even been to those homes where they are supposed to have originated from. Some cannot even speak the languages of those countries and yet they were being told they could not vote because they are aliens. They were being told that they must go to Zambia or wherever to vote, never mind that almost all of them were born in Zimbabwe.

In my rudimentary assessment, most residents of Harare, maybe 60 percent, cannot trace their origins to Zimbabwe. One old man told me that the building of most parts of Harare was done by these so-called aliens. Places like Mufakose, Mabvuku-Tafara, Highfield, and so forth were actually built to house the original so-called aliens who lived and worked in Harare back then, while our own "true Zimbabweans" lived in hostels only for the duration of the week before going to rural homes every Friday and relocating permanently upon retirement. This means that your Harare community has more "aliens" than so-called true Zimbabweans. This really shouldn't be such a big story because, after all, there was a time when colonial Zimbabwe, Zambia, and Malawi were actually one country, a federation of Rhodesia and Nyasaland.

We approached the polling agents over the matter and they said they were following a directive. This directive seems to have come a day before the elections or maybe even on the very day of the elections. From around ten a.m. to eleven a.m., many more were being turned away than

---

[10] Workers' housing, often very basic. Most black Zimbabweans have a traditional rural home. They may work in cities or on mines and farms, but they can go "home" (*kumusha*) to one of the communal areas. Immigrants such as these Tsitsi is describing, however, have no such home areas within Zimbabwe, so they are not connected into the web of traditional rights and authorities, chiefs, and the hub of social and political life.

actually casting votes. By now, it was too late to get the policy leaders to make an intervention.

Other groups were being sent from one polling station to another. The voter's roll was juggled to confuse people, and many did not know exactly where they were supposed to vote. This was because of the last-minute delimitation exercise. Let's say you live in Dzivaresekwa, your name might actually be registered to vote in Warren Park. And in between these two suburbs is Kuwadzana! Your name would be in the same constituency, but finding out the exact polling station where your name was registered for voting was a nightmare for many. Some people spent the whole day going round and round looking for the right polling station. As for me, I was moved by their determination to cast that vote. Imagine elderly people spending the day chasing around for their names just so they could vote.

As far as I am concerned, elections are a way of allowing people to express themselves. They are a way of assessing the health of a democracy. For us as Zimbabweans, we saw elections as the key for change when we fought—up to Independence in 1980—for the freedom of the people, freedom of the workers, freedom from hunger, freedom from oppression. From 1980, our country should have created opportunities for everyone, developing the country and opening up for the participation of everyone. But the Zanu-PF government set up a one-party state and even went on to destabilize those institutions that make democracy work, such as the trade union movement, the students' movement, the media, the churches, and so forth. So in a way, even though we were supposed to be moving forward, we went back to being a closed state.

We just changed oppression by whites to blacks, but in reality, on the ground, nothing much changed. Our expectation in the 2008 elections was that we could move to real change. Real independence.

As you know, that expectation was disappointed.

UP TO NOW, I AM STILL WAITING

I went to the Ministry of Agriculture and had my name listed to get land, but nothing came of it. When I lost my farm, I was at an age when I was used to being independent. You know, when you are trying to survive on your own, you can't impose yourself on family members. I was looking after my brother's child, too. I tried to highlight all those issues to the authorities and also how the land reform was supposed to empower blacks, but nothing made any difference. Up to now I am still waiting! I went to Chinhoyi where my mum was staying and registered my name there. They would say, *Oh, we know your case, you will be allocated land tomorrow.* But it has never happened.

When I think of that farm now, I remember most one place near the dam. It was just a grassy spot where I used to go and sit when all the workers had gone away to do their daily tasks and I was alone. It somehow became my resting place, and sometimes the farmworkers' children used to see me there and come to sit or play with me. I had applied for a license to establish lodges by that dam, and I was beginning to plan the building of the lodges. So it was sort of my dream corner.

I also remember the netball games that the farmworkers' wives used to play at the farm. I heard that many of my former workers have now gone into gold panning but, I am no longer in touch with them.

GEORGE

AGE: *42*

OCCUPATION: *Former large land-owner, now land manager*
INTERVIEWED IN: *Rural Zimbabwe, on a farm*

George, a white farmer, came of age in the 1970s, during the war that led to Zimbabwean independence. The son of a wealthy tobacco farmer, he led a privileged life, despite the ever-present threat of attack, on an estate in Karoi. George is dyslexic and always had trouble in school. He describes himself as a wild, hard-drinking polocrosse player as a younger man. Yet after marrying and taking over the family farm following his father's death, George began to settle into the life of a Mercedes-driving Zimbabwean farmer. He calls himself a born tobacco farmer, someone who has always been more at home in the fields than anywhere else. Things changed dramatically after his brother Henry's farm (adjacent to George's) was invaded by a group of war veterans. After barely surviving an attack by machete, his brother emigrated to New Zealand but George tried, desperately and ultimately unsuccessfully, to hold on to his farm. Eventually, he too was chased off and his land taken over. A candid, gregarious storyteller, George described his family's complicity (and the complicity of other wealthy farm families) in what happened to Zimbabwe before Independence—and since. After a few years in South Africa and Mozambique, George is now back in the country of his birth, working as a manager of a farm owned by a black Zimbabwean, something he says would have been unheard of just a few years ago. George spoke for many hours over the course of two days in the living room of his small house, as well as out in the fields as he inspected his current tobacco crop.

This all needs to be told from the beginning because it's all about who I was then, to who I am now. There's almost been a full circle.

My father came from South Africa. He went to private schools but still had a hard life; he had a stepmother who didn't like him. My grandfather was a director of an insurance company and served in the British Navy. As a young man, my dad struck off on his own. He came here to Zim—then it was Rhodesia—and started a new life.

He was working for a man named Jones. Jones was high up in the Rhodesian government and one of the richest farmers in the country. So he was a big part of the "blacks will never rule Rhodesia" crowd. Quite an eccentric guy, actually. My dad used to say when he first started working for him that all of Jones's labor used to come here from Malawi and Zambia. They used to truck them in, but they had a contract. They would get half their money here, then half their money was sent back to their families.

In those early days, there wasn't a big enough black population to provide labor for the commercial tobacco farms. If I remember correctly— just thumb-sucking, obviously—but I think in those days there were under a million black people in this country.

So my father worked on different farms as manager, and then leased in Sinoia[1] until he and my mother bought 1,264 acres in Karoi. It was hard for them a first—they lived in a shelter made of *hessian* (sacking).

So I was born in Rhodesia under the white government, brought up on a tobacco farm. I was the last child of three to be born on the farm.

TOTAL SEPARATION

In some ways we were very English. I don't remember working around

---

[1] Now known as Chinhoyi.

the house or making my bed or anything like that. We always had servants, everyone did. I would just get up, go down to breakfast, and there would always be eggs and bacon. From the age of six I was at boarding school, and on the holidays everything was laid on.

It was a beautiful time—that's why it's such a big comedown for all of us. When you've lived a life like that and then it gets stolen from underneath you, it's a shock. Maybe that's why it happened. Although a lot of people were fair and kind, when you've got all the power, people can be horrible. No one tells you that you are being a shit, you just are a shit. We were educated and had all those English rules, and the black people were uneducated and uncivilized according to the whites. But we didn't understand their culture. We were always the boss.

Some farmers, like my folks, struggled for most of their career. Some people even gave up. But some people did well and even had their own planes. I'm talking about rich farmers. All the money the country was generating was available to us to progress and make our farms bigger and better. I still can't believe what they managed to achieve, not only developing the farms, but the country. There was a lot backing us, and no control was given to the black man, who was still uneducated. However, most farms had a school built on it and a clinic. I was a child and didn't appreciate how hard it was for my parents. It was great running around in the bush with my pellet gun and going to the black compound. I got beaten for that. But to me the workers always seemed happy with their way of life. Life was harder where they had come from.

Our house ended up, after a lot of additions, resembling a Spanish villa. By the time my folks were finishing it, the war was already on, so they built the walls really thick. The house was on the top of a hill. My mom planted cactus to protect against the terrorists. That kind of cactus, with a long leaf, that has a spear on the end. You have to be very brave to walk through it; it's sort of a first line of defense.

A lot of my earliest memories are of the war. Where my bedroom was, there was a garden in front. My bed was made of bricks and concrete. It was like a cupboard with a concrete desk and a mattress inside. If we were attacked I only had to roll out of bed and through a kind of tunnel. Whenever we used to go to sleep, my parents would always leave a weapon by my side.

By the time I was eleven or twelve, the war had heated up. We were all so patriotic, I mean as far as believing in Rhodesia. I believed basically that some blacks are servants and laborers, and the others are the enemy.

My dad was a good guy. He was one of the first guys to give his black foreman a truck, and he had a totally different attitude from most of the white guys out there. But at that time, no black man could walk into any white crowd. There was total separation. You know how war does that. It was strange, I spent a lot of time with black people on the farm, yet we were also fighting these other unknown black people. We did not know who to trust, but we felt safe with our workers.

And then the atrocities started to happen. Local killings. Neighbors were shot. Our labor was tormented. It incensed everyone. If you're fighting a war and someone shoots your mate—that's when people lose control and do really bad things. I'm sure really bad things were happening on our side, but we only heard the one side of it.

We built a sturdy fence. We had listening devices on the security fence that never really worked properly. We had what they used to call an Adam's grenade, which is like four grenades put together on a steel pipe. My mom planted fourteen of them in the flower beds around the garden. My mother was a tiny, very elegant woman, but a strong woman.

When there's a war there's always excitement, big excitement. You live on the edge and there is something really nice to it. There is the shit part, but there is also this immense camaraderie. Oh, it was scary a lot of times, but also a lot of fun. We used to go fishing in convoys. The convoy would leave at ten o'clock in the morning, and all the cars would be in a line together and you would have two of those army jeeps going from back to front. At Kariba Dam, we'd fish, camp, be on holiday.

Through it all, we were like a community. Zimbabweans and Rhodesians have always been big drinkers, there was always a lot going on.

Even after the sanctions,[2] life didn't stop—that just put us more together. When people are getting attacked and you are in a war, you find people are merry, there are parties everywhere, because you might just die. Although my father wasn't a big drinker, most of my friends' parents were drinking. At that time there were a lot of parties. In town, in Karoi, there was also the golf course, tennis courts, and of course, the bar.

The terrorists used to strike at night. We lived quite close to the rural areas which they used to call TTLs, Tribal Trust Lands. But it was very difficult for them to coordinate a good attack because everyone could be in contact all night long. We had those CB-type radios. There was a whole lot of jargon. I could never remember it. I always remember standing there when it was my turn to speak on the radio. *You have to do it, George,* my mother would say. But I was dyslexic. I never got an A in school. So it was really difficult for me to get it together, even a few simple words reporting whether the family was safe or not. The Alpha Bravo used to confuse me.

A few times we got a message that they were on our farm. And then the dogs would be going crazy, really crazy. My dad would say that we must come to the passageway where he had all those Adam grenade things and all the guns. It would be my mom, my brother, my sister, and my dad sitting there with the lights off and the dogs going mad. We'd just be sitting there waiting for it. There were all these defenses, walls and walls, so that they couldn't shoot through the window at us. We were protected on all sides of the passageway, but I remember pissing in my pants.

One day we went to see a neighbors' house that had been attacked by RPG rocket launchers. The terrorists fired two of them, and they went straight through the house and exploded on the other side, but somehow they didn't explode in the house. There were bullet marks all over the wall. We used to laugh because we would say those guys didn't know how to use their weapons.

---

[2] See the timeline for more on international sanctions against Rhodesia.

Ninety percent of the time nobody was hurt. But other times people were. And you know then the Rhodesian forces would hit back hard. Now, I'm not bragging or anything, but the Rhodesian forces were brilliant. At one time, someone nominated them as one of the best anti-guerilla units in the world. The terrorists had a hard time getting at us; we were the elite. It was strange to me, but there were a lot of black people fighting together with the whites. We had the helicopters, and our air force was outstanding because Ian Douglas Smith was an RAF pilot during World War II, a great ace. But he also got shot down and had been a prisoner of war, so he had all of this to throw at the young men.

It was a psychological thing. We kept thinking these guys would never win. It was so stupid, because I mean the writing was on the wall.

DON'T LISTEN TO WHAT I'M ABOUT TO SAY

I was fourteen when the war ended.[3] We had to accept what was going on. Mugabe did give us the olive branch. But it was like this. Before those rallies, his people used to come and say, *Mugabe's coming up here, so please can you donate something? Can you get eight cattle together?* So the farmers, mostly white ones, would gather together eight cattle. At one rally my dad was there. Mugabe walked past and introduced himself to all of the people. When he got to my dad, he said, *Don't listen to what I'm about to say, I'm saying it because I have to say it.* Then he spent the whole meeting saying how horrible white people were, saying they've got all the land but their time will come.

It was like that for years. Whenever Mugabe thought he was losing popularity, he would come out with this land story and send notices out

---

[3] A ceasefire ended the fighting in late 1979, under the terms of the Lancaster House Agreement, brokered by the British. At Independence, the newly elected prime minister, Zanu leader Robert Mugabe, made a famous speech about reconciliation, saying: *If yesterday I fought you as an enemy, today you have become a friend and ally with the same national interest, loyalty, rights, and duties as myself. If yesterday you hated me, today you cannot avoid the love that binds you to me and me to you.* The full text of this speech has been widely reproduced.

that you might be acquired. So really, from the end of the war to when it all heated up in 1999 or 2000, there had been prior instances of him warning us. It got worse as the time went along. So we were all living with that.

I was sent far away to senior boarding school. I didn't do very well there. When I finished that school, the only qualification I had was for being beaten the most in school. I don't know what it is about paperwork but my brain just doesn't want to get a grip of it.

When I finished school I went to work on a stud farm with horses in South Africa. All the young guys my age were going to the army for the South African war.[4] And I thought, *Wonderful, I missed out on the Rhodesian war. Now I'm going to get a second chance at the South African war.* So I phoned my dad and told him, and he said to me, *You get out of there right now, get on the plane and get back home, I'm not going to have that.* I listened to my old man, I don't know why I did, but I did. At that point I'd been working for about six months without pay, so when they paid me a couple of thousand rand I went up to Sun City[5] and met up with a couple of mates I met in Durban. I blew it all. My folks were really angry with me when I got home. They told me to go find a job. I even went around to try and be a waiter. It wouldn't be bad in the U.S. for a twenty-year-old to go and be a waiter, but here it was a black man's job, so I couldn't do it. No one would hire me.

My parents said, *Come out to the farm, you useless little bastard.* They were away at the time. They said they'd pay me to farm-sit. At that time it was planting season, and I did a good job. You know when we talk about tobacco, tobacco is not like maize or wheat or flowers—this crop takes years to learn. It is a very intensive crop, it's a lot of money, you're dealing with a huge labor force, you're dealing with the weather and whatever, and I truly believe there is no other job like it.

---

[4] Primarily focused on the independence struggle in southwest Africa, then a territory of South Africa, now Namibia.

[5] A hotel complex built in one of the fragments of apartheid Bantustans, near Johannesburg, to allow gambling and other pleasures prohibited by the South African government.

But I found it easy because I had grown up on the farm. The people on the farm knew me as the boss already. It was hard because I was getting tested by sixty workers ranging between sixteen and sixty-five years old, and I had to get them to work. There are two ways to get people to respect and work for you. One is to pay them money, and the other is to be hard and unyielding. I couldn't give money, so the only way I felt I could be in control was to be hard and a bit violent. I did it, though... When the old man came back, he said, *You've got a job.*

My first season he had his best year. Then my second season, we had a drought, and the old man became very hard to work for because now he was pissed off all the time. Things were breaking down. Financially we weren't in a good position. He gave me two weeks' leave and he bonused me for the last season. I went out and bought a motorcar. Then I met up with a good friend from school and we got pissed in Harare for those full two weeks. We decided we didn't want to go back at all. My father came into town and told me to go overseas. So I went to England for about a year, you know, traveling, a working holiday. I became a laborer. I carried bricks, mixed cement, offloaded trucks. I was still thinking like I was a rich farmer. I spent all the money on drink. I had a mother of an experience in a red-light district. I had never seen anything like that. I was so naïve about the real world. You know, they show you a show or whatever it is. Then you order a drink and the drink is like fifteen pounds. Within days, I had no money. It was weeks before I got my act together. I was just sleeping on the streets. I found another job driving one of those ad vans, those big rigs with the billboard on the back. The job I enjoyed most was putting up rings for horses because I was outdoors in the country. I did all sorts of crap that you do over there.

We ran into Rhodesians that had left. We called them "whenwes." As in, *When we were in Rhodesia, we used to do things like this and this and this.* But we would say, *Fuck off, we're Zimbabweans now.* We'd definitely changed in some ways. In other ways, I've never changed. I kissed the tarmac when we arrived back in Zim. I refer to black people and white people in my story, not Africans and Europeans, because I consider myself an African. I am not a pommie.[6] My skin is burnt by the sun and I love my country.

I went back to work for my old man again. The difference was my brother was working for him also. But he'd taken a university degree, a BSC in agriculture, and so he now he started treating me on a different level, like I was under him. I became this overboard person again, whereas my brother was following my dad, maybe drinking a couple of beers, putting slacks on and coming to the clubhouse and getting abused by everyone for being like that. I really looked up to all those hardcore people that had been in the army. I was inside that mix because I was playing polocrosse and drinking a lot. I had already built up a reputation. I was fighting a lot. At the end of the night I would be that guy lying in the corner of the bar.

Still, I was good on the farm. I was much better with the people than my brother. And anything to do with working with labor, I was confident. Because I could get them to work, and I didn't take any shit. Also, my being a laborer in England had made me understand more. But anything to do with machinery, setting equipment, setting of applications, setting boom sprays, that confused me.

So my brother and I actually complemented each other. But the rivalry between us got to me. I went to find my own job. I went to interviews and got every job I asked for. I had this top farmer that wanted to hire me, huge, bigger than my father was, but I chose an old guy in Centenary because I was still hiding the fact that I did not know any technical stuff, I didn't want anyone thinking I was an idiot. Now I know it's all so simple. I was stupid to hide. But then I was hiding it from everyone, because at school I couldn't, I was the class fool. It was always my job to break in a new teacher, you know, harass him until he did something everybody could laugh at.

So there I was on this semi-rundown farm, working for this old couple.

---

[6] A disparaging term for a British person.

It was all basics. They didn't even have compressors to blow the tires up. We had to do it with bicycle pumps. Elephants used to walk past my house. Within four weeks on that job, that old man died. I was left in charge. We did all right, considering.

DIXON

I worked thirteen years as a manager on different farms. Once in Mhangura I worked for this big *oke*,[7] built like one of those guys from the World Wrestling Federation, ten or twelve years older than me. He'd been a Grey Scout, which was the horse unit of the Rhodesian fighting force— definitely old-school stuff.

He had a beautiful farm, lots and lots of water. He grew coffee, soybeans, barley, wheat—but he didn't grow tobacco. So he said to me, *You come and run the crop for me.* I was given carte blanche to run the farm, so once again I could hide my dyslexic problems. I started working for him that first night. I knew him from playing polo. He said to me, *George, I've got thirty horses here. You ride them, you train with them. Go to Harare for the weekend. As long as you sort everything out, you can go. You're young, sow your wild oats, but realize that I want hard work out of you.* So he was a great guy like that.

One day, I stole—borrowed—his car because there was a polocrosse tournament on another farm. I got really pissed there, and when I drove back I hit a bush pig. So I had to come clean. I said, *I took the car and dinged it.* He said, *Okay, it's not a problem, but next time just ask me. Don't do that again.*

I carried on with the job. But listen, the reason I'm telling you this is because something else happened. It's my first account of something I did then. Like I said, my boss was huge. When black people didn't do their job properly, or the sprinklers weren't turning properly in their

---

[7] Guy, man (South African slang).

irrigation scheme, he literally used to grab these guys and lift them off the ground. You know, that was very much the old way of treating a black person in those days, but he was nice to them most of the time. He had that line where he used to control them by force like a lot of us used to do. But they also still looked at him like he was their father, because he was the guy that when they got sick would take them to the hospital. If they ran out of money he'd supply it, and if they did their job properly they were favored.

There was a guy that worked in the workshop called Dixon, a black guy. I got to know him. He was a really nice guy, and he was built like a brick shithouse as well. Obviously he looked at his boss and said, *I want to look like that*, so he made up his own gym and had been pushing weights. So anyway, one day the boss was gone. I was riding horses and Dixon came to me and said, *There's a woman in the compound that's been bitten by a snake.*

I said to him, *Listen, I'm not taking another vehicle when he's away because I've already dinged this one. I don't want it to come back to me.* I said, *Tell her to go find a minibus and go*, because we were quite close to the town. We were only five kays.[8] But it was still my job. I could have taken the truck and driven myself. I wouldn't have got into trouble for doing that. It was just an excuse because I was riding and I didn't want to stop. Also I suspected that they just wanted a free trip into town. When you're in charge of two hundred families, there's always something.

So he went away, and he came back to me about two hours later and he said to me, *Boss, that woman's leg is swollen, please...* So do I go, or do I send him because he's got a driver's license as well and I'm really enjoying what I'm doing? I'm riding, practicing—I know it sounds harsh, but even when my brother was in a bad water-skiing accident we didn't take him to the hospital.

Eventually I give in to him and say, *No, you go, I'm enjoying myself too much*. I sat down with him and I said, *Please, you know what happened with*

---

[8] Five kilometers, nearly three miles.

this other vehicle, Dixon, please, I'm begging you, I'm not asking you to run and come back quickly, I'm asking you please, go slowly, slowly. Go with it nicely, don't put me into any problems, please.

I promise you, boss, I promise you, he said, and off he went.

I go back to riding. I had just changed horses. As I finish off one, they bring me another. Maybe forty-five minutes later, a young boy comes running and says, *Boss boss boss, there's an accident.*

There was a dirt road running down from the farm. Dixon had hit a neighbor's pregnant cow on the road, and the truck has gone down into the bush. The cow is lying in the road bellowing in agony. The next-door neighbor, who is an Afrikaaner, he was down there, and he's looking at the cow going fucking benzy, screaming and shouting, *Where's that kaffir?* So he quickly jumps into his truck, goes home, comes back with a rifle, and puts the cow out of its misery. The truck is there, but no driver. Dixon just up and ran away.

I never heard more about the woman and the snake bite. I think that was just a story. Now I have to find my boss and tell him about the car and that the fucking bastard's run away. I'm in shit again.

The next day, in the morning when I'm eating breakfast, Dixon's brother and two sisters come and they say to me, *Boss, there is something wrong in our family, we are worried about our brother. We need to find him, something has happened.* So I let them off work to find him. At one o'clock that afternoon I'm sleeping, because you wake up early on the farm. At eight you come back for breakfast and have eggs, bacon and a tomato. Then you go back to check on your workers, then tea at ten o'clock. At half past twelve you lie in your bed for an hour. So at one o'clock I'm still sleeping and someone comes, saying, *Boss, you've got to come with us.*

I go with them and they start walking me down a road that runs through the coffee. When I get to this tree, the two sisters started crying, screaming and hitting me in the face. The brother helps pull them all off and pulls me by the arm and says, *Look, up in the tree.*

Dixon had hanged himself with a piece of wire from the fence. I went and found my boss. He says, *Bring a ladder.* He went up there himself because no one else would, pulled the wire off Dixon's throat, and took him down. Air came out of him when he took him down, and he had his hat carefully folded in his pocket. I could see the top of that tree from my bedroom. The whole next year that I worked there, and until now, I've thought about that guy, Dixon. We had both crashed our boss's car, and he felt so bad he hanged himself.

I PHONED HER THE NEXT MORNING

By this time, I'm a guy who has a bad reputation. There are no girlfriends in my life because I'm always getting so drunk when I go out. I wasn't what a woman wants. I'm so over the top and all of that. When I lose control I lose control. I go to a party, I walk into groups, and everyone around me is listening. As I get drunker two or three of them pull out of the group. After a while everyone just disappears when I walk up.

Then I met my Sally. She was a Harare townie. She was brought up in the city. We used to have these bachelors' and spinsters' balls. If you haven't got a girlfriend you would go to these balls at this five-star hotel. I got dressed up in a suit with a bowtie, and because I'm from out of town, our ethic is that if there's ten people sitting around a bar, you buy all ten a drink. I ended up buying everyone drinks. I expected somebody would buy me a drink back, but those town people would snubble off. I went through a whole lot of money before the thing even started and couldn't get as drunk as I normally would. That's when Sally came and sat down. We danced and talked all evening, and she never saw the bad part of me.

She was my first proper girlfriend. When she told me she had a child, I said, *That's okay, I'm a farmer, we like good breeders.* She laughed. I phoned her the next morning. We have been together ever since. I met all her friends who were very different from army guys I used to hang around with. One even had an earring. We had a legend of a party at a game lodge near our farm. It was supposed to be a weekend but lasted a week. I had to sell my car to pay for it, but we're all good friends still.

Never having had a girlfriend in my life, let alone a child, to take both of them on was quite a thing. I know about being a step-parent. I know what happens to people in their heads when they're not dealing with their own children. As soon as I had my own child, I realized quickly what true love was and how many mistakes I had made with my oldest daughter. That's all subsequently changed and I love her unconditionally, like I'm her proper father, and I don't have any of those hang-ups anymore. She's such a loving girl, she made it easy. We're great, my eldest daughter and me.

Sometimes I don't know why my wife stayed with me, because I pushed her. I don't know how she stayed with me—God knows, with her little girl—I would go ballistic; I would fight; I was so jealous. I was having blackouts and couldn't remember anything in the morning. I was scaring my wife. She said that it was like another person took over me. So I tried to get some help. I went to an old white lady, a psychic. Some of it sounded like nonsense, but she also said some pertinent things about my life. And then I said to her, *The real problem is, I've come here because I get really jealous. People say there are two people inside me.*

She says, *I know what it is. You've got an evil spirit inside you. I can take it out of you.*

I just think, Wonderful, I can go and sort out a problem that I need to sort out. And I promise you: all the hair did stand up on the back of my neck. When she had finished, she says, *Oh my God, I've never seen something so ugly in my life.* She turns around to me and she says, *Did you know who that was? Has anyone in your family committed suicide? Not my family,* I said. *We don't even talk about that shit. We're too powerful, we're too strong. No one in my family would even contemplate going down that road. Doesn't matter what we went through.* But it suddenly dawned on me, about ten minutes later, what had happened on the farm, with Dixon. I mean, when I was alone in that big house, I used to lie there watching that window. And I thought, I'm still carrying this guy around with me? After the psychic, I felt a little uplifted. I'd still get bad sometimes, but not as bad as I was before.

LAND OWNERSHIP WAS STILL TENSE

My first partnership was with an Afrikaans guy. He looked after the paper-work and I did the farming. My father stood guarantor for me. It went badly. My dad got a phone call from the bank saying my partnership owed, I think, US$100,000.

I had built the barns, everything. It was my worst time because now I owed so much. My old man said, *Okay, you can come back to the farm and work for me, but you work in the morning, and in the afternoons you get all the paperwork from that farm and you go through everything until you work out exactly what I'm responsible for. We'll sell the cattle if we have to.*

You can imagine what kind of shit I was in. My folks couldn't even look at me, they were so pissed off, all their savings and their cattle herds might be sold because of me. Poor Sally now had decided to live with me, so she came to the farm under those circumstances, and got an evil eye from my parents.

Later though, when I explained things to the bank (I had found some errors), they said, *Your dad has been a client of ours for twenty-two years, we are going to let you walk away from this guarantee.* So in the end we sold the cattle and bought another farm that linked to the family farm. It made two farms of roughly the same hectarage for my brother and me. My brother was given the choice of which of our two farms he wanted to farm. Henry chose the other farm, not the family farm.

Land ownership was still tense. I bought my black manager a *bakkie*[9] and managed to get him on a small-scale ZTA[10] tobacco scheme. He went to the next-door farm to see his brother, and the owner of the farm went ballistic. He started shouting at me at my daughters' sports day. What an ass, but many people, including my brother, did not want strangers on the farm, even if they had to walk a long way around.

---

[9] Open-back pickup.

[10] Zimbabwe Tobacco Association.

IZZY

Nine months after our wedding, we had Izzy. My whole life changed. From the moment I saw her, I felt this surge of love and protectiveness. I thought child-rearing was about discipline. That went out the window. She is so like me, a wild child who rides her horse like a Red Indian. She refuses to eat meat and adores animals. Unfortunately, she also inherited my dyslexia.

I'M TEACHING YOU HOW TO FIGHT

I didn't quite hear it at first. My dad's telling me he's got leukemia. After he told me, I just ran off into the land and went and told some people to stop reaping badly.

He got nuked hard with chemo, really hard, and because I had to stay on the farm, I only saw him about six weeks after it started. He had already lost all his hair, and he was looking in a bad way.

Before he died, I said to him, *What have you got to tell me?* And he said, *I'm teaching you how to fight.* It was horrible. They'd give him some major morphine. The doctor told us he was going to die, there was nothing more they could do. They took all the machinery away. When he woke up, he turned around and said, *What have you guys done?* Ten minutes later he was dead. I watched him die in front of me. He went into these big convulsions of pain, almost rising off the bed.

THE REFERENDUM

Whenever we made money, we put it back into the family farm. After thirty years, the farm was a top-class operation. We had seven dams (enough water to last several droughts), underground piping to most lands, over sixty brick houses for labor, barns, sheds, and the house was a mansion. Our beautiful garden was five acres. I was called a cock holder by my friend, because I had inherited this farm and was reaping the rewards of my father's hard work. I told him he had a brown stain on his face from licking ass in the corporate company he was working in.

Then just before 2000, the vibe suddenly changed. We didn't quite know what was going on, but after the referendum happened,[11] which I'm sure lots of people have told you about, Mugabe got really pissed off.

I knew it all my life—it hung over us. Now it was going to happen. During the first wave of attacks on commercial farms, this one guy got pulled by his nose through his own house and told that it's not his house anymore, his land anymore. He was one of these high-class units, he'd fought in the Rhodesian war and all that. They obviously picked on him on purpose. They said, *Listen, my white friend, you'll just die, so don't give us any shit, your house is our house.*

We thought we could be involved in the politics of our country. MDC[12] came into the picture and we were all influenced. We supported it with money. We took our labor to meetings. Sally and I had MDC T-shirts. Mugabe was sitting there, watching, waiting, letting us show our true colors.

Then it happened. The first attack on our farm land. By then the farmers were quickly organizing themselves, forming security teams, electing members to handle this, to protect other farmers. It was like we were going back to war. Only this time we couldn't defend ourselves.

Like the old days, each farm would have a radio. So when anyone got hit, he would just get on the radio and go, *This is what's going down guys, I need help.* And within five minutes, you were in your bakkie and you were driving in. Then they came marching down the road at you, with spears and *pangas*, and with their drums, singing their *Chimurenga*[13] songs, war songs.

---

[11] Constitutional referendum, seeking a national mandate to change the constitution to (among other things) expand presidential power. See the appendix section on land invasions, as well as various stories, including those of Elizabeth, Boniface, and Briggs.

[12] See footnote 2, page 26.

[13] Shona term for the liberation struggle.

They used the divide-and-conquer strategy against us. Some farms were affected and others weren't. The white community would have these meetings on how we were going to deal with this situation. Some people thought we should have a no-tolerance policy. No speaking with these war veterans, no communication. In other words, no negotiation whatsoever. We were divided. There was no community closeness as there was in the war. And we were outnumbered. When the security people left, we were left with an angry mob that had been given carte blanche to do whatever they wanted. The police and army were backing them.

The second time they came, we got word from someone on the Security Committee. *George, I've seen these guys heading down your road, they're coming toward you.* My strategy was to agree with everything they said and show no fear. This totally disarmed them. Anyway, I drive them around, show them the place. They said, *This land is ours for the moment.* I said, *I've got no problem, where do you want to stay?* I can't even describe what I felt. I had to swallow my pride to keep my family safe. It nearly killed me. Also at that time we were made to feel bad by the white people who weren't being affected.

My farm wasn't a place you want to be staying and be sleeping at off in the thick bush. So by the next morning they came to me and they said, *Hey, we don't like this place.* And I said, *No problem. Got another farm, five kilometers down the road, why don't you go there? It's a more open area.* This got them away from our home area, but I tried to maintain a line where I didn't give into everything they wanted. And so began a year of negotiation and humiliation. I got quite used to being pushed around, and sticks and weapons being thrust in my face.

Well, you can imagine. I took a lot of heat for that from my friends and neighbors, and because I'm quite a truthful guy, I was openly outspoken and honest about it.

THE COLONIAL LOOK

My brother and I communicated all the time. We just had different approaches.

I kept quiet, I dealt with all my own problems. I said to my work-force, *Please, if something happens, I do not want you putting your neck out for me. Please, I don't want you to. Do not put your life on the line.* They did, though, it was their lives as well. My brother's people stood by him and paid dearly for it. My brother's compound got burned down three times. My brother—he was a very brave man during all this. That's the truth.

He'd become quite popular among our neighbors, and he liked that. He found himself being appreciated for having courage, for standing up for his rights. From my point of view, I felt he was being used by people who themselves wouldn't stand up against the war vets. I wanted to scream at him, *Stop standing up against them, because you can't win.*

My brother couldn't hide his feelings. And if you can't get rid of the colonial look on your face, they will eat you alive. In the end they got him. But the whole time, he kept moving forward. He didn't stop building: he was building new barns, he was building a tennis court, he was building a new house; he built a double-story thatch mansion while this was all taking place.

But he also loved his country, my brother. This is a guy who shot clay pigeons for the Zimbabwean national team. After the elections in 2008, he shot rounds of pigeons off his veranda. He was that sure MDC would win.

And then, one day, in 2008, he was out planting coffee. He had an overland irrigation scheme. Some war veterans came down the road and hit one of his pipes with an axe, so it started to spray water in the air and it lost pressure there where he was planting. My brother got on his motorbike and he went over there, and when he got off the motorbike, they surrounded him. Five of them. One guy pushed him from the back, pushed him into the next guy, and as he turned around to see who pushed him—I'm telling you they'd been given permission to kill him—another one slashed him across the top of the cheekbone with a *panga*. His whole face, it all fell forward. And his nose was gone.

My brother used to carry weapons. I never even thought about owning guns, I'd lost that long ago, but he had a shoulder holster. So he pulled that gun out and he fired it in the air. He still didn't have the right to defend himself. He knew that. He knew that if he turned the weapon on them and shot them, he would be dead. So he just took it out and he fired shots in the air, and then he got on the radio. Sally was listening from our house and heard him, but he couldn't speak properly because his whole face had come forward. Izzy also heard, she thought his leg had been cut off. We were quickly on the radios to everyone. So all the neighboring farms heard about it, and we all got together. We put a Cessna in the air, and we closed in on these guys.

We were all running toward my brother's farm, labor forces and everything. Don't forget: our black workers were with us at the time and putting their necks out for us. We're talking about an area of about five square kilometers. We closed in on them and we caught them. Four of our laborers caught them, and we tied them up, called the police.

Then the cops came. They just walked up to the people tied up and took off their ropes and said to them, *You can go.* They then handcuffed the four laborers and took them to the cop shop; they beat them severely.

We had a mini-riot. Everyone took twenty laborers from their farm and we all went off to the police station with black hearts and said, *Let them go! Let them go! What have they done?* But we had no power.

My brother was so loyal to Zimbabwe. An American facelift surgeon offered to sew him back up, and he said, *No, I want a Zimbabwean doctor to do it.* That's how patriotic he is. And he showed real bravery. He got back out there. My brother, he got his face cut off, he got his face sewn up, and he went back out there. He carried on farming. But by the end of the year he was out.

By then, things were even worse. Some people ended up having graves dug outside their houses. My mates, not me personally, but two of my mates, watched the war veterans spend the whole night there digging graves just outside his back door for him, his wife, and his two kids. They even went to the extent of taking flowers and putting them on the edges of the graves.

Now by this time, my mother had left the main house. She and a family friend had got together. My poor mum was facing *jambanja*[14] on her friend's farm, and she also found out she had cancer. Sally and I and the kids were living in our beautiful Spanish house, the house where I had been born and brought up. And these vets would stand outside the house for twenty-four hours; they'd make my own labor force stand with them and sing songs the whole night, a *pungwe*.[15] For months they'd make my laborers run around my house singing war songs. They said, *We have to re-educate them.* I'd just sit and listen.

There was this guy that was in charge of them. We heard that he had killed something like five people in Kariba. He actually beat a guy, a black guy, publicly in Kariba, in the shopping center, and he put him in the supermarket window and he said, *If anyone touches him, they join him.* The guy took, like, three hours to die in the supermarket window.

When he shook your hand, he would pull you within inches of his face and would look at you in the eyes. He had eyes like a lizard. He terrified the fuck out of me. Let's not forget that we had our two little daughters here, and he used to just walk into our house. I was on the closing end of finishing my crop. I knew that I was only a tobacco farmer and I was going to lose my way of making money, so I said to myself, *If it costs you some equipment to keep it until you've packed all your tobacco and sent it through to town, then you must try and fight for that.* So we had this deal that he would leave me for a while and I would help him with equipment. He wanted my brother's irrigation pipes, but I didn't want my brother getting hurt again, so I gave him mine.

Sally was sick then, vomiting all the time—she'd wake up in the morning and start vomiting. She was scared, terrified. They would steal those Motorola radios we used to have on a base set in our room. In the middle of the night they used to switch it on and go, *I'm coming to get you, you fucking white people.* Until the batteries ran out.

---

[14] Literally "confusion" in Shona, but now used to refer to the process of a farm being taken over by war vets.

[15] All-night meeting or forced rally, common during the liberation war. Zenzele describes *pungwes* in his story.

You know, people get very religious when shit happens to them and they can't defend themselves. We had praying groups at night, radioing in, and everyone would sit down and pray by the radio. It didn't always help. White people ended up hating each other, and people that were friends were no longer your friends.

It so happened that thirteen veterans were planning to finally take the place over. So I tried one last angle to keep my farm. I made a project proposal offering to turn the house on the other farm into a clinic, and that half the barns can be turned into a school, and the other half can be subdivided between the thirteen people. I can come over and teach them how to grow tobacco, etc., etc. I put it forward to the government. It didn't make any difference.

ALWAYS EASIER FOR A BLACK MAN
TO KILL A BLACK MAN

The police went on a spree of arresting people, even white women. They'd actually had me on charges for kidnapping and horrible things. They charged my dad as well. My dad had been dead long before that stuff even started. The police station smelled of urine, and there was a pile of what I thought was rags on the floor. It was black people that had been beaten. There was a lot of violence. It was becoming very intense. There were road-blocks of drunk and unruly war veterans and their hangers-on.

At the end of 2002 was the final invasion. I was watching rugby. The kids were playing in the garden. I can remember it so clearly—Sally walked out the door and saw them. There were about ten cops and ten war veterans, all with guns. The truck looked like a porcupine. Then I knew it was really happening. I didn't know what I was going do. They gave me a week and a very brave driver from my father-in-law's company came to load our furniture. I ended up selling my tobacco crop. But as far as all my equipment, my tractors, my trailers, my pumps—everything had to be left there.

I still had 150 people at my farm, and when I left, I remember my people standing around me, like thirty of them, and I was giving away things to them as well, saying, *You can take that motorbike, you can do this, whatever*. I gave one guy my guitar. All my servants and everyone was sitting around me, and Jacob, one of our workers, he got the guitar and he started strumming it and singing, and everyone started crying.

You know, during the year of this war veteran story, 1,500 white farmers in South Africa were murdered. I don't know how many of us died in Zimbabwe. I'm not saying we didn't—there was a guy executed just down the road. You must have heard about Stevens.[16] They shot him in the back of the head. My brother had his face cut off, almost got killed. There's a whole number of cases, but if you put them all together it wouldn't be anything close to 1,500. I'm disincluding the black people who died in droves—because here it's always easier for a black man to kill a black man, because a black man doesn't have a lawyer, he doesn't have finances or papers. Workers in my compound got as savagely beaten as my brother. We don't even know what happened to so many of them. Good people. Black people have suffered and been brave.

WE HAVE ALWAYS LOVED ART

So I'd sold my crop, I'd managed to pay my overdraft off—and I had a bit of pocket money left over, not much. We went into Harare, where Sally comes from, but she said, *I don't want to live here. It's a den of iniquity, we'll be divorced in a year.* I leased a house in Harare for about three months, and every night I was pissed out of my head, sleeping in the garden. All my friends that I've known have moved into Harare, all with the same big problems. They used to come around and we used to just drink and drink and drink. Everybody was looking for something to do or somewhere to go. Most chose South Africa or Australia. My brother chose Australia. We

---

[16] David Stevens, an MDC member, was the first white farmer killed during the land invasions, in April 2000. Notices of his death dominated the first major international press attention given to Zimbabwe's farm violence at the time.

chose Cape Town in South Africa.

We have always loved art. Sally is a floral artist and even represented Zim in the world floral art show. My dad, my mum, and mum-in law are artists. So if we couldn't be farmers in Zim we were going to open a gallery in Cape Town. We chose some incredible stone sculptures and some talented artists, and set up a beautiful gallery in a fantastic spot called Franschoek. We had no idea how to sell. I got lessons from an Indian guy that sold Persian rugs. He told me this story. The owner of a Persian carpet gallery had to go out one day and leave his son in charge. He told his son if he could sell a certain carpet for R165,000[17] he would be respected as a man. Well, he did sell it, and when he was finishing off the deal, his father came in and said, *What are you doing?* The son proudly told his father he had sold the carpet. The father slapped his son across the face and said, *You stupid boy, that carpet was worth R200,000.* The Americans that were buying the carpet were horrified and said, *We'll pay R200,000, don't hit your son anymore.* After they left the father turned to his son and said, *You can always do better than you think you can.*

Sally and I did not do well in our business. We got down to seven rand[18] and then our dog bit someone and this lady demanded R200. I tried to give her my bicycle but she wanted cash.

I needed to be myself again, in my shorts and T-shirt in the bush, the possibility of running into a python, talking to my workers, growing something. I tried Zambia and got a job teaching small-scale tobacco farmers, but then a mate phoned from Mozambique and said he would help me get a farm...

MOZ

It was like a history lesson driving through Moz. Although it had been

---

[17] Approximately US$16,500.

[18] Less than US$1.

forty years since the Portuguese had left, there was skeletons of their past everywhere. There was darkness in people's eyes, a legacy of a terrible civil war. Instant justice was common, and I witnessed a couple of public beatings for petty crimes that make me shudder when I think about it. Mozambique was hard. I felt like I was in that reality series *Survivor*, or worse.

The people were great. I met this worker on one of the farms I was looking at, he was as dyslexic as I was, and trying to hide it, but so intelligent and a real character. With the absence of peer pressure, I was finally allowed to become good friends with blacks. This guy, he helped me find my farm and became my manager.

But life in Mozambique was so hard. Sally had malaria six days after arriving, and then we all continually had it. We lived in a tent. I put a barn door on some bricks under a tree, and that was where you stayed when you got malaria. It was too hot in the tent. The one good thing about being sick with malaria all the time was that I didn't drink.

That October... disaster. Sally had a burst colon. I had to take her to Harare for treatment. She nearly died, twice. Izzy had a major epileptic fit, and my farm was hit by a tropical storm. For the first time I really appreciated what my folks went through when they were pioneering in Zim, and how much our farms in Zim were worth. I was in a daze, trying to look after my daughters, rebuilding, working and traveling to Harare to see my wife in hospital. Even our animals didn't survive that place. They had come from Karoi to Harare, flown to Cape Town, and then flown to Mozambique. Chippy, our little sausage dog with the heart of a lion, got caught in a snare. Our Alsatian was bitten by a snake and then died of cancer. The cats all eventually disappeared.

HOME

I realized it was time to come home, and so I started looking for farms back in Zim. This time I took my time. There was a smattering of white farmers holding on, and some people had already started leasing their own farms back from the blacks on them. Others were making a plan to lease anywhere. It was tempting to try and go back to my old farm. I'd been hearing that some blacks on the farms had found it wasn't so easy to be a farmer, and were ready to have us back. But I just couldn't go back to my old place. Too painful. I wanted to find something new.

I found a farm, was owned by a black man named Mr. Tuku. I was impressed by him right away. He knew about being a farmer and didn't have unrealistic expectations. He wanted me to go into a partnership with his eldest son, Kwashe. He made me do all the right things, not only for myself, but for the future of this country. When we met Kwashe, we immediately hit it off. He had been to the same university as my wife and my brother in South Africa.

I enjoy being in his company, he makes me laugh, and we have found a way of working together side by side. He and I went to the Zambezi valley together to do some tiger fishing and he made a DVD of the trip called "The Bold and the Shameless." Our relationship is not pretend. I wouldn't swap him for anyone, black or white. He does little things like SMSing my wife when she won a flower show. He even gave us his house to live in.

I still wouldn't change any part of my life right now, except I miss my brother. We seem to have got through all that happened and become a really close family. I have recovered from the bitterness toward the people that took our farm in Karoi. The people on the ground know that both blacks and whites were hurt in the land invasions.

Recently I heard that the war vets who took our farm took off and left the place. Apparently a lion was terrorizing them. My mum thinks it's my dad's spirit. I'm still not going back.

THE RURALS

MURAMBINDA

From a distance, the small rural growth point of Murambinda announces itself out of the plain as a set of unmarked hills: some rounded *kopjes*, one squat square-top, and a run of small cones rising. As you come closer, details emerge: lichen-splattered granite boulders, red earth, dry grass, and musasa trees. Then, gradually, houses, some no more than huts. Others, larger and more substantial, with tin roofs and fenced-in yards.

The market and shops of Murambinda, typical of many Zimbabwean small towns, straggle along a dirt road: a hair salon, a couple of general stores, a funeral parlor, a driving school. Beyond the buildings, a wide, slow river flows over slabs of granite and under a narrow stone bridge. A path leads out to The Irrigation, an agricultural improvement project from the 1960s where well-watered banana trees, sugar cane, vegetables, and maize grow, bright green, on square plots of land. At dusk, women work quietly up and down the fields. From the distance comes the slow thump of someone chopping wood.

There's more scotch-cart than vehicle traffic at the market these days. From stalls and under trees, women and boys sell vegetables, roasted mealies, homemade donuts, and loaves of bread from South Africa because there's no flour to bake locally. In the general store, stocks are low and shelves bare. Even the beerhall is relatively quiet: few people have money for beer, and there's no electricity to blare loud rumba through speakers on the concrete veranda. At this point (the week of U.S. President Obama's inauguration, to be precise), Murambinda has gone without electricity for two months. Unlike many others around the country, its hospital still functions, supported by the government, the Catholic church and, recently, Doctors Without Borders. A diesel generator is switched on only for surgery and other emergencies as fuel is scarce. Because cholera has broken out in the cities, people greet each other by touching forearms instead of shaking hands as is customary, to avoid spreading contamination.

Murambinda sits near the center of a large district of communal land, Buhera, a hundred and twenty miles end to end. Although it is only one of fifty-nine districts in Zimbabwe, Buhera features in several narratives in this collection. In the 1980s and '90s, the town of Murambinda was said to receive special attention—tarred roads, funding allocations—because it was the rural home, the *musha*, of a powerful cabinet minister. In the 2000s, Buhera also became known as the home district of opposition leader, Morgan Tsvangirai. And, as Briggs describes in another section, Murambinda is where two young MDC organizers, Talent Mabika and Tichaona Chiminya, were attacked and their car set alight in April 2000, a grim and fiery end to their lives and to a short-lived period of open protest that preceded elections that year.

ALICE

AGE: *42*

OCCUPATION: *Former provincial organizer, trader, domestic worker*
INTERVIEWED IN: *A neighboring country to Zimbabwe*

A former grassroots organizer, Alice is living in hiding. She seldom goes out, to avoid the local authorities and also any Zimbabweans who might be looking for her. Christianity and the internet sustain her. Over a year has passed this way by the time of these interviews, and more than that since she was raped by Zimbabwean soldiers, in a wave of political retribution through sexual violence.[1] In telling her story, Alice emphasizes the constraints that have held her, like a series of jails: poverty and family problems, the need for secrecy as an organizer, hiding out from government agents, actual detention, and now, though out of Zimbabwe, a kind of illegal exile.

My work in politics ended up hurting one of my children, beginning in 2006. I don't want to talk about the details. I went through terrible experiences myself, but it is my family that I am thinking of, it is concern about my family that causes me the most pain.

---

[1] In 2009, the advocacy organization AIDS-Free World published the first investigation to document "exceptionally violent rape" as a Zanu-PF election strategy put to use during the previous year's elections ("Electing to Rape: Sexual Terror in Mugabe's Zimbabwe").

My name is Alice. The surname I use is from my mother's family, but my ID and documents have my ex-husband's surname, Bhina. I grew up with my mother's family after my father and mother had problems. My brother was the eldest, and he and I were taken to live with my mother's family when we were young. My brother died there, when he was only in Grade 2.

I didn't manage to go to school past Grade 3. My mother married another man and I wasn't part of her new family. My stepfather didn't like me and my mother had no money for my schooling. She eventually left my stepfather and had two more children, a boy after me and then another girl. After that, my mother left her home area and we went to live in another small town. She worked at the market there and managed to buy a stand.

I grew up working in people's houses as a maid until I got married. By then I already had a son. He was two years old when I got married. I also took care of my husband's brother's children, Dorcas and Farai, his sister's children Robson, Michael, Sarudzai, and Tondirai, and my husband's children from his previous wife who had died, Joyce, Thomas, John, and Simukai.

My husband worked as a TV and radio technician, but he didn't make enough money to support the family, so I became a cross-border trader, traveling to Botswana, buying goods and going back to Zimbabwe to sell. One time when I came back from Botswana, my husband said, *Help me with some of your money so that I can go to Mozambique to open a shop. I will give you back your money as soon as I start making profits.* Unfortunately for me, he found another woman there after three months of working in Mozambique. This was in 2006. He didn't think about me or care. We had lived together for fifteen years.

MY CONSTITUENCY

Even before my husband left, I had been participating in MDC—the Movement for Democratic Change—for some time, but earlier I had to do it quietly. Where I lived, people had stopped coming out in the open because an MDC chairman was badly beaten up in our area by Zanu-PF people. Another person who was standing as a councilor was also beaten up by Zanu-PF youth. They'd go to people's houses in our area at night and beat them up. So people were afraid of getting killed.

I got involved in MDC because I was unhappy about the way we were living in Zimbabwe. A lot of kids were going to school and getting educated but with no jobs afterward. Only people in government were benefitting while others suffered.

As an organizing secretary, I'd go to rallies and talk to people about how difficult life had become and discuss the idea of having a new president. If we were planning to have a rally I'd be given all the information, then I'd tell the party chairladies and chairmen which wards[2] the rallies would be held at and when to tell people to meet. Then they'd tell the people that the MP[3] is coming to visit or Morgan Tsvangirai[4] is coming to see them on such and such a day. Before the constituencies were broken up, the area where I became an organizing secretary was very big.

From early 2008, I was heavily involved in the March 2008 elections. After voting, people from my constituency were beaten up. My MP called and said, *Some MDC people were arrested and need food.* I said, *Okay.* I made some food and took it to the police station. There was one guy who was badly beaten and had a serious nosebleed. Our lawyer tried to get him out so he could take him to the hospital, but the cops refused. The guy said to me, *My head feels like it's broken. If you can, please get me some Stopayne tablets.* While I went to the shops to look for the tablets, people driving a silver gray car went to my house looking for me. They asked the kids at my house where I was. The kids said, *She went to the shops.* So they drove to the shops. Actually, I saw the car drive past, but I didn't know they were looking for me.

---

[2] Except in towns and cities, areas are divided into village, ward, and district.

[3] Member of Parliament.

[4] Founding president of MDC, formerly secretary general of Zimbabwe Congress of Trade Unions.

At the shops, people told them I'd just left. They drove to my mother's house—I live in the same location[5] as my mother. When they went to my mother's, they said, *We are looking for Mrs. Bhina.* My sister-in-law was there and she told them I hadn't been there. They said, *Are you sure?* She said, *Yes, she never came here.* They said, *We are coming into the house to look for her.* They went in and looked for me but I wasn't there. They were carrying guns.

After that, they drove back to my house. Nearby, there was a car blocking the road. Its gears had locked and the owner was pushing it off the street. The guys in the car called out: *Hey! Move that car out of the way.* The owner of the car said, *It's up to me when I move it because this is my house.* They asked him if I was home. He said, *She is not,* because he had seen me leaving the house but he had not seen me coming back.

When I first heard about this, I was thinking it was MDC people looking for me because we had won. I didn't think CIOs[6] were looking for me. Our MP had just won in the parliamentary election. In our constituency, MDC had won three-quarters out of the seats for councilors, with only a few going to Zanu-PF, so we were happy. I said to myself, *This person is crazy to say I am not at home. What if it's MDC people looking for me, wanting to thank me? Why did he say I'm not home?* But later on, my sister-in-law came running and said, *Some people came looking for you,* and she described the car.

I said, *What did they want?*

They said I must tell you they and their friends are looking for you. And they showed us a gun.

I then became worried.

I made some more food and took it to the MDC members who were under arrest at the police station.

When I got to the police station, some people had been released and

---

[5] High-density suburb or working-class townships, formerly blacks-only, are often referred to as "locations."

[6] Officers of the Central Intelligence Organization are known as CIOs.

others transferred to the nearest town. Among the people who had come to see their relatives, there was a man who recognized me and greeted me by name: *Hallo, Mrs. Bhina.* A policeman heard him and said, *We are looking for Mrs. Bhina. She should be arrested.* I said, *Me, arrested, why?* He said, *You are beating up Zanu-PF seniors.* I said, *I've never beaten up any Zanu-PF seniors.* He said, *Let's go to the charge office.*

I waited for a long time at the charge office. At last I said, *If you are not going to call the people you say I beat up, I'm going.* They said, *So are you taking the law into your own hands?* I said, *No, but I have been sitting and waiting and I'm tired. I'm going because you are not sure about what you are saying and the person who reported me should be here to identify me. If you are saying I beat up old people and they are not here to say it's true, I'm going.* I picked up the bowls that I had brought food in and I went home.

Back home, I heard a car. I looked through the window and saw a Mitsubishi car arriving with some people in it. They were with a guy I know from our area. He was pointing out my house for them. Nothing happened; he just pointed out my house to them and they drove away.

It was difficult, as I couldn't move around freely and I couldn't let anyone see me. More MDC people were arrested and I needed to give them some food. I would take food to those people, trying not to be noticed, until they were released.

RUNNING

In May 2008,[7] another guy came to my house to tell me, *They are looking for you. If you don't leave now, those people could arrive any minute.* I had just got out of the bath and so I put away my towel and left in a hurry. As I was leaving my house, going to the neighbor's, along the fence, running away, I heard people banging on my doors. I ran away in the other

---

[7] As other narrators explain, the period between the March 2008 elections and the runoff presidential elections called for in June saw the most intense and brutal political violence of the decade. For further details, see the appendix section on the 2008 election.

direction, to my church priest's house. When I got there, I called my MP and told him that the situation had worsened.

He sent a car to take me somewhere far away, where I could hide with some other women. From there, I would call home to ask them to tell me when those people had stopped looking for me.

After about two weeks, when the children told me that things had quieted down at home, I went back. It was night and I slept. I stayed there for a week and no one knew. I had to use a chamber pot if I needed to go to the toilet. When I felt that things had really gone quiet, I decided to go to church. On my way, I got a phone call from the MP saying that more people were arrested from the villages and beaten up. About twenty people had been arrested that time. The police would arrest some, release some, and so on. In June 2008, there were almost five hundred MDC people in jail in the nearby town. He asked me to go and see them and to phone the lawyer. He said, *After you see them, you can explain to the lawyer what happened. Then if they need to pay fines, the lawyer will help them get released.* I agreed.

But when I got to the police station gate my heart was beating fast. I was too scared to go in, so I sent another guy I was with, Trust, to go and see the people who'd been arrested and find out how they were. He came back and told me that people were badly hurt and also really hungry. Some girls had been beaten on their buttocks and accused of going to visit Tsvangirai. This was in the villages, sixty or seventy kilometers from the nearest small town. Some had had their hair pulled out, and so they were in pain. I cooked food for them and I told Trust to go to town and buy them drinks.

He was taking a long time to come back and I was worried, so I decided to take the food into the police station myself. They delayed me, refusing to let me give the food to the people. I got there at noon and only managed to give people food at four p.m. On my way home, I received a call from the MP saying that Trust had been arrested and taken to the police station. I told the MP I didn't see Trust there when I took the food. He said, *You might have not seen him but he was arrested.*

When I got home, Trust's older brother came to my house and said, *I heard they are coming to get you today.* I said, *I'm tired of running. If they want to come and get me they can come.* Trust's brother left. Less than an hour later, they came. In winter it gets dark early. It was some time after six p.m. and it was dark. Three cars full up with people drove up to my house. This was the 7th of June, 2008.

VISITORS WITH GUNS

When I heard the sound of cars, I looked through the curtain and saw that it was bad. There was nowhere to run. They were wearing army uniforms, not the militia uniforms of the Green Bombers[8] but camouflage, the Zimbabwean army uniform, and they were armed with guns. They all got out of the cars. Some jumped over my gate and some went around to my neighbor's house where I used to go to hide. My house is a typical ghetto house—each one is attached to the neighbor's house. So they surrounded my house and the neighbor's house. There was a visitor at my neighbor's house and they beat him badly, tearing the skin of his buttocks. Then they went searching in the bedrooms in my house. In the other bedroom, they found my stepson and his wife sleeping. They started beating him but they didn't beat his wife because she was pregnant. After they beat him, my stepson told them where my other stepson was hiding with the keys. I'd given that second stepson the spare keys to my bedroom so that if I wasn't there, he could get anything he needed from my room, because I trust him. They beat him too, because he could not get the door open. He was trying to insert the key but he could not do it because I was inside holding the key. When I realized that they were beating him, I decided to unlock the door. I came out and said, *Please don't beat up my son. He has done nothing wrong. I am the problem because I am a member of MDC.*

They said, *Are you showing off with your MDC?* I said, *No, I'm not. You*

---

[8] Green Bombers, as Alice defines them, are Zanu-PF militia, the youth without jobs, trained to kill and be cruel.

are hurting someone who has done no wrong. They said, *Okay, open your bedroom. Why were you locked inside?* I said, *I was afraid because you came into my house with guns. I've never had visitors bring guns before.*

They went into my bedroom and started searching. They found twenty Morgan Tsvangirai posters and two posters for my MP, and flyers, and the *Zimbabwean* newspaper[9]—I had piles of them for distribution. I also had MDC T-shirts and bandanas, some were for distribution and some were my own.

They took all that and they said, *We want your phone.* I said, *I don't have a phone.* When I saw them coming, I had switched off my phone and put it in my panties. They searched my house and took some money that I was saving. I was hoping to use it to order stuff to sell after all this had calmed down. I had US$300 and R150.

They told me to carry all the stuff out of the house. I said, *I can't carry all that.* They said, *How did you get it in? Carry your stuff.* They wanted me and my other stepson to go with them, but one of the soldiers said, *Leave him.* So they left my stepson and took me in their open truck, a cream Mitsubishi. I was sitting in the back, in the middle, and they were surrounding me, sitting on the sides. They were all beating me, kicking me and hitting me with sticks and fists. Some were saying that they wanted to throw me into the dam. Another car stopped and someone inside said, *Did you find her?* and they said, *Yes, we did.*

They wanted me to tell them where the MDC MPs lived, the MDC youths' houses, the councillor's house. That's why they were beating me up—because I was refusing to tell them. They were saying, *So you are being like Jesus, who died for others? And now are you going to die for those people?* I said, *No. Whoever showed you my house should have shown you all the other houses.* They said I was rude. They beat me up so badly. After that they said, *Take off your clothes.*

---

[9] The *Zimbabwean* is an international Zimbabwe newspaper with a focus on freedom of expression, meaning that those who help distribute it in Zimbabwe do so at the threat of government retribution.

When I removed my clothes, just before we got to the Methodist church, they stopped the car in the dark and there they raped me.

There were many soldiers. I don't know how many raped me. I saw the first eight men who raped me but then I became unconscious.

I think they threw water on me because I became conscious just before we got to the police station. They said, *Put on your clothes.* I refused. They said, *You don't listen.* In the end, I put on my clothes. When we got there, they said, *Get off and carry your stuff.* I got off the back of the truck but I couldn't even walk. I fell down and they said *Get up* and I did.

Inside, when they got behind the counter in the police station, they threw a bullet at me and said *Kiss it* and I did, and they said, *That bullet is yours.*

THE COURT CASE

When they left, a man who knows me, another cop, said, *I heard you had gone to South Africa. Why did you come back?* I said, *No, I was here all along.* He said, *Your situation is dangerous. We were told to arrest other MDC members except for you and the councillor's son, because you are refusing to give them the information they want.* I agreed to pretend that he had not told me this. He said, *I will quickly write your name in this book and put you in the cells, because once I do that no one will be allowed to sign you out because it's against the law. It's better for you to suffer in jail than to be out there where your life is in danger.*

So I was put in the cells with two other girls who had also been beaten up, the ones I had visited before. The next day, those girls were released from jail and went to court in the nearby town. I remained behind and the lawyer came and tried to have me released from jail so I could go to the hospital because I was badly hurt. The whole time I was in jail—four days—I couldn't even eat. I started menstruating, but I couldn't get pads. They would say to me, *You are tough like a soldier. We are not giving you anything.* They took away all the blankets so I had nothing to cover myself.

One night, that good policeman came to me when it was dark—I don't know what time it was—and said, *I just slipped away so I could tell you this. I was told to write the statement about what you did. It's not easy, but I won't write exactly what I was told to write because it's wrong to accuse you of something you didn't do. What I will do in order for you to get out of this mess is that I won't come to court.* I asked him for blankets and he said, *It's not possible. You won't die, just be strong and God will protect you.* Then he closed the cell and left.

When my lawyer came to get me released, the police said, *Alice did not commit any crime—we would like to ask her for forgiveness.* But they didn't release me.

Every day for three days, I went to court. I bathed in cold water since I was in a smelly place. Before I got into the police van the first day, I asked them, *What am I accused of?* One of the bosses at the police station, the second officer in charge, said, *You talk too much. Get into the car.* I got into the car. When I got to the court in town, they read out my crime. I was surprised to hear that when I'd been to the police station to take food to the MDC people there, I had stoned police cars and fought with the police. I didn't say anything. My lawyer said, *Why do you say she committed these crimes? When I came to the police station and asked you before, you said, Alice didn't commit any crime—you even asked for forgiveness.* They kept on arguing with my lawyer. Like he had promised me when I was in jail, the policeman who wrote the report did not come to court. They kept on postponing, waiting for him to come, but at last they said, *The policeman is not coming.* The magistrate dealing with my case got angry in court. She said, *Since when do soldiers arrest people? You are bringing people who didn't commit a crime. I want to get into heaven—so Alice, go home.*

I went back to jail at around five p.m. I said, *I want to go home, I've been released. When can I remove the jail uniform and put on my own clothes?* But the prison guards told me that there were CIOs waiting at the gate. They said I must wait. After a while, they said, *Okay, now you can change your clothes and go. But when you leave here, don't use the road. Find other means.* I went through the bush and reached home at ten p.m.

LEAVING HOME

I hadn't seen a doctor to get treated, so when I woke up—it was a Saturday—I went to MDC offices in the city. I was told to go to the Medical Centre (they didn't treat MDC members at the general hospital) but the doctor was not in, so I went back again on the Monday. After I was treated they said I must have an HIV test so I went to the New Start Centre. I was tested and told that I am negative. Everything was done by Tuesday. On my way home, my children called on my cell phone to say, *Don't come home. They are looking for you. They came last night.* So I went back to the MDC offices and started living there.

While I was staying at MDC offices in the city, the Zanu-PF people kept on going to my house until all the children left. Those people took everything, food, pots, blankets, everything. As I speak, there's nothing at my house.

The people who did all this were Zanu-PF. They were mixed, it was like a joint venture: police, prison guards, soldiers, civilians, and the youth, all Zanu-PF. They also went to my mother's house and beat her. They hurt her chest and the side of her stomach. MDC people helped her go to the doctor. After beating her up, those people took my mother's food and her blankets. Then they went to the place my young sister rents at one of the railways houses. They smashed her windows. They were looking for me, thinking I was hiding there. My mother and my sister also came to the city, to the MDC offices, and we all stayed there together. When they were better, they went back home, but I couldn't go back because they kept on looking for me. Life in the city was safer, and we shared our stories with each other. We felt that the police wouldn't attack us as we were in our hundreds and lots of us had already been injured.

I stayed there for three months, from July to September 5th, 2008. We slept in the offices. Some people felt sorry for us and they would bring us food while we were there. There were lots of people there. I don't even know the actual number. Some had been burnt, some had serious wounds in their buttocks.

There was a time that I tried to go back home. I really missed home. On my way, I met up with the local Zanu-PF chairman and he said, *You are back here?* He and his youths started asking me a lot of questions. Some were saying, *Let's beat her up*, and some were saying, *No, let's not.*

LEAVING THE COUNTRY

I wasn't the only one to go through what I had gone through. A lot of other women also went through that. When we were at the MDC offices we were told that a woman called Betty Makoni wanted to help us. And she did help us. I don't know if MDC approached her and told her the problem or if she saw it on the Internet, but she called the MDC offices to find out more because she's got women's best interests at heart. When we heard that she wanted to help us, we caught the bus—nine women—and crossed the border to come here. Some had passports, some didn't so they had to jump the border. I have a passport. After the border, we carried on with our journey to this town and stayed at a lodge that MDC organized for us.

Betty told us that she wanted us to rest and stay in peace after what we had experienced. We stayed with her for one week at the lodge. She said we would go back home to Zimbabwe after that week. She said it hurt her that women have to go through what we went through.

When I got home after that week, I arrived at night. There was an MDC rally in our town the next day. This was September 2008, when they started talking about having an inclusive government. At the rally, the police officer in charge came and called me in front of the MDC MPs. The MPs said, *No, don't go.* But the police officer was very angry and kept on calling me. The MPs said, *He's the one calling you, so he should come here. Don't go there.* So I didn't.

After the rally one of the MDC cars dropped me at home and I just slipped into my house and closed myself in. The police didn't notice how I left the rally. Perhaps they thought I had gone with MDC cars. They didn't know I was at home. But it was impossible for me to keep staying there. Another woman phoned Betty and told her I couldn't stay at home. Betty called me and asked me to leave the country again. So I left and came here. Some other women came later. We are about nineteen, but some come and go. Betty still pays for food.

I applied for asylum in May 2009, but it's not out yet. I thought it would have come out by now. It's difficult to move around, it's scary, so I hide indoors. The house is very good, but my life is painful, because I can't go anywhere and I miss my family. I can't do anything to earn money for myself. I'm just someone who is sitting, doing nothing, thinking about my family.

LOVEMORE

AGE: *40*

OCCUPATION: *IT engineer and trainer, workshop leader,*
supporter of torture survivors
INTERVIEWED IN: *Harare, Zimbabwe*

*A philosopher-activist, a former drinker now as devoted to jogging as he once was
to beer, a teacher and IT expert, Lovemore is currently engaged, as a torture survivor, in helping others to heal through storytelling. He is a reserved man, tall and
lean, with a warm smile, but in a group tends to let others do the talking. Later,
in an interview, he describes his own history as it intertwines with that of the
country. Beginning as a boy pulling down election posters, Lovemore courted trouble
by acting on his critique of the politics of the moment. He went on to play a key role
in organizing the opposition party the MDC, only to find himself sidelined when
he emerged from his last, lengthy period in prison.* I was thinking too much, *he
says.* To think too much—kufungisisa—*is considered a worrying sign: you are
obsessing, unable to escape troubled thoughts, depressed.*

I was born on the 7th of May, 1970 in Makonde district. My father was
working for the ESC, Electricity Supply Commission, as ZESA[1] was called

---

[1] Zimbabwe Electricity Supply Authority, and now a general term for electricity: "We had
no ZESA for three months."

in those days. I grew up in what is now Nyamuka township, Nyanga town. But then it was still more like what we call a growth point.

The first year of primary education I did in Chinhoyi. As I am the first-born, I went to live with my grandparents when I was six years old. That's the tradition, that the first-born must live with the grandparents. To begin with, I liked it because I was living with my cousins, my uncles' children, all together, the whole lot of us, the same generation, and with my elder cousin-sister and my three aunts. I could play with other young children, one my own age, one a year older, one two years older.

It became a tradition for all of us to go to Chinhoyi Primary School— it was Sinoia Government Primary School then. But I only did my first and second year there. Then, because there were lots of us, I was not getting enough attention. I started crying for my mum. I wanted her care. So I went back to Nyanga for Grade 3. I didn't finish because of the war. We lived in an accommodation for ESC employees in the center of Nyanga, but the school was situated in a rural setting where the war had intensified. By that time the area was a liberated zone and the school was forced to close by the guerillas. They wanted to use it as a ZANLA base.[2] The Rhodesian soldiers could have tried to reopen it—it was something like five kilometers from the barracks—but they did nothing.

I was still young but I have memories of the war. My family lived near the Nyanga barracks. At night, we would be ordered to eat quickly. If somebody whistled, that was the signal to go into the bunkers. These were just thick planks and sandbags, above the ground. When there was mortar fire and we didn't have enough time to rush to the bunker, we would hide under our beds.

My father would order ESC overalls and *panga* knives for his work clearing the electricity lines. Then, traveling around in his Land Rover making repairs, he would give the overalls and the *pangas* to the guerillas and they would pretend to be ESC workers when they were actually

---

[2] The Zimbabwe African National Liberation Army was the armed wing of Zanu, the Zimbabwe African National Union.

spying and doing things like that. At that time most of the roads from Nyanga Centre were no longer functional because of landmines. When the war intensified, my father and his colleagues were escorted by the Rhodesian Infantry to go and lay cables and things. But they could no longer fix some lines, so many places had no electricity.

I was aware the guerillas were close by. They even visited our school. We were terrified because of the way they were dressed, and the *pangas* and the machine guns. To tell the truth, at that time I saw them as bad people. They would hold *pungwes*—all-night rallies—in the rural areas near the school. When they held a *pungwe* at the Nyanga Weaving Centre, they accused my friend's father of being a sell-out. The guerillas ordered everyone to gather round. Then they assaulted him till he passed out for good.

One time when they came to my school, they picked on a lady teacher who was married to a man we called a DA (although he was really the messenger, not the District Administrator himself). They took her away. Fortunately she was rescued, but because she was my teacher, I had bad feelings toward the guerillas, no matter what their cause was at that time.

When my school was transferred to a former hotel, Angel's Rest, my father decided it would be best to send me back to Chinhoyi. I did Grades 3 and 4 there, aged seven and eight. My parents used to come and pick me up by bus or train, to go home for the school holidays. I used to like the traveling part of it.

In Chinhoyi I felt safer. There was nothing happening. It was an urban setting, people moved freely. Most of my classmates in Chinhoyi knew nothing about war, so I told them stories about what I'd seen in Nyanga. Young as I was, I had once seen the Rhodesian infantry display bodies of guerrillas in the school grounds. Some of the fighters were alive but five of them, I remember very well, were dead, lying on the school field.

ZIMBABWE-RHODESIA

I was politically involved from an early age. I was detained by Ian Smith's police when I was nine years old. This was in Nyanga, 1979, at the height of the liberation war. There were elections for Zimbabwe-Rhodesia at the time.[3] My father supported Bishop Abel Muzorewa of the United Methodist Church.

All the ideas I heard at that time were about how Muzorewa is good and this Ndabaningi Sithole of Zanu-Ndonga is shit.

So, walking home from school that day, I pulled down a campaign poster for Ndabaningi Sithole from a pine tree. It was myself and two friends. We each tore a sign down. I didn't see the people who were nearby putting up the posters, tying them to trees with string. They came and captured us, these Zanu-Ndonga people. They bundled us into a truck and took us to a police station.

I was very scared. The police were hostile. They said, *These kids— where did they get the guts to pull down the posters? Somebody must have sent them.* They wanted to know: *What do your parents do? Who sent you? What party does your father support? How often is he at home? Have you have ever seen a guerilla?* Things like that.

But my father had always warned me at home, *Whenever you are asked, just say you don't know anything about the guerillas. Just say you don't know anything about Bishop Muzorewa.*

That day, we were detained from eleven a.m. to nine p.m. My parents were informed about what had happened. They came to the police station and negotiated with the officer in charge to have me released. Because my colleagues' parents were not there, my father helped to get them released too. That was the first of many times I was detained.

INDEPENDENCE

When Independence came I was still very young. I remember the day

---

[3] In 1979, Smith's Rhodesian Front formed a short-lived coalition government with nationalists including Ndabaningi Sithole (an early Zanu leader), James Chikerema, and Bishop Abel Muzorewa of both the United Methodist Church (to which Lovemore's family belonged) and the United African National Congress. The country was briefly known as Zimbabwe-Rhodesia.

the results were announced. I come from what I can describe as a democratic family. Each one supported a different party. My father's brother, my uncle, was Zapu. And my father, although he assisted the guerillas at some stage, was UMC, a Bishop Muzorewa person. My grandmother was Zanu. And my other uncle was Zanu-Ndonga. And my cousin-sister, the eldest of my cousins, was what was then Zimbabwe Democratic Party.

But though they supported different factions, there was a feeling of family unity at Independence. Everyone would come with his or her T-shirt. We knew that outside the family people would clash—there were skirmishes around Chinhoyi when UMC met Zanu-Ndonga, for instance—but in the family there was harmony. We would enjoy our meals together. We would know so-and-so's sister is not here today—she has gone to attend a *pungwe*. Bishop Muzorewa would come on a Friday and people would spend the whole night—you could call it a vigil—in Chinhoyi stadium, till Saturday morning. So we would know our cousin-sister is not here today, because she has gone to a rally. Ambuya is not here today, she's at the Zanu office. And our uncle is at his Zapu office. See?

At Independence, the first difference I saw in Nyanga was that the school reopened, St. Peter's Zvarabuda, the Anglican primary school. There was peace now in Nyanga. It was safe. Most of the teachers who had run away returned.

After finishing primary school in Nyanga, I went to boarding school at Hartzell, at Old Mutare Mission. I met a lot of different people there, some from as far afield as Bulawayo. We even had Zambians coming to our school, and students from Botswana. Some teachers came from America because Hartzell is a United Methodist center.

During this time, I witnessed what Zanu-PF can do. We had a printing press at Hartzell to print our school magazines, journals, yearbooks, and exams. But then the Methodist press was accused of supporting Bishop Muzorewa, who is a Methodist. Finally it was closed and the press was sold to the *Manica Post* newspaper. Also, Zanu-PF youths used to come and terrorize our matron, accusing her of being a Muzorewa person. When I was still doing Form 1, they used to come to our high school and disturb our evening study time by calling for a rally in Beit Hall. They would gather all the students. They wanted us to vote, but we didn't.

I am talking of 1983, 1984. That was the time when the Fifth Brigade[4] was being trained in Nyanga by the North Koreans. When I went home for holidays, we used to meet some of the North Koreans. It was only later we found out what the Fifth Brigade were doing in Matabeleland. So even from my schooldays, I wanted change in the country because I could see that something was going wrong.

I did enjoy senior school, though. I wrote my O-Levels at Hartzell and then I went to stay with my uncle, my mother's brother, and studied at Mutare Boys High. I managed to write the A-Level exams, but the results were not good. That's why I don't like to talk about them very much.

ZUM AND NEXT ARREST

At school, I got to know Edgar Tekere.[5] He was my senior at Hartzell. He was a friendly person, free with everyone. We used to visit him and enjoy his opaque beer. And then, after school but well before I went to Cuba, I became involved in the party he formed in 1990, the Zimbabwe Unity Movement (ZUM). I was one of the first people to sell ZUM cards in Chinhoyi. Chinhoyi was a no-go area for ZUM, while Mutare was Tekere's base, where people knew him.

One time, I took a back seat in a combi with a colleague, moving from a suburb called Chikonohono into Chinhoyi town, enjoying our opaque beer in the back seat. We started discussing politics. At the time there was a nurses' strike, so we were just commenting on that. And as a result, I was detained under the State of Emergency. We hadn't realized that there was an operative, a CIO, right there in the combi.

---

[4] A unit of the Zimbabwe Defence Force deployed to Matabeleland against the "dissidents" during Gukurahundi. See Section 2, "Matabeleland."

[5] A leading figure in Zanu in Mozambique and in the early days of Independence, Edgar Tekere left the party and formed the short-lived Zimbabwe Unity Movement.

I spent a week in solitary confinement at Chinhoyi Central Police Station. They didn't charge me. But I was in the cells and *alone* the whole time. They didn't beat me. They'd come and pick me any time, to interrogate me. They wanted to know my involvement with Edgar Tekere. The first two days, it was terrible. But it hardened me to some extent. I began to get used to it.

The guy from PISI,[6] the guy who took me, he's still alive. But now he's my friend. He has left the police force and he is now doing discos and other things. I even joined with him in doing discos, when I was heavy in the MDC. He used to joke about what happened back in 1990 when I was in solitary confinement. They would come at midnight when I was about to sleep and then they would start asking me all of a sudden, *Do you know Edgar Tekere?* and I would say, *I don't know him. I was just commenting on the nurses' strike, that's all.*

CUBA

I had always dreamed of being an electrician, like my father. But as time went on I began to change. In fact, it's only now that I have realized that dream, as I move into IT work. My parents didn't have enough money to send me to college, mostly because there were too many of us—seven kids, and I was the eldest. So by the time I needed the money for studies, my father was also looking after my young brothers, that's where his cash was concentrated. He was brave—I like my father for that. Five of us went to boarding school despite his meager salary.

When I finished school, I didn't get a job then and there. I tried my luck at a teachers' college. But I was beginning to resent authority, I was becoming sort of an anarchist. Quitting teachers' college seemed like a good idea. I started doing odd jobs here and there, and then, ironically, some teaching. I would teach at home—O-level mathematics—and some-

---

[6] Police Internal Security Investigations. See Zenzele's narrative for more on PISI.

times at a secondary school. The fact of not having completed my teaching studies always haunted me, made me feel inadequate. But I turned out to be a good teacher. The class was full of moderates. Not very bright, not dull either. But I produced quite a number of As, more than in the bright class. There was a bright teacher and his bright students, but here was a moderate teacher and his moderate students with sixteen As out of a class of thirty-four.

I was beginning to actually like school and to get interested in philosophy. The first philosophy book I read at that time was a Christian handbook on communism. That book influenced me. I began to read more about democracy, more about American history, Plato, the classics—Socrates was one of my favorites. That was when I met Bertrand Russell. I mean, I met his ideas.

In 1991, when I was twenty-one, I went to Cuba. This is how it happened. I was visiting an uncle and I decided to go and buy tomatoes and prepare lunch for myself. That's when I saw an advert for opportunities to train as a teacher in Cuba on the piece of newspaper that the old lady used to wrap the tomatoes. I responded to the ad and I was accepted. First I did four months of Spanish language classes with Cubans in Chinhoyi.

There were quite a lot of people from Africa in Cuba, a lot of refugees. At that time South Africa was still waging their independence war, so we had South Africans and Namibians, Congolese, not from the DRC but the other Congo. And a majority of Angolans, many Zimbabweans, many Ghanaians, a few Libyans, a few Nigerians, quite a lot of Koreans and Mozambicans, Venezuelans, Nicaraguans. We had a good time. It was not all Marxism. That was in about 1992, after the Soviet Union fell and Cuba was plunged into economic difficulties. There were no medicines and no electricity because the electricity in Cuba relies on imported fuel—they don't have hydroelectric power like we do.

I started to think that Marxism would not work for Zimbabwe. Actually, we didn't have any real Marxists. Our leaders called themselves Marxists, but I began to question what sort of philosophy they were following, because that was about the same time that ESAP was being introduced—the Economic Structural Adjustment Program.[7]

I thought Castro was wrong in following Marxism to the letter. There are, though, other tenets in his doctrine which I believed would suit us well in Zimbabwe. But I remember falling for what the South Americans called "liberation theology." It seemed to be somewhere in the middle. And I liked that—not to be extremist.

THE OPPOSITION

By 1999 I was back home and working as a fitter machinist in Chinhoyi. At that time, I started to be involved in unionism and the constitution thing. I was in the engineering workers' committee at the company, attending meetings of the Zimbabwe Congress of Trade Unions, and then of the National Constitutional Assembly, and then eventually the Movement for Democratic Change. I was part and parcel of the MDC when it was formed in 1999.

I used to travel with a colleague who worked for Guard-Alert, a security company, driving to places like Kariba, Chegutu, and Karoi. I would take the opportunity to explain to whoever else was getting a ride in the car that a party was being formed. At that time the name MDC did not exist yet, but the party was emerging out of the work of the NCA and other groups. I was interested in the idea of democracy in general, where citizens are allowed to be individuals without interference from the state. I had seen there was too much interference. Up to now, as an individual in Zimbabwe, you are not left alone to be yourself, to develop your potential. I thought that this new party, with the idea of people participating in their own governance, was the right way to escape from the jaws of this oppressive regime.

I was involved quite deeply in the MDC in Chinhoyi, in community

---

[7] To qualify for International Monetary Fund loans, Zimbabwe had to cut subsidies, charge citizens for health services and schooling, and cut tariffs on imports.

outreach. A friend and I used to drive by car during the night to distribute flyers and talk with some of the headmen, the local leaders in rural areas. The ideas of the MDC appealed to them at first, but when Zanu-PF started terrorizing people, some of them took a back step and withdrew. But many of them remained involved. Because I was employed as a fitter machinist, I would do most of these activities over the weekend and at night.

At first this kind of involvement was easygoing, but in early 2000 things started to deteriorate. First the elections were scheduled for February, but then they were postponed to June, and that's when a lot of violence began.

There was not much violence in the urban areas of Chinhoyi in 2000, but on the outskirts and all over Mashonaland West, there was lots of violence. In Chinhoyi town, I could wear my T-shirt freely, but in Harare and other places, you could not put on an MDC T-shirt at that time.

I was now in the provincial youth leadership, and we started forming committees to defend ourselves. We called them reaction units. Because most MDC guys had crossed the floor from Zanu-PF to MDC, we knew the tactics that Zanu-PF was likely to employ. Sometimes we were lucky, and we would get word that Zanu-PF was planning to attack so-and-so's house, so we would be there and stand guard. Sometimes they would come and we would repel them. We were armed with stones, catapults, sticks, anything. Bottles. At that time petrol bombs were not being used much. It was only after 2001, 2002, that we had lots of petrol bombs all over the country.

After that election in 2000, I felt cheated. I felt now was the time to finish this. I had been harboring ill feelings against this regime for quite a long time. But even at my parents' house, it was very difficult to convince my mother and father that this old man Mugabe is a dictator. They used to think highly of him: *You know, he is the best in Africa—he is the best the world over. He is getting prizes.* But I was warning them: *This old man is going to run this country down. Like Kaunda has done to Zambia and Nyerere has done to Tanzania.* But they still had blinders over their eyes.

REMAND

I was motivated to become more involved because there was a presidential election coming in 2002. As early as July 2000, we started planning and working hard for those elections. I was now employed full time by the MDC, getting a salary as security officer for Mashonaland West Province. I was instrumental to some extent in the formation of the security department for MDC at the national level.

I did a lot of research on the internet and in books to learn more about surveillance, about what intelligence is, and what information gathering is. A paper I produced in 2000 about intelligence got me into trouble. I put my ideas in writing and forwarded a copy to the party head office. Everyone was trying to look at how we could improve our security. My paper was a good contribution, I can say. But a copy of it leaked to the CIO and they arrested me again in 2001. I was in Chinhoyi at the time. They came and picked me up at my home with a copy of the document. I never denied that I was the author.

They wanted to know where I got information about some of the things I mentioned. These guys were convinced that I was somehow connected to the CIO because I wrote about things they were actually being taught at the CIO school in Goromonzi.

But I had done my research independently, without even thinking of the CIO. I wanted to know what intelligence is. I went on the Internet to see what the CIA were doing and the U2—that's the Cuban intelligence service. Those were my sources. And Ken Flower, this former Rhodesian chief intelligence officer—I had a copy of his book.[8] And one about MI16 in Britain, and one by a former CIA director, I forget his name. I had bought them from secondhand bookshops. So, fortunately, I had references. They were beating me, torturing me, but I stood my ground, telling them I never got this information from the CIO, nor from the

---

[8] Head of the Rhodesian CIO. See Samuel's narrative about the Rhodesian CIO's role in setting up Renamo in Mozambique.

CIA—the information is there on the Internet.

They would come to me at any time they felt like, take me out of the cell and start to interrogate me. When they didn't get much, they would beat me. I was being beaten under the foot and given electric shocks. They would make me dip my feet in a small pond and then they would turn on a switch to send an electric shock in the water. And waterboarding. They would take me to the river and dip me. Some of those ideas I had researched actually helped me at that time. I was interested in how to resist torture, and I had practiced things like deep breathing, so I could hold my breath underwater for a long time.

At first they scared me when they told me that they would make me disappear, telling me about all those stories about Rashiwe[9] and all those people they killed. *So it can happen to you, because no one knows you are here*, they said. And at first, it's true, the party didn't have much information of my whereabouts. One lady had seen when I was picked up. They warned her: *You have seen nothing!* But she later released the information to others. *People who looked like CIOs or police officers have taken Lovemore. But why they took him I don't know.*

I was held in custody for about three weeks. I managed to convince them that the information was not leaked out of the CIO—telling them about the books I had read—but it took time for them to release me, because of the bosses they were consulting. I was only released when the bosses were convinced.

This was the third or fourth time I was arrested, but my first time to be in Remand Prison. When I was released, my health had deteriorated. I was thinking too much. So I was thin. I could walk, but I was still feeling sore under the feet. I was taken to hospital and I recovered after some time. That was at the end of 2001. Psychologically, I was feeling bad.

---

[9] Romantically linked to a senior CIO official, Guzha disappeared in 1990, and state security forces are believed to have been involved in her abduction. She has since been presumed dead and, despite public protestation, her case has not been pursued by Mugabe's government and is infamous in Zimbabwe.

I would think that I wanted to see the guy who took me. I knew what he looked like. And I wanted to fix him, or set my boys on him. That was what I was thinking at that time: *These people who are harassing me, their time will come.*

ATTACKED

I continued to work with the MDC. The CIO now knew my ideas, so I had to re-strategize some things. But I continued. I was arrested twice in 2001.

One day, I remember, a group of us visited a drinking hole called Gwai-Gwai. While we were enjoying our beer there, a notorious Zanu-PF gang called Top Six came and attacked us. I was attacked with a knife deep into the spine.

On another occasion, in November 2001, we were taking a provincial leader to Mutorashanga in the party vehicle. When we arrived in Banket, we learned that there had been skirmishes there the previous day. The Zanu-PF Top Six were again terrorizing people. People were relieved when they saw us arriving in the party truck. *Salvation has arrived. Guys have come from Chinhoyi to avenge on our behalf what happened yesterday.* That was the next time I was arrested. At gunpoint. We were put in the cells. No food. No communications with the outside world.

My parents didn't know. My father was still alive that time. That was a month before he died. He was sick, he needed to be operated on. I had promised, *I am going to take you to Harare to the doctor.* I had arranged everything. But the operation was delayed because I was detained. In a way, it contributed to his death.

We thought we were going to be released, but they signed the warrant for further detention. So I spent two weeks in Remand Prison together with some other colleagues.

This time was different. I was not alone with criminals around me. There were fourteen of us this time. We could discuss things together, because they had arrested myself, who was the security guy, they arrested the guy who was our coordinator, they had arrested the chairman, the provincial chairman was with us, and the chairlady. They had the party driver, and some of the guys who accompanied us were in the party structures. So we could organize matters.

We were not interrogated that time. There was no sense in them doing that. They were accusing us of a crime we had not committed, so they didn't have any reason to interrogate us. The previous time they'd had the document and wanted more from me.

Because the chairman was diabetic, they treated him fairly well. He was in his room on his own and we would visit him there. We played cards during the day for the two weeks until we were released on bail.

Fortunately I was out when my father died. I saw my father for a few days before he passed away. I didn't see him enough. And that was that. We buried him. My other MDC colleagues were with me. It was raining. We buried him in Chinhoyi cemetery. It was hard, I do admit, but I had grown a thick skin by that time. Remember, I had been stabbed twice, and in Remand Prison twice. Soon after we buried my father, I went straight back into the trenches with the other guys because there was an election coming in March 2002. I didn't have any time for my family. We were working hard and we wanted to finish. Because we were encouraged by the fifty-seven seats the MDC won in 2000.

VIOLENCE

I was focused, but feelings of loss were ever-present with me. We were waiting for the day; we kept on promising each other that the day is going to come. I even said to Morgan Tsvangirai [10] when he was touring our office, *When you win, we want a week or two. We want revenge.* Those feelings were always with me, and they were building. I was feeding them, and also acting on them.

There was lots of violence in 2002, unlike in 2000. I couldn't move

---

freely from my place of residence to work—I had to use alleys to reach the office. Combis were hijacked and people were forced to go and beat others. They would just get into the combi and say, *All of you get down. Please beat this one. He is MDC. Beat him!* or they would take you take from the combi to a house and say, *Stone this house. There are the stones.* And they would stand behind you. We knew there were plain-clothed soldiers among the militias and the Green Bombers because—remember, I was in the security department—we had infiltrated Zanu-PF. We had sent some of our colleagues who were not well known as MDC to join Zanu-PF, be part of Zanu-PF, and give us information. If they got the chance to be in a meeting or hear from their superiors, they would feed us the information and we would sift it and see: *Is this true? If this is true, how are we going to react?*

Sometimes I would decide, *No, I am not going anywhere today, I am staying at home.* I had a party cell phone at that time. I would get calls and I would arrange things from home. I would phone the driver, phone the youth, send them out for reaction or to go and rescue somebody.

During my tenure as a security officer, I had to do horrible things. I would go and retrieve the decomposing bodies of colleagues who were murdered. No one else wanted to do it. At that time I was still drinking, so I just made sure I had enough beer. The driver was also a drunkard. Then I would ask who was courageous enough to go with me. When they saw that I was ready to go, I would get enough youths to go with me. Maybe our presence scared those Zanu-PF guys: *Ha, they've got guns!* In fact we had nothing. I don't remember actually throwing a stone myself at a Zanu-PF mob, but I would shout: *Go into them!* and they would start running away. Perhaps they thought I had a gun.

We went to Makonde in a truck we nicknamed "The Green Bomber" because it was green in color and they ran away as we arrived. They left the MDC guys who were injured and we took them to hospital. Another time in Chitombo, another body, a former spirit medium who had been murdered. By the time I arrived there, he was already dead. They had used picks and thick steel and iron bars. It was sordid.

So they were aware that I was driving in that truck. I would escape injury by staying at home, I would escape arrest. They'd be looking for me everywhere—they'd visit my parents, go to my friend's place, everywhere. And all the time I was at home.

That's how it was, the whole of 2001, 2002, 2003. Until I left the MDC anyway. That's how I survived. They thought I had gone to South Africa but I was just sleeping at home! I never went far. They would look for evidence of my presence, but I was using some of the tricks they use themselves. I would make sure I left everything as it was. If I cooked something I made sure I didn't use my own pots. I would borrow pots and plates, without touching mine. I would try to make the bed as it was. Throw papers on top of the cover as they were before. So they were convinced that I was not there.

One time I was actually still in the house when they arrived. I had locked my door and given the key to the landlord and I was about to leave when they came. I rushed into the landlord's daughter's quarters and straight into bed. They were given the keys and they went into my room. I could actually hear them talking to their boss on the walkie-talkie. *We are at his place, but he is not here.* That was the time when the Zanu-PF office were bombed and my colleague was arrested and in their custody. I was busy arranging for lawyers and things while I was outside.

TREASON

I handed myself over to the police after they detained my young brother. That was in 2003. They detained my young brother in order to get me. So I went and turned myself in. They held him in custody for three days while I was arranging clandestinely for lawyers for everybody else who was locked up. Most of the arrested were office-bearers within the MDC. I was the only one left from the administration side. So I ran around during the night making payments to lawyers and then gave myself up through the lawyer.

They held on to my brother until then. They had set a police dog on him because they wanted him to confess where I was. But he didn't know. At that time I made sure that even my mother, even my girlfriend didn't know how I was going about things. I'd just tell them, *I'm off*, not tell them where to. One time they terrorized my girlfriend but she didn't know where I was. Had she known she would have told them, because they set a dog on her and assaulted her. But none of those people knew. I would visit them and they would be scared, but they still wanted to see me. They would prepare food for me and tell me to leave. Sometimes they would give me somewhere to sleep and I would sleep soundly. But in the early hours, around four a.m., I would always leave. Maybe go to the river and think, meditate on my next move. And I would take that next step, exactly as I had meditated, and I would be safe that way.

When I handed myself in for my brother I was held for more than a month. That was the worst, because we were in "D" class, meaning "dangerous criminals," where those who had committed rape, arson, and acts of banditry or treason are housed. I was charged with treason and held there.

It was terrible because of the length and because of what happened to me while I was there. Like before, they would come and pick us for interrogation. But some of them were good. One officer, she was a lady, would tell me what to say to her colleagues during interrogation. That would stop them beating me. *They will be searching for this information—so if you tell them this, you will convince them. So keep on sticking to this. Don't change!* she said. And I never changed. I would keep on, I would repeat. She would tell me the techniques. *They will keep on confusing you. But if you keep on repeating yourself, they will change the subject.* Another officer would smuggle in the *Daily News* for us to read. He was also a good guy.

I was sharing a cell with other dangerous criminals. But when I was taken, I was interrogated by myself. Sometimes they would beat you. Sometimes there was no beating; they pretended to be friendly to you. But I knew that. I had researched on that. They would act as friends when they wanted you to feel free and then start giving them information.

The beating was worse this time around, worse than the other time, because they were under pressure from their superiors in Harare. That affected my health to some extent. But at least we were getting enough food this time from our colleagues outside, and most of the prison guards were friendly.

The people who were doing the interrogation and beating were police officers and CIOs. And they were always the same people. They would blindfold you so you wouldn't see who was beating you. They would handcuff you with your hands behind your back. If you resisted much then they would put you in leg-irons, and they had free rein to beat you now because you could not resist. It was horrible. It was just horrible. But we were tough. Most of us, by that time, we were hardened. Because of the earlier experience we were able to offer a bit of resistance so that we would at least survive and not break down, not just give ourselves away. In the middle of your sleep, you'd hear a cell being opened and know, "The CIOs are here."

I was there for a month. I got out of there because again they didn't have any evidence against me. So we won bail, but I had to report three times a week at the nearest police station, and surrender travel documents and not move out of Chinhoyi. I did stay in Chinhoyi, but of course I used to visit my friends in Harare.

This time in prison, though, the experience had changed me. It changed how I viewed things. I didn't want to go into prison again. Of course after that I was detained some other times—maybe two days, three days—but I no longer wanted to involve myself too much. Some of the things they accused me of having done, I am innocent of. Other activists managed to skip the border to South Africa. But we didn't. We were suffering in those dungeons. It was a turning point, actually. I withdrew a little from politics after that.

TREE OF LIFE

I had started working in computers when I was arrested. When I was detained, I lost everything. The books I bought for computers, those philosophy books I had—they were all burned while I was in. The two rooms where I had been lodging were petrol-bombed. All those books and a computer, all destroyed. And a camera and letters I was keeping for sentimental value, letters from as far back as my Grade 1. Some from my father. My stamp collection from Cuba, photographs from Cuba and from Spain when I was coming back. Yeah, photographs of the beach! All those things were destroyed. My birth certificate, my ID, my school certificate. And all the things I had worked so hard for.

When I handed myself in, I was wearing *mapatapata*[11] and old grey trousers and a T-shirt. When I was released a friend bought me a pair of trousers and a blue shirt and a pair of shoes. And that was that. I had to start afresh. I went to my parents' house because most people didn't want to see me at that time. I felt I was being isolated. Unwanted. Fortunately for me, because of my ideas about meditating, I actually enjoyed being alone some of the time. But then, then there were times when it just hurt. To visit somebody, spend a few minutes with that person, and then that person starts telling you, *No, I want to go and see so-and-so. I have to do this and that. Please can you come on such-and-such a day?* You know of course that this is an escape mechanism. This person doesn't want my presence because I'm just from prison.

I became involved with the Tree of Life[12] program just after I was released, in 2004, when I was still trying to stitch my life together. Nothing was working. I was still employed by the MDC, but the money was now too little. I was called to the office for a self-reporting questionnaire screening for the Zimbabwe Torture Victims/Survivors Project. There, I was chosen to attend a workshop at the training center at Lake Chivero. That was in August. That's when I became involved with the Tree of Life.

I tried with my own philosophy, with my practice of meditation, to help myself. But the first Tree of Life workshop I attended was another turning point in my life. I liked it so much that I never wanted to leave. I went there as somebody who was damaged. I didn't feel that I could

---

[11] Flipflops.

[12] A program of healing for torture survivors through storytelling.

contribute anything. I felt myself to be useless. My colleagues didn't want to see me. You suffered for the party, but when you came out from the prison, there was no hero's welcome. With changed situations, they were looking down on you, isolating you.

Of course the economic situation had deteriorated, but after the Tree of Life workshop we managed to keep on communicating. I felt safe when I had friends.

When I stopped working with the MDC, I went back to computer engineering. I wasn't earning anything from Tree of Life—we ran the story-telling workshops as volunteers, only receiving transport reimbursements. We still hope to reach out to others. There are two sides to these workshops. When you are facilitating you are helping others. But the majority of the time, you are also helping yourself. I saw that I was actually benefiting from every workshop I did. One, the diversity of the people and what you get from the people themselves, and two—I don't know how I can describe it—the strength I still get from each workshop I run. I go out of each workshop a little bit different than I was on entering.

I am still happy here. For some time, I will still be happy. The only time I will want to leave is when I think, for my health, I have absorbed enough stories, if I feel that they are going to affect me in a bad way. But not now.

The stories do not affect me because I wake up and jog and meditate and things like that. I have seen that the more workshops I do, the heavier I feel inside myself. So I have to release, to discharge that. I jog almost every day. If I miss jogging, say, two or three days in a row, I'll be in trouble. I try to balance physical and emotional things.

SECTION 5

MOUNTAINS

MUTARE

A beautiful, sleepy town set in a bowl of hills on Zimbabwe's eastern border, Mutare has long, palm-lined boulevards. Flowers by the side of the road bloom green and pink and red and yellow, and some ten thousand succulent aloes grow in its extensive public gardens. But Mutare has seen better days. At the main intersection, the four-way stoplight dangles precariously above the street from a nest of wires. A number of roads are cratered. At Market Square at the intersection of Herbert Chitepo Street and Robert Mugabe Avenue, would-be shoppers peer into shop windows. A bookstore is selling some of the latest titles from the U.K., including a biography critical of Mugabe (for thirty American dollars) alongside dusty textbooks, circa 1983. A sign in a bank reads: *Free Funeral Coverage If You Maintain a Balance of 10,000 Rand.*

In the green hills above town, mansions loom, a number of them half finished. A small branch of the National Art Museum of Zimbabwe—rarely open—exhibits valuable and striking examples of Zimbabwe's world-famous stone sculptures, displayed unguarded around its grounds. These days there are more essential things to steal. A sign posted on a billboard in town advertises jobs for private security guards. The salary:

800 million Zimbabwe dollars per day. Roughly, in American dollars, a dollar and a half a week. And yet on Saturday night, a crowd lines up at the Rainbow Vistarama to see the American film *Streetfighter*.

Due east a few miles is the border with Mozambique and Zimbabwe's nearest ocean access, the port of Beira. Early traders came this way, East African, Arab, Portuguese, Indian. When neighboring Mozambique gained independence in 1975, thousands of Zimbabweans headed over the nearby Bvumba mountains to join Zanu and train as guerillas in the bases there. This was the route that President Mugabe took out of the country after his release from Rhodesian prison in 1975. Guerrilla groups crossed back into the country through gaps in the mountains to mobilize support in the rural areas and to launch military attacks.

For all that it plays such a key role in Zimbabwe's liberation narrative, Mutare also gives the lie to ideas of national purity, ethnic uniformity and political consensus—the "unity" that politicians like to evoke when it suits them. In the town itself and up and down the eastern border, you encounter extremes, eccentricities, and exceptions. People in these mountainous borderlands are known for independent-mindedness. Take the Chipinge area for example, just south of Mutare. Firstly, the commercial coffee and tea estates here were famous for extremes of wealth, with farmers flying their own planes on weekend shopping excursions to South Africa. Then you have the Ndau-speaking spirit mediums of the Chipinge area, feared all over Zimbabwe for their potent medicines and spells. And thirdly, on the political front, Chipinge has always had an independent spirit when it comes to voting. For instance, the area voted Zanu-Ndonga[1] in the 1980s, when every other seat went to Zanu-PF or Zapu.

These days, Mutare tends to hit the headlines for a different set of reasons. From the mid-2000s and on, gold discovered on the Mozambican side of the mountains has drawn Zimbabwean panners and miners in the thousands. Then in 2006, diamonds were discovered in Marange, a

---

[1] An early opposition party, formed as a result of a split with the original Zanu party.

desolate communal area outside Mutare.[2] Research for this book brought us to Mutare a few months after the government and military had moved in to take control of the billion-dollar diamond fields. In laid-back cafes and township homes, people often said, *Ah, you should have been here when the diamond dealers took over the town...*[3]

---

[2] See Briggs's narrative.

[3] See Celia Dugger, "Diamond Find Could Aid Zimbabwe, and Mugabe," *New York Times*, June 21, 2010

SAMUEL

AGE: *34*

OCCUPATION: *Security guard, former farmworker and wood sculptor*

INTERVIEWED IN: *Mutare, Zimbabwe*

High above Mutare, a newish subdevelopment of large modern houses has been built into a lush hillside. The houses sit behind high walls, electric fencing, and are protected by dogs—and men. Nightly (from sunset to sunrise), Samuel walks the perimeter of one of these houses, listening for the noise of intruders. For a number of years Samuel provided security for a large white-owned coffee farm. After the farm was seized by war veterans, Samuel found a job with a security firm in Mutare. Each night he is sent to a different house in Mutare and to towns nearby. As he could not support his family with that job alone, he recently took on a second one during the daytime hours. Like so many other Zimbabweans who must work far from home, Samuel does not live with his family on a day-to-day basis. Samuel patrols with a German shepherd named Shaka on a leash and a rifle slung over his left shoulder. This interview was conducted, after midnight, in the garage of the house Samuel was protecting that night. Occasionally, Shaka barked during the interview, setting off other dogs in the neighborhood, but there were no other disturbances that night. Samuel began his story by talking about his father who was abducted when Samuel was young to fight in the civil war in Mozambique, never to be seen again. No matter the difficulties, Samuel is determined to be there for his own children.

My father went to war across the border in Mozambique in 1979. In the Burma Valley[1] there was a place called Mountain Lodge; that's where he was taken by the Matsangaise soldiers to fight against the government of Mozambique.[2] He was taken while he was working in the fields.

Years later, it was announced that the soldiers who had gone with Matsangaise were coming back. My father wrote a letter saying, *I'm coming home so buy a cow to feast.* He was in Maringe in Mozambique when he wrote that letter. Maringe is past Manica and past Chimoio, very very far from here. He wrote a letter and also sent us a picture of his new wife and family. After that, time went by.

Some people in our area came back, but he didn't. The war took him.

I have no idea if my father is still alive. I was very young when he disappeared, but I remember him, I know him. I would recognize him if I ever see him again.

My name is Samuel. I was born in 1976 in Mutare. In my family we are ten: six boys and four girls, all still alive. We all have the same father, same mother. I am the ninth born. The first born in my family is a girl; she is married and lives in the Chikurura area. She was followed by a boy, who is in Mozambique at the moment. He lives in a village there and has a family. He is a chef. Then a girl, who is married and is in Zimbabwe; she also has a family. Then a boy, who lives in Chigodora area called Chishamba; he works at Bikerama here in Mutare. He makes motorbikes. Another brother stays at Whitehorse Inn[3] and works there. He is a cook. My family sees each other. When I'm off work I go to visit them, and some of my brothers and sister also come to visit me at home. The one in Mozambique also comes to visit. When he comes he brings along clothes and fish to sell.

---

[1] Valley on the border of Zimbabwe and Mozambique.

[2] Samuel's father was, apparently forcibly, recruited by RENAMO forces led by André Matsangaise. RENAMO, the Mozambican National Resistance, was initially formed by Rhodesian intelligence and military. The resulting civil war in Mozambique claimed an estimated one million lives and uprooted many more, including Samuel's father.

[3] A hotel in the Bvumba Mountains near Mutare.

I went to Mutare primary school in Bvumba. When I finished my primary education, I went to Chitakatira. Chitakatira is in Chigodora. Just after Bvumba, coming this way, there's an area called Chigodora. There's a primary and secondary school there, and that is where I did my secondary school education, form 1 to 4. By the time I finished school in 1994, I already had a wife. She was at the same school as me.

I have three children. My first son is Moses. He was born in 1994 on the 26th of February. The second born is Memory, she was born in 1996. Another girl called Annia was born in 2001. Annia was born in Matengambiri. From here, heading toward Nyanga road near Manica Bridge, there is an area called Matengambiri. That's where my last daughter was born. All my children are going to school.

Right now my family is living in Buwerimwe, that's where I come from. Buwerimwe is in Chigodora, in Zimunya Communal Area. That's where they are right now, on the farm.

My place is about three hectares. It's a big place. The only problem is that there are a lot of rocks, but I have huge plowing space. My wife plows the field. The soil is red, but in some places it is also white. You do well on some of it and not on the other. People who live in Buwerimwe don't go hungry because they help each other. When I leave this security job in the morning, I will be going home to my farm for one day.

Then I'll come back to town for work.

SCULPTING WOOD

After leaving school, I met a white man called Stewart. This white man taught carpentry. He knew how to use the machines. When he saw me, he said, *Don't you want a job?* I said, *I do. I'm good with my hands and I can sculpt wood.* He said, *I'd like you to work using this machine cutting wood.* I said *Okay.*

I'd make things like rabbits and other animals out of wood. Stewart started teaching me to use a machine called a wood miser. It can cut wood as long as seven meters. It cuts all the way to the end and back. We sculpted a lot of wood, and he ended up hiring trucks and we would load them and send them to Harare and other places to sell the sculptures. I worked with him for two years. What happened was that he decided to move somewhere far away, and it was impossible for me to move with my family.

While I was not working, another white man called Peter Hall, a coffee farmer in the area, asked me to work for him. He wanted me to scout the coffee to see if there are pests in the coffee bushes destroying the coffee leaves. When there were a lot of pests, he'd spray. When the coffee grew and multiplied, it was ready for us to mix it together and put it into holes where it would stay for three or four days. Then it would be cleaned, dried in shelves, and heated with electricity. When dry, it would then be taken to Harare.

I worked in the coffee fields for three years. After that, the farmer told me he wanted the farm watched over. He said, *I want to teach you how to be a security guard.* I said *Okay.* At a place called Burma Valley, there was a ZRP[4] camp. I went there and spent twenty-one days learning about security. There were 150 of us training to be guards. Some came from Nyazura and other places. Every farm in the area sent a man to learn security. When I finished, I was given a certificate and a uniform.

When I went back, Peter Hall said, *I want you to take care of this place, overseeing and overlooking everything.* I said *Okay.*

So I started working security. I worked security for quite a long time.

LAND REFORM

In 2004, the land reform program was introduced in our area. There were land invasions. One day they came while I was working and said, *We have taken this farm, so you can't work here. Everyone who is here should go back where they came from.* It was the war veterans' association who said that. I thought, *I no longer have a job.* Then Peter Hall said, *I'm leaving.* He gave

---

[4] Zimbabwe Republican Police.

us all money for the work we did and gave us reference letters. Then the white man left his property.

There were about five hundred people working at the farm. Some people scattered. Others stayed working on the farm. As you can guess, the new owners wanted to find out what the place was like, how the underground pipes worked, etc. After the war veterans received all the information then those workers who had stayed left also.

SAFEGUARD

When I left the farm, I went into Mutare and starting looking for work with security companies. I found this job at Safeguard Security. I started working in 2006. Up to now, I'm still working for Safeguard.

Security is all about taking care of everything at the place you work, you know, making sure all is well. Let's take for example a fence. You have to make sure that it has not been cut or anything. After checking the fence, I also always check the taps in the yard. If there's a running tap, I turn it off. If there are lights that need to be switched on, I switch them on. I check the cars. We have a book, the OB, where we put down all our records in case something gets stolen. That's how we do our work. OB means occurrence book. We write everything that happens on the premises during work. When we leave in the morning, we also write down the time we leave in case something happens after.

The amount of money I'm earning, though, is not enough for me to manage to pay rent, electricity, water etc. When we were still using Zim dollars it was harder. Now we are using American dollars and South African rand. You need smaller amounts. It's better, and if this carries on it will be good because you know that at the end of the month you can at least plan to buy something—as long as you still have your job.

Another problem is that I stay in one place, and my family stays in another. Before Safeguard, my family stayed all at the same place. But now I can be moved to another place at any time. It means my bag is always packed. I don't know which place I'll go. When I worked as a private security guard on the farm, I was always based at the same place with my family. That's the big difference. Now I don't see them very often.

Not long ago, I met a man called Chinodya. He came to Safeguard asking for a security guard who would stay at his house during the day and also work as a gardener. Water and electricity provided. I decided to take the job and live there. Chinodya works as an officer at Dulux. He uses a company car to go to work. He is living well. He has chickens which he keeps at his place and sells. He doesn't pay me, but I stay there without paying rent. I cut the lawn, take care of the garden and the chickens. That's the way it is.

I go to work from Chinodya's place and return there in the morning. I do piece jobs and sleep until twelve. Then I feed the chickens. Except tomorrow. Tomorrow I am having a day off and am going to see my family. Tomorrow is a day I will see my family.

BRIAN

AGE: *14*

OCCUPATION: *School student, informal trader*

INTERVIEWED IN: *Mutare, Zimbabwe*

Brian attends a support group for HIV-positive children and teenagers at a church in the suburbs of Mutare. Technically, access to antiretroviral drugs (ARVs) is officially guaranteed by the government, but these drugs are either impossible to obtain or impossibly expensive. Some NGOs and researchers supply ARVs, but only to a few small groups. Born positive, like his brother Persistence, Brian's survival depends on keeping up with his treatment. As Brian explains, it's impossible to take the ARVs without food, and yet many Zimbabweans are forced to go without meals during this economic crisis. Operation Murambatsvina—a government cam-paign to destroy unplanned houses and stalls in urban areas that left thousands, possibly millions homeless—left Brian's family even less secure.

Today I woke up early to go to the market to sell. I do some vending there. After that, I went back home, took a bath, and came right here. My mother has a stall at the market. We sell tomatoes and vegetables there, and some macaroni and spaghetti that my mum gets for sale. It's not enough for bills, rent, and school fees, but it gives us some income. I'm very good with my customers, and most of them are very fond of me, so they keep buying from me. I can convince them to buy. That's how

I generate my sales. Sometimes, I make US $2 or $3 on a Saturday, and my big sales will be around $5 for the whole morning.

We face some problems at Sakubva market.[1] At times, the municipal police chase us away. We don't have a legal selling area because our names were not written down. There was a lot of corruption about registering vendors. We couldn't find a place so we just sell anywhere but if they catch us, they will fine us $20. They caught me once. I was about take my stuff and run away, but I had not noticed that there was a policeman behind me, and he caught me. At the police station, a policewoman said, *This one is just a small kid*, and told me to go home. They took a bit of my stuff, saying they would give it to their bosses if they were asked. They let me take the rest. The other guys that were caught, some of them spent two weeks in jail. This other man who sold with me—he sold soap and sugar—he was caught and his stuff was taken. When we went back to sell, he was still in jail.

A HOUSE FOR MY MOTHER

I was born in Sakubva in 1996. Most of the time I grew up with my mother. My father is dead. My mother treats me very well. I love her. We stay in a four-room house, but we only rent two rooms, half the house. I'm sharing with my sister. Her name is Madonna. She's nine years old, in Grade 3, and she's light in complexion.

What makes me happy is that we are together as a family. If there's little food, we all share it.

A long time ago, my mother used to work for whites as a maid. When I grow up, I want to buy a house for her. I want to be an accountant like my grandfather, my mother's father. He's retired now, in Rusape. I don't know my father's parents. They all died.

When I was growing up, my parents divorced. Sometime after the

---

[1] Sakubva is the largest and one of Mutare's oldest and poorest townships or high-density suburbs. The food and flea market, target of frequent raids by local authorities, is situated next to the busy terminus for rural buses.

divorce, my father passed away. Before he died, he worked on the train as a conductor and a controller. He was hit by a train when he was thirty-six. I was very young then. Sometimes I used to go on the train with him. When I think of my dad, I look at the photos on our walls. There's one where it's dark and he's by the railway line, controlling a train. I really like that one.

PERSISTENCE

I had a brother, but he is dead. He had a heart problem. He passed Grade 7[2] and went on to Boys' High. But in Form 2, his heart problem worsened, and he passed away last year. His name was Persistence. I miss him. Sometimes he would sell sweets so that we could find money to ride the combi to get to school. I often didn't have any money for the ride, but he would always share with me.

My brother, I loved him very much.

When Persistence died, I was with him. Our mother was not there, she had traveled to Mozambique to buy goods to sell. That's when his heart problem flared up, and that's when he passed away. My mother returned, but what could she do? He had already died while she was away. I was there. And my grandmother.

My mother is still very sad about my brother's death. She got counseling from Sister Nancy here at the church, and she was encouraged. We come to this same church on Sunday, from nine a.m. to six p.m. We pray, and Pastor is singing, and we have activities. Like how Jesus healed the blind man and the disabled people.

YOU CAN'T TAKE ARVs WITHOUT FOOD

When I started taking my ARV medication, people used to laugh at me

---

[2] The last year of primary school.

for being HIV-positive. I became ashamed of it, and stopped taking my ARVs. Other times, we would stop taking our medication because we didn't have food. If you take the ARVs with no food, it will make you sweat and feel very, very weak, so I don't take them without food. We came here to the church for prayer, and we also received food. Since then, we haven't stopped taking our medication—things are a bit better now. I am strong now.

Sometimes we go to the rural areas for the holidays, to stay with my grandmother and grandfather, the accountant. Sometimes, there is no food at their place because they have difficulties with the crops and droughts, and so we don't get anything to eat there.

Before my father died, we stayed at Dangamvura[3] and we went to school by combis, but now we don't. Plus, we sometimes go to bed without eating. When my father was alive, we would never go without food. Our problems now, as a family, are paying school fees, food, and rent. If you can't gather the money for rent, you find yourself with no place to live. And there are other things that are affected by this, even going to school. If the rent goes up, it might mean you can't go to school, or get books for school. Rent is $35 per week, and school fees are $20 per term for me and $20 for Madonna.

HISTORY, FISH, FOOTBALL

I go to Mutanda Primary in Sakubva and I am in Grade 7. I believe I am doing quite well. The last time we had our exams I was eighth in the whole school among Grade 7s. I like English best, English, and maths. That's why after I finish school I want to be an accountant.

Our headmaster is called Mr. Mudede. Our school was built in 1954. At the moment it looks a bit worn out, but when you are inside you'll see that it's beautiful and the people are friendly. Our teacher is Mrs. Chitsva.

---

[3] Another Mutare township.

She's an old lady. We're forty-two students in our class, and there are five classes of Grade 7. The number in the class depends on the number of people who are intelligent. For example, if there are a lot of intelligent people, there will be a lot of them in Grade 7A.

I'm in 7A, and next year I want to go to Mutare Boys High. That's where my brother went. If he were here we would be going together. They have good activities there, and also they may help you in the future. Plus, you can see that the pupils there have great ideas, unlike those from Sakubva High, who smoke marijuana.

There's a library at our school, so during our spare time that's where we go and read books about Zimbabwe's history. It's interesting to me, what used to happen in the past in Zimbabwe. As compared to what I've read, what's happening right now isn't fun. The history of Shaka and Nehanda[4] was much more interesting.

When I'm with my friend Owen, we focus on our studies when at school, but when we're at home we play a lot. We are like brothers. When we're walking from school, we ask each other test questions that might come up in the Grade 7 exam. It's about five kilometers from Sakubva High to Moffat. I walk every day. If you have money you can take combis, but for us who are poor, we just have to walk.

After school, I get home and play a little bit of football. Then I cook *sadza*[5] for the whole family. My sister is still too young to cook, so most of the time I'm the one who helps my mother. My mom usually cooks dried fish. I know how to cook it too. It's easy. When your cooking oil gets hot, you can just throw it in. It already has salt in it.

In Zimbabwe I support Dynamos, but in the world I support

---

[4] Shaka: legendary Zulu king. Nehanda: the 1890s medium of her spirit was executed for her leading role in the 1896 uprising against the British South Africa Company (the First Chimurenga), while her more recent embodiment inspired guerrillas of the Second Chimurenga, the 1960s and '70s war of liberation leading to Zimbabwe's independence in 1980.

[5] See footnote 5, page 31.

Manchester. I used to like Cristiano, but he's no longer on the team. I watched a game on TV once, when Manchester played against Chelsea. Manchester lost and I was very upset.

TOO MUCH POLITICS

When Murambatsvina[6] happened in 2005, we were living in the Singles.[7] That's like another location.[8] I was in Grade 2. The house we lived in was a shack. In the Singles, there would be a main house and the owner would rent out shacks at the back. Some landlords would have the house already made so a person could just arrive and move in, but my mother called a carpenter to make one for us, with one window. Those with cement can lay a floor. We shared that shack, me, my brother, and my mother. My sister was in the rural areas with my grandmother then. That's where we stayed until Murambatsvina came.

The government decided that shacks like ours should be removed. If you built your house on illegal grounds, your house was destroyed. Policemen and soldiers removed them. They burned the shacks if you didn't remove them quickly enough. Even the wood you used would be destroyed. That time was hard. We got help because if we took too long, our wood was going to be burned. Another car from the municipality moved around spraying stuff that made you feel itchy. Even if you took a bath you could not remove it. If you were found by the police scratching, you were then beaten up. I wasn't sprayed, but I saw people being

---

[6] Literally, "drive out the rubbish/trash," officially "Operation Restore Order," this was a large-scale government campaign to clear informal market stands and housing in towns and townships all around the country. Begun in 2005 and revived several times since, it is believed to have left more than 2 million people homeless. See other narratives in this book, including Boniface's and Briggs's.

[7] Labor systems under colonial and settler governments brought men to urban areas as factory and domestic workers. Women were not officially permitted to live in cities. Housing for men was called "Singles."

[8] An old-fashioned name for formerly blacks-only townships or high density suburbs.

sprayed. After Murambatsvina, many people ended up living at the marketplace and some were mugged and killed. That's what made so many people go to the rural areas.

When it happened to us, we looked for money to take our things to Dangamvura, to my grandfather's house. My grandmother gave us permission to stay there because she's the owner. She removed one lodger so that we could stay there. After we moved in, my mom and my uncles had an argument because my uncles also wanted to stay there. My younger uncle is a problem, he can even chase my grandmother away from her own house. He takes the lodgers' money from her every month.

After the uncles made us leave, we went to Zimunya, in the rural areas. Later, we moved to the house where we live now. My mother pays the rent from selling goods in the market, and from our lodgers.

Sometimes the police stop us, interrogate us, and ask what party we belong to. Even me, they stop me and ask me. I remember when we were asked to go and vote. They promised to pay our school fees. I wish people would stop doing party politics. I hope that Zimbabwe will become a one-party state and we will get peace. Zimbabwe is an independent country, but there is too much politics.

NICOLA

AGE: *25*

OCCUPATION: *Horticulturist, former farmer*

INTERVIEWED IN: *Mutare, Zimbabwe*

As a schoolgirl, Nicola's dream life on a large farm in Zimbabwe's Eastern High-lands was turned upside down by the land occupations in the early 2000s. Her father, the head of the powerful, and mostly white, Commercial Farmer's Union, was arrested in 2001 for the crime of remaining on his farm. After his release from prison, he promptly left Zimbabwe for Mozambique, but his two headstrong daughters—then nineteen and twenty-one—decided to remain in the country and continue to farm a small piece of land that had not been taken over. Nicola was in charge of the farming; her sister Linda managed the business side. For a while, the farm was quite successful, and the two sisters exported bananas and other produce to South Africa and the U.K. Eventually, however, this section of land was also occupied. As a young white woman attempting, on her own, to manage the day-to-day operations of a farm as Zimbabwe was torn apart by political violence—a small but significant aspect of this violence being directed at wealthy white farm-ers—Nicola's is a unique perspective. Although not living outside, Nicola's story is one of internal exile. Currently, she lives and works as a horticulturist near Mutare, where this interview was conducted. On the same evening, in a separate interview, we also spoke with Nicola's sister, Linda.

We tried to keep as much under the radar as possible. But as you can imagine, two young white girls farming here doesn't stay under the radar for very long. I think this is only an extraordinary story if you don't live here. I mean, you talk to anybody in this place and they've got a story to tell. The only reason why people find this one a little bit more unique is because we're young and we're girls—we started farming on our own in 2003 when Linda was twenty-one and I was nineteen. I think when you're nineteen, you don't see the big picture—you see your childhood and this happy life you have. You really don't get the big idea of what's going on.

I was born and raised in Burma Valley, Zimbabwe. My grandparents were from Burma Valley, my father was born in Burma Valley, so I had more of an emotional attachment than anything else. During World War II, a friend told my granddad he'd heard about this place called Southern Rhodesia that apparently had the most incredible farming in the world. That's why he came down to see what Rhodesia was all about. And he settled in Burma Valley.

Burma Valley is the most beautiful place in the world. It's hot and humid and has almost rainforest-y characteristics—beautiful rivers and raffia plants and the rarest butterflies in the world. The game and the wildlife are incredible. There's beautiful farming, and the valley is surrounded by amazing mountains full of bushmen paintings. It's a really unique place.

As a family, we moved onto our land in 1996. I went to school in Mutare very happily, and had a very fortunate childhood; I never went without anything. For somebody like me who loves the bush and the outdoors, I had it all on our doorstep, with mountains to climb, and horses, and every animal under the sun: goats, sheep, donkeys, rabbits, dogs, cats, you name it. I was a great animal lover as a child, so every birthday gift was a pet of some sort. We had the whole collection.

Burma Valley was mainly a tobacco area. Tobacco and bananas, really. My dad in his prime was probably one of the biggest early tobacco growers in the country. He got Burley Tobacco Grower of the Year a couple of times. He was a fantastic farmer—well, *is* a fantastic farmer.

TWENTY-FOUR HOURS TO LEAVE

In 2000, the land invasions started. My father was chairman of the Commercial Farmers Union at the time, which they generally thought of as a white union, because most of the commercial farmers were white. He was one of the first targets.

It started off pretty peacefully. Farmers were asked to give up patches of their land, which we did. I remember a whole section of the farm that we gave up. People slowly moved onto that land, black families. I remember my dad saying that we couldn't go horseback riding on one piece of land that we loved to ride into, because he'd given that to the government. I was fifteen at the time when it started, and I remember court cases coming up, challenging the farm occupations, but my father kept us very sheltered from all that. He'd crack the occasional comment like, *Oh, that's a war veteran or something.*[1] I didn't really pay much attention to what was going on. You don't as a teenager. Even then, we knew that all these things were going on around us, but it was one of those "that will never happen to me" kind of feelings.

I was sixteen or seventeen when they started arresting farmers and the first farmers were murdered. My dad was arrested in 2001. I couldn't even tell you the charge. I don't even know. Basically it was just a trumped-up charge. After his arrest, the other farmers came down to the farm and they said to my sister, my mom, and me: *Pack your bags, you're going now before they come after you.* They said, *Just grab valuables,* jewelry or whatever it was, and we did that and we all jumped into the car. I kept thinking, This can't be happening—not to us. You read about these things, you hear about these things, but you don't expect them to happen to you. At that point, when it first started, it sounds so unbelievable: how could people just walk into your house and take everything that you own and everything that you worked for?

---

[1] Ex-combatants and others claiming to be ex-combatants led the early land occupations. See the appendix section on war veterans and land invasions.

We were given about twenty-four hours to go. Everybody helped. Every neighbor was there with a truck loading our stuff. Everyone we knew arrived to help us move. We got everything off the farm—the horses, the animals, all of us.

We went to court so my father could get sentenced or whatever it was they were doing, and he was standing there in this box, handcuffed, and his only crime was to be a farmer. And then they said, *You have to go to jail.* Bail was denied. They put him in the prison truck, and my sister and I were standing on the corner outside the courthouse, and the prison truck drove past. They'd put him right in the front: the prisoners had to stay shackled, they had to keep their heads down, they weren't allowed to look around, and they were sitting on the floor with their knees up and their heads down. And I remember my sister, she shouted his name, she shouted *Dad!* from the corner. And as he looked up to see us, this guard hit him in the back of the head with the butt of his gun. It was like somebody had stabbed me in the stomach, seeing that, seeing my father being treated like that for no reason at all.

They kept my dad in jail for a couple of days before we could see him. When I went in to see him, there was this awful jail guard there who kept hitting on me in front of him, just to try and make my dad's stay a little more unpleasant. With the farmers being in jail, the wardens tried to wind them up to be aggressive or to misbehave, so that they'd stay in there longer. I know a lot of comments were thrown at my dad, about how they were going to go to my house, how they had my address, that sort of thing. And you know, Linda and I are Daddy's little angels—you don't say anything about us to him. So I know that was pretty horrible for him to hear because I'm sure he sat there night after night, wondering if we were okay or if people were coming to the house.

In jail, they had my dad shackled, and we had a kind of window to talk to him through. It was probably the first time I ever saw my dad cry. He's a manly, macho man—you know, cowboys don't cry. I was trying really, really hard to smile, saying, *Oh Dad, don't worry, tomorrow, you're getting out tomorrow, everything's sorted*—you know, lying through my teeth.

He was in jail for about a week.

They let him out on bail, but on the condition that he was not allowed to go to Burma Valley, and that he signed over the farm. It's not an inherited farm or anything like that. My grandfather had sold his farm and moved to South Africa when we were very young. My dad worked his whole life to be able to own a farm—he started off as a bossboy,[2] a foreman, and worked his way up to the point where he could actually afford to own his own farm. He really brought himself up, and for somebody who's worked that hard, to have everything taken away in an afternoon because he's white? It just doesn't seem right. My father basically said that he wanted nothing more to do with Zimbabwe.

FARMING SOUNDED LIKE A GOOD IDEA

They took the main farm, a couple of hundred hectares with the main house on it, and left a very small section in the valley, separated by a dam, with only forty hectares of arable land and a manager's house on it. This patch of farm would have been left to my sister and me, so therefore it was our decision what we wanted to do with it. I remember distinctly we were all at Leopard Rock Hotel, all hungover after my sister's twenty-first birthday, sitting on one of the hills that overlooks the whole valley, and we said, *No, we can't not go back to our land.* Being nineteen and twenty-one, we thought, *Well, we'll go farming.* We were both unemployed at the time. I'd just run away from a job running a restaurant, which I hated, and Linda had just come back from England, which she hated, so farming sounded like a great idea.

Initially, three of us moved onto the small piece of our farm that had not been occupied—Linda, her friend Maureen, and me. Maureen was there for six months, and then wisely moved on to better things. Linda and I stayed for another five years.

---

[2] Worker overseeing the other workers. (Not usually a white person.)

There were some other people staying in the house at the time—an elderly couple who had worked for my dad many years before and stayed on. So we rented a little A-frame cottage just down the road until we could find them another place to live. Because of the weird wiring, everything metal in this A-frame electrocuted you if you didn't have shoes on—you'd get electrocuted by the taps when you'd try and brush your teeth. It was quite an experience living there. It was a great little house, though. It had a little dam in front of it, and it was perfect to get started in. We got robbed enough times there—I remember getting back from an outing, and they'd even stolen the curtains. We didn't have much at the time, and it was funny more than anything else. After six months at the A-frame, the elderly couple moved out of the house and we moved back onto the farm.

I had a beautiful view from the house on that piece of land. We got the sunrise—it came in through my bedroom window—and the day would change to the tune of the bird life. You get morning birds, afternoon birds, evening birds, night birds—weavers and fish eagles getting up in the morning, and in the evenings the starlings and the nightjars, and then later at night you get every owl in Africa hooting outside your window.

We had incredible floods this one year, and all the crocodiles from the Chikamba river moved into our dam. Then every year during the mating season they'd come and nest in the swamps in our dam. We'd watch them without fear of being eaten. Hundreds of babies and about three or four huge mothers, just watching. And if you go there at night and you shine your torch, it's just eyes everywhere, all these eyes staring at you. At night the dam was magical: the glow bugs on the banks would look like Christmas lights.

The only car we had was this ancient, beaten-up Peugeot 504 truck that lost its doors somewhere along the way, and this was how we drove around. We named it Percy, Percy the Truck. It didn't have a starter motor so we had to start it with a piece of wire under the bonnet at five o'clock in the morning. The brakes always used to fail, so we used to have to stop every fifteen kilometers to bleed the brakes so it'd actually work. Trying to get that stupid truck anywhere, we were the laughingstock of the whole town. But that's how we used to get around.

A typical day on the farm would start between five and half-five. At that point, it was so cold, it was gloves and jeans and tracksuit pants over boots and socks, beanies and scarves and all you could see of us was our eyes, and we'd head off on our motorbike. When the Peugeot broke down we had a beat-up little 125 motorbike, which we would go to work on. The day would start with roll call, job allocation, sending the workers off on various jobs. We had about seventy people at that point working for us and living in a compound. It was always exciting, the best couple of hours in the morning: getting everyone fired up and everything sorted. Come half-past eight, it's so hot that you're down to your shorts and no shoes, vest, shirts, big hats. Knee-deep in mud and dirt and fun. It was always an adventure, always something going on there—fighting snakes and chasing monkeys and bush pigs off the land. Never a dull moment.

Before this, Linda and I hadn't had anything to do with farming as such. We both did business for A-levels[3] and accounts and things like that. But I had always tried to learn about the farming and the agronomy side of things. And I picked it up pretty quickly. Watching the things grow, the crops come to life, was always so rewarding. I figured out that it's actually perfect for me and exactly what I want to do. Right now I'm in the final year of my Bachelor's degree in horticulture, which I've done through correspondence, through the University of Zimbabwe.

By the time my sister and I moved onto the farm, tobacco had kind of crashed from all the commercial growers being *jambanja*-ed,[4] the whole deterioration of farming in the country. For tobacco to make money, you need huge hectares of it. Subsistence farmers were only doing one or two hectares, so they had to close down the tobacco floors because there just

---

[3] Final year of high school, required for entrance to university.

[4] Literally "confusion," the Shona word *jambanja* has come to mean "invaded." It's sometimes used as a verb, as in "when that farm was *jambanja*-ed."

wasn't tobacco going through there. Linda and I really picked an ideal time to go farming in Zimbabwe!

When we started, we were growing vegetables and fruit for a huge exporting company. They sent all of our produce to Tesco's and Marks & Spencers in the U.K., and Woolworths in South Africa. And we did very well off them, until a new policy came out and that company got taken over the year after we started farming. We then did a couple of seasons of tobacco, which we didn't do very well from, just because of the way things were going. Then Linda and I managed to borrow huge sums of money as outgrowers, doing bananas. Well, it was really Linda. I do the hands-on farming, and she does the marketing and the banking and deals with people and paperwork and all the things that I hate. Bananas was a way forward, the only thing that picked up with inflation, really the only way to survive. So we managed to borrow huge sums of money, and finally got our bananas planted, and we were invaded shortly after. As soon as we were about to reap, they came into our house, and that ended our farming.

EVERYTHING YOU OWN IS NOW HIS

What a farm invasion is, basically: one day you're farming, you're getting on as normal, and then a vehicle arrives and somebody walks up with a piece of paper to say that everything you own is now his. And if you don't comply with this piece of paper, you're going to jail or worse.

At that point, the power cuts were getting bad and the phone lines had been stolen. There was no communication on all the farms, so Linda had moved to town because she needed communication to do her job, and I was still living on the farm. They'd come a month before, people from the Ministry of Lands, and they'd given me a Notice of Intent to acquire everything I own. And I went to the lawyer and he said, *No, no, no, it's nothing to worry about*—because at that point we'd already been in and out of court so many times. *No, no*, he said, *it's nothing to worry about, because you've got all your ducks in a row. You've got all your legal documents. Don't worry, they're just trying to scare you because they know it's just two girls.* Blah blah blah. But at that point they'd seen the bananas, and that was enough for them. Then a month later, they arrived with another piece of paper and this gentleman, and they said he was the new owner.

I said, *Not legally. He's not legally the new owner.* They said, *No, your farm's been acquired, and we've given this gentleman an offer letter for your property.* I said, *I've got a pile of paperwork to say that you can't do that.* No, no, that didn't matter. They left that day, and I went to town and saw the lawyer and filed another appeal, booked our court cases, spent a fortune getting nowhere. And then over that weekend the gentleman moved onto the farm. He moved into the grading shed about a hundred meters from the house. And he brought his whole family in, cattle and goats, and all his earthly belongings. That hurt a little bit. And he started plowing up the fields right in front of my house. He was a tough guy, full of bullet holes. He'd fought in the Congo.

We went to court and got a high court order very quickly to say that he wasn't allowed on the property. He was issued that, and he said he didn't care. So the police said that's all they could do, despite the fact that the high court order had told them that they could use any force necessary to remove this man off the farm. So anyway, that never happened. But it did quiet him, and we both basically lived like that for just over a year.

At that point, I was spending most of the time down there by myself, and Linda was spending a lot of time in town. She's always really been in and out, always on the move. It got incredibly lonely at some points, especially when all the power cuts started. You'd finish work, and it's that period between five and nine where you'd stand alone with a candle in the dark. Sometimes I'd go horseback riding in the evening, or I'd read. I'm a reader. Huge Stephen King fan. I've read every one of his books.

I didn't feel very safe, for obvious reasons. But I guess I was obstinate—I'm not gonna run away that quickly, which, I mean, looking back now, is absolutely foolish because of the things that could have happened. People were being raped and beaten, having animals kicked to death in front of them—all sorts of atrocities going on all over the rest of the country, and there's no reason why something shouldn't have happened to me.

Initially, a couple of our workers jumped ship and joined the war vets. But most of them stayed pretty loyal to us, until push came to shove. When we had to move off the farm, none of them really did anything. Instead, they all threw up their hands and wanted to be paid gratuities before we left, which was quite disappointing, because when there's sixty of them and one of him, you kind of think it could work in your favor. But it so seldom does. A lot of them had been my dad's workers, and a couple of them had actually been my grandfather's workers. We had a couple of generations there, they watched us grow up, so there was a huge history with our family and a lot of the people there, which is why it was quite disappointing the way everything turned out. I can honestly say 60 percent of them were illiterate, and I think they just didn't understand. They hear things on the radio, people tell them it's their right, and the white people stole everything from them, and, you know, they hear these untruths and believe them.

The war veterans sat on the farm for a year with us—the main guy and a group of others. It was a strange kind of relationship that developed with this man and me, the war vet living in the grading shed. He had a couple of people there, mistresses or whatever they were. They came and went a lot. And I met one of the sons, who really didn't want to be there, on the farm. I think the war vet was one of those people that genuinely believed in what he was doing. I'm not going to mention his name. He's over fifty, a liberation war hero. He's been at the head of every major *jambanja* in Zimbabwe. He's responsible for the deaths of several white farmers, which I only found out recently, after we moved off. At the time, though, he said he wasn't going to move, but when I'd pass him on the road, he'd tell me that he would never want any harm to come to me because he respects me and he respects what I'm doing and how I've done things. He often said that he'd never let any harm come to me. So we had this kind of strange understanding almost.

YOUR LUCK HAS FINALLY RUN OUT

The 2008 elections didn't cause so much of a problem. It was the rerun, because that was when the youths just ran rampant through all the farms.[5] And then when there was that whole period of lawlessness, and when none of the police were responding to anything, that was when the group of war vets moved into our house. I was in town. The war veteran had taken all the keys to the main gates, the farm, the house, everything. He'd beaten up a bunch of our workers, and he'd somehow gathered this bunch of youths that had all come down, a bunch of other war veterans, too, to wreck havoc throughout the valley. So I first went to the farm and we had this conversation. He said, *I'm very sorry to tell you, but pack your things and go.* I said, *You know, by law you can't do that.* Blah blah blah, we had this long conversation. He said, *I'm warning you, Nicola. I'm warning you. Pack your things, just go.*

So I thought, Whatever—what are you gonna do? And we went to the house and we were walking around, and one of the workers came running up, and he was like, *Madam, madam, please go, now, the youths are coming, they're coming for you right now, just go, just go.* So I grabbed the computer and the dogs and left.

Then a few days later, I went back to the farm with my mum—she was living in Mutare all this time—because now we'd gone to court. We drove to the farm with police protection, two armed policemen with AK-47s. Eight war veterans followed my mother and me into the house, and the police stood outside. The war veterans were walking around the house, kind of leaving my mum alone, but they were really trying to get me riled up. They started following me all around the house. And then I went into my bedroom, which had a bathroom attached. As I walked out of the bathroom, all eight of them came into my bedroom and they

---

[5] When the contested results of the 2008 elections did not determine a presidential winner, a runoff was set between Morgan Tsvangirai and Robert Mugabe. The period before the runoff contained some of the worst political violence in Zimbabwe's history. See the appendix section on the 2008 elections.

closed the door and they leaned against it. And I remember saying to myself, *You know what? Your luck has finally run out. You've been stupid until now, and this is it. You're going to meet the same fate as every other white farmer who tried to be clever.*

They started shouting and swearing, *You must go, pack your things and get out of here.* And they loved spitting at you. Their favorite thing to do is to spit. At this point, my mum had seen them push into the room. What they didn't know was that there was another door into my room on the other side, and my mum managed to come in through there. The only thing I thought to do, to try and knock this guy down, was just to introduce myself. I was like, *Well, I'm sorry if you are the new owner and you are taking over. I am Nicola, and you are?* And fortunately for me it worked, it knocked him completely off balance, and he didn't know what to do with himself. I remember walking out through the house and seeing my cat. I grabbed my cat, and I walked past my wine rack, and I took a bottle of wine, and we left.

I was so livid with the policeman. I said to him, *Did you not see?*

Ah, don't worry, nothing would have happened to you.

Fuck you, you knew exactly what was going to happen to me. And we left then, and I remember my mum and I got to the tar road and we both packed up laughing because we didn't know what else to do. It had been such a close call and could have gone so, so horribly wrong for us, like it has for so many people.

At that point, my sister was safe, my mum was safe—we all got off safe, we hadn't been beaten or raped or hurt. I've had friends violated, they've been tied up and threatened with rape, watched their father being slapped around in front of them. I've been very, very lucky, had some really close calls. Somebody up there's watching, because most others haven't been as lucky as we have.

The next time we went down to the farm was to get my horse. And by then, they'd cut her legs open and her neck open and split her ear and starved and beaten her, and when I finally got the SPCA—they rescue horses—she'd been stuck there for four months. And I had never seen such a case of neglect and abuse. She was this beautiful sixteen-and-a-half-hand thoroughbred. Bay with black points. In her one foot, the wound was so deep and so infected with maggots that I could fit my entire hand inside her leg past my wrist. She couldn't even walk, she hardly made it to town she was so exhausted from standing. She even had ticks on her eyelids. She had this scar from ear to ear across her neck. There'd been slashes and cut marks all over her legs. She was skeletal, absolutely skeletal. She had so much mange and so many ticks on her body you couldn't see what color she was. The SPCA finally found her down at the dam where she was hiding from these people. She'd obviously managed to get out of wherever they were trying to starve her to death.

I could smell her from the horsebox—she had so many maggots inside her, she was so rotten. I stepped into that horsebox and she looked at me and she started whinnying, a "Where the hell have you been?" kind of thing, and I couldn't put her down. We saved her ear, we saved her foot, and she's managed to recover, I don't know how, and I started riding her again. She's a tough horse.

UNFORTUNATELY, I LOVE THIS PLACE

Now I work at a seedling production place on the outskirts of Mutare. It's really nice, and the people I work for are wonderful. They're very accommodating. They took my dogs and my horses and me and all my problems and troubles and everything in. My mum and dad often mention, since I moved here, how much happier they are to know that I'm safe, that they don't have to go to bed every night worrying if these guys are gonna come for me or not.

Everything that has happened has caused such a racial shift. I'll give you an example. Some black guys that were in my sister's class came and wanted some seedlings. I said to them, *So when did you start farming?*

Oh no, they said. *We just took the farm down the road.* They were talking about my friend's farm. You hear that, and you don't want to be racist, but somebody that's had the exact same upbringing as you and they can go and do that to somebody else because they're black and Zimbabwean. You're white and that means you don't have rights? I try not to be racial. I mean, being in Africa you can't be. To a certain extent you have to try and be as accommodating as possible. But then when you hear that, you can't help but get angry.

I don't expect anything from the Government of National Unity. I think it's possibly the worst thing. I think that's a general feeling for a lot of Zimbabweans. A lot of people had their hopes on a new government, not a unity government. I met an old black gentleman in the street the other day—he was selling newspapers on the side of the road, and we started talking, and I think he put it into perspective: it might be a new driver, but it's the same old car. And I think that just says it. It doesn't matter who you put in the driver's seat, if you've still got the same engine running, you're not gonna get anywhere.

I still think of myself as Zimbabwean, unfortunately. No changing that. But there's nothing very hopeful here. I don't see a future for me in this country. The company that I'm working for is a great stepping stone while I find my feet and a bit of direction, which I'm still trying to figure out right now. I know Africa. I know how to farm in Africa. That's not really gonna help me in Europe or anywhere else. And, unfortunately, I love this place.

REARRANGED

Recently, I went to the sheriff, the one who was supposed to remove the war veteran from the farm, and I said to him, *Hey, you know, we've done everything by the book, could we not at least go down there and see if we can get some of our stuff?* And he went down there and I gave him a list of the stuff that was there, and when he came back he said that every single thing on the list was still at the house—this war veteran had apparently taken every single one of my belongings and put them in a room and locked it, which is really bizarre and peculiar. And he was very willing to let the sheriff start bringing stuff out. It's been a year now, and I'm finally starting to get some of my belongings back: bits of furniture and my photos and paintings and things like that. Even clothing, which I thought would have gone, and bedding and stuff like that, has come back. But everything has been tampered with, even photo albums—all the photos have been rearranged, which I find very creepy. In the picture frames, photos have been put upside down. Everything has been touched and he's been through everything. But nothing's missing so far.

Initially I didn't, but now I feel lucky and almost grateful to not be down there dealing with it all the time and having that constant, constant fear. I never slept properly, because I never knew... everything that went bump in the night, you know? It causes a huge amount of emotional stress, and you don't even realize it.

EDMORE

AGE: *Early thirties*
OCCUPATION: *Former gold miner and political activist,*
now an asylum-seeker doing piece jobs
INTERVIEWED IN: *Musina, South Africa*

Edmore has tried all kinds of schemes to get ahead, to break out of the double bind—political and economic—in which he finds himself. The only time he made real money was from informal gold mining. First, he tried the dangerous fringes of gold prospecting, one of thousands braving floods and landslides, armed rivals, Mozambican authorities, and the Zimbabwean military for the chance at a few grams of gold from newly discovered seams in the east of Zimbabwe and across the border. When he did find gold near the town of Kadoma, Edmore admits that he drank away the profits. Back in his home area, he was swept up in organizing ahead of the 2008 elections, as politics pitted opposition-supporting relatives against ruling-party stalwarts among his extended and polygamous family. Six months after he crossed the Limpopo River into South Africa, Edmore still finds it difficult to recall that journey. He is staying in a church shelter in the border town of Musina.

All in all, we are thirty-six children in my father's family. I myself am the thirty-sixth. My father died at the age of one hundred and four. He had many wives, six of them. He was a rich man. He had lots of cows, some grinding mills. He was actually famous in Buhera as the first person in our area to own an ox-plough. But you know how it is with polygamy. My mother was the last wife, and I was the eleventh of her eleven children. The other, older wives looked down on her. Those who enjoyed life in our family were the children from the first few wives. The later ones didn't have much say. There were tensions. My father paid attention to his last wife and the others didn't like it. That's life in a polygamous home.

When I was very young, I was given a bursary and sent away to Nyashanu Mission School, but then I was expelled because I was naughty. Instead, I went to St. Albans where I stayed for many years. After school, I thought of joining the army because some of my brothers were soldiers. But they didn't want me to be killed in the DRC,[1] so they discouraged me. I didn't know what to do. I said to myself, what next?

Back home in Buhera, people suggested that I get a teaching job, but no one would hire me because my family was too involved in politics. You see, some of my brothers are Zanu-PF members, but other brothers who had gone to the university started causing problems for the government even while they were students. First, they were involved in ZUM in the late 1980s.[2] When they grew older and MDC was formed, they joined. They became known as people against the government. That affected the whole family. And so at the schools they would say, *Your family are members of the opposition party, so no work for you.* Even Mugabe knew about our

---

[1] The 1997 anti-Mobutu rebellion overturned Zaire and renamed the country the Democratic Republic of Congo. In 1998, Mugabe committed Zimbabwean troops to the rebellion's attempt to thwart an overthrow of the DRC government by neighboring Rwandan soldiers, and, it is alleged, to protect his interests in the diamond mines.

[2] The end of the period of reserved white seats in Parliament promised by the Lancaster House Agreement and the merger of Zanu and Zapu in 1987 created a situation in which Zimbabwe began to move toward being a one-party state. The leading opponent of this, initially, was Edgar Tekere, a former Zanu leader, who formed the Zimbabwe Unity Movement party (ZUM) to contest elections in 1990. However, ZUM made only limited progress.

family from Buhera. He said, *Down with that family!* If you don't know our family, you are the only one who doesn't.[3]

These were hard times, the late 1990s. Food was hard to come by. Some donors used to bring food, but when we went to collect some, we would be screened. The chief would say, *This family should not get food. If they do get some, they should be the last ones to get it.* This happened to other people, not only my family. Other opposition party supporters were denied food as well.

GOLD OVER THE MOUNTAINS

When I finished school, I had no opportunities—no work, no way to feed myself.

When I heard that there was gold in Mozambique, I decided to go. I traveled there with a group of other men as a syndicate, each man carrying ten kilograms of equipment, a shovel, a pick, and a range—a tool that looks like a spear, made from steel and used to dig hard and stony surfaces. We went to Chimanimani and climbed up the mountains and over the border. Days and days of walking. Mozambique is surrounded by mountains. You have to be strong and keep climbing, even if you are in pain. We walked a distance of one hundred kilometers to get to the place. We called it Kumandofa.[4]

That first time, I stayed in Mozambique for about two weeks. There wasn't any food there. We had to carry our own mealie-meal with us. When we noticed that our mealie-meal was almost finished, we knew we would have to go back home. The rain came often, and our mealie-meal got rained on. There were no trees in that part of Mozambique, so no firewood and nothing to cook with. There were no houses in that area either, so we lived in caves. It became very cold. When people get cold,

---

[3] Edmore's surname has been omitted to protect his identity.

[4] Translation from Shona: a dangerous place, possibly deadly.

they become even more hungry. Water got into the caves, rivers of water. It was difficult to sleep. When we realized that the situation was going to cause death, we decided to go back home. So you see now what kind of life we were living there. We left. When we got back to Chimanimani, we heard that some of the men who had remained had died.

When I came home I met a girl and asked her out so I could start a family. But still there was no work, so I decided to go back to Mozambique. Gold was the only chance I had to make some money, so I climbed over the mountains again. When I got back to that place, I found a person buried like a dog inside one of the caves. Covered with grass with just a stick to show there's something buried there. You feel so sorry for someone buried like that.

I often had to hide from the *matembeya*. I'm not sure if they are Mozambican cops or what—they secure the border, trying to stop foreigners from coming in. That second time we went there, we managed to find very little gold. Later, what little money I had was stolen by Zimbabwean police at Chimanimani.

IS THIS ME?

I've done so many things. I've always been someone who wanted to do his own thing. I thought if I made a little money then I would be able to sustain my life. The first time I went to Harare, I got a house at Joshua Nkomo Housing Cooperative in Kambuzuma.[5] Then—not too long after—the government came and destroyed those houses. Oh man, why? I had no choice but to go home back to Buhera. I tried farming at home. That was in 2006. There was a severe drought. Farming didn't work out either, so I returned to Harare to look for work. I did find a job that time, and I worked for Colcom Foods for almost a year, in the boning department

---

[5] Kambuzuma is a township outside Harare. The Joshua Nkomo Housing Cooperative was destroyed on June 6, 2008 as part of the government's Operation Murambatsvina. Brian and Boniface describe Murambatsvina in their narratives.

where sausages were made. But that was a tough life and jobs were not secure. I realized that I had no future. And time was passing.

Then one of my cousins came home for a visit. He comes from Buhera but he lives in Canada. He asked me, *Cousin, what are you doing?* I said, *I'm suffering.* By that time I had left my wife. Things weren't going well at work or at home.

My cousin was a miner too. He'd made money in Kadoma and then moved to Canada. But now he needed more money. I told him about my time in Mozambique, and he said he wanted to experience that kind of mining for himself. I said to him, *Look, people die there. But if you are brave enough, we can go to Mozambique.* So we went.

That time it was raining even worse. Two weeks of it, cold, cold weather. But we were strong. We worked extra hard and managed to get four grams of gold. We said, *Praise the Lord* and went back to Chimanimani to exchange it. We got a reasonable amount of money. I said to my cousin, *It's not bad, but it's not a lot of money. I can't go back home with only this.* My cousin said, *We'll go to Kadoma—it's a city of gold.* We got on a bus looking so dirty, after two weeks of not bathing. Some of our clothes were in sacks. We took buses from Chimanimani, through Mutare, Rusape to Harare, and then from Harare to Kadoma.

I didn't know Kadoma, but my cousin even had a house there that he used to share with his brothers. His younger brothers had claims. That means you peg off an area to show you are mining there. It means, "This is my claim, from here to here to here." No outsider can come and take it.

At that time I was desperate for money, but I was still strong and I got lucky. I managed to get my own claim and I came across twenty-five grams of gold. I had never managed to make that much money before. You know how it is when it happens for the first time? I was happy. I said to myself, Is this me?

Back home in Buhera, they thought my cousin and I were still in Mozambique. When I got home, I bought cows for the family. But I said, *I can't be here for long. I need to back where the money is.* After a week, I went back to Kadoma. Luck came my way again, and I started making even more money. I started finding kilograms of gold. You know there's a difference between kilograms and grams. A kilogram is not a thing to play with.

For the first time in my life I had enough money. I bought blankets, a nice bed, clothes, a TV. But money easily goes, and I am a drinker. I ended up using taxis all the time. I'd tell the taxi driver to wait for me all night, parked.

WE WERE SURROUNDED

Money is a bad influence. Money can hurt you. We were spending money, and we didn't want to stop. The government was starting to become interested. Obviously, Zanu-PF knew what was going on because they are the bosses. They started deploying soldiers and police at our claims because they knew we were finding gold. "Operation no more gold panning" was introduced.[6] Whoever was found mining would be severely punished. The government said we were taking gold that wasn't ours. We were supposed to take all our gold to Fidelity. That's the government's dealer. We did take a certain percentage to Fidelity, but not all of it. Because Fidelity underpaid us, we felt it was better to keep part of it and find a better market. We weren't in mining to make Fidelity happy.[7]

When they started to control gold panning, we tried to resist. To protect our claims against people who wanted to steal from us, we would get guns from a nearby farmer. They often have guns on farms for shooting wild pigs. They aren't usually for shooting people. We didn't shoot thieves, we just threatened them. We'd sign for the guns in the morning

---

[6] In December of 2006, Zimbabwe began a crackdown on illegal gold mining. Farmers had been hiring villagers and farm workers to illegally pan for gold, often leaving the land barren.

[7] Modifications to the Mines and Minerals Act, which required small-scale prospectors to sell their minerals to the government-owned refinery Fidelity, afford the government large control over the minerals market.

but the farmer needed his guns at night, so each evening at five p.m. we'd bring the guns back. At night we had weapons but not serious ones, only catapults, sticks, and *sjamboks*.[8]

In open-cast mining,[9] you dig holes to a depth where you expect to find gold—around one and a half meters. If you don't find a sample at that depth, you dig another hole. At night, we would climb into those holes to sleep and also to avoid the cold until morning. There was room to spread your legs. Four or five people would sleep together. We would camp out there in the bush for three days at a time, and then go back to the locations,[10] to our homes, then back to the bush to keep panning for gold.

I don't know who leaked the information about where our claims were, but the police raided us. They arrived early one morning when we were still sleeping. A car arrived and they told us to put our hands up. We were surrounded. We didn't even know how they got there in the grass. "Hold each other's pants!" they shouted. You know, when a person has a gun there is nothing you can do. Even if you think you are clever. We held each other's pants, for sure, and when they said, *Get down!* we did get down, for sure. *Hands up!* They pulled us up and searched us.

One guy had the idea of trying to escape through one of the deep tunnels that we had dug panning for the gold. But the police decided they'd tear gas him, and he thought he would die in there, so he shouted out that he would come out.

Then, from everywhere around us gold panners started running toward where we were, shouting, *Cops! Cops!* Wrong move, running toward us, because the cops were surrounding us. When they tried to run in the other direction, the cops said, *No! Hands up!* It was chaos.

---

[8] Traditional heavy leather whip with strips of cowhide.

[9] In open-cast mining, also known as strip-mining, large strips of land are excavated in order to extract materials without subsurface tunnelling. This can cause short- and long-term environmental damage.

[10] "Locations" refers to townships, formerly restricted to blacks-only housing.

This other group realized that there was no way out. The cops said, *Let's beat them, let's beat them.*[11] And so we watched our friends being hit. We thought they were also going to beat us. Our hearts were thumping. But it turned out that the police were after these other guys. After the police allowed us to leave, we went back to the location. We decided to stop panning for gold because we didn't know exactly when police cars or even soldiers might suddenly arrive. It's like this: Kadoma has gold. We knew the big guys—I cannot state who exactly; all I can say is it's the big guys—they now wanted this gold for themselves.

I went home to Buhera. Where else was there to go?

TEA WITH MILK

One of my brothers said, *Do you remember when we used to drink tea with milk and sugar? Not any more. Remember when Dad used to tell us to wait for him at the bus stop so we could help him carry groceries? No more. We no longer enjoy the things that we used to enjoy because of what is happening in the ruling party.* Yes, the ruling party educated me, but what had I achieved so far? Nothing, and time was ticking away. So, I started campaigning against Zanu-PF, mobilizing people, old people and so forth, saying, *We used to drink tea with milk every day. Now look at what has happened.*

This was in February of 2008, the time of the election. There was a lot of conflict at that time. In my big family, some of the older ones are actually war vets[12] who are supporters of Zanu-PF, and they turned against those of us who supported the MDC. This election divided families, including mine. I began to worry about my safety. Zanu-PF sometimes hired guys from other districts, like mercenaries. They would come and beat you. But you couldn't identify who'd beaten you, because you didn't know them. They would swap: people from our area would

---

[11] By 2009, indiscriminate beatings in gold towns like Kadoma were a well-known and terrifying occurrence, at times described in the press as a "nightmare."

[12] See footnote 1, page 172.

beat up people from another area; people from another area would beat up people from our area concurrently. It was politics. It happened to me. One night I was beaten up by outsiders, by people who were unknown to me.

I left home late that same night. I went through the bush to a place called Gaza.[13] I walked on foot the whole bloody night. But the situation in Gaza didn't seem right. There was a crew who were killing people. My sister was married in that area, so I went to her house and hid there before I went back to Harare.

On my way to Harare, I got a phone call saying that the night I left, some of my family members, old men and old women, were beaten up by Zanu-PF supporters. My brother's son was at home when the black boots[14] rushed in. He knew it was too late to run away, so he hid in his bedroom and they used tear gas to get him out. They beat him with a baton stick and broke his foot, crippled him for life. He has had to use a walking stick since then. It's politics.

After all the beatings, many of the men fled, so what those thugs did was attack their wives. They went door to door. They had a list of people who they thought were activists. Why did they beat the wives when they couldn't find the husbands? Why, because these monkeys are all the same. I decided then, *I'm no longer coming home. You are making me fly to some other place.*

THE NEW SLOGAN

I went back to Kadoma. This was around the time of the run-off election. I wanted to check things out and go back to work panning for gold. But the situation in Kadoma was not good either. The government had introduced a curfew where people were forced to be indoors by six

---

[13] A small center in Buhera.

[14] The police.

o'clock at night, with the doors closed. But gold panners like myself, we often work at night and finish late. Soon I was in trouble again. One night, I'd just come back from the mine. I had made some money and I wanted to go enjoy myself after all the hard work. I was on my way into town when I ran into bad hands—people were singing liberation war songs on the corners.

I had no idea what was going on. Suddenly, I see people with sticks, chains, *sjamboks*. They grabbed me and told me to sit down. At first I thought it was a joke. Then I noticed more and more people coming. Real mafia, about fifteen or sixteen of them. They asked me to tell them the new slogan.

What slogan? I told them I spent most of my time in the bush. I didn't know there was a new slogan. I was trying to reason with them. Before I knew it, they bashed my head with a stick. Then they beat me with a chain on my buttocks. I wasn't the only one caught. There were three of us. *Roll!* they shouted. So I rolled in the dirt. You can't reason with these kinds of people. After beating me up and then telling me to roll, they said, *Run, run and don't look back.* Then they released me. I couldn't report them. I was crying. From that attack, I have ten stitches in my legs.

When I got home to Westview,[15] I met other miners who were also beaten up. They were also crying. Then we heard more singing. We all climbed a mango tree to hide. We were silent. No one says anything when things get that bad.

That night they didn't find us. But the violence continued. In Westview, Zanu-PF members went door to door and took people away. Some of those people never came home. Some are still missing to this day. Maybe they were burned. Maybe they were thrown in the river. It was a frightening time. We were supporting MDC and I think that's why we got into trouble at Kadoma Westview. Of all the miners I knew, only three were Zanu people. It became known that if you lived in

---

[15] A suburb of Kadoma.

Westview you liked Tsvangirai more than Mugabe. And people were dying for that reason.

I didn't vote during the re-run election in 2008. I felt it was of no use to vote again and win again and then the next thing you are told, you didn't win. But on election day the government introduced the red finger operation. When you go to vote, they put ink on your finger. Later, if you were found without the ink, you would get into serious shit.

To get away from Westview, I went to Harare during the re-run election. As I told you, I have some brothers who are Zanu war vets. When you have a family so big, people are going to be on different sides. When one of my war vet brothers saw me in Harare he asked me about the red finger operation. He said, *How come your finger is not red? The ink doesn't come off. If you voted, it will be red.* That's when I realized that some of my family was against me.

TWO REASONS TO LEAVE

People were being attacked with petrol bombs. Houses were being burned. Always, it was by people who you didn't know. They would find people to do the jobs for them, youths. They'd say, *Go and burn this place, I'll pay you.* So because these youths don't have money, they would just do it. Some were not paid; some were just given alcohol. They'd buy them crates of traditional beer and say, *Gentlemen, go and kill sister so and so. She's a problem.*

I got a call. People at home in Buhera were being made to repent for supporting MDC. Some of my brothers were beaten up by the war vets.

I couldn't go home. I was known as a troublemaker for MDC. (I may appear very simple, but I have the ability to persuade people.) And so I heard they were looking for me. I knew if I went back to Buhera they would say goodbye to me.[16]

---

[16] Kill me.

I went back to Kadoma and tried to work for a while. But I looked at the economic situation in Zimbabwe, and at the rent that I was paying. I used to pay low rent, but by that time the rent I paid had increased to two grams of gold, which was equivalent to R600. I had always told myself that if I became financially stable, I'd like to go to South Africa, buy water pumps and other equipment, and then come back to Zimbabwe and mine my own claim. Much of the gold underground is at the water table. You need a pump to remove all the water so you can take the gold. Plus, I needed to get married again. I knew I wouldn't be happy or build a sensible life without suitable help.

In December 2008, a friend of mine who works at ZESA[17] came to my house in Kadoma while I was watching my claim in the bush. He persuaded me to go to South Africa the next day. I wasn't prepared for the journey, but I decided to sell my bed and my TV and a nice Monarch suitcase I had. What do I need all this stuff for?

What really, really made me leave home was, one: Life was hard. We didn't have work and couldn't buy much with the money. Two: People were after me. I was afraid for my life. Zanu-PF made me run away.

NO-MAN'S LAND

We leave Zimbabwe carrying the wrong impression of South Africa. The South Africa in our minds is very different from the South Africa we saw. We thought it was so easy to cross here to South Africa. We were not aware of *magumaguma*.[18] When I think about it, my heart starts beating hard.

We started our journey at night, four of us. On the train from Kadoma to Bulawayo, we were drinking all the way. I'd never been to Bulawayo. I phoned some friends who work there and told them I was thinking of

---

[17] Zimbabwe Electricity Supply Authority.

[18] Gangs who assault and rob border-jumpers. See Section 7, "The Border," and the appendix section on Zimbabweans in South Africa.

going to South Africa. One of them started telling me about people who'd died on that journey. Still, they took us to the place where you get taxis[19] to South Africa. That was around three p.m. We got into a Mazda pickup with a canopy. They said it would cost R60 to get to the bridge, Beitbridge.[20] We were tired and hungry; we had nothing to eat.

When we got to the bridge, we were carrying nothing except for a second set of clothes each: two pairs of trousers, shirts, and a jacket. We wore the trousers one on top of the other. No bags, nothing. We got to the bridge at around one a.m. When he dropped us off, the driver warned us about thugs and so on. It's bad to look like an innocent villager. So we made ourselves look strong. We started acting cool. What could they do to us?

When we got there, we saw people sleeping outside on verandas at Beitbridge. We joined them and slept. The next day, a dreadlocked guy approached us. We said, *Comrade, we want to cross over.* I was looking serious, smartly dressed, and he liked my style. He said, *Comrade, are you not a gun man from Kadoma?* And I said, *Yes, that's where I work.* In this way, I was instilling fear in him. He thought I'd worked at the bridge before. We paid him R50 each for the four of us.

We were made to walk along the bridge in no-man's-land. When we got there, we were told to wait. We were hungry, sweating and holding our jackets in our hands. There were about fifty Zimbabweans just waiting there in no-man's-land. Some had lots of luggage, some with kids, trying all different ways to leave.

After paying our money to this guy, he paid some soldiers there, telling them he has four guys only. We didn't know he was *magumaguma*. Four of us went down quickly through the fence, escorted by this guy,

---

[19] Minibuses or other vehicles that run a certain route, often waiting until they're full before they set off.

[20] Beitbridge is a border town in the province of Matabeleland South, Zimbabwe. The name also refers to the border post and bridge spanning the Limpopo River, which forms the political border between South Africa and Zimbabwe.

and the others were supposed to remain behind.[21] But some people took a chance and followed us through the fence. If you did that without paying, you would end up very sorry. One man was with his wife and kids. They told him to lie on the ground and then asked that woman to lie on top of her husband. Then they did whatever they did to her. Yes, the kids saw what happened. Some other women were unfortunate too. Some of them were limping afterward. Those people who stayed behind, we never saw them again. When I think about it...

WHAT COULD I DO?

We continued with the journey, with the same guy, but we stopped in the bush many times. You know, stealing is not straightforward. If they want more money, these people can make you pay thirteen times. The guy led the way, telling us when to run and when to walk, to avoid being seen. The dreadlocked guy was liaising with people, working out how much to pay at the forced entries—these are open, with someone there, guarding the space. When we went through the fence, squeezing under razor wire, my jacket was torn at the back, but I couldn't stop to check it. I carried on running. I was always the last one because I was still a bit drunk.

When we got into South Africa (the first time in history for me), we were told to stop again. By now, we were dying of hunger and thirst. The guy seemed to like us, I don't know why. At the taxi rank[22] at the bridge, he said, *Gentlemen, I will make sure that you get into a taxi to Musina.* He bought us cold water and we drank. He gave us his phone numbers and

---

[21] The vast majority of Zimbabweans entering into South Africa do so through undocumented means, typically traversing the Limpopo River and making their way through the rows of fences with a wire cutter or using pre-existing holes into South Africa. See the Section 7, "The Border" and the appendix section on Zimbabweans in South Africa.

[22] The bus stop or bus terminus. Minibuses or old Peugeots run informal bus services. The taxi rank is usually also an informal food market. Travellers often sleep at the taxi rank, waiting for the next bus.

made sure we got into a taxi.[23]

We were true border-crossers for sure—we had nothing and we don't understand Venda, the language they speak here. There were bad vibes at the taxi rank. We didn't understand what the drivers were saying to us. We paid, but when we tried to get into a different combi, people poked us with sticks. I don't know if they were city council people or taxi rank marshals. We got separated and ended up being only three. One of our friends went ahead. He had no idea where he was going because it was his first time. We didn't know where he'd gone or how to find him.

I had had enough of being poked by sticks. I didn't understand their language and my money was almost gone. So I carried on walking, down toward where the big trucks were. There's a place where they sell buckets, it's like a valley; that's where I went because I was thirsty. I saw a tap with a little water coming out. I didn't care even if it was sewage water, I was dying of thirst. So I crouched and drank and drank and drank.

My two friends found me. We saw a car with Zimbabwean number plates and stopped it. The driver was coming from Rusape to Musina and then proceeding to Pretoria. We asked for a lift and explained our situation. They understood and we jumped in. The soldier at the barrier at the South African border said, *Kill yourself before I kill you*, meaning give me some money before I ask you for some. So we paid R300 each, the three of us. Then he let us pass.

After the driver left us, we didn't know where we were going. We walked from the cross-border inspection to Shoprite where trucks are parked and sat there. We bought one banana and some buns to share.

One of my friends met a woman and started talking to her. Luckily for us, she told him about a church that takes care of Zimbabweans. She managed to get us in the line for the shelter. She said, *Guys, you won't starve here*. That church is where we are staying right now, the I Believe in Jesus Church.

---

[23] The distance between Beitbridge, Zimbabwe and Musina, South Africa is about 16km.

Before we got there, it hailed, a big storm. The woman who brought us there got us some food. I slept on a chair that night, covered with my wet jacket.

WAITING FOR ASYLUM AT THE SHOWGROUNDS

People told us we needed what is called an asylum. Because we had no asylum or traveling documents, we could easily get deported. We were like bush dwellers. We couldn't expose ourselves. The situation was tough. We would see a lot of police cars going to off-load people at the Zimbabwe border.

We used to walk up the hill every day, from the I Believe in Jesus Church to the showgrounds.[24] We would spend the whole day there and then come back to sleep at the church. We were trying to get asylum, but they introduced new systems. We were more than 4,000 people at the showgrounds—it was packed. There was a lot of corruption. Some would pay R400 in order to jump the queue, back door. We didn't have money, we were always broke.

Sometimes I would sleep at the showgrounds, trying to get my asylum back door. We slept in the open. They set up bowser tanks.[25] There was no privacy when bathing. You would just bathe while the next person is sitting there.

The bible says, *There's time for everything, there is an end to everything.* I agree with that. I never thought that my situation was going to come to an end, but it did. Asylum took forever.

---

[24] The showgrounds in Musina is a large open field where 3,000–4,000 Zimbabweans wait to seek asylum. The systems and rules for asylum there change as South African immigration laws change. The conditions are unsanitary and have recently been subject to a major cholera outbreak.

[25] Water storage tanks.

REFUGE

After I got my asylum, I worked at a refugee camp for three months, cooking for people. It's a refugee camp for all, not only Zimbabweans—from Burundi, DRC, Rwanda, wherever. So I was working with lots of Vendas and four of us Zimbabweans. Just before getting our salary, they said, *You have the wrong papers.* Our contracts were terminated. Up to now we haven't been paid. That was a month ago.

Mine is a very big family and my brothers drive big trucks. If I buzz them, they call me back. That's how I communicate with them. Last Saturday I heard my child is fine. I am hurting a lot. I want to go back to Zimbabwe. I want to get into the salon business, a hair salon or a barbershop, so I bought some hair clippers, hair dryers, hair oil, braids. They are at my sister's house, back home.

At the church, we have blankets and a supply of food. If anyone gets there hungry, we can usually feed them. People come and go. They seek asylum, and when they get it they move on. Passersby come to the church when they don't have anywhere else to go. People get here with nothing because it will have been taken by magumaguma. People take risks—even up to now. Some people arrive at the church after being attacked by crocodiles, or robbed by thieves; some are fainting from hunger, some say, *We were one hundred when we left, and now there's only three of us left.* Women arrive having been raped and not able to walk, needing a doctor. Our pastor supports them all.

THE CAPITAL

HARARE

It has been raining in Harare for the last few days, and the city is overgrown and green. Summer weeds grow tall beside the roads. All is quiet, as if the entire capital were holding its breath, waiting.

Driving across the city at night, there are few streetlights. Headlights pick up people walking by the side of the road. Others walk down the median. Most traffic lights no longer function. They're hollow eyes in the dark. Just a few other cars on the road. At intersections, people are polite, hesitant. *You go. No, after you, please.* Nobody hoots their horn at anybody else. Drive by Harare City Hall: completely dark. Drive by Harare General Hospital: completely dark.

Only certain government buildings have power tonight, notably the President's official residence in the center of town, State House, the lights of which are only dimly visible through the thick trees.

Some statistics estimate that at least one-third of the population has fled to neighboring countries, mostly South Africa, but also Mozambique, Botswana, and Namibia. And every day the Zimbabwean diaspora becomes larger. They're leaving because of systemic political violence, lack of jobs, the almost total breakdown of education and health-care systems, and rising rates of deadly disease, most notably cholera. It's impossible to know if this one-third estimate is correct, but the city *feels* emptier.

Harare, called Salisbury during the colonial days, used to be a bustling, up-and-coming African capital, a regional and cultural hub in a country that was feeding itself and educating its people.

Literature, a good indication of the health of any country, used to thrive here. Bookstores were well stocked with books by such great Zimbabwean writers as Dambudzo Marechera, Charles Mungoshi, Tsitsi Dangarembga, and Chenjerai Hove. No bookstores are left in Harare, even in the still-posh northern suburbs. A few of the remaining stationery stores sell dusty books, but the titles are mostly by popular American and British authors. Now it is difficult to find books by Zimbabwean authors.

This week, the government issued a trillion-dollar note. Yet no matter how often new denominations are issued, inflation (due to, among other factors, the collapse of agricultural and industrial production) keeps rising. Today's rate can be found on the chalkboard at a favorite coffee shop: 34 trillion Zimbabwe dollars to one American dollar.

Word in the coffee shop is that soldiers are paid in bundles of cash that are dumped out of trucks like hay bales. Someone else mentions, laughing, that people are driving by State House and throwing Zim dollars out the window of their cars.

And people laugh and laugh over the zeros. What choice do they have but to laugh? An article in the *Financial Gazette* (known locally as the *Pink Paper*) laments the nation's loss of identity, as their currency has become a national and international joke.

On the street, now it's almost completely an American-dollar economy. Milk is two American dollars; bread is one. A Mars Bar at the gas station can go for as much as three. A bag of maize is between eight and ten. Most people, though, don't have many dollars. In the shops, as on the roads, people tend to be quiet. They wait patiently with their few dollars gripped tightly in their hands. Only crisp clean bills are accepted. A sign at the Bon Marché supermarket in Harare reads: *Dear Valued Customers: Please note, soiled, torn, written on, or stamped notes are not accepted. Thank you.*

Cashiers examine each bill with the concentration and intensity of jewelers. Often, they reject them. And yet even then there are few confrontations, no raised voices. These supermarket cashiers hold an immense amount of power in Zimbabwe these days, but they don't tend to abuse it. They simply shake their heads sadly at the bills they can't take, and wait as the person separates out the groceries he or she can't live without from what they can now no longer afford.

A woman, a young mother, tells us she's proud (and also lucky) to still have her job as a secretary; it's only that she's hardly being paid. She says she fears for her children and prays that she'll be able to scrounge up enough dollars to pay for food through next week. Another man, a former teacher at an elite school, tells us he had to stop teaching. *How can I love these children*, he says, *if I know what some of their parents do?*

FATHER JOHN

AGE: *38*

OCCUPATION: *Former Catholic priest (suspended), human rights defender*
INTERVIEWED IN: *Johannesburg, South Africa*

Father John has round cheeks, a warm smile, and a very busy schedule. Called to the ministry as a faithful Catholic, then promoted to run the respected Catholic Commission for Justice and Peace, Father John became deeply involved in documenting rights abuses and supporting people as they lost their homes in Operation Murambatsvina or were attacked for their political beliefs. (In 1997, the CCJP's groundbreaking "Report of the Disturbances in Matabeleland and the Midlands, 1980–1988" was the first historical account of Gukurahundi and the first time this secret war was brought to public attention.) The government put increasing pressure on his superior in the church to silence him, and his bishop did, finally, suspend him. Much as this distressed him, Father John continued to be active in civil society in other ways, while repeatedly asking his bishop to reinstate him. The violence of the run-off elections of mid-2008 finally pressed Father John to leave Zimbabwe. In Johannesburg, he joined the Solidarity Peace Trust and is able to continue to serve people, only now in a parish with no boundaries.

I am quite lucky because, in this whole story which I am about to share with you, through God's protection, I was never beaten, nor was I tortured in any way.

I am a suspended Catholic priest. I haven't been expelled. When they expel you, they write to you. I haven't received an expulsion letter so my proper status is that I am a suspended Catholic priest.

As you know, becoming a priest is a calling from God. So I simply responded to that call, and offered my life to God.

When I was in Grade 7, this Franciscan priest came to talk about priesthood vocations. When he said, *Those who wish to become priests, come and register your names*, I felt the urge, not just out of immaturity or being excited, no—I could feel it. I could feel the urge to serve other people. By the time I finished with Form 3,[1] I had already applied, and was accepted to the seminary.

I went as far as Form 4 and then I did a diploma in philosophy. After that I did a four-year program and acquired a Bachelor of Arts honors degree in religious studies, philosophy, and classics at the University of Zimbabwe. I started my Master's degree, but then I froze it.

The bishop at that time loved me so much and trained me to become an altar server, and I used to work with him and travel with him, serving his Masses, especially during confirmations.

I did my first year of formal education as a priest in '91 in what is called the year of formation. I was born in 1972, so I was nineteen at the time of my year of formation. That is the year when you decide if you are really really determined to become a priest.

In 1995, I took a year off from religious studies. They call it probation or working experience. You are either given a teaching post or you become the librarian, you know, as part of the training. They want you to gain working experience.

That year I worked as a teacher and school librarian at a Catholic mission in Wedza. It was also a time when I started to see injustice and

---

[1] Equivalent of tenth grade.

to ask myself what I could do to help create a just and peaceful society. You could say I grew up in Wedza, working with the poor and the needy.

BECOMING AN ISLAND

My father died five years ago. He had become a leader in the Catholic church. He was a full-time catechist when he died.

He was very active in politics when he was younger. He was arrested during the liberation struggle, and he used to share with us stories about sharing a prison cell with the likes of Robert Mugabe and Enos Nkala and others. My father believed in justice, in fairness.

With his political background, my father used to highlight the injustices he used to see every time he read the newspaper. He used to tell me, *Look, society used to be very democratic, but this president doesn't seem to care for the people at all. He kills people willy-nilly.*

He'd say, *We are becoming an island. Look, we have been shut out of the commonwealth. What kind of country are we going to become?*

Now, my father had his own ideologies and his own beliefs about what he saw in the political scene. But for me, I concentrated on my day-by-day service to the people.

WORKING FOR JUSTICE AND PEACE

By 2004 I was already a deacon, and I was asked to become the assistant spiritual director of the Catholic Commission for Justice and Peace, the CCJP.

That is when I started working for justice and peace in Zimbabwe and in the archdiocese of Harare in particular. During those years when I was appointed, political violence was increasing all the time. The 2002 elections were quite violent; many people died and many rights and values were shattered in Zimbabwe. The government had become more and more dictatorial. The president and civil society were fighting. Some people were already falling by the wayside, but many others remained brave. When I was appointed, we had a great many tasks on our hands as a commission.

First of all, we had to empower the people, and that had to do with carrying out voter education workshops. Also, we discovered that most of our citizens didn't even know their rights and what they meant, so we took it upon ourselves as a commission to teach this information in our parishes. We even reached out into the rural areas.

But as the church became more involved in politics, our actions were always misconstrued by the government, so we used to clash quite a lot with the police. Many times, they cancelled our workshops. We the leaders were especially targeted. The government thought we were working on behalf of the opposition. As you may know, civil society organizations in Zimbabwe have always been labeled as siding with the main opposite party, the Movement for Democratic Change.

The other thing is that, as the peace and justice commission, we were deeply concerned about the deteriorating economic situation, with the government overspending while its people lower down in the hierarchy were suffering. Actually, three-quarters of the country was in dire straits: there was no food and we were also not getting good harvests from our fields, so as a commission we set out to look for donations in terms of food and clothing. And we managed to cover most of our people, those who were in our dioceses, distributing food we were getting from donors, and clothes.

The health sector had begun to collapse way before all this, in 1996, 1997, so we also sought medical equipment and medications to give out to people. By 2004, we are talking about a health sector which was next to nonexistent. Doctors were often on strike, and there was no medicine in the hospitals, so people were dying. We started distributing food, distributing clothes, and also helping those who did not have shelter.

CLASHING WITH THE GOVERNMENT

Let me take you straight to 2005, when we had the so-called tsunami,

Murambatsvina,[2] the operation to clean up, which our commission had discouraged even before its implementation. When the government started to implement it, we joined with other organizations in denouncing it.

But we also had to do something: denouncing was one thing, doing something was another. So, as a commission, we agreed that we needed to locate places where people could be relocated, and we needed to erect temporary shelters. We needed to source food, clothes, and blankets, which we managed to do with the help of donors.

Now, in trying to do this, we again clashed with the government. Their view was that they were trying to pull down illegal structures, but at the same time they had no alternative settlements for these people. Murambatsvina was more than unjust; it was inhuman.

The government used a heavy hand against civil society, and the church was not spared, but that did not deter us from doing our work. Civil society groups then linked up with the churches and, from that time, only the churches were allowed to distribute things, which meant that our commission had to take a leading role in sourcing supplies, and then linking up with that organization to go and distribute.

All the food was channeled to the churches and us priests who then helped to distribute it. As a leader, I had to lead by example, spearheading many of our operations as a commission, and I continued to clash with the government.

SOLDIERING ON

I remember, on several occasions, when a truckload of stuff would be delivered to whatever area and, especially in my own parish, it would always be misconstrued as coming from the opposition, the MDC. The

---

[2] See Boniface's and Brian's stories. In Operation Murambatsvina, the government destroyed an estimated 100,000 dwellings and trading stalls in urban areas around the country on the grounds that they were not properly planned. The first round of destruction—what Father John calls the tsunami—took place in 2005, and political violence aimed at urban areas has been repeated since then.

government set up some tricks to frustrate us in our work. For example, when we received some supplies, especially foodstuff, an official would say, *How was that cleared?* and *Where are the clearance papers from the border?* Or they would say, *This food has not been tested for germs—where are the papers?*

One thing we avoided was handing over those foodstuffs to the so-called Department of Social Welfare. Giving it to that department was as good as handing the food to the ruling party, and the ruling party would certainly use such things for political mileage.

So we would rather wait and keep those supplies until they were cleared by the police, or by the CIOs.[3] Then we distributed them ourselves. I was always on hand, and other volunteers as well, and we managed to reach out to many people who were displaced, many people who were suffering, many people who were hungry.

We went through a long spell of drought, and that affected our people enormously. We were now dealing with a two-pronged problem, with Murambatsvina on one side and the economic collapse on the other. In dealing with these two things, I can assure you that we were crossing swords with the political leadership, both in my own parish and in the dioceses.

On several occasions, I was detained at police stations. I could be picked up by the CIOs at any time, any hour, for questioning about this or that. But in all these instances the British Embassy and the American Embassy always supported me in every way. They always made sure they made follow-ups to ensure my safety until my release.

ONE YEAR SUSPENSION— WAITING FOR THE DUST TO SETTLE

Come the 2006 elections. As a commission we also had to carry out voter education, encouraging people to go and vote, and vote wisely, which was

---

[3] Officers of the Central Intelligence Organization.

also misconstrued as campaigning for the opposition, MDC. By then, the Catholic Church was labeled as being pro-opposition, and it was also the time when Archbishop Pius Ncube was very vocal in terms of denouncing Zanu-PF's misrule.[4] He also denounced the human rights abuses taking place in Zimbabwe, the lack of all the freedoms one can mention: freedom of association, freedom of speech, and so on. There was no work we did, whether approved or disapproved by the political leaders, which was not endorsed by our leadership, by the bishops.

But by mid-2006, the government cooked up a story that the people no longer wanted this priest—me—in our area, Mashonaland Central. The truth of the matter was that we were really challenging the government, we were defending human rights left, right, and center, and that did not go down well, and so they made up all these stories: this priest here, he is womanizing, and he is not doing his work as a priest because he is too involved in politics.

The fact was that people's minds were opening. They were starting to know their rights. Due to the work we were doing in terms of empowering the people and carrying out workshops and so on, people began to see the light, and I became a threat to the political leadership.

The Provincial Governor told me directly in person, *Father, Mashonaland Central province has been 100 percent Zanu-PF, but we no longer enjoy that monopoly. Due to the work you are doing, we are losing a lot of political support, and one of these days the president is going to fire us, because he has always been proud of this province.*

The governor was trying to protect the president's image of the ruling party still being in control, still commanding the support of the majority in Mashonaland Province. The governor was concerned that the election results might reflect otherwise. That would pose a serious challenge to the

---

[4] Pius Ncube has been a human-rights advocate and an outspoken critic of the Zanu-PF government. He resigned as Archbishop of Matabeleland in 2007, after images from within Ncube's bedroom alleging an affair with a married Bulawayo woman appeared in the Zimbabwean press. Ncube has stated that the allegations were politically motivated, retribution for his public anti–Zanu-PF stance.

governor himself, and that's why he pushed the bishop, who was now in charge of me, saying, *Look, if you don't remove your man, maybe we will kill him.*

My bishop then put me on a one-year suspension. I tried to lobby my colleagues, to get them to realize that what was happening to me could happen to one of them one day, but people were not eager to even call the bishop to sit down and talk about the matter. I tried also to lobby with the Nunzio, the papal representative, but the Nunzio said that the only thing he could do to help was to push my bishop to look into the issue and investigate it thoroughly.

At the expiration of my year-long suspension, one year without my saying Mass, my bishop still failed to reinstate me. He kept on telling me, each time that I wrote a letter or booked an appointment with him that he'd get back to me. *John,* he would tell me, *John, please bear with me, we must keep waiting for the dust to settle. You need some breathing time.*

That went on and on and on, until in 2008, in March, when I started thinking about my life, I realized that we were approaching two years and I had just been idle.

I'LL GET BACK TO YOU

Every week I would go to the bishop's office asking him to reinstate me, because I cared for my vocation. I was losing weight due to stress and embarrassment. I had offered my life to be of service to the people, and I was being denied the chance to do so.

During the first year we would sit and talk for twenty or thirty minutes, but toward the end it would last less than five minutes. He'd say, *If you don't follow what I am telling you, I question your obedience as a priest.*

Actually, two or three times I became very angry and emotional before my bishop. Of course I would not insult him. But it became a heated argument with me trying to convey to him, *Do you realize the kind of pain and stress that I am going through?*

I think about May or June of 2008 was the last time I saw him. I told him I wanted to go to South Africa. He said, *If you need any assistance to go to South Africa, to get some breathing room, we will assist you. What do you want?* I needed a letter so that the immigration could provide me with a visa, and he gladly provided that letter.

I applied for my visa, and it went through. I provided my bishop with my email, my cell numbers, and my address, but since that time I have received no communications from him.

During the time of my suspension, I decided to resume my work in human rights. I was incapacitated in terms of being spiritual director of the CCJP, but I began to attend other civil society meetings and activities in the country in general, especially in Harare. I also continued my work with Harare Ecumenical Working Group, HEWG. I also was engaged with AFCAST, the African Forum for Catholic Social Teachings, which advocates for the dignity of the human person. At AFCAST, I was also engaged by Veritas, an NGO which asked me to run their peace desk. So I was going out into communities, teaching them conflict resolution because violence was so rife in the country.

We were also trying to solve disputes between tribes, disputes among families, and above all disputes among political parties. There have been so many clashes, especially between the opposition MDC and the ruling Zanu-PF, so as Veritas we joined other peace players in Zimbabwe in trying to go to those areas where disputes were really volatile, then trying to bring those people together and get them to talk and do their politics in peace.

But it didn't end there. There were also conflicts even between chiefs and their subjects. There were conflicts between, for example, ex-combatants clashing with people, war veterans clashing with farmers, even inter-party disputes. Another important role we took on was tracking down people who were tortured, people who were displaced, trying to get the statistics.

I had to go out into the rural areas. When I received reports that people had been murdered in whatever place, I had to go and verify it. Of course, other colleagues would go out as well, since I couldn't investigate every incident myself.

When we would visit an area where people had been displaced, we would certainly not go with our pen and papers. But we would carry one or two parcels of food to give to those people, because it doesn't make any sense when you go to people and say, *Tell me your story*, and they tell you that their last meal was last week—*It has been nine days and we haven't eaten a thing*—so when I visited people like this I would bring some food—but it often wasn't easy to give a loaf of bread to certain individuals. That person might be an MDC leader and he was beaten because of his political activities. Giving such a person bread would look as though you sympathize with him. It wasn't easy, but we still had to do it. But our policy was: whether someone is Zanu-PF or MDC, we are looking at the individual, we are looking at the human person.

Sometimes we would meet war veterans and clash with them in the villages. For instance, I was looking into the abduction of someone, and the war veterans would want to block the investigation, because very often they were the people carrying out the abductions.

Now, when you release a report that Zanu-PF has beaten up people in such and such an area—well, that wouldn't go down at all well with the ruling party. So time after time they would visit our offices and threaten me and ask questions. Time after time they would pick me up before I jumped into a taxi and ask me to jump into their car and answer a few questions. You know, *What are you after? You want to know who was beaten, why? What for? You must be working for the MDC or you must be working for our Western enemies.*

In Zimbabwe whenever things were getting hot, my mother's advice was always, *Stay out of trouble*. At this time, I was still living at home with my mother. When I came home, there were some things I could not talk about. I didn't tell her, for instance, that on the 11th of March, 2007, I witnessed the killing of Gift Tandare.[5] She knew that I had been out

---

[5] Zimbabwean police shot and killed MDC activist Gift Tandare at a public Highfield prayer meeting in 2007. Two days after his death, two individuals attending Tandare's funeral wake were also shot by police. See Lovemore's narrative: he and Lovemore were good friends.

there and that things had turned out violent. She said, *I heard there was a guy that got killed.* And I said, *Oh, I didn't know about it.* But she knew what was going on, about the barbaric behaviors of the riot police, you know. And she would always voice concern.

REEDUCATION

There was an area where the militias, the war veterans, went for reeducation exercises. We organized transport and went out to investigate. When we arrived at the local school in that area, eyewitnesses told us what had been going on. They told us that the whole village had been gathered at the school and that all the teachers were told to come in front of the person addressing them, a person in an army uniform. He said, *You see these people—they are sellouts. These people are selling out. And we want to show you how sellouts are treated.* These teachers were taken to a classroom, and in this classroom they were beaten so thoroughly under their feet that when they came out none of them could walk. They were told not to cry, to just come out and join the meeting. Meanwhile, the other soldiers and war veterans, those doing the reeducation, were saying, *You want to betray your father? Mugabe?*

We started collaborating with the Progressive Teachers' Union to get statistics. Many teachers were tortured, beaten, and displaced. I remember meeting one man. He was on crutches, and he had come to the Progressive Teachers' Union to get some money because he wanted to go back to his homeland. The story of this man was quite moving: He was beaten and then he ran away. While he was running away, Zanu youths pursued him. He fell into a hole and broke his leg. After that, they beat him more. Finally he was helped by some well-wishers who took him to the hospital. He left his wife and children and property in the village. He called using his hospital neighbor's phone to check that his family was safe. He wanted them to come to him and leave that place. But his family was told never ever to move out. *If you move out, if we see you attempting to go, we will kill you, so you must stay here.* Do you see? They were trying to force this man to return home to his family and perhaps be killed. The man said, *Look, it's a matter of life and death now. I'm just praying that God will protect my family and my property.* He had been a teacher for five or six years at that place. Now, nothing, and he couldn't go back to his family.

That's only one story that I recorded.

MARCH 29 ELECTIONS

We became involved in the March 29 elections.[6] Now, during that time, I was staying with my mother, and most of the time I just stayed away from home. The state agents were harassing people like me, and I didn't want my mother to be targeted as well. Up to now, she's been safe. But two weeks before the March 29 elections, I moved to the Holiday Inn for security reasons.

During election time things were very tense. There were many reports of people being harassed and tortured. In so many areas people died when Zanu-PF unleashed a reign of terror countrywide, sending out militias, ex-combatants, the so-called war veterans, and even soldiers, our army, to go out beating up people and in some instances killing people. Some were raped, others were displaced.

Our job was to prepare a report on the election. We couldn't pronounce it a free and fair election. Soon after the election, we released a statement that told the truth. However, the African Union quickly rushed to conduct a press conference where they pronounced the elections free and fair. As church organizations, we denounced that, because we knew what was happening in the constituencies, prior to the elections, during the elections, and even after it was over.

When the elections were over, the government refused to release the results. Under Zimbabwean law, parliamentary results are supposed to come out within three days' time; presidential results within seven to

---

[6] See the appendix section on the 2008 elections.

nine days. When that didn't happen within the time frame, we as a civil society started to raise eyebrows.

We gathered together as civil society and said, *Look, this is unfair. Why is the Commission not releasing the results? Let's call for a special campaign. Where is my vote?*

We decided to try and march. *Those who are priests, put on your regalia; those who are pastors, put on your collars. Let's hold our bibles. Let's go to the streets.* But so many people were afraid to go into the streets. You know, maybe fifty people arranged to march—then all of a sudden there are only three of you. And you start to doubt whether to go ahead or not.

Very often, the march wouldn't go.

DAYLIGHT ROBBERY

When we arranged to have a meeting to compare the government figures with our own, someone found out about it. Before that meeting even started, the CIOs arrived. They rushed into the room, overturning tables, chairs, everything. Then they got us all to sit in one corner. No one was allowed to say anything, no one was allowed to answer any phone. We were told to sit on the floor like that... nobody moving.

They threw all our information into these bins and took it away.

That meeting was at a hotel in Hatfield. After about an hour or so of us on the floor, they began to give us a lecture. The word they used was *reeducation*. They wanted us to understand that they were intent on the reeducation of people. They said: *You know what you guys are doing is against the state, against your own country?* They started telling us about the liberation struggle. *Do you know what you are fighting for? You want to bring the whites back?* So we were given a reeducation lecture. This guy who addressed us was holding a gun, but he wasn't dressed in any army uniform. After the lecture, he made us repeat the Zanu-PF slogans.

One of our guys, he was very, very stubborn. He refused to say the slogans. The man hit him in the back with his gun. Then we were just told to go straight home and never ever to meet again.

It took the government a whole month to release the results. I can testify that the opposition won the March 29, 2008 elections soundly, but the ruling party played around with figures to give Robert Mugabe a percentage he didn't deserve leading to the so-called run-off, which made a mockery of our electoral system.

I regard what happened after the March elections as daylight robbery.

WHERE IS MY VOTE?

We caused a very big commotion when we called on the whole nation to put on white clothes—a white T-shirt or a white *doek*[7] or a white cap or a white armband. And the message was, *I voted, so where is my vote?* We were saying white represents peace. *I don't want to fight. I am not using violence.* We thought white was the proper color. WOZA, the Women of Zimbabwe Arise, tried to join us, and I heard they wore white. They came and marched in town. When the riot police attacked them, they all went on their knees and raised up their hands. We had said, *In the event that you are attacked, don't try to be a macho or anything, get down on your knees, raise up your hands.*

All the focus was on this so-called run-off between Morgan Tsvangirai and Robert Mugabe. As the government began preparing for the run-off, that's when things became intolerable. The government unleashed a reign of terror. People were beaten for having voted, both in rural and urban areas. People were arrested, some people were forced to move from their homes, a lot of people were displaced. A lot of people had their homes and property destroyed, and during that time, people were raped, people died. Morgan Tsvangirai saw that violence was flaring up again. Therefore he said, *No, no, I am pulling out,* and then there was no run-off, leaving Robert Mugabe the sole candidate for the presidency.

I knew the statistics and I had seen the violence first-hand, and it

---

[7] Headscarf or dhuku.

moved me. So when Morgan pulled out, I supported him, because it was the only way to lessen the suffering on the part of the masses. Even if he had contested, who would have dared to go to the polling stations to vote? I think pulling out of the run-off was the only thing he could have done to save lives.

GOING TO SOUTH AFRICA

It was becoming very tough for me to continue staying in Zimbabwe. We knew the government was monitoring our activities, listening to our cellphone conversations. You'd receive a call and there would be this *shhh* noise that means these people are listening in or that the conversation was being recorded. We'd arrange our secret meetings and then receive a phone call, someone saying, *If you value your life, you'd better not attend.* Having been seen in a team for the churches, which was still being branded as working hand-in-hand with the opposition, it was not safe for me to stay in Zim. That was when I decided to link up with my friend and come to South Africa.

My family—my mother, my brothers—were never threatened. I am glad things didn't deteriorate to that extent. I was afraid that it would get to that point. For me, the deciding factor was of course the fear of getting physical pain, and also the inability to perform, to work freely. Also, sadly, the economic factor was hitting me like everybody else. As a suspended priest, I had to fend for myself.

I met a religious leader from South Africa, a man who was also a renowned leader in the ANC[8] Youth League. He was interested in my situation. I shared with him my story, how I was being frustrated out of the priesthood by my bishop. He also knew of my work prior to the elections and about the police harassment. He was very sympathetic and he told me that if I ever contemplated coming to South Africa, he personally and as an ANC member would welcome me.

---

[8] The African National Congress, the ruling party in South Africa. The ANC is Nelson Mandela's party.

I believe this was in late May or June 2008. A number of my friends were already in danger. They had been picked up, and now their whereabouts were not known. Others were beaten, tortured; some were made redundant, fired from their jobs. They were rendered useless because they would be told to stay at home and not get involved in any activities.

Finally I said to myself, Besides the fact that my life is at risk, I think I may be able to use my efforts better elsewhere. I started just to move out quietly, unannounced. I left. I didn't even bid farewell to some of the friends I used to work with. I only sent them emails when I was already in South Africa.

Now, when I arrived in South Africa, I was welcomed by my friend and some of the other ANC youth leaders. At first I was living in a small rural place. They asked me to help out there because the people who were living there were quite poor.

I was teaching in schools and counseling youths because in this rural area the youths were very, very unruly, drinking, involved in drug abuse, and so forth. So I was doing my best to help, for free, conducting informal conferences, seminars, basically talking with them.

My only problem was that I am not conversant in Zulu or Sotho, but with the help of interpreters I could talk even with those who couldn't understand English. In the meantime, I tried to link up with my colleagues back home in civil society and in the religious realm. I did the same here as well, tried to link up with other priests here in South Africa. I continued to have a serious problem, however, because of the Catholic church rule that if you are not transferred by your own bishop, other diocese cannot accept you. It's what they call incardination and excardination.

Incardination is the process of being accepted by another diocese, and excardination is the process of being released by your own bishop to be accepted in another diocese. So, since my bishop was unwilling either to reinstate me or to excardinate me, I had to begin a new life. And that is when I hooked up with an NGO called the Solidarity Peace Trust (SPT), which then engaged me as one of their volunteers.

As a priest, I am used to working with the people, offering spiritual services, and from those first days it has been difficult for me to wake up each day knowing that I won't be able to perform my religious duties because I was—I am—on suspension. For example, I am filled with sorrow at not being able to conduct Mass for the purpose of saving God's people. But when I started working with SPT based in Johannesburg, I discovered that what gives me joy is that I am still working, still able to reach out to those that society casts aside, the underprivileged.

So that consoles me a great deal. Another thing which is amazing is how God works in our lives. As a priest I used to serve only one parish, but now the work I am doing with SPT allows me to serve an even bigger parish, one with no boundaries. I serve people of all tribes, all nations, of any color. Right now, I am working with Zimbabweans living in exile in South Africa, but I also serve Congolese, Malawians, Mozambicans, Somalis...

SO MANY WOUNDS

Think about all the people who are coming here, having that political stress on their minds, being overburdened by the economic strife back home and the troubles they had to go through in traveling from Zim to South Africa. So our mission is to not only give them a plate of food, but to be there to support them.

We are trying to restore the dignity that has been shattered on their journey from Zimbabwe. We are trying to help people understand what they are still capable of doing, that their potentialities have not been wasted. For example, so many trained teachers have been forced to come to South Africa. But here they are employed as maids and gardeners. The talent of trained and resourceful people is being wasted.

There are so many stories. I hear them on a daily basis. People who come here often lose sight of where they are going. Some fall pregnant. Young boys start to lead a life of debauchery. They become thieves, robbers, even murderers. Our aim is to rehabilitate these individuals. So we spend time with them, listen to their stories, try to bring them back to a normal kind of life. Our aim is to empower them today, so that they can be self-sufficient, self-supporting tomorrow, and be able to serve and uplift the shattered nation of Zimbabwe.

I am very grateful for these opportunities, because I too could have given up. I lost my priesthood; I could have lost my vision in life as well. I've suffered, but I've tried to stay focused.

PAMELA AND THEMBA

AGES: *27 and 28*

OCCUPATIONS: *Marketing for small companies (Pamela)*
Entrepreneur (Themba)

INTERVIEWED IN: *Harare, Zimbabwe*

When they first met, Pamela and her husband Themba were both employed in middle-class jobs in Harare. As the Zimbabwean economy started to falter and inflation skyrocketed in the early 2000s, the parallel (illegal) market took over. In 2002, seeing an opportunity to leave his office job, Themba began to import foreign cars illegally from across the border and sell them in Zimbabwe. To supplement her regular income after the birth of a new son, Pamela too entered the "informal" economy, selling clothes and food. Eventually, Pamela and Themba decided to form a small company that provides horticultural products to farmers. While so many Zimbabweans, and a number of people in this book, chose to leave the country, either for economic or political reasons (or a complex combination of both), many like Pamela and her husband have chosen to remain in the country, for better or for worse. Today, they own and run a small business in Harare, where they live with their two children.

PAMELA: I grew up in a nice house. And we had a modest life. Every day, you know, we had bread, tea with milk, sugar, a good sandwich, cold milk, eggs, everything. The whole works. Yes, we went to good schools—but then, everybody could do that. Because the money had value. Zimbabwe had one of the best education systems in this region. And now we are trying to send our kids to South Africa for them to get a good education. It's totally the other way around. And Zimbabwe was also regarded as the breadbasket of Africa. We used to export our produce to Botswana, South Africa, Mozambique, all those places.

I'm not saying there didn't have to be changes. Take land, for instance. Black people, communal farmers, had all the poor land. And then in the fertile areas, the land was reserved for the white commercial farmers. So of course the land had to be redistributed.

But the horror stories that we heard, some of them were so terrible. I mean, here in Harare we are so removed from it all. But you would see it on the telly. Say, for example, a white commercial farmer owns a farm. He employs many workers. He provides food for these workers. Then the veterans come and take the farm. The white farmer is not given time to even pack his things. They say: *Right now, leave this place, we're taking over all of it.* You know? And he had to leave everything that he's worked for his whole life. He's been in Zimbabwe since I don't know when. Just like that. And he has to go. If he refuses, then repercussions.

CHICKEN AT THE DRY CLEANERS

THEMBA: There was no transition. It was just, *Look, we're taking it right now, we're moving in.* So the method of acquiring these farms was harsh. And the result was a significant change in the environment, in the business environment throughout the country. Economically, things became unstable. Costs went way up. Then things started going bad. Not only the cost of transport, of fuel. Prices across the board were changing. Inflation started to rise at that time. There was so much happening. Everything was just going too fast. Shortages. Food shortages. There was no production on the farms. There was no production in industry. Different sectors were suffering. Inflation started rising.

We called this new era of high inflation and all the problems that went along with it "the black market." In the beginning, I was very ambitious. At that time, if you wanted to survive, you had to be experimental. Things—groceries, commodities that weren't obtainable in the formal markets—you'd find them outside. You had to go out hustling.

You had to go to the person dealing sugar. Sugar was a good business because, in fact, almost no one could find sugar. People couldn't find fuel either. So there were people dealing in fuel. You could deal in almost anything. I remember once I was at a soccer match and my friend said to me, *Hey, if you want chicken, go to Second Street. The dry cleaners, they have chicken.*

The dry cleaners are selling chickens! It was true, they were getting chickens from the farmer who was afraid of taking it to the supermarket because he was forced to sell it for the price that was below his production price so he was selling it from the back door of the dry cleaners.

Because, you see, prices were being controlled. Now, when this happens, the value of something increases. The control on certain commodities reduces the supply, so the people are forced into using the black market.

Now, if you got caught you could get penalized. If you're caught with the maize or rice, you know, it would be confiscated by the police. Same of course with sugar.

PAMELA: I remember even Orange Crush got on the market. A lot of the time, you could never find anything anywhere but on the black market.

THEMBA: Amid all this, the corrupt environment thrived. There were only a few powerful people who had access to commodities. For example, those in marketing control boards.[1] These top officials would channel certain things—grain, sugar, and fuel—to the black market. And that's how the black market thrived and the powerful became richer and richer.

But with corrupt activities going on from top to bottom, the economy itself started falling. Production suffered. The government started losing

---

[1] The ability of those with political power to make fortunes on the parallel market and in foreign exchange is discussed in the appendix on economic decline.

lots of money. The currency started falling as well. Then, within a few a years, we got to a point when the unemployment rate was over 90 percent or something. Industry wasn't functioning at all.

No products, and no imports. It was difficult to manufacture. So, when that year started, I think we're talking late 2003, people would start bringing in things. There were a lot of cross-border traders going to the regional countries—South Africa, Botswana, Mozambique—and bringing back commodities to sell. And then inflation just shot up, kept on going, higher and higher.

Yeah, it was hard. And I was involved in it, buying and selling on the black market. There was a lot of risk. You could be raided, your product could be taken away. In time, it became more and more dangerous. There were police raids. I knew I had to get out of it and into a more legitimate business, something more formal.

A BANANA FOR 10 TRILLION

THEMBA: The Zim dollar first crashed in 1997, and ever since it has just been dropping. This is a situation that we couldn't imagine, that we didn't think of. Right now, we are taking zeros[2] away from our currency. We're into the trillions now.

Zim dollars now? I give you 10 trillion Zimbabwean dollars, and you can't even buy a banana with 10 trillion. No one wants that money. It's painful, but, hey, I'm a Zimbabwean. We should be using our own money. At one time, it was quite a strong currency. We've sort of adjusted. We know our money is useless. We are not looking to the Zim dollar for anything.

We have money in the bank, but it's just Zimbabwean money. It's not

---

[2] Along with frequent devaluations of the national currency, the Reserve Bank of Zimbabwe redenominated the Zimbabwe dollar in August 2006 (one revalued dollar equalling one thousand old dollars) and again in 2008, when ZW$10 billion became equal to ZW$1. Overall, ten zeros were cut from the currency in this way, but the numbers soon climbed back into the trillions.

doing anything, and it's pointless for me to go and wait in line for two, three hours to get 10 trillion dollars, which can't even buy a banana. It's all about foreign currency today.

But then, some people really have no way of getting the foreign currencies. So they go to the bank every day to get their 10 trillion dollars and you always wonder how they do it. But the money, it's not making sense.

PAMELA: People out there are hungry, people are very hungry. And then you're thinking, How are these families surviving? How difficult it must be—especially for the men, the breadwinners—they can't buy a loaf of bread at work, to eat at work, and then their families are starving at home. In Zimbabwe, it's almost as though you are either poor or you're very rich. The poor, they can only afford just one meal of sadza a day. That's in the evening. I suppose in my family we are lucky, because we are able to eat every day. We are really not that hungry—yet. And the very rich? It's like they are not living in Zimbabwe.

When I think about it now, I think back to the liberation war. It's sort of history repeating itself, you know? We are in another war. I will say this is a sort of war too. It's a war because every day you are struggling to survive. When you wake up, there's no electricity, there's no water, there's no food.

For the first four years of the recession, my husband and I were on our own. We didn't have so many responsibilities. Who knew it would go on for over ten years? We used to think, *Oh, maybe next year it will be over.* And then of course, we got married, had kids, and you're not thinking about leaving when you've got young kids. We stay here because we have young kids.

Sometimes you really do think about it though. You think, Okay, so what am I supposed to do? Stay with the kids and watch them die of hunger? Or leave them so I can go and work in maybe South Africa, and every month send back money for food?

A few months back we almost left for South Africa. Because, yes, that's what you're thinking. You wake up in the morning and there's nothing. There's no mealie-meal, there's no sugar, there's no cooking oil, there's just nothing in the house. And you're thinking, *Why shouldn't I go to South Africa and work? My kids would be living a better life because I'd be able to provide food, clothes.* But I never did leave, because we thought we could actually make it.

THEMBA: And look, there are things you have to believe in. I'm a very patriotic person. I love Zimbabwe. I've been to other countries in the region. They don't compare to what I have here. Someone has to stay behind and protect it. So yes, I still do have hope.

PAMELA: We are not working for ourselves anymore. We are working for our kids, because we want the future to be brighter. Now, if we give up, or if something was to happen to us and we leave our kids where they are, they would have a really difficult task. They'd have to start from the bottom.

BRIGGS

OCCUPATION: *Director of Campaigns, Africa Action; former student leader*
INTERVIEWED IN: *Washington, D.C., USA*

It's easy to imagine Briggs leading student protests, as he used to do, or singing at the front of trade union marches, or moving up and down a train, educating passengers on their political rights. It's harder—and sadder—to imagine a man with so much to offer his country being imprisoned and interrogated along with so many hundreds of others who risked criticizing the government. After one too many brushes with the authorities, Briggs went underground and finally left the country in 2006. His two-year-old son was born in the U.S., but Briggs and his wife are packing up their Washington, D.C. lives, getting ready to take their boy home, aiming to keep working for a more just Zimbabwe and to raise him there.

I got my name "Briggs" from my days as a student leader in Zimbabwe. It comes from "brigadier." We were organized in a militant way and I was called Brigadier Bomba. In 2000, I was imprisoned the first time. There were four of us. When they took us to the court for sentencing, a huge crowd showed up. They had to bring out the riot police. Outside there were students waiting, chanting, *Brigadier! Brigadier!* I think the fact that we had so many people out there was intimidating. We ended up being granted bail, a very small amount, and remanded out of custody.

Right after that, we continued. I remember going back to campus with my arm in plaster. I said things like, *With this firm hand, I demand our right to education. We demand democracy.* This turned into another huge protest, with thousands of people marching to the library, the admin building, all over campus. Freedom Hall was packed, people sitting on the ground, singing the song we used to start meetings: "Iva Gamba"—*Be a fighter, be a warrior, face the enemy.*

My father was very distressed about what I was doing. I remember him telling me on the phone, *Son, you can be anything that you want to be. But this is not the way. You do your school. That is your path.* For him, this was such a terrible thing: the son that he had raised should not have done these things. My name was now on the news, on television, in newspapers. But my mom was the one who was completely shattered. Panicked. She thought I was already dead.

As student activists, we were prepared to deal with it. But we never really thought about the impact on our parents. Our real, new family had become the activist community—they would look for the lawyers, would campaign for solidarity internationally. But our parents were left on their own to deal with all of this. Up to now, my mother is full of fears for me. She tells me, *Don't come back.*

NUMBER ONE

I was a very curious child raised in a very authoritarian family. My old man was firm: by six we had to be home. My father—and my mom as well—valued education a lot and we were encouraged from the beginning to prioritize that. Education and the church. So I always fought, from primary school on, to lead my class, because every time I came home and said, *I came number one in class*, there'd be a big celebration. My mom would slaughter a chicken for me, *muurairei huku*. She has a very strong traditional background—not so much my dad—so even when she distributes the pieces of the chicken, she gives this piece to the head of the household, this piece to mom, these pieces to the kids. But on those days, she would go against cultural protocol and make sure I picked the pieces I wanted first. My old man would give me some cash to be able to do whatever I wanted. I wanted so many things: Korn Kurls, or this candy called *chiponda moyo*, "something that smashes your heart."

My mom is from Manicaland. Her home area is called Chikonzo, the same as their last name, which means it's their land. Like all royal families, she can trace their origins to the very beginning of the world. I always used to be fascinated visiting my mother's place as a child, seeing this completely different life, working the fields with ox-drawn plows, traveling by scotchcart, milking cows. A rural set-up was so novel when I was very young. I remember big rivers, forests. Now, if you go there, those rivers are just gullies, dry sand. The land is unproductive. There are no trees, no fruits. Everyone used to have a lot of cattle, but now the area has become barren and desolate.

I'm still tracing my dad's family history. His brother was born in Hurungwe, and my dad always talked about how we were related to Chief Chipota in Guruve, but my father was a city man. My old man passed in 2006, before we had explored all of these questions. I still have to piece the story together.

My old man had become one of the first senior managers for National Foods, a big corporation. He employed hundreds of people on the stock-feeds production side. And he was very kind. I remember one day right after high school. We are driving. There's an old woman on the side of the road, at the place where trucks deliver maize to his depot. And she is picking up all the little kernels that have fallen on the side of the road. I remember my dad stopping, getting out, talking to her, and giving her some money to go buy a decent amount of maize for her family.

HEAVEN AND HELL, SIDE BY SIDE

My father was very interested in farming. Right near the end of Rhodesia, toward Independence, he'd gone back to farming in the rural area, when the first white folks vacated, those who didn't feel like they could live in an independent Zimbabwe. He was able to get access to some of that land in Macheke through his church. Part of our lives was on the farm and farming, and part of it was living in Harare, work, and school.

Surrounding that farm were white farmers of Macheke. It was a really productive farming area, the heart of the Virginia tobacco farming sector. Those neighboring farmers were super wealthy. We would see their private planes. Sometimes they would spray the crops, and sometimes just flying around. Beautiful houses. And the latest Nissan hardbody when it's released. Horses, some for riding, some for herding the cattle, a boat, motor bikes. It was like an all-around package of paradise. Sort of.

The other side was the life of the farm workers. Tiny little soot-filled hovels, that's where these workers lived. They'd all wear overalls, most of them torn, and worn-out boots. Every morning, at every farm, you'd have this bell, a big metal gong, that someone would go and hit at three a.m. Then people would wake up to go to the tobacco fields. We are talking about huge farms, thousands of hectares each. At every farm there would be a farm store, where workers would borrow *matemba*[1] or a packet of sugar. Then, when it's time for your salary, whatever you borrowed is more than you earned, so you head into another cycle, indebted to the farm store.

Sometimes, my mom would sell things to the workers on surrounding farms, like tomatoes, or she would bake bread. (She is an excellent baker.) Come end of the month, I'd go to collect payments. I was able to see how completely miserable their lives were. It was like heaven and hell, living side by side.

In Kasipiti—the huge farm in Macheke belonging to my father's church—we had huge rivers running through the farm. We would fish. I learned to swim in a dam. The forests had big thick trees. There were many seasonal wild fruits, *mazhanje, matohwe, matamba.*[2] The soil itself

---

[1] Small river or lake fish, dried.

[2] These are, respectively, wild loquat/Uapaca kirkiana (*mazvhanje*), snot apple/Azanza garckeana (*matohwe*), monkey apple/Strychnos pungens (*matamba-usiku*).

is very productive and there is a lot of good rainfall, so the fields produce and you are able to harvest. Contrast that with my mother's area, Marange, where there's no water, basically. All the rivers are silted-up gullies, except for a few rivers like the Save which are seriously threatened. Trees are sparse, only very robust trees that can survive without rainfall are left. Grazing land is very little, too. Sometimes your cattle eat another person's crops, and it's always sparking disputes, which can become fatal. Each time I go to visit my grandparents, even today, there is always a dispute about *muganhu*.[3] People are always fighting about the boundary: *Your field ends there.* Even within the same family, the younger brother and the older brother fight over *muganhu*. And it's worse with neighbors. People are really crowded on small pieces of land that are not productive, even for grazing their animals. And water is a huge problem.

And then as a child I would see the contrast with the paddocks in Macheke. Those commercial farmers were thoroughly organized. Like clockwork, farming season: The tobacco fields are prepared. The seedlings are transplanted. Come harvest time, there is the maize. The farms were broken into paddocks. You are grazing in this paddock, then after a while, you move the cattle to graze a different area. You keep moving to allow the land to regenerate. The land was really managed, so it did not deteriorate. People were not allowed to cut green trees. Only the dry trees that have fallen can be used for firewood. Of course, all of that changed when the whole disorganized land reform took place later on.

Land is owned in different ways in Zimbabwe. In the commercial areas, our farm Kasipiti for example, it's large pieces of land with individual titles. It's commercially, privately owned, and the titles are transferable. So these farmers were able to leverage those titles to access money from banks to invest in their farming activities. Then, in the rural areas, the land is communally owned and held in trusts by chiefs. There, it's the chief and all their sub-structures, the *sabhuku* and the headman, who

---

[3] From Shona: the boundary.

oversee and allocate the land. When your son comes of age—you never really talk about the daughters—you can go to the chief and say, *My son needs a place to build his own home and grow his own crops.* My mother's father has one, two, three, four, *five* boys, so he's had to cut his farm to give each one of them a piece of their own land to grow their crops on. Five of them. No one has title to any of that land. You cannot use it as collateral with a bank. Because it's overcrowded, people cultivate close to the river. The next thing you know, all the soil is washing into the river and the river has died. People will chop whatever tree is there, leave it to dry, and then use it for firewood because that's the only fuel they have. So you end up having completely barren pieces of deforested land.

Of course, that land did not just deteriorate in the time since I started visiting. The history of colonialism in Zimbabwe was about folks being pushed into areas with low rainfall. Some commercial farming areas border on communal areas. As you leave Marange, for example, you get to commercial farms in Odzi, where the rainfall is better, and the forests are still there. People in the villages, the chiefs and the kings, speak of it as their land. *Oh, our land used to extend beyond those farms before they were farms and before we were moved out here.* They know it as their land because there is a very strong oral tradition in those areas.

Commercial farms, which have always been mainly white owned, also got a lot of government support. For example, government graders used to come and pave the farm roads around Kasipiti. I'm telling you, to get a telephone line to our house, government workers had to lay poles for more than thirty kilometers, but it was done. Those lines went through rivers, bush, whatever.[4] On that ten-thousand-hectare farm, there were only three telephone lines: one for us, one for the head of the church who was the primary owner of the farm, and one other. All that work for three telephone lines. The government had set up all those services, facilitated all that support. But there was nothing like that for my grandparents in the rural areas.

---

[4] See Lovemore's story—this is the work his father did in the government's electricity supply authority.

So those were the three images I had growing up. First, the experience in my own grandparents' area, where land is the biggest issue. Then, the experience of the commercial farming area where there is so much wealth. Those farms were huge, with so much support. And third, that picture of the farm workers themselves and how miserable their lives were.

BREAD RIOTS

My family had lived in a middle-class neighborhood in Harare called Waterfalls since I was very young. It was one of the first whites-only places to be opened up to Africans, black Zimbabweans. My family were among the very first people to move there. I was living there and going to school in Highfields, which is the working-class township, very historic in terms of the nationalist struggle in Zimbabwe and of the post-Independence struggle. That's where groups like Zanu-PF were founded. Even Mugabe's original house is there.

In 1993, when I got to Form I,[5] I was still living in Waterfalls, going to school at St. Peters, walking around five to seven miles each way. Quite a trek, now I come to think of it. My brother had just started a job with my father's company, doing an apprenticeship. He was renting a single room in Glenview and he invited me to stay with him. And that's when protests broke out—the first of the bread riots.

I remember one day coming from school, early evening, hearing people running through the streets chanting a slogan: *Five bhobho chingwa! Five bhobho chingwa!* meaning *Five bob[6] {fifty cents} a loaf of bread.* Over and over and over again. People were raiding shops, first taking bread, and later anything they could get their hands on. At that point, 1993, the price of bread had gone up so high, close to a dollar, or in some places maybe even a dollar fifty.

---

[5] The first year of secondary school, equivalent to ninth grade.

[6] "Bob" is slang for "shilling." Rhodesia converted from pounds, shillings, and pence to dollars and cents in 1970, but many people continued to call ten cents "one bob."

This is the thing in the township: when there is some excitement going on, everyone joins in. Immediately, me and this other schoolboy joined the protestors, running through the township from one tuck shop to the next tuck shop, from one shopping center to the next shopping center, chanting, *Five bhobho chingwa.* It became a big protest and we were running around the whole night. Later in the night, we saw riot police deployed into the township. They were quite merciless when they cornered people. We saw people lying down on the tarmac and being seriously thrashed. Every time a group of people grew large, tear gas would be fired. People were running. The houses are so close together in the township, and there are so many alleys, it was difficult for the police to pin people down. People were able to come and dare the cops and then suddenly disappear and regroup and keep chanting.

After chanting and running for hours, now we are walking back home to go and sleep, maybe three a.m. As we're walking home, me and this other guy, we hear, *You! Come here.* We realize there's a group of cops and they have people lying down. They yell, *Where are you coming from? Where are you going?* Luckily, the guy that I was walking with actually knew one of the cops. He told him, *We are just going home right here.* And the cop was like, *Okay.*

Protests of that kind were not common at that time. It was the beginning of the wave. This was three years into the structural adjustment program,[7] so things were already beginning to get bad.

What we found out later on was that this protest had actually started in Mabvuku, which is another poor working-class township, by women who sell vegetables at the *musika.*[8] They were the ones who said, *Enough is enough*, and they came up with the slogan, *Five bhobho chingwa, five bhobho chingwa.* Like a veld fire, it quickly spread to all the townships.

---

[7] The structural adjustment program is discussed in the appendix section on Zimbabwe's economic decline.

[8] A Shona word for "market" used in English in Zimbabwe.

NO RUBBER BULLETS

Other protests were starting. As I continued high school, teachers often went on strike. In Form 3, 1995, we had a long stretch where teachers were not coming to work because they were protesting.

I finished my O-Levels in 1996.[9] I moved back to Harare, and was living in another township, Mabvuku. Mabvuku became the center of the next food riots, which broke out in 1997 and 1998. What we had seen in 1993 now looked like a tiny little tea party. This was a huge protest. That's when, even though we were in high school, everyone started to know who Morgan Tsvangirai was because he was the Secretary-General of the Zimbabwe Congress of Trade Unions, ZCTU. When these protests were breaking out, Tsvangirai emerged as the leader, organizing the call for stay-aways. People would stay away from work, and those who ignored the call and went to work would meet resistance. In the late 1990s, they say up to a million people would stay away when those stay-aways were called.

I remember going to the shopping center and finding everything smashed, people running out with the hindquarters of a bull or a television set, raiding supermarkets, and the military being a constant presence on the streets of Mabvuku. Stories went around about how brutal they were. If they caught you during the rainy season, they'd make you lie in a pool of water and then you'd be thrashed, or they'd get two of you and make you beat each other, observing you and making sure you were brutal to each other—it could be husband and wife walking and they'd call them to beat each other. It got to the point where they criminalized just being on the street.

We had very few civil-society organizations in Zimbabwe at that point. ZCTU was one of the central, leading ones. The communication with the outside world was minimal. People just felt, *Oh that's the nature of the military, or the soldiers—don't mess with them.* It's not like now

[9] See footnote 8, page 59.

where it sparks this outrage. It was before email and Internet, where you can quickly send a message—*There's this abuse going on*—with pictures. The military felt that they could act with impunity. My high school was colored by protest, left, right, and center. Many days, my parents would deem it not safe to leave the house. The government even released military tanks into the townships. Dumiso Dabengwa[10] was Minister of Home Affairs then, and he said something to the effect that, *Our army does not use rubber bullets, they are armed with live bullets and they will shoot to kill.*

YELLOW CARD

In 1998, toward the end of the year, my parents moved to Chegutu, because my father was promoted to become the head of National Foods in that region. That meant having a fiefdom. When you're head, you employ whoever you want. You fire people the way you want. I used to see long checkbooks, thirty centimeters[11] or more. He could sign a check for a million dollars on the National Foods' account because he'd be buying in bulk for the depots, moving maize around the country. Our life completely changed. You would have security people saluting you each time you walked onto the premises.

After exams, I moved from Harare to Chegutu to follow them. Between the time you finish your high school in November and the time you are supposed to go to university, there's a long break. You wait for your results to come in around March. I had my ten points.[12] I was really excited. In March 1999, my old man put me on a train to go to university in Bulawayo.

I had studied maths, physics, and chemistry in high school. And my

---

[10] A ZIPRA leader locked up for five years during Gukurahundi, and later a powerful presence in the Zanu-PF government.

[11] One foot.

[12] A-level results are accorded points. Admission to university is highly competitive and points-based.

father wanted me to be an engineer. Or a doctor. That's what he was pushing for. I applied to do civil engineering at both the National University of Science and Technology in Bulawayo (NUST) and the University of Zimbabwe in Harare. I was offered places at both, but I chose to go to Bulawayo. I think I wanted to get far away. Bulawayo was the farthest I had been and I was on my own—renting a place for the first time.

This is 1999. Things were really heating up. The Working People's Convention had been held in February, where all these groups said, *ZCTU must spearhead efforts to form a new political party to challenge for political power.* So we were already in a totally defiant mood. People had already turned their back on Mugabe, feeling that he was illegitimate.

I get to the university two weeks before the beginning of school. The vice-chancellor is supposed to meet us for orientation. I see these very radical and defiant young men, who don't seem to care about authority. Suddenly they climb up onto walls and shout slogans, *Ahoy comrades! Ahoy comrades!* On that very first day, the message from the Zimbabwe National Students' Union was, *Listen comrades, we have issues to fight for. Ignore the vice-chancellor's orientation. When you want to discuss your problems, you will never see him.*

I blame the three student leaders I heard that day—Nelson Chamisa, Hopewell Gumbo, and Takura Zhangazha—for shattering my father's dream for me to become a civil engineer. Because from that day, I was like, *Forget everything else. You are my comrades.* I ended up very close to all of them, especially Hopewell Gumbo, president of the Zimbabwe National Students' Union and also a student at my university, NUST. I looked for him that afternoon, before I went to my first class, to say, *What books do you read?* Because they really blew me away. That was my introduction to university.

From that moment, student organizing was my priority. Every day we had activities: a study circle, a campaign against corrupt campus caterers, and meetings and discussions about national issues, such as the constitutional debate. I would move around with Hopewell, educating people and becoming an activist myself.

Later, I was elected the president of the Student Representative Council. From the minute we were elected, we restructured the students' union, putting it in a combative mode. We saw ourselves as waging a struggle—to get President Mugabe out of power and to bring in a new political dispensation, one in which people's basic bread-and-butter issues were addressed, and the rights to education and the rights of workers secured.

We would go back and forth to Harare for conventions around constitutional reform and for meetings to prepare the launch of the Movement for Democratic Change, MDC. On the train from Bulawayo to Harare or back, we would move from coach to coach, educating people about the issues. Sometimes, there would be war veterans on the train, too, singing revolutionary songs, while our songs would denigrate Mugabe. We had created the Ahoy Choir, and myself and Msavaya[13] were always composing new songs and teaching them to people.

The main thrust of our organizing at that time was around constitutional reform. This is what got civil society mobilized in the late 1990s. The president had appointed a commission to rewrite the national constitution. Most of the members of that commission were aligned to Zanu-PF, so we didn't really feel that a democratic constitution would emerge from that. We wanted a process for writing the constitution that was open, that would allow people to participate in it, and that would have a legitimate authority presiding over it. Over time we initiated a parallel process through the National Constitutional Assembly (NCA).[14]

By that point, I had become a student leader at NUST, so I was working with the NCA in Bulawayo to educate people around constitutional reform issues, but also to organize a boycott of the meetings that the government's Constitutional Commission was trying to conduct. We would go around from school to school, we would go to neighborhoods, speaking

---

[13] One of Hopewell Gumbo's names.

[14] A number of narrators in this collection were involved in the NCA. See Elizabeth's narrative for example.

about what a truly democratic constitution-writing process would look like and why people should boycott this version.

When it came time for actually voting for or against the new constitution that the government was proposing, February 12, 2000, I was a monitor at a polling station at one of the schools from morning to evening. And the following day, I was part of the tallying process, where we were counting the yeses against the nos. We were thoroughly thrilled to see President Mugabe on TV conceding defeat, saying that the new constitution had been defeated. It was this completely incredible moment: *We have won.* We had organized and this was really our first taste of political victory against the entrenched machinery that had looked so invincible up to that point. So it really boosted people's confidence: *We can actually change things in this country.* Which is why, right after that, we started calling it a yellow card.

Soccer is the people's sport in Zimbabwe. Everyone knows that if you commit a fault while on the field, the referee gives you a yellow card as a warning. If you do another fault, you get a red card. So, we were saying, *Okay, this is a warning. The next time*—the elections in June 2000—*it's a red card.* Once you get a red card, you are booted off the field.[15]

It was a huge wake-up call to Zanu-PF to realize for the first time, *We could actually lose power.* Right after we celebrated that victory, the political landscape changed drastically. That's when the war veterans marched on the farms. That was the response to the people who voted against the constitution, who had opposed the clause that says, *We are forcibly taking land for the people.* That's when Zanu-PF teams were organized in the rural areas to make them impenetrable to the opposition, remobilizing all the arms of violence, especially the war veterans at that point, and later the youth militias as well. Zanu-PF took it very seriously, changed everything. Within the blink of an eye, it was very dangerous to go out to Uzumba Maramba Pfungwe and try and hold an

---

[15] See Boniface's story for more on yellow and red cards as activist tools.

opposition rally. Some places became completely sealed off. You could not go there.

Before that, teachers were actively involved in spreading this message around: *You have the political right to choose your leader. If life is hard, you can choose a different way.* Things had not yet been destabilized as much as they were later, so farmers were speaking to their workers. Basically, everyone was involved in the political process. But right after the referendum, when war veterans occupied the farms, farm workers were intimidated with terrible violence and told, *You cannot vote in any other way, you are becoming an agent of imperialists.*

The biggest shock was the death of Talent Mabika and Tichaona Chiminya. They were part of Morgan's very close circle, campaigning for MDC ahead of the elections. In Murambinda, in Tsvangirai's home area of Buhera, they were cornered by people claiming to be war veterans, and their car was petrol-bombed. They were basically burned alive.

The people who did this were very well known, the leader's name is known. But there was absolute impunity. Not a single person has ever been arrested for this incident. This incident foretold what was coming: people would be defenseless, they could not rely on the police for protection. These acts were meant to reverse the momentum of the successful referendum and to ensure that the red card was not delivered come election time.

The killing of Talent Mabika and Tichaona Chiminya—their shocking, brutal deaths—marked the end of a glorious period of organizing.

THE NEW CHEESEMANS

I knew we needed land justice in Zimbabwe. You have to understand how it was for people like my maternal grandparents, forced to eke out a living on a barren piece of land, knowing that the green, productive areas that border their villages are, actually, part of their own land. Some of their ancestors were buried in those hills.

But I did not support land reform when the war veterans invaded the farms and when President Mugabe launched his Fast Track Land Reform.[16] In my eyes, he had lost his mandate to do anything for Zimbabweans. So much had changed in a few years. So, for President Mugabe to say, *I'm going to deliver land reform*, when our mood had already swung from *five bhobho chingwa* in 1995 to *Mugabe must go* in 1999—well, we were not prepared to hear it.

The pressure to get land was not only coming from someone in Zanu-PF scheming, *Okay, now we issue a call to take over those farms.* There had been other farm occupations by villagers in other parts of the country, too. In 1997, villagers from Svosve area occupied commercial farms adjacent to their communal lands, but they were thrown off those farms by Mugabe's riot police: *Out, out!*[17] And now the government was pushing land reform, at a time when it would be used as a political gimmick. The urban areas were up in arms, so the government needed something to take to the rural areas, to rally their support there.

The situation that we need to correct was a racist land ownership set-up. But when you get to the point of completely denying part of your population the right to citizenship because of their race, I think you are simply creating another problem, a big problem. Some commercial farmers who paid money for their farms[18] lost everything simply because they were white. Some of them had only owned that land for ten years but still lost it, and lost their property too—the tractors that they'd bought, things like that. It just did not make sense.

You cannot turn back the wheels of history. The white community are equally Zimbabweans at this point. My friend Comrade Fatso,[19] for

---

[16] For details of Zimbabwe's Fast Track Land Reform, see the appendix section on war veterans and land invasions.

[17] Zanu-PF would subsequently deem these villagers heroes in initiating the Land Reform program.

[18] As opposed to those who were allocated land by the earlier colonial and settler governments, notably when the country was being "settled" from the 1890s onwards and as reward to white soldiers during an immigration drive after World War II.

[19] A dreadlocked rap poet and cultural activist, son of long-established white Zimbabwean families.

example: he was born there, his family has been there for over a hundred years, Zimbabwe is all he's known.

As I was growing up, I noticed that one farmer would usually own three or four adjacent farms. That was one option: to simply say to commercial farmers, *You are left with one farm each.*

One of the big issues now is repeating this multiple-farm phenomenon. The new privileged class, those who are really highly connected politically, now own three farms, four farms. I don't subscribe to the story that *all* the land was given to politicians, because I know that thousands of very basic, rural people got land too. But the privileged political class accessed the choicest pieces of land. And you now have the new Cheeseman with four farms, basically repeating the same exploitative conditions from before. Or even worse.

THE BULAWAYO FIVE

The referendum on the constitution—our great victory—was in February 2000, and the elections were in June that same year. By the time of the elections, we had seen the killing of Mabika and Chiminya, we had seen the violence on the farms, which displaced so many people. But still the opposition got 48 percent of the seats in Parliament. So we knew it was very close. Without the violence, the opposition would have won outright. ZCTU talked about protesting the results and making demands for workers, and we at NUST called for a protest to coincide with it.

There was pandemonium on campus, with more than a thousand students marching to town, out of a total of 4,500 students in the whole university. The level of political mobilization was that high. The police moved quickly to stop us by sealing the campus. It was a drizzling wet day, with dark birds flying above and a certain mood. The police panicked when students released fire extinguishers—*boom! boom!* spitting out powder—but finally they subdued the student union building.

I was with five people from the union in our office trying to plan the next move. Someone had come to tip us off that the police were now doing a door-to-door search, so we shut everything and stayed quiet. Then we see a baton stick opening a window at the back and they shout, *Open up or we're throwing tear gas into the room.* We ended up opening the door and they put five of us in their truck.

The minute we get to the central police station in Bulawayo, without saying anything, they just start viciously thrashing the others with batons. They were not beating me at that point. I was saying, *What are the charges? We have the right to appear before a judge.* They just said, *You kids, you don't know what you are up against. You are trying to challenge the president.*

These were police in full uniform, the riot police and the response unit. PISI people were also there—the Police Internal Security Intelligence folks who were always following us. They beat everyone, making them bend over a bench and thoroughly thrashing them like that, but I would not let them do that to me. So five of them came and randomly beat me all over, very viciously, breaking my arm. Being hit like that, the intense pain, a minute is the equivalent of three hours. *When is this going to end?*

They threw us into a cell with three *bhanditi*, complete outlaws, from the notorious maximum security section. They don't fear anything, they're serving long terms. One of them said, in Ndebele, *I'm going to fuck one of you tonight, but I'll choose later.* We quickly realized that we needed to band together to survive this, and stand our ground.

The cell was small. In one corner, the toilet, just a hole where you had to go and squat, that could only be flushed from outside. And we packed that space—at least twenty of us at all times. There was literally no room to lie down. The floor of the cell was covered in a red blanket that had turned black and brown, all caked with filth. It was cold at that time, in the middle of winter, and that was the only blanket. It had a label: *Dreamwell*.

A hierarchy emerged. The weakest ones found their nose in the toilet hole, in the corner, which reeked. Even now I can smell it. There was no window, only a little grille at the top, where we would go and beg the prison officers: *Chef! Chef!*[20] *Tokumbira flush!* which means, *Chef, can you please flush this thing?* They would take their time. A few times a day, you would go out to get your food, porridge caked up on aluminum plates and some tea. We were counted four times a day, the last time at around eight-thirty, and then we slept at nine.

CIO[21] people, wearing dark shirts, would come to take us away one by one for interrogation. Everyone in the cell was becoming interested, because it was not the regular police dealing with us. *What did you guys do? This must be something intense.* We played on that because it gave us some cred in the cell. We got some sort of respect from the bandits. We created our own corner of the cell, we had access to our Dreamwell, and no one got raped in there. We actually built friendships, staying in that cell for five days. We ended up teaching people the songs from our protests outside.

By the third or fourth day, we all had diarrhea. That created new tensions because we could not wait to relieve ourselves according to the timetable. There was a lot of shouting, we were at each other's throats. *You are killing us in here! This place is unbearable!* I had not had medical attention for the cracked bone in my arm, so I was in intense pain the whole time.

We were interrogated every day. This guy comes in wearing dark shades and calls your name. The minute you walk into the interrogation room, he pulls out a gun, puts it right on the table. There are three other people in there and marks of blood on the walls. *We know what you guys are up to. We know you want to overthrow the government.* Once in a while, someone else comes in. They ask, *Is he speaking yet?*

They had been trying to get hold of me for a while. Now they said, *Look at this little boy! He's the one who's giving us problems.* They'd do it with everyone. Each one would come back with different stories. Some would

---

[20] From *chefe*, Portuguese for "head" or "chief"—adopted into Zimbabwean English from the period of the Independence struggle, when Zanu operated from bases in Portuguese-speaking Mozambique.

[21] The Central Intelligence Organization, the state intelligence wing.

get lashed again to make them speak. Luckily, they kept putting us in the same cell.

The first charge against us was treason, which came completely out of the blue. But we basically kept to our story. We said we were simply demanding that the government reinstate funding to university students and stop privatizing education. They were cancelling grants at that time and imposing loans, so students had to borrow from private banks.

In the meantime, because people saw us getting arrested, there was a campaign, *Free the Bulawayo Five*, that sort of became international. Luckily, I had a comrade from the U.K. who was in the country doing research on student politics. He was very active, mobilizing solidarity, setting things up online. We were still very young on the Internet, but he was able to get people phoning, sending faxes from as far away as London.

On the third day, they eased off on us. We were just waiting. At that time, support was not well organized—we didn't have Zimbabwe Lawyers for Human Rights coming to take our case. Some of our colleagues on the outside had to go and find a lawyer. Our lawyer was not that experienced at this sort of thing, but his presence made us feel better, more confident.

On the last day, we were ready to go. But then we got word through the lawyer that they were going to oppose bail. I'm telling you, we were not ready to spend even one more hour behind those bars. Remember, this is when we had diarrhea. It was chaos in there, begging for the flush. I saw my comrades break down in tears, really crying.

That's the occasion when the students chanted outside court in big numbers, when we were released on bail, and when we headed back to campus to keep organizing.

What I remember is the darkness in the cell. Even at twelve midday, it was dark. Our only connection with the outside world was the clock at Bulawayo City Hall, chiming the hour.

A DIRTY BROOM

By the time I left university in 2005 and went back to Harare, my father had moved the whole family down to Mutare, to my mother's home area in Marange. He had a piece of land there for a long time but he had never used it. So now he reoccupied it and tried to raise an income from it.

His circumstances had changed. He had left National Foods in a terrible way. Basically, he was forced to resign. His whole empire crashed, and this had a huge effect on the family. He lost his job when the economy was tanking, so whatever money he had saved was blown away, becoming valueless fast. He tried various projects—a big garden, a chicken project, a bakery—but nothing really worked. My father's last days were very stressful for him. He had always been at the top, and now he was completely shattered. We had no money at all.

I was now on my own and my life became 100 percent activism. In Bulawayo, we worked on national constitutional issues. Any civil society agenda, we were at the forefront. At that point, almost everyone who was opposed to Mugabe was part of the Movement for Democratic Change, MDC. There was really no division between civil society and the emerging party. We were up in Rufaro launching the party. I was at the first congress in Chitungwiza electing the first leadership of the party... all of that. Up to that point, the opposition was a coalition of all these civic groups—ZCTU played a role, the students' union, we were all part of it. It was a movement when it started, but when the political party was formed, it started to take on a life of its own. A distance emerged between the party and civil society.

"Operation Murambatsvina" (sweep out the trash) was on at that point. In an article I wrote about it, I put the question: how can a dirty broom possibly sweep anything clean?[22] People called Murambatsvina "the tsunami" because it devastated so many ordinary people's lives.

---

[22] The article is titled, "When a Dictator Is as Devastating as a Tsunami." Briggs drew on this article to describe Murambatsvina in this account.

I quoted some statistics in my article: that Murambatsvina displaced over a million people, leaving them refugees in their own country; that 300,000 kids dropped out of school; that over 22,000 poor people trying to survive on informal trading were arrested by the police, and their goods, worth millions of dollars, were confiscated or destroyed. And all of this at a time when the informal sector was the only option people had.

The first day, I saw riot police driving into Mabvuku in Defender trucks, singing and drumming as if they were psyching up for war. The next day hundreds of cops drove around the township with sirens blaring and all their tools of violence on display. They were giving instructions to residents to destroy all informal structures. If they came around and you had not destroyed your own cottages and tuck shops, you would get it. They would beat you up for resisting and ask you to start demolishing while they watched. Sometimes they rounded up everyone in the vicinity and forced them to take down the structures. Tuck shops, cottages, market stalls—they were all coming down in dust and smoke. People did not know where to sleep that very night. Many of these houses—now ruins—had sheltered people for over two decades. Late into the night, I saw women with kids strapped on their backs pushing everything they had saved in carts. Some lit fires and slept in the open.

In Chitungwiza, there was heavy rain after the demolitions, so it was even more depressing. At my brother's house, another family was sheltering on his verandah with all they could pick up from the rubble of their home. Another neighbor's kids were sleeping in the lounge. Their mother was away at a funeral when their place was destroyed. I heard terrible stories from all over Harare and all over the country. In Tafara a kid died when a wall fell on her. In Gweru a man committed suicide from the stress and desperation of the situation. The media carried stories of a mother who had to drag her terminally ill son from a burning hut torched by the police. People living with HIV/AIDS couldn't take their drugs. This was almost like an execution, because with antiretroviral drugs—ARVs—you have to stick to the course 100 percent, otherwise you become resistant to the drug and die.

In Harare, vendors came out at night to try and sell something: tomatoes, onions, bananas, avocados. They had no choice. Selling was their only means of survival. I saw vendors, mostly women, begging passersby to buy their vegetables, and looking out for the cops who might raid at any time. On their regular night raids, the police would beat up and arrest the women and seize their goods, just keep them. Their fringe benefits. One vendor was beaten with a wooden plank in a police interrogation room. While beating him, the cop shouted, *You are being told go and work on the farms but you are refusing.*

The cops were rounding up people from the streets and dumping them on certain farms. One of my good friends went to one of these farms. He said people there were under twenty-four-hour police guard. No journalists were allowed in, and aid workers had escorts to censor what they were allowed to discuss with those inside the camps. No cameras, no cell phones. My friend described terrible scenes in there. The mentally ill tied to trees to restrain them. No safe drinking water, people drinking from the same dam they use for bathing. No houses or toilets—people sleeping in the open. Tents donated by aid groups just heaped somewhere—the police said the tents would be illegal structures if they were pitched. The terminally ill in desperate need of medication.

HOUNDED

After the 2005 presidential election, Zanu-PF had a two-thirds majority in parliament. The MDC was in disarray, not really offering leadership. ZCTU again came up with an idea to protest harsh living conditions. I worked on a flyer listing our demands, things that we wanted resolved.

At around one in the afternoon, we all head out on the protest. I'm like the MC, leading the singing, right in the front, moving things forward, as we march near Town House in central Harare, and then, from nowhere, we are surrounded. Out of all the people marching, one hundred and twenty of us are arrested. They seal the streets. They spring on us: *Everyone sit down!*

Munyaradzi Gwisai was part of the protest, a high-profile person because he had been a member of parliament, a very controversial one. He tried to say something, and a policeman beat him with a baton. An elected leader and there he is, being beaten.

They pack us into a truck: Wellington Chibebe (ZCTU Secretary General right now), Lovemore Matombo (the president of the ZCTU), a lot of ZCTU people from the regions—all of us arrested. They take us to Harare Central Police Station and file-march us to cells. I had been arrested during Murambatsvina, so some of the policemen knew me: *Oh, Bomba, you again?* We were eight or so per cell, so it wasn't as packed as other times, or as stinky. But in no time, bedbugs came swooshing down on us. The cell was infested, unbearable.

At midnight, we hear gates opening. Everyone must come outside. We are made to line up and told to go outside the building, in the pitch-black night. Guys wearing overalls, looking like farm workers but all holding AK-47s, force-march us into another truck, packed to twice its capacity. We don't know where we are going, but eventually we find ourselves at Makoni Police Station in Chitungwiza.[23]

This police station had not had water for two weeks. Even by prison standards, the facilities were too unhealthy to hold people. They packed us in what I can call two cages: men on one side, women on the other side. A number of people there were living with HIV/AIDS, and they were being denied medicine, denied water. There wasn't enough room to sit down, so we took turns, some seated, some standing. There was no hole for a toilet. We had to beg the guard for a bucket. Woman were right there and men right here, so there was no privacy. In no time, the bucket overflowed. We tried to keep our spirits up, singing revolutionary songs, but they shouted, *Everyone quiet!*

I think they started allowing us to have food from outside the second

---

[23] Chitungwiza is a dormitory city on the outskirts of Harare, a large city built before independence as a dormitory for black workers. The relationship between Chitungwiza and Harare is something like the one between Soweto and Johannesburg.

day, food that relatives and other activists brought us. And you could relieve yourself the few times you had to go outside—when they took your information or if they selected you for questioning by the CIO. I was one of those taken for questioning, and so were the ZCTU leadership. By now, things were a bit better organized, so Zimbabwe Lawyers for Human Rights were there constantly.

They moved us into individual cells the next day. I was in a cell with six other people, no water, and a burst sewer overflowing onto the floor. We had no shoes. The beds were bunks made of cement. No blanket, no Dreamwell. One police officer, a very young guy, appeared to be sympathetic. We didn't know whether to trust him or whether he was a plant to try and get to us. But he did end up getting us moved from that awful sewer to a bigger cell, with the whole leadership there, so we were able to hold a meeting.

We were released on the fourth day. We were not even taken to court that time. They just changed their position and released us. But after that, I became a real target in Harare. Police officers used to come to the Zimrights Center on Fourth Street where I was working, so I decided to go underground.

When I changed phones, I gave my old phone to a colleague. He told a caller, *I'm right here at Quick and Easy,* a popular internet café. In no time, four guys appear at Quick and Easy and one dials his number. When his phone rings, they lift him, throw him in a car, and drive him to Rhodesville Police Station. He tells them, *I'm not Bomba.* Luckily he had his ID. But they wanted to know, *Why do you have Bomba's phone? Where is he?* He did not know where I was—luckily for me, because they beat him under his feet, trying to get information from him, and detained him for the whole day and the night. He ended up going to CSU, Counseling Services Unit.

I stayed underground for a while, still meeting everyone I needed to meet and writing. Being underground meant being in a very safe house, but still feeling an overwhelming sense of insecurity. You don't really feel like you can go outside. Very few people know where you are, or what number to reach you on. (With just your cell phone number, they could run the coordinates and pinpoint you.) You see things lurking in the shadows at night. There was even an earthquake at that time, February 2006. I'd been hounded out of all my safe zones.

I did have to travel sometimes. Once was when WOZA[24] was convening their first national grassroots gathering, a few hundred people from all over the country, and they asked me to come and speak. WOZA had emerged later, so they had learned a lot from what had happened in the past. They had a lot of secrecy and were very well organized. Around one thirty or two a.m., I'm being whisked off with three women in a car, through the bush, with no cell phone reception, to the remote place where the conference was taking place. I did not know where we were going, I was just keeping my head low, literally abducted by my comrades. I made it to the conference and back. It was strange, but worth it.

Finally, some people helped get me out of the country. I found myself in South Africa one day, able to breathe freely and walk about outside. I think I had even started becoming white from lack of exposure to the sun! I realized that my reactions were different from other people's. Even now, when I walk into a building I don't put my real name when I sign in at the front desk. You become cautious, especially in your relationship with the police. If I saw a group of people walking to me down the street, I would think, *Oh, something is about to break out, or it's already broken out.* I would feel like I had to run away or join in, like it's a march or a mob.

I ended up working at the Centre for the Study of Violence and Reconciliation in Johannesburg. I continued mobilizing for solidarity with Zim and supporting youth groups. I got busy organizing resistance concerts in South Africa. Everyone chipped in: someone contributed their truck, someone designed the posters.

---

[24] Women of Zimbabwe Arise, a group formed in 2002. The word *woza* also means "Rise" or "Come forward" in Ndebele. This Bulawayo-based organization is famous for creative non-violent protest actions, and received the 2009 Robert F. Kennedy Award from President Obama.

That was my path. I left Zimbabwe in 2006, lived in South Africa that year, and then came to the U.S. in the beginning of 2007.

DIAMONDS

My mother is still living in her home area, in Marange. And Marange in Manicaland is where the diamonds were suddenly discovered in 2006, 2007. Quietly, local people started panning. Most of the diamonds were really close to the surface. In no time, that forsaken place was bustling with activity. People left everything else to come to the fields, which were not producing anything, to pan for diamonds. At one time, there were over 30,000 people gathered in the fields, digging with their hands, with sticks, with hoes. The first panners would exchange diamonds for maize meal or clothes. They didn't know the value of those diamonds. Some went to Mozambique or South Africa and exchanged diamonds for groceries, cooking oil, salt to bring back.

But then word spread. You had Lebanese, Israelis, you had dealers from Yemen, all sorts of people showed up. The minute it became clear that this was an opportunity to make serious money, that's when big political players started to get involved, to band together in a syndicate. They would deploy police units or army units to take over an area and then get a bunch of panners to work for them. A guy called William Nhara—a leading personality in Zanu-PF—was arrested at the airport as he was trying to leave with a bag full of diamonds. He tried to bribe a cop to let him go. But the whole syndicate was against him, and they were more powerful. It was clear that a lot of senior politicians, especially those connected to the military, the police, and the mining ministry, were becoming very rich from diamonds from Marange and places nearby like Chiadzwa.

When I was in Zimbabwe in December 2009, I drove down to visit my family for the first time since diamonds were discovered. I passed through a police checkpoint and they were asking a lot of questions: *Where are you going? Who is this person you are visiting?*

For the villagers, for a minute, it provided a break from their very miserable conditions. You can still see thatched houses with solar panels in Marange, or hear someone playing a radio—big luxuries. Some, mostly young people, were able to buy cars and leave the area. But this "blessing" ended up becoming a curse. In 2008 there was a huge crackdown, which involved helicopter gunships. The full story has never been told. My relatives talk of seeing people brutalized, beaten all over, as politicians tried to drive out villagers from the diamond fields where they were trying to "eat."

The community never really benefitted from that wealth. Things for my mother's family are still just as difficult. You didn't have projects; no one said, *Okay, now we can tar your roads, now we can build a better clinic, now we can build an orphanage, take care of these orphans.* No, there's no investment in developing the community.

All kinds of people had relocated to Mutare to make money from diamonds. Sex workers moved all the way from Bulawayo and Harare to the hotels in Mutare. Other people came and set up stalls in Marange. It was a whole economy. Some were cooking food for the panners, some were selling drinks, some were setting up tents to rent out for board or for sex workers. Right there in the middle of the most desolate bush you can think of, a huge market just sprang from nowhere. Like the birth of Johannesburg. Then these guys came and smashed it.

MEANS AND ENDS

On March 29, 2008, I was back in Zimbabwe as part of an informal election observer mission. We were meeting with people in civil society to understand how they were viewing the election process. We went around different suburbs of Harare but I also took a trip to Mutare, met activists in the high-density suburbs there, and went into Mozambique for a couple of hours to see whether Zimbabweans were crossing back to vote.

Many times we've had elections in Zimbabwe where people thought, *Maybe the opposition will do well, maybe it will be fifty-fifty,* but in March

2008 there was a sense that a lot was changing, even in areas that were traditionally Zanu-PF strongholds.

Things were largely very quiet when we arrived. The first thing we did as we drove from the airport was to go to Mbare[25] to buy some vegetables. There we noticed a young woman holding a child and wearing an MDC T-shirt, on her own, not in a crowd. It wouldn't have been possible earlier. And all the way to Bocha in Marange area—this is deep, deep rural—people openly threw MDC signs and wore MDC T-shirts.[26] In fact, Chris Mushowe of Zanu-PF had been the member of parliament for Bocha forever. But, in that 2008 election, he lost. Finally the rural community was ready to break ranks.

Things seemed so desolate to me. You walk into a shop in town and there's just one bottle of Coca-Cola there, one bar of soap there, and maybe one packet of salt. And that's it. Shelves were bare. Try to imagine how people were able to make it from day to day in such a dire situation. Things like fuel, you could not get. Because I had to drive around, I always had to go in the middle of the night to see who could get us some. Everything was on the parallel market, the black market, being sold out of people's trunks or in someone's backyard, illicitly and exorbitantly priced. Even eggs were coming from South Africa, and bread, perishables. Basically, nothing was coming from the local industry. Local beer had completely disappeared from the stores. People had to change their drinking tastes, as I learned on my first day back, when a colleague took me for lunch at Kebab Centre in Harare. Zimbabweans like to drink Lion, Castle, Bohlingers, Zambezi, but everyone was forced to drink Hunters. People were complaining.

People of my generation have vivid memories of a completely different reality. At primary school, every break time we would get a

---

[25] Formerly called the Harare Township, Mbare was the first black township in the capital and has the best known *musika*, or market.

[26] Zimbabwe's rural areas are traditionally strongholds for Zanu-PF, while MDC largely grew from urban areas.

sachet of milk. When you had filled up your school notebook, the teacher would sign it and you would go to the stores room and get a new one. But this time around, schools were shut, teachers were leaving en masse to go to South Africa, Botswana, and do menial jobs there. Even before the schools were shut, people could not afford the fees. I believe that the statistics say that more than 80 percent of kids did not go to school that year.

For the most part, you would just go without electricity, without water. Students, including some of my relatives, were dropping out of college because they didn't have money for transport, or for food to eat, or even to pay the fees. In the hospitals and the clinics, people were dying. We were not counting the numbers the way we would if they had died from outright violence. It was a silent wave that was taking lives.

A whole generation was not being given the slightest chance in life. All doors were being slammed shut in front of them. Crime—armed robbery, violence in the communities, domestic violence—everything was going up. Pedestrians walked blindly onto the street without even looking, like they had a death wish or something. Would it be possible for us, as Zimbabweans, to find a point where—even while we continue to have differences—we are not hanging on the edge of a precipice, knowing very well that we all have a rope strapped around each other's necks? If someone falls, it's everyone going down that cliff.

As you'll remember, the March elections were really quiet. There was a minimum of violence. People really felt that they could freely express themselves. The opposition ended up winning in so many rural areas. This was the first time, it had never happened before. But the run-off elections, which followed in June, were the complete opposite. The opposition actually pulled out of that election because of the violence.

We called our report "The Dream Deferred: The Zimbabwe Election 2008." We put an image on the cover of a pair of hands tearing up a ballot paper, surrounded by darkness. We start the report with Langston Hughes's poem, which is a good depiction of what had happened.

A Dream Deferred
by Langston Hughes

What happens to a dream deferred?
Does it dry up
like a raisin in the sun?
Or fester like a sore—
And then run?
Does it stink like rotten meat?
Or crust and sugar over—
like a syrupy sweet?
Maybe it just sags
like a heavy load.
Or does it explode?

The way Zanu-PF as a movement operates, the end justifies the means. At the schools they went to, they were taught: *Shoot one in public to scare away a thousand.* This is partly why, I think, they do not flinch as they inflict that much pain on you. For them, you are threatening the revolution. *If it means that I have to smash your head in, and regardless of what a certain piece of paper called the constitution says, I am going to stop you.* If you are dissenting, then you are threatening the potential for this whole movement to succeed. It happened during the war, the liberation struggle. That's where this whole thing began of dropping burning plastic on people said to be traitors, digging them into a hole. Imagine: you are a new combatant in the Zanu forces. You've been recruited. There is a war to fight, a war to win. Every other thing becomes subordinate to this cause.

It's not just a Zanu-PF thing, and that's why we make a lot of mistakes, because we personalize it. It's very much a part of our own history. Within our student movement, as we were protesting for freedom, we would coerce other students to take part in some march: people would set off fire extinguishers to disrupt you, or carry large branches to beat you if you did not join the march. Dissent was not tolerated there either. And we've seen, later on, the fights within the MDC, where again violence is deployed against one another. It is all this baggage that we inherit from the background of war, where the stakes were high.

We need to exorcise this out of our systems. It doesn't happen automatically. We need a national healing and reconciliation process. It's a very complicated story.

SECTION 7

BORDER

MUSINA

The last town on the South African side of the Limpopo River, Musina is cold, dry, windy, and dusty in wintry July. The town of roughly 57,000 people has an additional 15,000 temporary foreign residents, the majority of whom are Zimbabweans.[1] A constant flow of trucks, farm pickups, city cars, minibus taxis, and bicycles clog the main road north to the border of Zimbabwe. During our visit, striking municipal workers empty trash over the streets. We drive through a knee-high wash of newspaper, packaging, and plastic bottles and bags.

But through the eyes of a Zimbabwean border-jumper, Musina is a town of plenty: supermarkets full of groceries, clothes on sale in Truworths and Jet Stores, fuel in the pumps, and, all along the street, stores stocking car parts, cellphone SIM cards, gumboots, seeds, buckets, notebooks, and pens. A couple of Zimbabwean kids are working the cars at the intersection, begging at each driver's window.

Musina is the gateway for Zimbabweans making their way into South

---

[1] *New York Times*, "Desperate Children Flee Zimbabwe, for Lives Just as Desolate," Barry Bearak, January 23, 2009.

Africa by foot across the bridge, by car, or by swimming the Limpopo River. It is in this bottleneck of Musina that you see Zimbabwe's problems close up. No one really knows how many Zimbabweans attempt to jump the border, nor how many make it, surviving crocodiles, drowning, and attacks and rape by bands of violent thieves known as *amagumaguma*.[2] Many who cross the border here move on to other places in South Africa to look for work. For some, however, Musina is as far as they are able to go. If you have money or relatives in South Africa, or speak Ndebele as your home language (giving you a shot at blending in with Xhosa and Zulu speakers), you stand a better chance of heading to Johannesburg, Cape Town, Durban, or a farm in the Northern Province. Sixteen kilometers from the border, Musina is full of Zimbabweans without even these meager advantages. It is a town full of men, women, and many thousands of children waiting—but for what?

---

[2] See a *New York Times* video from March 9, 2009, "Reporter's Notebook: Confronting Rape on Zimbabwe's Border" by Barry Bearak, Joao Silva, and Vijai Singh.

OSCAR

AGE: *25*

OCCUPATION: *Self-employed entrepreneur, making sandals
and creating sculptures*

INTERVIEWED IN: *Cape Town, South Africa*

Oscar explains that he doesn't want to talk about the reason he left Zimbabwe, except to say that it had to do with politics and that his livelihood—he ran a small-town nightclub—was ruined. Nor does he want to talk about what has happened since he made his way to Cape Town, where he ended up as spokesperson for one of the camps for people displaced during the xenophobic violence of 2008.[1] But he will tell the story of his crossing illegally into South Africa. What someone like Oscar is prepared to undergo in trying to cross into South Africa underlines the intensity of the pressures that propel Zimbabweans to leave.

---

[1] The year 2008 saw the eruption of dangerous and sometimes lethal hostility between working-class citizens and new immigrants across South Africa, killing at least sixty people and displacing an estimated 100,000. As South Africans' expectations collide with the slow pace of change and failures in service delivery, foreigners are often blamed. The Forced Migration Studies Programme at the University of the Witwatersrand estimates there are about 1.6 to 2 million foreign-born residents in South Africa, out of a population of 48 million. Other figures have placed the number of migrants originating only from within Zimbabwe as high as 3 million. For more, see the appendix section on Zimbabweans in South Africa, and see Nokuthula's story for more on the experience and fears of xenophobia.

I left Harare on the second of January in 2007 with my sister, who had come from South Africa. She was assisting me with fares and because, basically, I had nothing. She had 2,000 South African rand,[2] which we expected would be enough to take us all the way to Musina. She was working someplace halfway between Musina and Louis Trichardt.[3] So we boarded my sister's friend's car from Harare to Beitbridge,[4] together with another friend of the driver. We knew we had to work out something at the border post, because she had a passport that had no visa, and I had nothing. I did not even have my Zimbabwean ID on me. I just had my bag of clothes and a few million Zimbabwean dollars.[5] I was quite nervous because I knew I was going to have to cross the border, whether by the bridge or by swimming across the river. I was just not going to go back to Zim.

Before we left Zim, my sister had bought me a pair of sneakers. These were the shoes I was using when I was walking. Three weeks later, the soles of those sneakers were totally worn out. You could see the soles of my painful, swollen feet.

TRICKS FOR CROSSING THE BORDER

My sneakers were still new when we left Harare in the late afternoon. We traveled overnight, and got to the Beitbridge border post in the morning. The driver and his friend had their papers all in order, so they carried on

---

[2] Approximately US$200.

[3] Now known as Makhado.

[4] Beitbridge is the border town on the Zimbabwe side; Musina is its equivalent across the Limpopo River in South Africa, as explained in the introduction to this section. Oscar's sister risked making this crossing a second time, as many do, to help get her brother over the border.

[5] With inflation reaching thousands of percent, it is hard to pinpoint the exact value of the Zimbabwe dollar at this point, but as an example, one British pound was trading on the informal, parallel, or black market for Z$400,000 in July 2007. Ten years before, in 1997—before the Zimbabwe dollar began to fall dramatically—one British pound was worth ten Zimbabwe dollars.

with their journey, leaving us to figure out how we were going to cross. They dropped us off at the border post, on the Zimbabwean side, the part where the trucks are. My sister went to speak to the border guards. I think she put some money in her passport. It was actually very easy to cross the Zimbabwean side. When we got to the South African side, that's when we faced a problem. Most people who try to walk across are apprehended and put in police vehicles for deportation. But there are these people called *malayitshas* who help people get across the border. That's what they do to earn money. They walked across with my sister and managed to get her across, and then they came back for me. The one who got me across was a South African lady.

There are these booms[6] at the border, you know. Before the trucks go through the boom, the driver has to sign some papers. The *malayitsha* told me told me to go and stand on the passenger side of the truck. I was supposed to walk alongside the truck, so that I couldn't be seen. And then when the truck drove off, I would just walk on. I was twenty-two years old. I had never done such a thing. I am someone who never had to pretend or lie or anything. So my heart was beating quite fast. I walked over and stood on the side of the truck, while the guards were getting the driver to sign. Then when the boom lifted and the truck moved, I walked beside it at the same pace. Then I just walked off.

But that was not the final toll gate. Before you leave the border post, you face one last toll gate. Many people get caught here and deported. The police here are very strict, and they treat people badly. My sister and I had met up in a flat, open area some distance from that gate. We were just sitting there, thinking of a way to cross. People had told us that it's a little easier, maybe, to do it when it's dark, when the customs officials are tired.

While the *malayitsha* was trying to bribe somebody, my sister and I got into a heated debate. I was so nervous, so worried about two people crossing together when they are both illegal. I thought it would be better

---

[6] Barriers consisting of a gate with a pole that lifts up.

for us to cross separately. I was telling her that if anything happened and we got caught it would be easier for her because she had a passport and she was going to work. I kept telling her that I could get across on my own, and then we could meet at the place where she was working. But she was not comfortable with that. She was feeling responsible as my older sister. But I didn't want her to lose her job, and I was sure I was going to follow eventually. Many people have to try more than once. But she wouldn't give me the phone numbers or the money because she preferred that we stay together, since we left Zim together.

There's this trick, when you're crossing the border. The officials call you to walk toward the toll gates, and when you're just about to approach them, you receive a phone call. It's just make-believe. You start speaking on the phone, but in fact you are waiting for a moment when the guards face away, sort of like a blind spot. When you see that, you go through the gate and then you sprint to the other side, hoping they don't see you and catch you. My sister managed, but when I was following her they called me and asked for my papers. They are very suspicious of males. I decided to tell the truth, that I had no papers and was just trying to get across. They were about to put me in a police van when my sister came back. I'd asked her not to. But she tried to talk to the policeman, asking him to please release me, saying, *He's my brother. I need to go with him.* It was a foolish thing to do, because then they put the two of us in the police van and took us to this filthy place called the Musina military base or SMG.[7]

THE ONE WHO OPENED IT

SMG was a concrete, two-story building, with two sets of burglar bars on the windows. The roof was tin, held on by thick iron trusses, and

---

[7] Soutpansberg Military Gebied (SMG), a disused military base outside Musina, served as an immigration detention facility for several years. Sustained pressure from human rights organizations, along with a cholera outbreak along the border, finally resulted in the closing of SMG in 2009.

between the roof and the walls was razor wire. Inside, there were more than a thousand people. It was the first time I'd seen so many people in this kind of military-style building. You could not walk without stepping on someone's feet. There were two sides: one for males and one for females. They put me on one side and my sister on the other side. The wall between the sides was made from metal sheets, welded on, about half a centimeter thick. There were holes in the sheets, so you could see the women's side, but you could not manage to have a conversation with anyone because there was confusion on both sides. Unfortunately for me, my sister had all the rand and the cell phone. I had no phone, so we could not communicate. I thought they would be reasonable enough to deport people at the same time, because people might be dependent on each other, maybe husband and wife. But they didn't care.

It was evening when they caught us. We slept there that night. The place was smelly and filthy, sweaty and musty. Once every three or four hours, a policeman would come and ask people if they wanted to go to the toilet, but by then people would have urinated all around the place. People were getting sick. Some told me they had been there for three days without being deported. They didn't give us any food until about eleven a.m. the next day, when they opened the door and let the men out into a fenced area and gave us half a loaf of brown bread and some water.

I tried to talk to someone on the ladies' side, but no one could hear me. On the men's side, there was a door. Each time they opened the door to deport people, the men would stampede to the gate to try to get out. Some fainted. It was unbelievable to me that they were begging to be deported. The police could not control the men. So they decided they weren't going to deport us at all; they were only going to deport the women.

I was very worried because I couldn't speak to my sister and I didn't know whether she was there or had been deported already. So that morning when I saw the people trying to stampede out the door, I decided that if I didn't get deported that day, I would have to escape.

The whole day passed without anyone being deported. Night came. It was about one a.m. and I was standing by the door. The men were banging at it, asking the police to open it for them to go to the toilet. The police just ignored them. I looked up and saw this guy had climbed up, past the razor wire. There appeared to be a hole in the razor wire. I don't know how he managed to make that hole. He was pushing at the tin roof with his palm, trying to open it, and the roof was slowly giving way. This guy was taking advantage of the noise and commotion, banging at the tin roof while the men banged at the door. I watched him do this for about fifteen minutes. He seemed to be worried that the police could hear him, so when he came down I told him that I was going to watch the door for him. I said I'd whistle to him if any policeman came so that he could jump down. So he carried on, but eventually he came down and told me the roof was not giving way and now he was tired. So we swapped positions.

While he was watching the door, I climbed up. But instead of using my palm, I used my feet. I held on to the angle iron and swung my body back and forth like a pendulum, using my weight and kicking the tin roof with my feet. Whenever someone banged at the gate, I would swing and hit the roof hard. I did this four or five times, until finally the roof opened. There was a gap about forty centimeters wide. Suddenly people started waking up and pointing at me. They started realizing that there was actually a possibility of escaping. I climbed down told the guy, *Okay, it's open. You can get out now.* But he was too scared. He said, *No, you are the one who opened it! You can go.*

I made an announcement to the men that there was a possibility of escaping. Lots of people were just too tired, had spent such a long time in there, and didn't want to take the risk. And some must have been traumatized by the treatment they were receiving from the police. For most of us, the question was: What would happen to somebody who tried to escape and got caught? The police would want to make an example of this person, to show everybody what happens when you try to escape. So nobody took the chance to get out.

I decided to climb up, just to see what the outside would look like. So I climbed up and looked out. I began to think about the contrast between the outside and the inside. Outside it was quiet, open. Inside there were 1,200 men falling asleep in sitting positions because there was no space to lie down, the place filled with the stench of urine. I decided to take the risk. I jumped.

I landed on the outside. There was a policeman at a desk. He was dozing. I just sprinted past him. He was awakened by my passing, but I did not turn back. I heard lots of noise, lots of commotion behind me, but I was running too fast to even think of turning. I was just hoping they wouldn't shoot me. But I knew that on foot no one was going to catch me. I ran in the direction of the N-1,[8] and when I got to the N-1, I turned. I don't know how long I sprinted, but when I finally stopped I was under a bridge along the N-1. I had been running through short, thorny bushes that tore my clothes. When I finally stopped, I saw that my shirt was all torn and my hands, arms, and chest were bleeding.

I rested there. I just intended to sleep for two hours or so, but I slept for a very long time. While I was sleeping I had that feeling, you know that feeling, when you know there is something bothering you but you are too tired to think of it, then when you wake up it suddenly springs at you? That's how it was. A heavy truck passed over the bridge and I woke up. I wanted to celebrate having escaped, being the only one out of 1,200 men who escaped. But I was suddenly aware of the fact that I was in a foreign country and I had no money and my sister didn't know where I was. I didn't even have my clothes. My sister took everything. All I had was 8 million Zim.

EVERYTHING EXCEPT OXYGEN

I decided that I was going to look for the place where my sister was working, a place called Ridgemount Farm, but she had not given me clear directions. At first I was walking along the road, but after seeing a few police cars, I decided that the road was definitely not the way to travel.

---

[8] The main highway south to Johannesburg and the rest of South Africa.

So I walked to a distance of about eight kilometers from the main road, and started walking parallel to the road. I would climb a hill and locate the nearest farmhouse and then walk in that general direction. That's how most border jumpers walk. If you have a path, it's obvious, and the police can catch you. So you just note the general direction of the place where you are going and you walk that way.

It's mostly game ranches, not farmland there. On each farm you have one main house and a small compound that is close to the main house. The rest of the area is just bush. I had to climb over high fences, but I would often find that people who'd come there before had sort of stretched the wire to create a space for someone to pass. There was evidence that people who had walked that way got too tired and decided to leave some of the things that they were carrying. Once in a while I would see an old bag, a few clothes, stuff like that. There were also lots of wild animal footprints. On many occasions I saw cat family prints, so I was just hoping I wouldn't meet any lions.

When I got to a farm, I would try to find where the compound was. The population of workers in that area is mainly Zimbabweans and South African Vendas, and most of those people are very kind. I think maybe because they came the same way, they understand how people travel and the circumstances that make people leave. I would get to one house and they would give me food and water to wash. They would tell me how I could avoid the police and where I could get water on my way. They would also ask me where I was going. But I only knew the name of the farm. Unfortunately, nobody seemed to know the place I was going. I might walk for thirty kilometers in a certain direction, and when I get there, it's not the right place. Then they direct me somewhere else. I turn in an angle of forty-five degrees and I walk another twenty kilometers, and when I get to that place, it's not the right place either.

When I left Zim, I wouldn't eat a lot of things. But in a matter of a few days, I wasn't so choosy. And after some time, I was eating wild food. I would eat almost anything. I was in a very desperate situation because I was very, very hungry and tired. I had traveled for four days trying to find Ridgemount Farm. I probably walked over two hundred kilometers in total.

On the fourth day I finally decided I was not getting anywhere. And I remembered my sister was pointing me in the direction of the farm. The first time they went across, they had not gone via the border. They had crossed the river and walked in a certain direction. She had pointed in that direction. So I decided to go back to the border, get myself deported, spend some of the eight million Zim that I had, and try to cross again that way. When you are so hungry, almost starving, you don't make reasonable decisions. So I started walking, but this time I was walking on the road.

Unfortunately, the police seemed to have lost all interest in me. But I was definitely looking like a border jumper. When I left home, I had this huge Afro. It was combed and had gel in it, but after four days my hair was full of grass. I didn't care anymore. When you leave, you think the travel is not going to be a problem: just bribe a few police officers, take one bus ride and then another until you get where you're going. But then you are in the wild bush and you have nothing: no phone, no food. Life is basic. All of a sudden you don't care much about what people think about you. You just think about the next place where you are going to get food, get water.

And when you meet somebody, you ask them for something, and you are so thankful to so many people. When I was working in a nightclub in Harare, I was too proud to even borrow a CD, but at this time I depended on other people for everything except oxygen. On one occasion, I got to this compound, it seemed deserted. But I knocked on one of the houses and somebody came out. I tried to speak to him in English. He did not understand English. I tried to speak to him in Shona. He did not understand Shona. I spoke to him in Ndebele and hand gestures. But he wasn't getting any of that. Finally I just held his hand and pulled him into his house and pointed at a pot, and he understood. He just laughed and he prepared me something to eat. In a matter of days I lost all my pride, and I became a very simple person who needs very simple things. *Can you tell me which direction is this farm? Can you give me some water?*

I walked and walked along the road toward Musina from Louis Trichardt, and police vehicles were passing. I tried to wave them down, but they did not stop. I walked until I got to Musina. I was very angry at those police, because they just didn't seem to notice me. I felt like I was going to die of hunger if I didn't get back to Zim. When I walked into Musina town, everyone was looking at me. I had grass seeds all over my pants. In Shona we call them *tsine*. I had lots of those in my hair as well. Finally a vehicle pulled over, a blue 4×4. I walked toward the vehicle and opened the door and I got inside. The police were very surprised. Because in that area, each time they see a border jumper and they turn toward him, he sprints, like I had been doing. But this time I just got in and sat down. They asked me, *What's wrong?* I just said, *I want to go back home.* And they said, *You've been living in the bush for a long time. We're going to take you to a place where you're going to be given food, and you'll be taken back to your country of origin.* I just nodded. They drove to the military base again.

When we got there, I walked a few steps and stopped by the door. I was hesitant to go in. I was worried that people were going to point out that I had been the one who had escaped. But it was all new people. I did not recognize any faces. It was less populated this time. Once I was inside, everybody was greeting me. I was not sure why, but people seemed amazed to see me. I just went to the corner and sat. Some guy came over to me with a CD and said, *Look at your reflection on the CD.* I had to smile. Imagine some Afro hair that's big, and that has not been combed for close to a week, and has got all that grass in it. And I had been sleeping in the sand. I just said thank you and gave back the CD. I was beyond embarrassment.

I pointed at the opening in the razor wire in the roof. It was still slightly opened, just an inch, and I asked the guy what had happened. He said, *Twenty-six people escaped last week.* I said, *What?! Twenty-six?* He said, *Yes. They say two people opened the roof, they let everybody out.*

AN ISLAND IN THE MIDDLE OF THE RIVER

This time they were suddenly very quick to deport people. It seemed like some people had died in there. Maybe they'd found out that when you put so many people together, something bad can happen. So two hours later, I was back in Beitbridge, Zimbabwe, holding a 500-ml can of milk and a loaf of bread. I was just walking in town like those street kids. This definitely would not have been acceptable for me a week or so earlier. I was raised in a family where people always talk about manners, looking presentable, not doing anything that is embarrassing. But I just didn't care.

I thought my sister had probably waited at the IOM[9] place to see if I got deported, and then she probably got tired and went across. I knew she would not go back to Zim. I did pass by the IOM, but she was not there. I slept that night at the taxi rank. There were a number of other people sleeping there. Some were waiting for buses. I slept on the ground on a stoop between two bus roads. And the next day I left early in the morning and walked on my own to this place called Chiwara, where the river is shallowest.

As I was passing the last rural area before Chiwara, I noticed some kids waiting on the road. There are robbers in that area, and I think these kids inform these robbers when there are people coming. After I walked a few kilometers into the bush, approaching the river, the vegetation got denser and I saw two guys in front of me. When I turned, I noticed two other guys behind me. So I knew it was trouble. One of them advanced toward me, but I was not going to be attacked first. So I gave him a kick in the ribs and he retreated. But one of them had a knobkerry,[10] and they all jumped me. Luckily for me, a car came along and the guys ran away. The driver told me to jump in. I jumped in and he drove back toward Beitbridge.

By then it was midday. At the taxi rank, I heard some guys speaking

---

[9] The International Organization for Migration, which provides services to Zimbabweans deported back across the border.

[10] A wooden club with a large knob at one end, used as a weapon.

of going to see whether the level of the river had fallen. Eight of us went to look, and when we got there the water had actually risen. The moment you put your foot in the water you could feel the force of it. One of the guys tried to swim a few meters to test it, and the water took him almost fifty meters down the river. He came back, saying, *No, it's not worth trying.* And the whole group decided they were going back. But I didn't want to go back. I knew if I stayed in Beitbridge without money, it was going to be very difficult for me. I told the guys I was going to try to cross anyway. They said they would wait to see what happened, so that if I drowned, they could take the news back. Most of them were telling me not to try it, but one guy said, *You never know. Maybe you can make it.*

I went up the river because I had noticed an island in the center. The river was about 150 meters across. I'm not a good swimmer. I knew I would never make it across in one swim, so I wanted to swim as far as half of the river, and then let the water take me down. I got into the water about fifty meters up the river from that island, and I started swimming.

The water was stronger than I thought, and my muscles became painful before I got to the center. It suddenly became clear to me that there was a good possibility of drowning, because the water was taking me down too fast. I was almost going past the island and I was not in the center yet, but I managed to grab on to some *tsanga*[11] and then climb onto the island. My heart was beating heavily. My hands were bleeding from pulling the reeds.

I knew I might die when I made the decision to cross, but it was never something that I believed could actually happen. I sat there and I cried. I didn't think that on the other side of the border there could be soldiers watching me. I didn't care about that. I was just thinking of either dying or living. And I was feeling sorry for my sister. The most stressful thing is that there's somebody who does not know where you are.

Now, if I chose to swim back there was still a possibility of drowning,

---

[11] Reeds, in Shona.

because I was tired. The guys on the other side were cheering me. They said I'd been submerged under the water for some time, and they were just about to go back and report that I had drowned.

I stayed on the island for twenty minutes, and then I swam across to the other side. This time I began with heavy strokes, because I was thinking, *What's the point of managing to come all this way to the center and then I can't make it across?* When I got to the other side, I had no energy left to walk or anything. I just rolled in the mud and lay there for a few minutes. It's fortunate that no patrol soldiers came that way, because I was quite close to the border bridge.

When I finally got up, I began to jog. I wanted to go down the river to the side opposite Chiwara, because I knew from there the direction I was supposed to follow to get to the farm. On my way I met some soldiers. The first time, I saw them before they saw me. But the second time I was in thick bush and almost bumped into this soldier. We just stood there, surprised. He was wearing a military uniform and holding a gun. I looked at his face and then looked at the gun, considering, *If I just sprint now, will he shoot?* I took two heavy breaths, but then he asked me where I was coming from. I actually told him the truth. *I'm a border jumper, I'm coming from Zimbabwe.* He said, *You should go back.* And I told him, *No, I won't go back,* stepping away from him while I was speaking. Then I turned. He asked me, *Do you want me to shoot you?* And I just said no and began jogging in the other direction. There is a human side to everybody. And most of the time you can see from their eyes that a person feels some compassion. So I took advantage of that.

THEY'LL NEVER HEAR THANK YOU

I walked for eleven days to get to the place where my sister was staying. This time I was closer to the area and I had remembered the name of the mountain where the farm was. Once in a while I would meet somebody who knew the mountain and they would give me directions. But I was in a place where there were fewer houses, fewer people.

It was very hot during the day, and there were lots of mosquitoes biting me. I was walking through game ranches. Sometimes at night I would hear lions roaring. I was eating wild fruit and drinking water from animals' water holes where there were buffalo prints. But I was so grateful to see a place where there was water that I would almost dive into it, forgetting the possibility of getting anthrax from drinking water that buffaloes have drunk. I drank a lot of dirty water at that time, but I never got sick. Sometimes I thought of getting a job somewhere because I was too tired to walk. But I knew if I got a job, my sister would not know where I was until I could get a cell phone and give her a call. So I had to keep on walking.

On one occasion, I got to a compound and there was no one there. But the door to one of the huts was half open. I was almost starving then, and I'd gone a long time without seeing people. I felt like the first person I was going to meet had to be friendly, because I needed something to eat desperately. So I opened the door of the hut and there was no one inside, but there were red-hot embers in the fireplace, showing that somebody had been cooking recently. I sat for some time waiting for the owner to come back, but nobody came. Then I took a look around. There was a pot and some mopane worms already roasted. Mopane worms are caterpillars that appear seasonally. To prepare them you have to boil them for a long time, and then dry them, and then you can fry them. So in order to prepare it and salt them, I took the pot and put some water in it, put it over the fire, and made myself some *sadza*.[12] I ate that as if I were in my own house. I was thinking that when this guy comes, I'm going to give him an explanation, and he'll just have to understand. Because it's better for me to explain when my stomach is full than to die of hunger. So I just ate that pap and slept in that house, waiting for the owner to come. I waited for a few hours, and nobody came. So I took a 500-ml container from there and put some water in it. I washed my face and left. I forgot to wash the guy's plates. I just continued with my journey.

---

[12] See footnote 5, page 31.

I went as far as the Venetia Mines, on the road to Alldays. At the mine they gave me directions to the mountain. And when I got there, I climbed the mountain. At the top of the mountain, I met someone and asked him if he knew where the Ridgemount Farm was, and he pointed it out to me. I had spent nearly two weeks trying to get to this place, so when he pointed it to me, the aerial view of the place, it was like I'd discovered paradise. Because that's where my life in South Africa was supposed to begin.

When I got to the farm, it seemed like everybody knew my story, and they were all very willing to take me to my sister's place. She was no longer working at Ridgemount. She had gone to some other place and was working in a house. A guy took me to that place, and when I got there I asked to see my sister. I knocked at the door of her room and she was there. She cried when she saw me.

I discovered that these bad experiences make you strong. My parents died when I was twelve, and after that, I stayed with an uncle who is quite rich by Zimbabwean standards. The way I was brought up, you don't get desperate. Fees are paid on time; you go to boarding school; occasionally you maybe take a flight from Hwange to Kariba. Until the time that I crossed the border, I had that pride when you think that you're just all right, you think you don't need anybody. I learned a lesson that in life people depend on each other. Back when I was running the night-club, I would look down on this kind of person because *he's just a farm worker*. But you meet these people and they're so helpful. They do much more useful things than I was doing when I was back home. What was I doing? I was going to buy beer at Delta Beverages, bringing it to the nightclub to get people drunk and playing them music, getting them to spend lots of money. But this guy here, he sees somebody who is walking, who is starving, and he gives him something to eat. And these people, I don't know how many people like me they have helped, but I don't think they'll ever hear any of those people say thank you, because they just never come back. I mean, I will never go back to those places.

BERNARD

AGE: *28*

OCCUPATION: *Former banker, now a day laborer*
INTERVIEWED IN: *Musina, South Africa*

A former banker who describes his family as solidly middle class, Bernard found himself torn between his career goals and his politics. An outgoing and at times lighthearted young man, Bernard believes his future in Zimbabwe looks fairly bright despite everything he's endured since he was arrested and later beaten by Zanu-PF youths. Since he crossed into South Africa, he has been laboring on building sites in the small town of Musina, but he hopes to complete his advanced accounting studies and go back to work in the financial sector—when he's able to return home. His parents still live in Harare; his sister has since moved to Namibia. After the interview, Bernard headed back to the minimal comforts of a men's shelter run by a church. Very early the next morning, he would be back on his construction job.

I'm twenty-eight years old and still single. Not that young anymore. I'm racing with age!

I was born in the eastern highlands part of Zimbabwe, in Mutare. My father used to work for Johnson & Fletcher, a company which was involved with carpentry. He was the production manager and used to travel quite a lot for his job. We moved a few times when I was young. My father had quite a lot of opportunities in those days. I can say that in Zimbabwe there are three classes. Isn't it the same everywhere? The poor, the middle, and the rich class. My family was in the middle. We're a small family. There's only me and my sister.

We lived for a time in Bulawayo. I did my primary school up to Grade 6 there. I actually speak a little bit of Ndebele. In Bulawayo, we lived in one of the new suburbs there in New Luveve. I would have to say it was a pretty normal childhood. I played a lot of soccer, hung out with my friends, the usual things in a ghetto area. And I had every support from my parents. But I have to say my mother was very strict while I was growing up. We were members of the Seventh Day Adventist church. My father was Adventist also, but he didn't go to church. He used to drink quite a lot when we were still young. He quit drinking in 1990. But he still doesn't go to church.

When I completed primary school, my father was transferred again, this time to Harare. It was then that he bought our first house. Even then it was difficult to finance it. Things were already changing. We weren't doing quite as well as before. I remember I had to iron my own clothes. And we were more crowded than ever before. Moving to a different area, to the city, is difficult. You have to meet new people, have new experiences. It was then decided within the family that my sister and I should go to boarding school. My sister went to Lydia Chimonyo in Chimanimani. I went to Nyazura Adventist High School.

I must say I always liked school very much. I was a pretty brilliant student, though at times I was a bit too playful. I had a very small body then. As I was one of the youngest guys in class, I would always be trying to make jokes. I used to sit in the back of class and make comments. But when it came to my schoolwork, I was serious. I had quite a lot of ambition then. I actually wanted to be a pilot or an engineer. I was planning to join the Air Force of Zimbabwe after high school, to train as a flight engineer or as a pilot.

I think that's when it all started. It was because of my family. My father was a finance guy, he had a financial background. When he first started out, there were no jobs because of segregation. And yet he made it all the way to management. My father's brother is a chartered accountant. He runs an accounting firm in Harare. My mother went to college in Bulawayo. She also studied accounting. Also, my parents were from this Christian background. They didn't want me to do something that was dangerous. I don't come from a family of risk takers. My parents didn't appreciate my dreams of wanting to do something different. They actually forced me to change my plans.

TO BE PART OF HISTORY

That's when I can say I became involved with some quite naughty boys. My father was summoned often to my school. I started airing my views, you know. I started talking too much. The food in the school dining hall was not that good, and I would just say so openly, without any fear of teachers or anyone. One night, they gave us beans. Cooked beans. They weren't done well. They hadn't used any oil. I said they tasted like stones.

Another time I was involved in a strike. I knew this guy in Form 4,[1] he was hit by a teacher with a bamboo stick and the blow broke his hand. I remember then we got a few guys together to protest. We took off our shirts. We wrapped towels around our faces. We threw some stones and broke a few windows. They brought in someone to mediate, a guy who used to work at the school. He talked so nicely to us. We appreciated it. The teacher who hit my friend was asked to leave the school. Of course, we were sent to detention afterward.

Besides being involved in such activities, I would also miss home so much. The high school was only three Ks[2] from the main road, in an

---

[1] Equivalent of eleventh grade in the U.S.

[2] Kilometers.

area of bush area behind a mountain. Sometimes I would run away from school, jump onto the train back home to Harare.

Finally, my father decided to transfer me to another school in Harare. That was in '98, when everything started, the year of the food riots in Harare.

Things were getting tougher and tougher in Zim. Food prices were increasing too much. The trade union was still so active then. Morgan was still the president of the ZCTU[3] and they were organizing strikes. I remember one strike. It was November and I was about to write my O-Levels.[4] They actually cut off all the transport into and out of town. People were stoning buses, burning old vehicles, that kind of stuff. There were battles with the police, tear gas. My new school was out in Belvedere, Christ Ministries School. I struggled to get there so that I could write at least my final paper. My father told me, *No, it's better to miss it and write it next time.* I said, *No, I have to do it.* Luckily, I jumped into a truck that was going in the direction of my school. I made it. I wrote my O-level that day.

When I got back into town, around five in the afternoon, the chaos was still going on. I was caught in the middle. I saw it all live. The street life of people throwing stones, destroying, burning, looting. The exhaustion of frustrated people. There was smoke all over. Actually, I even threw some stones myself. I had heard about strikes before. But I'd never been in one. I wanted to experience it, to be part of history, to say I was there. I remember the songs people were singing.

Vana venyu mhai varamba kudzokera Ijipita nyika yeudzvanyiriri. (Your children, mother, have refused to return to Egypt.) That's a biblical song—when the children of Israel left for the promised land, they refused to go back to Egypt.

I remember that day. I must have walked something like twenty-

---

[3] Morgan Tsvangirai—who went on to lead the Movement for Democratic Change—was secretary general of the Zimbabwe Congress of Trade Unions at this point.

[4] See footnote 8, page 59.

seven Ks because I had to go around the police in order to get home to our suburb. I went through Mount Pleasant, Vainona, Mabelreign, Sanganai Inn. By the time I got home, it was past one. Everyone was so worried.

I realized we were all going to be affected. Things were changing so fast. Even my family was feeling the rise of the food prices. We normally went for groceries toward the end of the month. My mother would buy in bulk, put everything in the freezer. But she no longer went on those big grocery trips at the month's end. She began to only replace things when they ran out.

WHAT ELSE SHOULD I BE AFRAID OF?

After my O-level, I proceeded into A-level. I had good grades. My father was happy. In 2000, I wrote my commercial subjects, accounting, management, business—all subjects pertaining to finance. That was the time of the first parliamentary elections. I was a big boy by then. That's when the Movement for Democratic Change was gaining ground. Even so, people were still afraid of being known as part of those people, of being someone who was too vocal. At that time I was beginning to drink quite a lot, so I didn't care much about anything. I had that attitude. I didn't care about trouble. And I believed in speaking up. Things weren't going right in the country. So I joined those guys. I went to one of their meetings. That was the first time I got arrested.

We were locked in cells for about two days, but we were never taken to court. There was all kinds of commotion in the cells. They'd come and ask us all questions. *We received information that you were going to attack somewhere and hit some people and disrupt a rally for Zanu-PF that is going to come. We need to know who sent you. Who is organizing it?* That kind of stuff. They were abusive in their language. They would say so many bad things about your mother, about your families, everything. They would beat you and say you were just being troublemakers. *We just want to teach you a lesson so that you never do this thing again.* They beat us with those baton sticks, on the feet and on the bum.

There would be a shift change. And the new guys, before they would start asking you anything, they'd hit you first. They'd tie you in handcuffs, you know, on to the burglar bar. I experienced it. I have even some scars. See?

So we tried to talk. We told them, *No, this was just a simple meeting. We were just organizing some party events—how to run our programs, our campaigns, that kind of stuff. We're not trying to disrupt anything...*

After I was released, that's when the actual fights started with my family. They never wanted me to get involved in that stuff. And my parents were saying I was dragging the family into the mud.

But let me say, for myself, it was a very terrible experience. I've never been a thug before, I've never been involved in any criminal activity. And there I was in the same cell with real criminals. I knew that I was not the kind of a person who was supposed to be held. I was in the wrong place, and justice wasn't being done to me. But one thing I know for sure—it made me stronger. I lost the fear factor. I've been beaten, I've gone through it. What else should I be afraid of?

But my parents were afraid. When I was released my mother couldn't speak, she was crying so much. My father shook with anger. They were so worried for me. There were rumors I was being sought. They thought I might be picked up again. So they suggested I move to Botswana for a while. I went there with my mother. She rents a room on the other side of the border because she was working as a cross-border trader. Each month she would go over and buy some supplies, then sell the stuff to her customers in Zim. She did this even before the economic crisis. For us, it was an alternative source of income. I stayed in Botswana three months. I didn't do anything exciting there. The company I worked for was BTC, Botswana Telecoms. They were developing a new telecom system. I was a site clerk which means I recorded the number of hours people were working, kept the register for the tools and the materials onsite, that kind of thing. Not very exciting. I wanted to go home, and so I did.

When I came back, it was time to get a job. For a time I worked at a place called Gainsborough Properties, a real estate agent. I was replacing someone on maternity leave. I worked as a bookkeeper for a few months. I also was continuing my studies at Zimbabwe Open University for my undergraduate degree.

WILD, WILD, WILD

In 2006, I was hired at ZB Financial Holding Company in Harare. I joined as a ledgers clerk. Later I became a bank officer. It was interesting work, but it's also true that the banking sector doesn't pay that much. Even at the bank, you could see most of the people—except for the top brass—were experiencing hardships.

But then came mid-2008. Everything then was all about foreign currency dealings. I'm talking about U.S. dollars, South African rand. That's when I made a small fortune—temporarily. I could change money. Almost everyone in the bank was doing it.

Foreign currency was scarce, and everybody needed it. Maybe 5 million Zim dollars for the dentist, or for medication. People who needed foreign currency would have to make an application. You cannot simply go up to the counter and say, *I need to buy such and such amount of dollars or rand.* You have to make an application and you must specify the reason you want the money. Normally, the bank would turn most of the applications down. But they would, of course, approve government officials who, let's say, needed surgery outside the country. Also, they would approve applications, for the right people, for school fees, for those who were in universities out of the country, and also those in the mining sector who were sourcing raw materials. But for most people it was difficult to get approval.

Of course, there was a thriving black market. Buying forex[5] on the street with hard dollars, if you had enough Zimbabwean cash, was actually cheaper than going to the bank. But in most cases you could not get

---

[5] Foreign currency, officially purchased on the foreign exchange market.

that cash to buy the forex on the street. There were limits on how many Zim dollars you could withdraw from the bank. So lets say they tell you that you can only withdraw five hundred dollars. But with five hundred Zim dollars you can make only one trip into town because it costs five hundred Zim dollars for a bus! For a one-way ticket! And to get that five hundred dollars that doesn't buy you anything you have to wake up at three a.m. to get into line!

But I had an idea. I would say to my friend, *Can I use your account?* He says yes. So I transfer some monies into his account so that as a banker I can cash those amounts.

So you would have a brother, sister, friend, whatnot. Anybody who would do it. They'd just sign those slips. Then I'd go to a teller and give them the verified slips and take out the money, say 5 million, and for 5 million, you could buy about US$50. Now you have something to work with.

Now, we have large corporate companies that are involved in trading. They are selling stuff, right? They're being paid in checks and in bank transfers. They have billions and billions in those accounts, right? But they cannot access that in hard cash. They need forex. So I would say, you guys, listen, I've got this $50 US. I will give you this fifty at a rate of one to two hundred. See? So they transfer to me at one to two hundred. Now I've got access to even more cash.

For a while everybody was needing forex, and I could get it. The nation's industries needed it. There were few exports going out of the countries because they were based on agriculture—and agriculture was not producing. The mining industry was going down. The embassies too needed money.

Even the government itself needed forex. The governor, Gono[6] himself, would send some guys. They would come to the bank with a BMW full of new notes. These guys would come with their full bags of money

---

[6] Gideon Gono, controversial head of the Reserve Bank and close advisor to President Mugabe.

and pay the highest rate for U.S. dollars. And so that's how finally the inflation rate went wild, wild, wild. And Zanu-PF, maybe they needed money to campaign, buy new vehicles. They'd phone Gono and say, *Governor, we need US$100,000*. And Gono would go to his machine and just print all night! Then the following morning you would see his little boys in their flashy cars and clothes coming over to the bank with new Zim dollars...

So I did make a bit of a fortune dealing in forex. It didn't last. I was still with MDC. I still believed in change. But for now I had to survive, right? Everybody has to.

MARCH 2008

Things started to unravel for good. That was the year I felt I had to express myself. 2008. That was the turning point. We were at a rally at a stadium. 2008 was the year when Morgan challenged Mugabe in the elections. This was the final rally before the vote. When it was over, people were going home, trying to make it to the taxis. It was a big crowd. Some people started running. They were singing, they were chanting songs. They were blocking access to the transport. People were over-excited. So the police, instead of just trying to talk to people nicely, they just started to hit people. We scattered. Later that night I went to a party, a birthday party actually.

That night, after the party, I walked home with an MDC friend. I remember one side of the street was very dark because of the blackouts, the power cuts. The other side had electricity because it shared the same substation as the army base which houses the Presidential Guard. It was about two in the morning when we met some guys, about fifteen of them. They were part of a Zanu youth militia. Normally you could get by them if you just repeated one of their slogans. If you held up your fist and said, *27 June, Mugabe must be in office! 27 June, Mugabe must be in office!*

But that night they didn't believe us. One guy grabbed my friend by the collar and slapped him. Then this other guy kicked him in the waist and he fell. Another guy grabbed me and said, *Ah, I know this one. This one, this enemy, he's a snake. It's Bernard. We've been looking for this guy.*

I was hit in the back. Then I'm not exactly sure what happened, but they took us back to their base. They have these bases around Harare. This one was a house in Dzivarasekwa.[7] They pushed us through the house into the back part, behind the house. They were drunk. Some were smoking *dagga*.[8] They slapped me first in the eyes. I could smell the blood before I started bleeding, bleeding from the mouth. And they had those *sjamboks*,[9] the long ones. They made us jump. They made us sing the revolutionary songs. You couldn't react fast enough. By the time you try to respond to their question, it might be too late. They kept asking my friend and me different things at the same time. And they expected our answers at the same time. They were looking for Tendai.[10] He was the MDC secretary then.

They clapped me in the face with something—a hoe, I think it was the back of a plowing hoe.

I lost some of my teeth. They also broke my arm. While they did it, they sang songs, their own stuff. Then they hit me with something—how can I describe it?—it was hard plastic with a ball in front of it. They jabbed me with that.

And then I fell. When I fell, I fell together with my friend. My friend actually fell on top of me. They tied us together. That's when lights came on, the electricity. They told us now they needed names. That they weren't playing any more. They said, *You know the exact guys who assaulted our friends when they were coming from Kuwadzana, when they were close to the Bulawayo Road.* We said, *We don't even know about those things. We're no longer involved.* We tried to explain we didn't know anything. They said, *You're lying.* They started kicking us with their boots. It went on for about three hours. A guy would pour some water on us. Then they would take a break before coming back to beat us again.

---

[7] One of the high-density suburbs or townships on the outskirts of Harare.

[8] Marijuana.

[9] See footnote 8, page 289.

[10] Tendai Biti, MDC Secretary General, MP, and Minister of Finance in the so-called unity government of Zanu-PF and MDC as of 2009.

My friend was bleeding seriously. He had a cut under his eye. He said to me, *Bernard, we're going to die here. What we have to do is jump and go.* At the back of that house was a fence and a small sanitary lane.[11] We managed to jump over the fence together. Then we managed to untie ourselves. I said to my friend, *Let's make our own ways. Let one of us be caught, but not both of us.* He went one way, I went another. I wasn't even seeing clearly by then. Everything was hazy, you know? So I think I ran and hid inside some sort of a drainpipe. It was dark inside. Whatever was inside there, I never even thought about it. I just went inside that drain and slept.

I woke up early the next morning in pain. I knew it was morning because I looked out the hole in the drain and saw a lady going to market with one of those big baskets, you know? I crawled out and looked at my shirt. It was just full of blood. Even my trousers. And my mouth—my teeth were so sensitive. No saliva or anything. My teeth were broken into pieces.

Still dizzy, I went to my cousin's place and I told Jimmy what happened and he phoned my dad. I was in so much pain, I couldn't concentrate. I went to the hospital, then the issue was reported to the police.

I think the police just opened up a general docket but they didn't take any other action. They said I was attacked by some thugs. That kind of attack.

A BLIND ADVANCE

After the beating, that's when I had to leave my job. For safety, I went to Bindura and stayed briefly with my uncle. But Bindura was a Zanu-PF stronghold. So I moved to Mutare and stayed with another uncle there and began doing my distance education through Zimbabwe Open University.

I was still a guy with ambition. I'd always wanted to go back to

---

[11] A small path between the houses where sewage runs.

studying. Now I was into trouble. There was nothing I could do about it. I tried coming home for a while. I thought I might be able continue my studies in Harare. But there was talk in the neighborhood of a blacklist. They were coming for people, rounding up organizers. And everybody knew I was back, *Bernard is back, Bernard is back.* A friend I used to drink with told me that those guys were looking for me again.

I had to make a hard decision, you know. I sat with my family. They didn't want me to leave. They wanted to rent me a house out of town, out of Harare. They wanted me to be in Zim. But I just felt like, No—I really have to move. I couldn't live a normal life. I was scared then.

I was actually labeled the problem kid within the family. They talked about me like I was creating my own suffering. But it's not like I wanted to create trouble for the sake of it. Some consequences push you, they end up advancing into events you can't stop. It's a blind advance. Not something you plan. I wanted to speak out. I didn't plan on endangering myself or my family. I only thought, *I have to do something.* Now the consequence was that I had to leave my country.

My father finally said, *Well my son, you're grown up. You can do whatever you feel you have to do.* So I just packed my small bag. That was stolen on the journey, that small bag I had. I didn't use public transport. I hitched a ride in a truck. We arrived in Beitbridge about midnight.

I waited until the morning when some guys came around and offered to take me. They said, *If you pay us a R150, we'll just take you over the border.* They said, *We have some guys who have contacts on the Zim side with police. First we pay them, then we cross at the old bridge.* That's how they explained it. I agreed to pay. To cross, that's what's on your mind.

There were about nine of us. It's actually a chain. You move through people. Everybody has to be paid something. On the Zim side, the police, the soldiers on the border; on the South African side, the soldiers there. When we were about to cross the bridge there was a problem. We waited for almost an hour. Our guides were supposed to know the South African soldiers. But there were different soldiers then. Our guides told us we would have to wait until the shift changes to pass through. They said we would have to wait by the river. We waited three, four hours for the shift to change. They came to us and said, *We don't know this new shift either.* So they said we were going to have to cross the river in the water. By then it was dark. We men took off our trousers; the ladies, they pulled their dresses up to their sleeves. As soon as we crossed the river, we were about to jump over the last wire. Just beyond the river there's a security wire. Before you can reach the road, you have to cross it. Before we crossed the wire, we saw a car coming. It was a Toyota. About six guys came out. They were wearing those woolen hats and those big heavy winter jerseys. And it was still hot, you know. They started producing weapons. One had a shotgun. It was brown, short. The other had a knife.

They said everyone should empty his pockets, lie down. One guy tried to run away. They caught him and started hitting him so much. I didn't fight with them. I was just afraid. At that time I wasn't feeling too well. In my pockets I had about US$150. I put some in one pocket and handed them US$80. Most of them were Zimbabweans. They were speaking Shona. But a couple of the other guys, I think they were speaking some Zulu, but Zulu is similar to Ndebele. So I really don't know. They may have been Zimbabweans also.

This was on the South African side, along the old All Days Road. It's the road that goes to the border with Botswana.

So they emptied us. Clapped some people around. Two guys though were seriously beaten. Then they said, *You can go now.* Everyone took off in his own direction. I made my way to Musina in the back of a truck and was dropped off at the showgrounds.

I was so fearful. And of course angry. But at some point I felt like not blaming them. I actually know that what they were doing—of course it was wrong, to take our things, to beat us. How could my own brother do this to me? But I think you have to take these bad experiences and, you know, put them into perspective. You have to get over the accusations. I mean, this wasn't a political thing. They were just mere robbers. Trying to survive.

RUBBISH EVERYWHERE

In Musina, I found the Abbey Church. There were about 4,500 people staying there in a kind of camp. It was in South Africa that I could see, up close, the real problems in Zimbabwe. This was during the time of cholera.[12] There was so much death in the camp. There were tents all over. The guys from Doctors Without Borders, they were the ones who erected the tents there, and they couldn't even handle all of the corpses. Some of the people were sent to hospitals and treated. But the others...

You would see people being taken by ambulances in unconscious states. There was rubbish everywhere. Water everywhere. People would be urinating everywhere. There weren't enough of those moveable toilets. And people started to avoid them because they were so dirty. Of course, they tried to clean them, but they couldn't keep up, you know?

I escaped the cholera. But diarrhea was a real problem. It was the food. There wasn't enough for the people. It was the Red Cross in conjunction with another lady, a white lady, I forget her name, that was providing food here. Those soya beans. They put some soya in a lot of water and just add flour to make the soup. Most people had diarrhea. Some people had both diarrhea and cholera, but everybody had diarrhea.

IS THAT BERNARD?

You know, I've only been here six months. I'm still trying to settle. I do some piecework at Messina Steel as a general laborer. I work on the construction of sheds, and help around the company. Yeah, I'm learning a new career now.

---

[12] Cholera spread during 2008 as basic services—including water and sanitation—collapsed in urban areas all over Zimbabwe. With so many Zimbabweans crossing the border into South Africa, cholera was then reported in Musina too. Images in the press of ailing Zimbabweans on drips on camp beds in the showgrounds helped fuel the concerns that led to some policy changes, including the ninety-day visa and the closing of the SMG detention facility (see in particular Oscar's story).

It's embarrassing. Sometimes when I'm in town working I see people from home. The other day I was helping erect a metal billboard and some ladies who knew me from Harare called out, *Is that Bernard working up there?* They weren't used to seeing me do such work.

At the moment I'm trying to refocus. Because, you know, when you go through such experiences—beaten up, running away—you get confused.

I'm actually planning to move to Cape Town. Cape Town or Port Elizabeth. I haven't finalized my plans yet. I'd like to make some money before I go back home and pursue my studies again. As you can see, Musina doesn't have much of an economy. There's not much chance of getting decent employment here.

THE CONFLICT NOW

I've caused my family some deep, deep problems. Being the only son, I often feel like I've failed them. But here I do a lot of talking with friends from the party.[13] I feel that we have to be people who stick to values. And I believe we deserve better leadership. I believe we are the type of people who should be given a chance.

I mean, Mugabe is, what, eighty-five now? He might leave office, but I don't think so. He might run for another term after 2011. So we're scared.

But the truth is the MDC has had some problems. There's been a split in the party, which is a painful thing. It's not worth it. I support MDC President Tsvangirai. But I also have to say that there are other guys who have been a real source of inspiration. People like Welshman Ncube. I mean, think about it, Ncube's a Harvard graduate, a man who helped draft the Namibian constitution. And these guys have squabbled with Morgan, who has made his own blunders. They tried to replace him. He's a difficult man to replace because he has the support of the labor movement. But Welshman and the others were saying the party needed

---

[13] See footnote 2, page 26.

someone who was a bit more educated than Morgan. That was what it was all about. They didn't have that much faith in the president, especially as time went on. You see, it was because Morgan was not consistent, the kind of guy who couldn't be firm on any one thing.

I can't go home anytime soon, because Zanu-PF is still fighting. They've started beating people again. I'm sure you've heard that. And the government is having trouble accessing forex in order to fund their campaigns. They can't use forex to pay their own supporters because there's no way they can get enough. Now they cannot print that useless paper they used to finance everything in the past.

AMOS

AGE: *16*

INTERVIEWED IN: *Musina, South Africa*

Soft-spoken and shy, Amos is the third of six surviving children—three boys and three girls. Another brother and both his parents died at home, in Masvingo Province. Amos's left foot is swollen to twice the size of the right one, with a horrible wound still festering from a stick he stepped onto as he crossed the border in the dark, after being chased by magumaguma. *Other boys focus on ways to make money; Amos dreams of school.*

This story I'm telling you, I want people to know about it.

My parents were farmers. They had their own farm. My father became ill and his whole body hurt. My mother became sick also. She was sick in the mouth. When my father died, my mother had already passed away. I was very small, seven years old. This was in 1997. I started staying with my grandmother, my mother's mother.

I was good in school, but when my father's family came and took me away, my father's mother didn't want me to go to school any more. Later, I went to live with my older sister in Rutenga. Rutenga is a rural area, and my sister stays at a farm in a mud house. She didn't have money for my food or school. She said I should come to South Africa to try to earn money. She found one hundred rand[1] to help me to get here. It was a lot of money for her. That's the last time I saw my sister, when she gave me the money.

When I got to Beitbridge, I met some older boys. I asked them if I could walk with them to South Africa and they said okay and we started walking together. We walked to South Africa through farms.

While we were walking, we met *magumaguma* and they took all the money I had. It was early in the morning, maybe around four a.m. They suddenly came out of the bushes. There were six of them and they held us. They had knives. One took money out of my pockets and another removed my trousers and also took my shoes off. They didn't take the shorts I was wearing inside. After they'd taken the stuff they said, *Go*, and I ran away. That's when I was pierced by a thorn on this foot. A big thick thorn. It went into my foot and came through the other side.

We had already gone through the river to cross the border. We went through the border gates and I saw a taxi. I asked for a lift and to go to the hospital. That's when they operated on my foot.

In the hospital, I was in a bed and there were three other people in the room. I was the only Zimbabwean. They weren't nice to me because I couldn't walk. I struggled even to go to the toilet. I was in the hospital for two weeks. I was worried about where I was going to go after discharge, since I had nowhere to go and couldn't walk.

When I was discharged, I slept for a night in the yard of the hospital. Then I met Emmanuel. He is seventeen years old. He was coming to the hospital to get treatment for an ear infection. He said, *If you can't walk, come with me where I stay, at the shelter.* On that day he didn't get treatment because he brought me here on his back—he went back to the clinic on another day for his ear. Yes, Emmanuel was carrying me on his back. I was in pain so he brought me inside and I went to sleep.

Some of the children here go to primary school. They said they will

---

[1] Approximately US$10.

take us to secondary school, but I don't know when. At school they speak Venda and I can't speak Venda. I need help to go to school.

MATTHEW

AGE: *15*

OCCUPATION: *Building assistant*

INTERVIEWED IN: *Musina, South Africa*

Matthew sits across from us on a plastic chair at the far end of the dusty yard of the boys' shelter. Economic deprivation has forced this fifteen-year-old to cross a dangerous border in search of opportunity. Yet he is matter-of-fact in tone and detail as he tells his story. But with some prompting and listening closely, the outline of a complex and difficult life emerges. Matthew is not animated, but he is not defeated. He sees possibilities for himself, ways he can find work, send money back to his father to help his sister through the schooling he has been denied. The interview was conducted in Ndebele.

We are from Mberengwa, but I grew up staying with my father in Harare. I am the first born of two. My mother passed away in 2003. My father brought us up. He stays with a white man in Milton Park, Harare suburbs. My father is employed there as a gardener. Money has always been a problem. I was sent back to Mberengwa in 2007 because my father didn't have money to send me to a local town school. My sister stayed in Harare. So we weren't staying together anymore. My sister remained in the city with my father.

In Mberengwa, the situation isn't rosy. We stay in the communal areas,[1] we don't own a farm. I was living with our grandmother on my father's side. But we had so little. It become very difficult for my family to put bread and butter on the table as we didn't have foreign currency, South African rand.[2] At one point, my grandmother asked about when I was intending to leave the country. I couldn't stay back and watch anymore—my family had no food, no money. I had no employment. So after the schools were closed, I decided to move to South Africa for greener pastures. My grandmother encouraged me, saying, *Yes, go, my son.*

FIRST CROSSING

I crossed the border with a friend who also wanted to find a job. We paid R150 each. We crossed the border over the bridge in a taxi. As soon as we reached the South African side, the driver took me and my friend to the Musina taxi rank. There we then looked for buses to take us to Johannesburg, but to no avail. After a while, we decided to start walking. We passed a place better known as *imbobo zama juba*[3] and continued walking along the road passing farms. A haulage truck stopped and the driver offered us a lift to Louis Trichardt.[4] As soon as the truck driver dropped us off, we went into the bush, where we stayed for sometime. We started looking for jobs but had no luck for a long period of time. During the

---

[1] The 1920 Land Apportionment Act divided the country into commercial farmland—for deeded ownership predominantly by white farmers—and communally held areas, first called "Native Reserves," later "Tribal Trustlands," and now "Communal Areas." Traditional authorities—chiefs and sabuku—still allocate land in the communally owned rural areas. For more on how the legacy of land division affects Zimbabwe today, especially in regard to commercial farmland, see the appendix section on war veterans and farm invasions.

[2] South African rand commanded purchasing power in Zimbabwe even before the Zimbabwean government adopted foreign currency as legal tender.

[3] Literally a pigeon hole or tunnel, this refers to a point along the Zimbabwe–South Africa route where many Zimbabweans are caught by the South African police. Roadblocks here are said to be bad news for those transporting Zimbabwean nationals and cross-border goods.

[4] A South African town located south of Musina in Limpopo Province. Now known as Makhado.

night, we slept at the garage.[5] I wanted to proceed to Johannesburg, but due to financial constraints I ended up staying in Louis Trichardt.

I was very dirty, I didn't have a place to bathe, I was unemployed. I was given food by well-wishers. A certain person, I can't remember his name, gave me cabbages, sugar, cooking oil, tomatoes and a 2.5 kilogram sack of mealie-meal.

In that first year, I was arrested for the first time. The South African police took me on the grounds that I was a foreign national without proper documentation staying in the bush. I was incarcerated in Louis Trichardt prison for eleven months. It wasn't easy. That's all I'll say.

Thereafter, I was deported back to Zimbabwe. We were dropped off at Beitbridge border post and taken into buses manned by Zimbabwean nationals, which took us to our destinations.[6] In my case I was taken back to Mberengwa. I was back in Zimbabwe for more than a year. I spent most of my time doing nothing. I returned to South Africa in December toward Christmas, 2008.

This time, I crossed on my own and paid a bribe to the South African police who man the border gates. But as I reached the fence at the final border post, I was arrested. Instead of being deported, I was brought to the showgrounds.[7] After obtaining papers to apply for asylum, we joined other Zimbabweans staying in a church.

I started working manual jobs. I stayed for twenty-one days in Thohoy-

---

[5] A common sight in Musina and other parts of South Africa is Zimbabweans sleeping at the 24-hour petrol stations. See Rudo's story.

[6] Part of the support provided by the International Organization on Migration, IOM.

[7] Many Zimbabwean and South African towns hold an annual agricultural show and set aside an area for it. The showground in Musina was taken over by South African authorities as a place to process asylum applications by border jumpers. In late 2008, with more than a thousand Zimbabweans crossing every day, cholera broke out along the border. Hospitals and clinics in surrounding areas refused entry to "undocumented" non–South Africans, so hundreds of cholera patients were treated in the open, in the hot December weather. Due in part to this disaster and attendant media attention, the South African government introduced a ninety-day work or asylum-seeking visa for Zimbabweans with passports.

andou[8] doing part-time jobs before again being arrested and deported back to Zimbabwe, this time to Harare. I was very happy to see my father and my sister, and they were happy too. This was during the hardest time when all of Zimbabwe was affected by the shortage of foreign currency. I left my father and sister and headed back for Mberengwa. I wasn't specific with them about my plans of coming back to South Africa, I only hinted to them jokingly that one day I wished to be back in South Africa. When I reached Mberengwa, I then headed back to South Africa, and here I am again.

On my arrival this time I came to this shelter, June 2009. I was shown this place by a friend who I came to Musina with—he asked me to come with him to this church.

I'm actually in need of a better job so that I can support my family and relatives back in Zimbabwe with money and food. Currently, I work as a building assistant here, employed by a construction company. I wish and hope to continue working here, but the problem is that this part of the country doesn't pay as well as other provinces, like Gauteng. My friends have been telling me about employment opportunities in Pretoria. They are saying a builder's assistant like myself would get R100 per day. In Musina, they pay R30 per day.[9] I work seven a.m. to six p.m. every day. There is no off day.

NOW AND THE FUTURE

I have a preliminary asylum document, only valid for six months. I would like to get a proper permit or a passport. I was hoping to get a Zimbabwean passport. Unfortunately, it's expensive, and very difficult to get.

I think I last communicated with my family in September. I lost their contact numbers here in South Africa. Currently they don't know where I am. I'm hoping to go back again to Zimbabwe. I'm also planning

---

[8] See Boniface's narrative for more on Thohoyandou, an agricultural area where undocumented Zimbabweans live in the bush and work on farms, often at exploitative wages.

[9] Approximately US$10 and US$3, respectively.

to bring groceries for my family. I know that the situation at home has not yet improved. My father's job has not changed. I feel very sorry for him, a man who works as a gardener earning only R200 a month.[10] I'm sorry to say these words, but there are no miracles that I can perform to improve his situation except to work very hard in South Africa and assist him. Imagine surviving on R200 a month.

---

[10] Approximately US$20.

RUDO

AGE: *32*

OCCUPATION: *Informal trader*

INTERVIEWED IN: *Musina, South Africa*

A gifted entrepreneur, Rudo has always found ways to support herself. She began to work at the age of ten and hasn't stopped working since. She's sold, among other commodities, mealie-meal, pork, sugar, light bulbs, dried fish, chicken, biscuits, and paraffin. When her brother, traumatized by a beating from Zanu-PF youths, suffered from severe mental illness, Rudo supported him, emotionally and financially, even after his behavior became nearly unbearable. But when the Zimbabwean economy began to collapse, Rudo found the challenges overwhelming. Resourceful as she was, she couldn't continue to care for her disabled brother and carry on a successful business in such an economic climate. Like so many other Zimbabweans, Rudo opted to cross into South Africa to earn enough money to survive. Rudo's tenacity won her financial success and political asylum in a difficult environment on the border. However, things took a disastrous turn after she met a man who called himself a pastor and whom she accompanied to Johannesburg. Now back in Musina at a woman's shelter, Rudo shared the details of her story over the course of a long, dry afternoon.

Before my father died, my mother had already started buying and selling paraffin, sweet potatoes, and tomatoes. I was young and my mother was always buying and selling. She would also go to Mutare to buy second-hand clothes to sell in the village. She would do her selling in the rural areas while my father worked in Harare at the tobacco floor.[1] My mother would visit my father, and other times he would come to the village during the holidays. They used to help each other. It was hard for them. We didn't have a fancy lifestyle—we just survived.

We are four in our family, two girls and two boys. The first child was born in 1974. She is called Lucia. She was followed by a boy called Innocent, followed by another boy called Energy. I am the last born. I was born on May 27, 1982. We are all from the same parents. Most of the time we were staying in the rural areas while my father worked in Harare. I left school after Grade 7 in 1996, which is the year my father died.

I started school late because life was hard for us. I think my father wished I could go to school earlier, but there was really no choice. In 1992, my father stopped me from going to school and told me to find work. That was a hard year. There was a drought in Zimbabwe. I went looking for work as a house girl. I was young, ten years old, but I just worked. I worked the whole of 1992, and my mother would take the money and use it to buy food. When drought was over I went back to school. My father was still alive, still working then, but his health was getting worse.

He could walk but his brain was affected. He was sick for a long time but he was still going to work. I was fourteen and I had just written my Grade 7 exams when my father died. I was interested in school, but at that time my mother told me that she no longer had the money to pay for my education. She only sent my brothers to school. I don't understand why she did that. It bothers me that our life was like that, that we lived that way.

---

[1] Tobacco auction house, where the annual crop is traded.

MY MOTHER'S TUCK SHOP

When my father died, my uncle, his brother, wanted to inherit my mother (*kugara nhaka*[2]), to become her husband. My uncle also lived in the village. He would come to our house and say that he wants the family to plow, and this and that. Even today, I don't understand what was going on with him. I was very young. Maybe he wanted my mother to agree to become his wife in order for him to rule everything, or maybe he wanted to start a new life with my mother. I don't know.

So my uncle started giving my mother rules. My mother used to go to Chiredzi to sell peas, but my uncle started refusing to let her go. He would threaten to lock her in and burn down the house. He would say to my mother, *If you don't want to follow my rules, you can leave.*

My mother eventually decided to leave. We didn't stay at our house for long after my father died, only two years. My mother refused to become my uncle's wife, so he told her to go back to her parents' house. But she was already doing her own business, so she decided to go to Harare to start her own life. My mother, my brother Energy, and myself packed and left and moved to my oldest brother Innocent's house in Harare.

We didn't stay with him for long because Innocent only had one room. Luckily, my mother had cash from selling her stuff, so we started looking for our own house. We found a place to rent in Chitungwiza.[3] Then she opened a tuck shop business.[4] The tuck shop was near a school called Chaminuka in Chitungwiza.

My mother would also go and sell things to people on the farms on

---

[2] This controversial tradition became even more contested in the HIV/AIDS era. Inheritance law has been the subject of advocacy and education campaigns since Independence. Widows often end up homeless and destitute as the husband's family claims all the deceased's property and the children.

[3] Chitungwiza is to Harare as Soweto is to Johannesburg, a large city in itself, built before Independence as a dormitory town for black workers.

[4] A tuck shop in Zimbabwe is an informal stall selling food essentials, often out of someone's house.

their payday. At first it was okay. My brother and I would stay in town and help at the tuck shop. But then people went on strike to protest the government. During the commotion, we hid in our shop. Some people, maybe the police, noticed that we had locked ourselves inside the tuck shop, so they sprayed tear gas. When we came out, some people came and looted everything we had, including all the cash.

After losing her tuck shop, my mother decided to move back to the rural areas. She went to live on a commercial farm, in Shamva. There she married another man. I stayed in Harare with Energy and started to work as a house girl again to support myself. Energy began working as a carpenter. By 2000, I was working at Gazaland,[5] selling at the market. I was staying with my two brothers and my older brother's wife.

One day, when I came back from work—I remember it was a payday—I started thinking about home, about our village. For some reason, I decided to take all the money I had and move back to our village. This was in 2001. My brothers didn't know where I'd gone. I didn't tell them. I didn't know or understand what made me go there. I just found myself at home, in the village. I think I needed to be there.

I went to my uncle's house and I told him, *I have come to fix my father's house.* It was the year of Cyclone Eileen, so the house had been destroyed. It needed a lot of work to build it back up. My uncle agreed. He said, *Your father has been bothering me at night, saying, "Where are my children?" So it's a good thing you came. You can go ahead and fix the house.*[6] So I fixed the house and after that I phoned my brothers telling them I was at our village.

I stayed at my father's house for a while, but because I didn't have any food or work there in the village, I went back to Harare. I left my uncle's house after I realized I wasn't happy there, because of the way he treated me. I went back to Harare. When I got there I went back to Innocent's

---

[5] A trading area in Highfields township, Harare.

[6] Rudo's uncle is referring to the spirit of Rudo's dead father.

house. This must have been 2003. Soon, my sister-in-law had trouble with me. Before, when I had a job, she was nice. But when she saw me with my bags and no job, she became moody. She actually got sick after I came. For two days she stayed in bed, saying, *I'm not feeling well.*

So I tried something else. I went to the farm, to Shamva, to where Mother was living. It was then that I started my own business. I bought a bag of mealie-meal and started selling it, weighing it on a plate and selling it around the rural area.

MY OWN BUSINESS

When I was staying on the farm a man asked me out. At the time he seemed single, but it turned out that his wife was away somewhere. This man had a tuck shop and a bar and a scale for weighing gold. Thinking he was single, I fell for him. Within two weeks of my falling for him, his wife came back. I saw him holding a child that looked like him, and I asked someone and they said it was his child.

I explained everything to my mother and you know what she said? She said, *You can't leave him. Even if he does have a wife.* I was hurt. I began thinking about my background and I said to myself, *Why is my mother telling me things like this?* I think it was because he had money.

I didn't listen. I carried on selling my things. I bought pork from a nearby farm. I would do a *braai*[7] and sell the meat to gold panners at night after work.

Then my mother got sick. She had herpes. I gave her all the money I had and put her on the bus for treatment in Harare. When she came back, she was still pressuring me to go back with that married man. Whenever she saw me with another guy she would shout at me because she wanted me to be with the married man. I knew I couldn't stay with her any longer. I had to move again. This time I moved to Masvingo. I decided to go to

---

[7] Barbeque.

the house of a pastor I knew. I used to do Bible studies with him. I needed my spirit uplifted. So when I went to Masvingo, I told the pastor that I would like to stay with him while I looked for work as a house girl.

The pastor said I could stay with him and his family, and that he would try and pay me to work for him. But life wasn't easy there either. They too were suffering. We would eat vegetables without cooking oil and we would have black tea in the mornings and sometimes porridge without anything. But I just said, *All I want is to praise the word of God. You don't even have to pay me. I will work here as your child.*

So for two years I learned more about the Bible. There was a day when the pastor went to town and bought a case of sugar from OK.[8] When he brought home all the sugar, I told him, *You know, I used to sell sugar in the village. If you like, I can go sell some for you.* He said, *No, not for me, you go and sell some for yourself.* So I went to Gumbo and sold the sugar in that neighborhood.

The pastor said I could take the money and use it to continue the business. So I would then sell shelled groundnuts at the market and at the bus rank. They sold very well. So I started with a case of sugar and people would ask for more. Then 1.5 liters of paraffin when fuel was hard to get in Zimbabwe. I bought it in Masvingo and then went around to the villages selling. From the profits, I would buy bread, meat, cooking oil, or veggies for the pastor and his family. I also sold small fish. I would buy a 250g can, open it and make ten small packets out of it, and then charge for an amount that would give me profit. So it was working out. My business was growing and I was living with the pastor.

I started seeing this guy who was studying mechanics at the technical college. I felt that it would be a good thing to get married. I would have a family and forget about the situation at home in my family. So in August, 2004 we eloped. Within three months my husband went to pay *lobola*[9] to

---

[8] OK Bazaars, one of the main supermarket chains in Zimbabwe.

[9] See footnote 5, page 130.

that uncle of mine. My husband and I were together in 2004, and then in 2005 I fell pregnant and had a miscarriage at three months.

My husband was an only child and he wanted children. My mother-in-law took me to prophets[10] so that we could have a child, because after the miscarriage I didn't fall pregnant again. It didn't help. By the end of 2005 our marriage was over due to the fact that I couldn't conceive.

The pastor I'd stayed with before had moved to Gokwe. So after my marriage, I started renting my own room. That year, 2005, I told myself not to be involved with men. I wanted to concentrate on business. I was selling light bulbs, candles, matchboxes, dried fish, and other things. Even though I only had a small table at the market, I would say my business was growing. I ordered light bulbs from Harare, I ordered dried fish from local shops in town. I bought it in bulk because everything sold fast. I thought if I sold more I would go and do a dressmaking course. I could also buy a machine at the flea market to sew bedspreads or seat covers.

SHAMVA INCIDENT

2006 was a time of many political problems, especially in Shamva where my mother was living. She is still there up to now. I couldn't go visit my mother because I was afraid. I'd heard that people were getting killed there.

My mother was a Zanu-PF member. In Shamva, there was no choice. They force you to be a Zanu-PF member whether you like it or not. If you want to go to that village, you need to have a Zanu-PF card or you will be beaten up. If you have an MDC card they beat you up.

One Friday, my brother Energy, together with a cousin of mine, went to Shamva to visit my mother. Neither of them had a Zanu-PF card and they didn't care. My brother was involved with MDC at that time.

They spent the night at my mother's house. The next day there was a Zanu-PF meeting. My mother went to the meeting with her husband.

---

[10] In some of the independent African churches in Zimbabwe—especially among the Apostolics or Vapostori—healers are called prophets.

Everyone in the village was expected to go, but my brother and my cousin refused to go. Energy said, *I will not go to a Zanu-PF meeting.*

So they stayed in the house, but one of the Zanu-PF youths passed by and heard them talking in the house. You know how these Zanu-PF are. This youth knocked and went inside and talked to my brother and my cousin. This guy said, *Look, this house will be burned so get out, leave.* He said, *Get out of here and use a different route, not the main one.*

My brother and my cousin started running. They took a different route from where the meeting was taking place. They had to take the long route, the one that went high up through the hills. They climbed and climbed and then sat under a tree to rest. That's when the Zanu-PF people at the meeting saw them. The road was high up, and people down below could see them through the trees and tall grass.

The Zanu-PF ran up there and caught them. My brother and his cousin were tied together, hands at the back, and brought to the meeting. When the meeting was over, they were beaten. They were beaten while my mother was present. There was nothing she could do to stop them, because if she did they would involve her too. They were beaten, and the youth were singing. My cousin died in the beating. They dropped his body in front of my mother's house, just left it there. He was buried there in Shamva because no one had money to take him to his home area in Zaka.

Energy survived. That day my mother took him to the hospital. She said he was coughing up blood and looking very confused.

My brother stayed in hospital for three months. When he was discharged he still wasn't fit. He was a little better but had scars. He still has those scars now. He also started to show signs of suffering from mental illness. I believe the beating affected him mentally.

When he was in hospital, I would go to see him, and he would always start talking politics. He would say, *You Zanu-PF people, you want to kill me? Well, you guys are murderers. We MDC people are going to rule.*

Zanu-PF wants to kill him, he would say over and over, Zanu-PF wants to kill him. When he would talk like that I would think he was seeing what happening during his beating all over again. Even now, he is afraid to go to see my mother in Shamva because in his head he is still thinking about what happened there. When my mother went to visit him, he didn't want to see her. He would say to her, *You are the one who sent people to beat me up.*

Not long after Energy was discharged from the hospital, he started becoming violent. Whenever it all came back to him in his head, he would beat up his wife. He was even violent toward his two children. Because of the violence, his wife's parents asked her to come back home to Harare. So then she took the two boys and left him.

He stopped going to work at his carpentry job. When he couldn't pay the rent, the landlord told him he couldn't stay in his house anymore. So my brother lost his house and his wife and children.

Sometimes you can have a proper conversation with him. Sometimes he talks like he knows what he is doing to his life, but I guess that's part of his illness also. Because he just changes and diverts to politics, saying, *Zanu-PF wants to kill me but I'm just like God. I am God, and the year you lose I am going to stop everything. And if you kill me I won't die, I will come back to haunt you.* It was so terrible. Sometimes he would say to me, *I am not related to you. I want to have sex.* The problem was that if you argued with him he would start talking about the beatings and then he would start crying with his head facing down.

HE NEEDS HELP

Other things were going well for me then. I had a good job and I was living in a two-roomed house in Masvingo. I even had a maid working for me, unbelievable for an uneducated person. So when my brother came to the village, I would pack up some food for him and then go back to my place in town. He did all right for a little while. He was selling carpets in the village.

But he became worse. He would come to my house and ask for money. If I told him to leave, he wouldn't. Three times I had to call the cops so they could tell him to leave. When the cops came, he would always negotiate with them, sounding like a sane and healthy person. He would say, *If you give me some money I will go back to the village.* But he never stayed in the village for long.

In July 2007, Energy came to my place and said he didn't want to stay at the village anymore. *Zanu-PF people are becoming a problem.* It was during the election campaign. People's houses were being burned, and it was true, many bad things were happening. My brother sometimes behaves like someone who knows what he is doing. At that point, he said, *I want to live here,* and I said, *What will you do?* He said, *I can sell things just like you do.*

I took out some money and paid rent at another house for him. I gave him some cases of salt and sugar and told him to start selling. He sold for one day, then another day, but on the third day he started talking strangely again, saying, *I don't want to stay there anymore, I want to have sex with you, you sent Zanu-PF people to kill me. I was sent by God to sort things out here on earth.*

I ended up having to explain to my landlord the situation, because sometimes Energy would just start screaming or making other noise. The landlord understood. He advised me to take my brother to a traditional healer for treatment: *He needs help.*

My sister is a traditional healer, a prophet, staying in Bikita. So I got onto a bus and went to get her. I brought her back to Masvingo, and explained what was going on with our brother. I told her that since sometimes he is all right and knows what he's doing, I thought helping him would be a good thing. But now I'm afraid he might overpower me and rape me.

I also phoned my mother to come. I told her, *Please come, he's got worse.* She finally came. So my mother and my sister were with me, and we spent the night discussing what to do about him. The thing is, sometimes he was fine. My brother had a guitar. He always carried it with him, and he would sometimes play and sing. He even wrote songs. That night, with my sister and my mother, he played. So he was playing and because my sister was drinking, she gave him some money to buy alcohol.

Everyone stayed in my house that night. In the morning, I remember, he asked for some Colgate toothpaste. I gave him some and he brushed his teeth. Then he said, *You sent Zanu-PF people to beat me up*, and all of that story. He started screaming and walked down the road. We followed him, but he picked up stones and threatened to kill us, so we were careful. We didn't get too close to him. In the end, he disappeared. We didn't see where he went to. He ran away. He must have used the money my sister had given him for drink for transport.

We were looking for him all over. We even went looking for him at Masvingo Police Station where he is well known because he's been there before. We asked the cops if he'd been there and they said no. We suspected he might have gone to the village.

Energy came back after two weeks. He was sitting in my kitchen, saying, *Zanu-PF people will kill me.* I told him, *No one is looking for you.*

Again he wouldn't leave. So I went to the police station, and five guys from the neighborhood watch were assigned to help me. They asked me, *Is he violent?* I said yes. I went home with the five young plainclothes police. He said, *Are you cops? I will go to the police station to find out because you are not in uniform and you don't shave your hair.* They threatened to beat my brother up and he started crying. The police said to him, *Go back to the village. Your sister will come and visit you or she will send you food.* Finally he agreed and he left.

My sister was not around anymore. She'd gone to South Africa herself. She said she was only going for a short time, but she didn't come back and I didn't know how to get in touch with her. My mother couldn't help me. I was left to deal with my brother's problem by myself. He kept coming back. I stopped letting him inside my house, because whenever I let him in, he wouldn't leave. He would sleep outside. At the shops where I sold at the market, he would also come and either sleep or sit next to me while I worked.

One day my door was open and he came into the corridor. When I told him to go, he refused. That day I was brave enough to push him. So he took his guitar and bashed my head with it. It broke and I got cut. I went to the police. I think it was the fourth time that week asking the cops for help with my brother. My brother was afraid of cops and soldiers. Anyone who wore a uniform he thought was Zanu-PF. I went, wounded, to the police station to report, and they gave me a letter to take to the hospital for treatment. I went to the hospital and then went back home. By that time, the police had managed to chase my brother out of the house.

I DIDN'T SAY GOODBYE

By 2008, the Zimbabwean economy was going even further down. The Zim dollar was devaluing every week against the rand. We were now buying everything from South Africa. I sold my stuff in Zim dollars and then changed my money to rand to buy more stuff. For those buying with U.S. dollars or rand, I would just use the going rate to sell to them.

Life was becoming really hard. I had no one to talk to. My uncle didn't understand and my auntie said that my brother was only pretending to be mentally ill. It hurt me that she said that.

The devaluation continued and I had debts to pay back because I'd bought some things on credit. I started thinking about my life and where it was going. I knew my brother wasn't going to get better. Soon, my business would be nothing. I made a decision on the 9th of December to come to South Africa to try and start a new life.

I didn't even tell anyone or say goodbye. A girl I knew agreed to come with me, and together we got onto a truck at nine that night. It was a big truck, a long-distance truck, but we were packed in there. Another dozen people got onto the truck in Ngundu. Women and kids, too.

We got to Beitbridge before twelve midnight. We were dropped off at the Total garage next to the border. It was my first time there. My friend got off the truck first. She said she was going for a quickie in order to get more money for transport. I had no idea she was a prostitute. She said, *Wait for me at the border, I'll be back.*

There was a man walking with his brother and his wife and children.

I joined them because they didn't seem like robbers. So I was walking with the two men, the woman, and the two kids. One was a baby. The woman carried him on her back. The other child she carried on her shoulders because he was too small to walk such a long distance. That woman's husband and his brother were leading the way.

I'd be lying if I said I remembered the road we used. We were walking through the bush. We moved slowly. We walked from twelve midnight until morning. We went backward, away from the border in the direction where the truck had come from. I don't know the name of the place where we eventually crossed.

When we were walking I had faith and prayed for a safe journey. In my heart I felt like this was going to be fine. Back then, I didn't know the stories about people getting killed crossing over, which is why I wasn't afraid.

In Musina on the South African side, I slept overnight in front of a petrol station. There were other Zimbabweans who were selling plastic bottles also sleeping there. The next morning, I woke up and went to the showgrounds.[11] There was a church service going on when I got there, which I attended. Then I waited in the queue for asylum. Women with children went first, but those women with no children had to wait. That night I slept at the showgrounds. We slept there on the ground in the open air for two more days. On Thursday, the 19th of December, I got my asylum papers.

The next day, I started looking for piece jobs at the locations.[12] I was walking around with another girl who I'd met at the showgrounds. We didn't get any work so we went back to the showgrounds, but the food was finished there. Some women would go out and be picked up by truck drivers to go have sex and then get food from them. I never did any of that, so I went hungry.

---

[11] Gathering place in Musina for migrants coming from Zimbabwe.

[12] An older word for formerly black-only townships or high-density suburbs, still commonly used.

SELLING SADZA AND BISCUITS

I didn't have any food or anywhere else to stay. I still slept on the ground at the showgrounds. Each day I would go to look for piece jobs but wouldn't find any. I also sometimes went to the Roman Catholic Church where people were getting food. One day I was in the queue at the church, sitting down, tired, and hungry, and a man who was driving a car came and said, *I need someone to do my laundry.* So I got up and ran to his car. He said his house was near the showgrounds, but when we got there I was surprised to see another woman wearing a uniform and an apron. He said, *I'm sorry, she works here every day but I thought she was not coming today.* He gave me twenty rand.[13] It was obvious that I was hungry and penniless and still sleeping at the showgrounds. I used five rand for the taxi and for some food and saved fifteen rand for myself.

I was told I might find help at the I Believe in Jesus Church run by a man named Pastor Sithole. Pastor Sithole was kind, he welcomed me. Another Pastor, a Zimbabwean who I knew from Masvingo, was also there. There were some girls who had been raped. They were staying at Pastor Sithole's as well. I didn't go back to the showgrounds to sleep.

One morning, I told the other girls at Pastor Sithole's that I was going to town to look for piece jobs. They gave me twenty rand to buy them panties because they'd been raped and they needed new panties. I thought about the fifteen rand that I had and I said to myself, *God won't let me down.* With my fifteen rand and the new twenty rand, I went to town and bought a box of biscuits, lemon creams. I went to showground and started selling them. The box was finished at around eleven a.m. I'd made sixty rand. I was selling again. I thought about it. Why only biscuits? I bought two kilograms of chicken at Score, which was something like thirty-seven rand. I felt the pastor wouldn't refuse for me to use his pots to cook, or his plates, dishes, and so on. By then the shop for panties was closed, so I couldn't buy those girls their panties.

---

[13] Approximately US$2 at that time.

I told them what happened and they did not mind because I still had their money.

I spoke to Pastor Sithole and the Zimbabwean Pastor. I said, *Please can I use your pots to cook so I can sell food at the showgrounds? When I have money I will move on and support myself.* They told me what I was doing was good. They said, *Go ahead and use them, it's okay.*

I began selling chicken and *sadza*[14] and biscuits. After three weeks of staying at the church, I'd raised enough money to buy clothes and get my hair done. My hair needed it. You need to look good when you sell food. I'd also raised some money for rent so I told the pastor to let me know if he heard of any free place. He helped me find a place which was R360 per month to rent. On the 15th of January, I paid my rent and moved.

THE MAN FROM DRC

I had a lot of customers at the showgrounds. There was this one man from the DRC.[15] I won't say his name. He was given asylum papers while I was selling there. I never used to speak too much to people from the DRC because they behaved in a proud way. He would only buy food from the Somalis.

Then one day I met the man when I was going to buy chicken to cook with *sadza*. I was walking to town and he was too, so we started walking together. He started asking me out, saying he was a pastor and that he came from the DRC. He said his bibles were stolen while he passing through Zimbabwe. He said, *I am going to Joburg where I have a furnished room. I am going there to open a restaurant. I'm looking for someone to marry. We should come to an agreement.*

I asked myself why the pastor wanted to marry this way. Since I once lived with a pastor, I know that normally a pastor would approach

---

[14] See footnote 5, page 31.

[15] Democratic Republic of the Congo.

a family first in order to marry their daughter. But I did agree to go out with him.

I didn't see him for a couple of days. When I met him again, he was with a man he called his brother. He said, *I live with my brother and his wife and we all sleep together in one room. We are waiting for money for transport to go to Joburg.* He said, *If you can, please help me with accommodation for now. It's not a good thing for me to sleep in the same room with my brother and his woman.* I said to him, *Okay.* But I knew my status, because when my husband and I divorced I went for a blood test and I was negative. I had never slept around. Whenever I dated, I'd tell a guy, *First, we have to go for HIV tests.* If they refuse, I'd leave them and maybe we'd just become friends. So I told this man from DRC—my new boyfriend—*I won't have sex with you until we go for HIV tests.* I said, *If you are strong we can just stay together as brother and sister in one room.*

He said, *Okay, we can just live together.* So he stayed at my house for a week. For sure we stayed like that, like brother and sister, and he would pray at night, and it seemed real. We communicated in English but he said he also spoke Swahili or French. The whole time we stayed together he never asked to have sex with me. I would just cook and go to the showgrounds and leave him at home sleeping. I would get back home and find him reading this Christian book in English which was given out by the pastors at the showgrounds.

Sometimes he'd go to town to check his email to see if his money had gone through. He would tell me that he had this white friend who had promised to send him money on such and such a day. One Friday when I was walking from town to buy my chicken, I met some people who told me there were free train tickets being given away to whoever needed them.

I told him about the tickets. On Saturday he left the house saying, *I'm going to tell my brother that there is free transport and also check email.* When he came back he told me, *We can't go together now but in two weeks I will call you so you can come to join me.* He said, *I will phone you,* and he seemed honest. I was surprised and I said to myself, *God is with me and being with this pastor will lessen my problems.* On the 21st I packed my stuff and gave the man from my church the keys. I sold my pots, stove, and washing baskets in order to get transport money. I was going to Joburg! The taxi left at seven p.m. and arrived in Joburg at around one a.m. We all slept. The driver parked, locked the doors, and we slept in the taxi because it was too dangerous to move around at that time. When we woke up in the morning I phoned my boyfriend. When he came to get me, he took me to the place where he was staying. I was surprised. He didn't tell me his room was in a shelter for refugees. I know I should have asked more questions. I don't normally say much because I'm not that good at talking.

His room at the shelter was upstairs. It had nothing in it but two mattresses and a chest of drawers. There were two other people living in it, a woman and her young child.

He asked to have sex with me and I said we should get tested first as per our agreement, so we just prayed and slept. On the second day, I said, *I don't know Joburg. It's my first time. I don't even know South Africa very well.* I didn't know where to go for HIV testing in Joburg but he said he knew.

I thought we were going to go and get tested but we never did. On the second day my boyfriend went drinking. He came back and showed me his true colors. He said, *You want to go for blood tests to do what? You know what, you are not clever.* He started shouting at me and became a different person altogether.

That night he demanded sex. I didn't know what to do or where to go, and because people had seen us staying together I knew no one would help me even if I screamed. I didn't know then that he had given my name to the UNHCR and the owner of the shelter, saying that I was his Zimbabwean wife. He forced me to have sex with him.

On the third day, he started saying other things. He said, *You know, I don't love you. I want to get another wife. I don't like sleeping with you.* He said, *I want to get another woman to have sex with right now. Go back to Musina.* He started hitting me and shouting at me. He said, *Do you have a marriage certificate? Do we have children together? You are forcing me to marry you.*

When I got to the shelter he'd taken the R900 voucher which was meant for me. Other women were also getting the same for food. He'd changed my voucher to cash and he gave me R300 and took the rest. He gave me the money and told me to go back to Musina. But I thought if I went back to Musina I'd be forced to walk around in the streets and maybe meet another man who would give me HIV. I didn't want to risk my life.

I started thinking about everything I'd lost, all the money which I had spent to travel here. I went outside the gate and cried, and then I went back inside to speak to the person who ran the shelter. He said, *I don't like people to go to the police without talking to me first. I will listen to your story and tell you whether to go to the police or not.* He asked me to tell him what happened and I did. He sent someone to call my boyfriend and he came. He said, *I love my wife, I don't know what her problem is. Maybe she has a problem but I love her.* The man in charge of the shelter told me to go back to my room and be good.

After that time my boyfriend treated me badly. He would hit me and I would cry. He would follow me down the stairs hitting me. He'd beat me up anytime he felt like it. Whenever I told people about it, he'd refuse and say, *I don't know about that, I love her, I love my wife.* That woman who was also staying with us in the room would hit her child if she came near me.

Whenever my boyfriend felt like having sex with me he would, and then he would shout at me afterward. Yes, even when the woman and her child were in the room. I worried that this man had really messed up my life and all my plans and maybe given me HIV.

On the 10th of June he hit me and I went to the shelter office to report him. He denied it all again. I went back to the room and took a belt from my bag. I wanted to commit suicide. Someone who lived opposite our room saw me and ran to call my boyfriend who came and removed the belt.

I am trying to explain to you the story of my suffering. My boyfriend told the man who ran the shelter and he said, *We have to remove her from here.* He told me, *I want you to refresh your mind and move away from your boy-*

friend. My boyfriend went to get my stuff. When I was leaving he mocked me, saying, *I'm happy now.*

THE TIN HOUSE

The man who ran the shelter was a South African. He took me and two other women, a Nigerian and another Zimbabwean woman, I remember her name was Sue, to his car. He dropped the other two women off somewhere. I had no idea where we were. He said, *Are you hungry?* and then he bought me some chips and chicken. I was hoping he'd help me and I was feeling better, thinking he'd help me find somewhere better to stay.

He then stopped the car and said, *I want to sleep with you.* I was afraid because he was a big guy. But since he was helping me, I didn't say anything bad to him. I just said, *Today, no.*

He dropped me off at some other house which was not a shelter, even though he'd said he'd take me to a shelter. He said he owned a lot of shelters where refugees stay. He dropped me off at this place where one woman lived with her child in the main house. Behind it was a small tin house. He put me there. The place was dusty and very dirty. I didn't sleep that night because I was worried about the shelter owner. I stayed there for four days without blankets. I slept cold, on the floor. I didn't have food or anything. I had no knife or a wooden spoon for cooking. I just stayed alone in that room without electricity. I was hungry. I had a cell phone but no one to call for help. After four days, the owner of the shelter called me before five in the morning. He told me to get ready, that he was coming to get me. When he called, I thought I was dreaming, so I checked my received calls again and still didn't know who had called. After thirty minutes he came and asked me if I was ready. I said, *I'm not ready because I didn't know it was you calling me.* He wanted to give me a hug and I refused. Then he drove me to my asylum interview in Pretoria. They were asking how I left my country and how I was living now. The interview was for refugees. In the office were Congolese, Ethiopians, and

Somalis. Only two of us were Zimbabweans. I don't know the name of the organization, but white people were in charge of the interviews.

While I was waiting, my boyfriend, this pastor, came into to the office. He said he wanted to talk to me because of the interview. I told him I wouldn't talk to him. *You chased me and you said you don't love me. And why are you writing on the form that you are married to me?* He started shouting at me. He went to another Congolese girl who was there and they started pointing at me laughing. He started saying, *I'm married to someone else. This one is just a girlfriend. I don't love her.*

He was so loud that a white man approached us and took us to another room. There was another white person there. They said, *Tell us your story*, and I told them my story. My boyfriend also told them the story. They said, *You brought her from Musina?* He said yes. Then this other white person, a woman, said, *Why lie that you want to marry her and treat her like this?* She sent him out.

Then the white man said, *Okay, today let's do the interview and then we will look into your story another day.* She said, *You must come tomorrow when we are not busy so you can tell us the whole story.* So we did the interview. Then Sam, a driver for the UN, took me back to the tin house where I'd been moved to by the owner of the shelter.

In the car, I made a big mistake. I decided to tell my whole story to Sam, and I also told him the owner of the shelter wanted to have sex with me. I was crying when I was telling him the story. I made a mistake because the UN driver was friends with the owner of the shelter. He knew that if I reported my story, his friend would get into trouble.

Sam had told me that he'd pick me up the next day after the interview to go back to Pretoria to report my story. But he didn't come. No one came. I think Sam was now afraid to come and pick me up. I called him and he kept on saying *I'm coming*, but he never came. I'd been given money by the woman who was staying in the main house but I'd run out. I went to her again and told her my whole story.

She said her name was Comrade Elizabeth something. She said she had connections high up in the government of South Africa. When I was with her, I phoned the pastor in Musina to explain what was happening. But I couldn't really speak to him—I kept crying. So Elizabeth spoke to the pastor.

The pastor referred me to a man named Sabelo, a human rights lawyer originally from Zimbabwe. Sabelo came to where I was staying and then we all—myself, Sabelo, and Elizabeth—went to the shelter where I used to stay. Sabelo asked what was going on. The owner of the shelter said, *She was beaten up and abused and has reported to me before. We can't give her money because she stays outside the shelter.* I said, *You are supposed to be helping me. Even the UNHCR isn't helping me because the driver, Sam, is a friend of yours.*

BACK TO MUSINA

I was still living behind Elizabeth's house. She wanted to take my story to the government because I had tried to commit suicide. She said as an ANC[16] member, she was going to take it into her hands. She said, *We have a duty to help because these people in the shelter are abusing refugees.* She drove me around and I reported my story to various comrades.[17]

I told Elizabeth that my asylum was expiring on the 25th of June. I was afraid of looking for a piece job in case I got arrested by the cops. So I wanted to leave and go back to Musina to renew my asylum. *I'm not doing anything here. There's not even electricity in my room.* She said, *Okay, if you have any problems just call me, and let me know how things are going.* The following morning I went to Pretoria. I phoned the UNHCR offices when I got there. They gave me money for transport from Pretoria to Musina. UNHCR referred me to this women's shelter.

I just wanted to explain—what has hurt me most was the time in South Africa, when I started staying with that man, my boyfriend, at

---

[16] African National Congress, the former liberation movement and now ruling party in South Africa.

[17] Other members of the African National Congress.

the shelter. It was only a month that I was there, but it was too painful. Here in South Africa, I'm only waiting for my asylum to be renewed, always waiting. Maybe my life will change. I don't know how things are at home. The last time I talked to my mother, I was still living in Joburg. I asked her how my brother is. She said he's still at the village.

SANKOH CHARI IS STILL ALIVE

The title of the last section of this book refers not to a geographic location, but rather the direct statement of one man. Sankoh Chari, against many strong odds, is not only still alive, but willing to tell his story.

SANKOH

AGE: 36

OCCUPATION: *Security guard, barber, T-shirt salesman,*
MDC youth Leader

INTERVIEWED IN: *Johannesburg, South Africa*

Sankoh[1] is a quiet but forceful storyteller. He doesn't raise his voice. He never becomes emotional or angry. He can quote passages of the bible from memory. He has a remarkable memory for dates as well as certain details, such as the colors of cars. His tone rarely changes even when he is describing, in detail, being tortured. A former security guard and barber, Sankoh, by his own admission, is an unlikely man to become a serious political activist. Yet, after his tuck shop was destroyed in Murambatsvina,[2] he joined the MDC early on and rose quickly through the ranks to become head of Morgan Tsvangirai's security detail as well as a leader of the MDC youth wing. Soon he found himself a wanted man. At times his story is a kind of harrowing adventure, complete with great escapes and even a caper where Sankoh and his best friend Gabriel attempt to elude police capture by detouring into a barber shop and pretending to be shaved. He was imprisoned and tortured

---

[1] Sankoh Chari is a name the narrator gave himself. He told us he picked it up years ago when one of his friends likened his fearlessness to the Sierra Leonean rebel leader, Foday Sankoh.

[2] Operation Drive Out the Rubbish.

on numerous occasions. Not one to back down if he disagrees, Sankoh often found himself not only at odds with the government, but also with the leadership of his own party. He considers himself a man with enemies across the political spectrum. Now isolated from his family and the movement to which he nearly gave his life, Sankoh struggles to get by in Johannesburg, broke and alone. This interview was conducted in various places around Johannesburg, including a number of hours at a table in the back of a Nando's Chicken Restaurant.

As a child I was very quiet, maybe stubborn, and somehow intelligent, you know? I didn't want to talk too much, always kept quiet. It might appear as if I am a slow learner, but at the end I'll catch up.

I call myself Sankoh. I was born in 1974, on the 20th of May, in Norton. We lived on a farm called Someyb. I was the third born in my family of six.

When I was nine years old my father was working in Norton at Gulliver's and United Tippers as head mechanic. On the side he built a boat together with his boss. One day the boss wanted to go test it in Lake Mcllwaine—now it's called Lake Hunyani. It was a Sunday. They went to the lake and tested the boat. But when they were putting the boat onto the trailer, the trailer swerved and hit my father. My father died there, on that spot.

We were at home and we heard the message that father had passed away—my mother was preparing lunch with dried fish. Up to now, I don't feel like eating dried fish.

When my father died, my mother was pregnant with my brother, the sixth born. His name is Last. After my father's death, my mother said she didn't want to stay in Norton anymore, so our family moved to our mother's rural area near the Mudzi army barracks. There is a dust road, some huts, mud houses. We used to go fetch water from the boreholes and bathe at the dam. We were planting maize, sorghum, groundnuts, and millet. Mudzi was a good place.

As a child, I loved reading or just fiddling with things. I'm a person, who, if I see a cell phone is not working I just try to fix it. Even a radio.

And I was good at making some car-wire toys. I also drew some cartoons. If somebody was treating me bad I'd draw him in a cartoon. I remember one day there was a soldier called Mutani who fell in love with a girl called Senzeni. I was also in love with Senzeni. I was only a schoolboy. He was in the army. He was taking out my girl, or the girl who I wanted to be my girl, so I cartooned him and Senzeni. I put the pictures around the ground where we used to play football. This guy was very angry and he tried to beat me, but I showed him that I was stubborn. I resisted.

THE MOST PAINFUL THING IN MY LIFE

I moved to Harare in 1994. My older brother Simon was already there. I liked it there because there were a lot of activities. I used to go to the halls and train in martial arts there. I didn't specialize in one thing because I wanted to have many styles. Because of my small body, I wanted to keep myself physically fit for self-defense. I trained tae kwon do, karate, kung fu.

For a while I was staying with Simon, but he was already married so I didn't stay long. So I moved in with my Uncle Chester. I was twenty years old.

Then I received the news that my mother was very ill. So I went back to Mudzi to see her. When I arrived, I understood she was dying. In the rural areas people who become ill often don't go to the hospital, because the hospitals are usually too far away and expensive. They just die in the house. We didn't even manage to take Mother to the hospital, because we didn't have the funds. That was a most painful thing in my life. I arrived on a Friday, and on Sunday my mother passed away. It was around four in the afternoon on a Sunday in October of 1995.

We missed her a lot because she used to teach us life. When my father died, my mother was there for us. She taught us how to work, how to live with others, so many things. She was a very lovely mother.

After we buried her, the headman said to me and my brothers, *Now that your mother has passed away, you must find your own ways. You must move from here. This is not your area. You do not belong to us.*[3]

Again we had no place to go. I left my young brothers staying with our grandmother's relatives in another area called Kawere.

TARIRO

I went back to Harare and trained as a security guard for Rapid Results Security Company. I learned how to supervise other security guards and how to patrol areas. They also taught me how to handle dogs and to use guns. But the money was very little, so I started my own business on the side.

I used to see other people cutting hair, and I knew that I could do it also. I thought, *Why not become a barber?* Even now, here in South Africa, women sometimes come to my place to have their hair fixed by me.

So with the little money I had I bought some scissors, a hair dryer, and I employed two girls. I also bought some bricks and hired some builders to help make a nice tuck shop in Budiriro.[4] I had one big room for cutting hair and a smaller room for charging batteries for people without electricity. There was not a lot of competition, because in that area there were no big shops.

In Harare, I met and fell in love with Tariro. We were married in 1997 and we have one lovely daughter called Chiedza. Chiedza was born on April 28, 1998. As for my wife Tariro, she is a God-given wife because she always stands beside me in the difficult times. Also, like my mother, she has helped to unify my family. Before I married her, my family was not in unity. My brothers and I weren't visiting each other. Tariro brought us together. My younger brothers came to Harare to live with us. Of course Tariro and I have had some misunderstandings here and there, but she has always stood with me.

---

[3] In rural areas of Zimbabwe, women often lack property rights and cannot inherit land.

[4] Budiriro is one of the newer high-density suburbs on the outskirts of Harare.

WE BEGAN DESTROYING OUR OWN SHOPS

In 1998, the government came and said, *No, these tuck shops are illegal structures*. It was not Operation Murambatsvina, but it was the same idea. They said if we didn't destroy our tuck shops they would bring a bulldozer. So for fear for our asbestos, doors, windows, and other materials, we began destroying our own shops. For the others, the ones who refused, the bulldozers came and that was it.

Things were difficult. I rebuilt my shack, but business wasn't good and I could not find other employment. After the destruction, that's when the people from the trade union came and said, *Together we must fight these government policies*.

So I joined up with the trade unionists in their opposition to the government that had destroyed my business. In the beginning I was just helping.

It soon became known that I had joined the opposition, so the Zanu-PF youth came and destroyed the shack that I had just rebuilt. They stole all my material, my scissors, my hair driers. I was grounded. I turned to politics full time.

VOTE NO

On September 12, 1999, the trade unionists formed a new political party called the Movement for Democratic Change. It was launched in Rufaro stadium in Mbare. It was then that I became more involved. I was elected to be organizing secretary for ward three in Budiriro and began mobilizing people to join the MDC.

In February 2000, we were campaigning for the NCA.[5] Mugabe wanted to pass a referendum about the constitution that would expand

---

[5] The National Constitutional Assembly, a group of civil society organizations that began a campaign for a new constitution for Zimbabwe.

the president's powers. The MDC was against the new draft constitution.[6] Our position was that the constitution must be written by the people— not by a few individuals, or political leaders, or the select committee. Eventually our Vote No campaign won the election against the government's Vote Yes.

So Zanu-PF and Mugabe lost that. That's when they started beating up people and invading farms.

WE NEED SOME STRONG GUYS

By mid-2000, the MDC was in full swing. We were going to have parliamentary elections in June.

In April, two members of MDC, who were called Chiminya and Talent were petrol-bombed in Buhera. Buhera is the area where Morgan Tsvangirai comes from. Chiminya and Talent were campaigning there. One day they were driving and members of Zanu-PF chased them. Then the Zanu-PF guys threw a petrol bomb into their car.[7]

When we were at Chiminya and Talent's funeral, the provincial chairman told me, *President Tsvangirai wants to go to Murambinda in Buhera next week to address a rally. You know what happened there, and a lot of people are afraid to come out. So can you go there to mobilize people to come support Morgan? We need some strong guys brave enough to go.*

I volunteered. I went to Murambinda with my best friend, Gabriel, who I had met through MDC. Gabriel became like a younger brother to me. He was a very intelligent person. He also liked talking. As I say, I am the quieter one. If Gabriel was still alive, he would be a good leader of

---

[6] The constitutional revisions were a general consolidation of centralized presidential and governmental power. They would have allowed Mugabe to remain in office for two more terms, ensured political and military leaders immunity from prosecution, and authorized the government to confiscate and redistribute white-owned land without compensation.

[7] The men who were allegedly petrol-bombed by Zanu-PF youths and members of the CIO are Talent Mabika and Tichaona Chiminya, Morgan Tsvangirai's campaign aides.

the opposition. A man like him could even have been the future leader of Zimbabwe. That's not possible now.

That day we were both so excited. It was our first time campaigning in a rural area. The situation was tense because of the bombing. We arrived at eight p.m. at night. We couldn't find a place to sleep because all the hotels refused us. They all kept saying they were fully booked. So we went on to sleep in the bush near the river.

The next day, Gabriel and I and some others started going door to door, to the bus stops, even where people were sitting drinking their *ndari*.[8] We went to the people and talked to them. *You know what?* we said, *This government is not good. Why don't you join this new party?* They began to listen to us. That's how we were interacting with people.

The following morning, around five, we started singing before the sun came out. We sang, *Maria and Marita kudai magara pano Chiminya haaifa*. It's a song which derives from the bible when Maria and Marita were begging for Jesus Christ. *If you were here Lord, Chiminya would not have died*. About twenty of us were singing, and we went to the Murumbinda growth point[9] to begin campaigning. We said to the people, *Just come. Your President Tsvangirai is coming, and he is a son of Buhera. He was born and bred here, so why are you afraid? You must come to the rally and be addressed by him and hear what he has to say to you.*

That afternoon, people were coming from all different directions to see us. Morgan came and he addressed the rally. Afterward, we all went to Tsvangirai's homestead in Makanda village, and there were a lot of people who were waiting to meet with him. That night we didn't sleep. We all enjoyed. After three days we went to Masvingo because Gabriel and I were now on the advance mobilizing campaign team for Morgan. Our primary responsibility was to do surveillance, to go ahead and assess

---

[8] Home-brewed beer.

[9] An area of markets and shops.

any danger to Morgan.[10] That's what security is all about, knowing all the facts. But no, I didn't carry a gun or any other weapon.

Wherever Morgan was going, we went first. We would scout the place, hand out pamphlets and fliers, and, always, sing.

So there was a lot of things happening. The Zanu-PF people were trying to fight us, but we were resisting. We had no guns, only our voices.

FLAMES OF FIRE

On December 19, 2002, we got a call from headquarters that we must go to Masvingo in Bikita West to mobilize for the by-elections.[11] When we arrived we had a clash with Zanu-PF war veteran[12] leader Chenjerai Hunzvi.[13] He said to us: *Some of you will not see Christmas Day, because you will be dead.*

For safety we slept in a different place every night. We were guarding MDC vehicles and our members' shops. On December 24, about four o'clock in the morning, I was sleeping near one of our cars and someone came and threw a petrol bomb. I woke up in the flames of fire. The clothes I was wearing and the bag on my back were on fire. I managed to remove the bag and burning jacket. I began to run. I didn't know where I was running, I was just running. I heard others screaming. I ran until the light of the morning. I made my way back to the car at around 6:30 a.m. My colleagues were looking all over the area for me. They were certain I was dead.

But I was lucky that time. My burns weren't too serious. Only my

---

[10] Especially during times of heightened political tension, assassination attempts on Morgan Tsvangirai have been a frequent danger. Though attempts at assassination may be disguised as "accidents," Tsvangirai has stated that he has survived at least four. Shortly after Tsvangirai's 2009 inauguration as prime minister, Tsvangirai's wife, Susan, was killed in a suspicious car crash while Morgan was also in the car (as mentioned in John's story).

[11] An election that occurs when there's an unexpected vacancy in parliament, as when a member dies in office. In the U.S., it is often called a special election.

[12] See footnote 1, page 172.

[13] Hunzvi's biography is detailed in the appendix section on war veterans.

hair, my jacket, and my bag were burned. The car didn't burn. Some of the other guys had minor burns, but they were okay also. We did report the case to the police. I told the police that I suspected Hunzvi because of his remarks the previous day, but they did nothing.

The violence was becoming worse. One day, during a rally at Baradzanwa business center, a guy named Gara was killed. He had been wearing two T-shirts, one Zanu and one MDC. Maybe he thought he could stay on both sides, I don't know. But that day we were having a rally and all hell broke lose. The police fired tear gas and Zanu-PF youths started beating people, and this guy Gara was murdered in the mayhem.

Gabriel and I were accused of killing Gara. We were taken to the police station.

Now they were claiming that Gara was a Zanu-PF supporter. Outside the station, we were ordered to sit down under a big tree. I remember a ZBC[14] film crew was shooting video of us. From that tree we were called into different rooms where they beat us. They beat us with the butt of a gun and also a rubber stick while handcuffed. They put our heads into a bucket full of water. There were condoms, and they put the condoms on our private parts. They were doing this in order to force us to admit that we had killed Gara.

On the 19th of February, Gabriel and I were released on bail. We went back to Harare. By that time the election had already passed, and Zanu-PF had won. Six months later we were formally discharged. The magistrate had found that there was no evidence against us. A witness, the Governor of Masvingo, a man named Hungwe, confessed that the CIOs had fired some bullets into the crowd to shoot the MDC supporters, and that most likely Gara had been killed by them.

We kept on working. Gabriel and I, we were placed in charge of the MDC youth.[15] We began forming what we call CDUs, community de-

---

[14] Zimbabwe Broadcasting Corporation, a state-controlled radio and television network.

[15] MDC Youth can refer to anyone from their teens to their thirties. Similar to ANC Youth in South Africa.

fense units. I know it sounds like a military thing. When the CIO[16] heard about it, they sensed that maybe we were planning for war. But for us we were just talking about organizing for simple defense and resistance of the police. These were in areas where Zanu-PF youth were moving around, scaring and attacking any member of MDC.

The CDUs were part of the action campaign. We wanted people to rise up against the government in mass protest.

But before the proposed dates of mass action, a ZUPCO[17] bus was burned.

At that time, some of our own more overzealous youth were active in the Glen-Norah area.[18] They were boasting, claiming that they were the ones who had burned the bus. That's when police took them in and started beating them. The police asked, *Who are your leaders?* They told the police, *Our leaders are Gabriel and Sankoh.*

SIX MONTHS FELT LIKE SIX YEARS

I was visiting Gabriel at his house. It was on Saturday the 17 of February 2003. All of a sudden the whole house was surrounded. Gabriel was called outside. He was dragged to one of their cars. This was in daylight, in the middle of the day. Gabriel started screaming, saying, *Sankoh, come help me!*

When I came out they arrested me also. At the Glen-Norah police station, they started beating us and accusing us of burning the bus. We said, *No, we don't know about this thing at all.* Our words were falling in deaf ears. We spent about seven days being interrogated. They didn't torture us much that time. They interrogated us, asking a lot of questions. Many different types of people would come and interview us. They were asking us about the CDUs.

---

[16] See footnote 1, page 172.

[17] Zimbabwe United Passenger Company, owned by the government of Zimbabwe.

[18] A suburb of Harare.

We were taken to Harare Remand Prison. We were held for six months. Every two weeks we went to answer our charges in court, but each time we were sent back to prison without our case moving forward.

I'd been locked up before in the Gara case, but this was my first time at Remand. We were treated like animals. We were eating one meal a day, sometimes only bad porridge and, if we were lucky, some boiled cabbages. It's the type of food to feed a cow. I became thin like nobody's business, and I also became ill with a disease. Up to now I don't know what type of disease. I spent two weeks in the prison hospital. My wife brought me food and helped me so much during my incarceration.

A cell in Harare Remand can sleep more than a hundred people. The way you sleep there, it's what they call Ndimba-Ndimba. People lie on the floor, one facing one direction, the other the other. I've heard from people here about South African prisons. Here they are living a luxurious life. In Zimbabwe it is living in hell. You have no rights. When you go bathe, the guards will beat you. When go to have your lunch, you will be beaten by the guards. The time you receive your food you will be beaten, the time of inspection you will be beaten.

INTELLECTUALS AND TRADE UNIONISTS

We were finally released on bail on the 4th of June, 2003. A month later, they arrested Tsvangirai at his house. They accused him of treason, and he was taken to court and was remanded in custody. They said his protesting was in order to topple the government. So Gabriel and I didn't have anything to do at that time. We just went home and relaxed—for a while. Then we began campaigning for parliamentary elections scheduled for 2005.

People within the MDC started disagreeing. It became an issue between the intellectuals and the trade unionists. The intellectuals were saying we mustn't be led by Morgan Tsvangirai because of his lack of education. Our General Secretary, Welshman Ncube, was an intellectual. In 2005, the MDC had a national meeting, and there were private discussions. Some people were trying to remove Tsvangirai because he was not a learned man and he'd failed. They were saying he'd had his chance and now the MDC was losing seats.

Me and Gabriel saw what was going on because we were part of the security. We went and talked to Tsvangirai. We could always get a meeting with him because we were like his sons. We told him what was happening. *Welshman and other guys, they want to remove you*, we told him.

But Tsvangirai said, *You guys you are lying. My general secretary doesn't do this. Why are you saying my secretary can do this?*

We kept on telling him the truth, but he just wouldn't listen.

At that time, Gabriel and me were still not employed by MDC. We were working for free. We felt left out. We were always there, always working for the party. We wondered, *Why are they leaving us behind? Why are they not employing us?*

Meanwhile, people inside MDC were selling secrets. Whenever we wanted to have a demonstration, someone would always alert the police. When we investigated, we found out that the new head of security was releasing the information. And we went on to tell Tsvangirai, *Look, this is what's going on.* But still Tsvangirai didn't agree with us. He just did not believe in us anymore.

I don't know why he didn't believe us. He is just a man himself. Sometimes he just didn't want to see the truth.

THEY DIDN'T WANT TO EMPOWER YOUTH

One day we decided to protest our bad treatment and to draw attention to problems and abuses in the party. One of the abuses was misuse of MDC vehicles. Some high officials used the cars for private use. So we collected the party vehicles from various places in the city and parked them at Harvest House.[19] At that time Tsvangirai was overseas, in Australia. Then we

---

[19] Harvest House holds the national headquarters of the MDC.

closed Harvest House. We chased away all the employees and other staff members who were opposing our demands.

When Morgan heard that we had closed the office and took all the cars, he abandoned his trip and flew back to Zimbabwe. He met with us in the big boardroom. All the youths, more than three hundred of us, were there. We told him our grievances against the party leaders and their abuse. We said the MDC didn't want to empower youth.

This is the reality. They didn't want to empower youth. They just wanted to use us as their political tools, or political condoms. You know what I mean? They don't want to get dirty. When they are in power, they get whatever they want; then they dump you. We work hard, campaign, get arrested. Then they are all in parliament, driving nice vehicles. They give their relatives money to start projects, send their sons and daughters outside the country on scholarships to get a better education.

So a lot of youth were protesting, saying they were being neglected by the party leaders. And Tsvangirai finally said to us: *I hear what you are saying and heads shall roll.*

You know what surprised us then? They had their meeting, and they went on to fire about twenty-four of us in the party. Twenty-four of us, including myself and Gabriel. They said, *You are fired. You are no longer MDC members.*

After that, many youth stopped participating in MDC activities. In Harare and other parts of Zimbabwe, the youth were not doing anything. They weren't mobilizing the people because they were angry we were fired.

AN IN-BORN THING

Eventually we were reinstated, but even before that we began meeting with the youth and organizing again. Personally, myself, I'm not a coward. I felt that I mustn't leave the struggle of the country because of the greediness of other people. I'm not a big man. But I had to keep on. We were fired on paper, but on the other hand we were the only ones who were able to mobilize the youths. Say Tsvangirai wants to go to Bulawayo—if we don't go, he doesn't see anyone. We felt important because people were listening to us. If the party didn't always support us, it didn't matter.

MDC officially split in October 2005. There was a faction behind Welshman and there was a faction behind Tsvangirai. By this time, Gabriel and I were reinstated. Gabriel went on to contest as a general secretary for MDC youth, and he won the election. But the leadership was still afraid of him. Because if Gabriel became the general secretary, he would have too much power.

Gabriel and me were powerful, of course. I don't hide that. Zanu-PF was afraid of us also. Not because we had money or whatever. Only because we were brave enough to challenge powerful people. If someone did a wrong thing, we told them. Even if you are a leader, we are not ashamed or afraid of saying, *Ah no, Mr. President, what we are doing is wrong.*

Gabriel, they said, lost the election. We accepted it. Even Jesus, when he was eating with other people who didn't like him, he just said, *Come on guys, let us eat together.* I think it's an in-born thing. I can't explain it except to say MDC isn't Tsvangirai. It isn't Welshman. MDC is bigger than any individual. Even now, even right now, though I feel betrayed, I'm still MDC.

TO THE STREETS FIRST

In 2006, the congress of MDC made a resolution that created the Democratic Resistance Committee (DRC). The goal was to bring Mugabe to the table to negotiate. Screaming, kicking, or whatever. The leaders were advocating for a certain way. They had been taken to watch videos from other countries, which have done democratic resistance. You know, the likes of Mandela and Mahatma Gandhi. But we as the youth were saying, *No, we must establish a Zimbabwean thing, not follow what other countries have done. We are not South Africa. We are not India. This is Zimbabwe and we must do what is suitable for us. We have to go to the streets first.*

And the leadership said, *You guys are sabotaging the program of DRC.*

But we said, *No, we aren't sabotaging, we are just not agreeing. We favor work-ing directly with the people.*

We had a meeting with a top MDC official. He told us he understood what we were saying and gave us the green light to do it our way. And so we became involved.

In Zimbabwe, because of this POSA,[20] people have guilty minds already. Our goal was to educate, to say, *No, you are not guilty. It's your right to feel free. It's not a crime to have a demonstration. It's not a crime to* toyi-toyi,[21] *to sing, dance.*

We organized a major demonstration in Harare. It was the 17th of February, 2007. The police were all over town. People were afraid, and so we had to lead by example. We went onto the roads. We started singing, we started calling people, and people started coming.

We led. We said, *You must be out in front if you want people to follow.*

So we taught the people and we taught our leaders. We held our demonstration and the police started beating people, arresting people, and we resisted. It was a big crowd, and people were gaining composure.

One police officer arrested an MDC member, and the youths started to beat the police. This happened at the Ximax mall in Harare. Other people became over-excited and also started beating police officers. The police ran away. They weren't used to people defending themselves.

On that day, people managed to defend themselves and defeat the police. Two days later we were planning an even bigger Sunday rally to be held at Zimbabwe grounds in Highfield. But the government was say-ing, *No, there must be no rally.* After the beating of the police officers, the government announced a curfew, saying there would be no more public gatherings in Harare.

---

[20] The Public Order and Security Act is a set of laws listing offenses for speaking or acting against the government or the "public order"; its enforcement has been used as a pretext for much of the Mugabe government's anti-opposition action.

[21] *Toyi-toyi* is a genre of music and dance that can include political slogans. The govern-ment outlawed it just before the 2008 elections.

That day we marched and protested from Harare Gardens to Julius Nyere Road.

A lot of people were surprised. The leader is saying no, and people are going out into the streets. There is no food in the shops, we are not paid well. Why should we be afraid? The only difference is that they have guns and baton sticks. If we go in big numbers they will do nothing to us, but if we go in small numbers they can arrest us and beat us.

We began planning for another large rally on the 11th of March. We found another venue, outside Highfield. If you are coming from South Africa it's on Masvingo Road. People call the area *paMbudzi* because many people sell their goats there.

We said all the youths must come and gather, and they did. People came that day in taxis and any other vehicles they could find.

The police were starting to intensify the harassment. They put up barricades to prevent people from entering Highfield. But about three hundred of us managed to enter and were heading for the main venue when we met another line of police officers. They were holding baton sticks and shields. They were getting ready to throw tear gas.

We stood about a hundred meters away from them. Gabriel and I ordered the others to stop and be silent. I began chanting the MDC slogan. Other members joined me and began singing a song. The police felt that maybe we wanted to attack them because this song goes like *"shuwa shuwa tovabvondora here tonobvunza kuvakuru vechinja..."* Which means, *Can we attack these police officers?* And we were also singing a song called "Twenty." It goes: *ten taramba, zvaMugabe taramba, nzara mumba mangu.* Which means, *We are refusing to abide by Mugabe while we are suffering with hunger in our houses.*

We started running toward the police, running fast like we are chasing something. When we were about ten meters away, the police they dropped their sticks and shields and ran away.

So we were a very big number; even small boys and girls had joined us. We were calling out *Ngonjo! Ngonjo!* which means *Police! Police!* The police were running away. When we were about fifty meters away from the stadium, that's when a police Land Rover came and started firing bullets at us, live bullets.

We starting fleeing in every direction. The police were becoming vicious. They were also using those vehicles the government bought from Israel, the ones that spray stingy water and have the power to floor people down. If that water hits you, you will regret it. So those vehicles were being driven all over Highfield, and people were scratching their bodies and running all around. That's when we heard that Gift Tandare was shot.[22] And then more disturbing news, Morgan was arrested again, and now he was being beaten at Mchipisa police station.[23]

We managed to escape from Highfield that day. That night, we were phoned by a friend, a contact inside the police. He told us, *Ah, Gabriel and Sankoh, the police are looking for you again because they are saying you are the leaders who are causing all this havoc.*

On the 12th of March, Marimba police station was bombed. At the same time, another bomb went off at Gweru Nehanda police station. Once again we got word that the police were saying we—Gabriel and myself—were responsible for these bombings. We were now on the most wanted list of the police.

So we went to hide in Marlborough, in an area we used to call Mazvikadei. There is a proper area called Mazvikadei, but it's far, far away from Harare. When we said we were going to Mazvikadei, people thought we were going to this other place. But the truth is that this Mazvikadei in Marlborough is close to Harare. It's sort of a small farm, a plot of land.

We felt that it was a secure place for us to hide because there were some rooms there. We knew a lady there. Sometimes we went to provide

---

[22] As mentioned in Father John's and Lovemore's narratives, Zimbabwean police shot and killed MDC activist Gift Tandare at this public Highfield prayer meeting in 2007. Two days after his death, two individuals attending Tandare's funeral wake were also shot by police. Tandare became a martyr, and his death a means of inspiration for MDC organizing.

[23] This was the third assassination attempt on Tsvangirai described in a footnote on page 436. Details on the fallout from this event can be found in the appendix section on the 2008 elections.

security for her. It was a personal relationship, not politics. So we went and told her we needed help, and she said, *Take these rooms, guys, you always help me.* So we hid in Mazvikadei for about a month.

HE IS DEAD AND YOU ARE ALSO DEAD

One day we decided to go back—quickly—to Harvest House and collect some our stuff. You know, Gabriel and I, we used to print some T-shirts there to make some money for living since we weren't being paid. So we wanted to take our silk-screening equipment from the office.

But that day the whole of Harvest House was surrounded by the police. Even the roads were barricaded. So we went through the window and found a pipe, a draining pipe for the toilet. On the other side of Harvest House, on the ground floor, there was a beauty salon. We slid down the pipe to the salon. We took a seat in the chairs and pretended we were there to get a shave. We were seated being shaved and it was okay. Well, we thought it was okay. But then the police came and started harassing the staff of the salon and one guy said, *These two guys are not customers.*

So we were arrested again. They started asking us our names. I kept quiet, Gabriel kept quiet. They searched Gabriel and found his wallet. They saw his ID and said, *Ah, it's Gabriel!* They searched me and I didn't have anything. They took my phone and asked my name and I said, *I am Joshua Mashayanzvimbo.* I just created a name, Joshua Mashayanzvimbo.

We were about 157 people arrested at Harvest House, men and women. They questioned us the whole night. The police kept asking, *Where is Sankoh Chari?* Even though I'd been arrested and in prison before, these police didn't really know what I looked like. And I have that kind of face. I am able to mix into a crowd. I'm not easy to remember.

They began to beat Gabriel badly. *Where is Chari?* they asked. *You are always moving with Chari, where is Chari?* And Gabriel said, *You arrested me alone and you took me from the salon. I was being shaved. Why are you keeping on treating me like this?* Even the ladies who knew me, they just kept quiet.

They charged Gabriel and some others with the bombings. They still didn't know who I was. So they released me. That's when I ran away to Norton to stay with my father's younger brother. But I couldn't stay away from politics long. Soon I made my way back to Harare. I went to the courthouse where the case of my colleagues was being heard.

It wasn't safe to go into the court, so I sent a girl—her name was Joyous—to bring me information. So she was coming and going and telling me what was happening.

Gabriel and the others were remanded to prison. But the magistrate said, *These people must go and get treatment in hospital before they can go to prison.* This was because they were so badly beaten. But the police didn't follow the orders. The prisoners were just brought to Harare Central Prison without getting any medical attention.

So this girl I was with, Joyous, she said, *Let's go through town, I want to collect my passport photos.* She was applying for a passport to leave the country. In town I was approached by two people. One was an old person without teeth. He greeted me. I said, *Hi.* The next moment he pointed a gun at me. This was on Mbuya Nehanda Street. He ordered me and the girl to hold each other's belts. Another man came. They weren't wearing uniforms. They took our phones. He asked our names, and at that time I told them my real name.

So we were told to sit between two taxis. I was just feeling guilty. This girl, Joyous, she didn't commit any offense. Talent's mother was an activist of MDC, but this young girl, she didn't commit any crime.

So I was thinking this, and I just started running. I ran like a mad person. They started shouting, *Thief, thief, thief!* Then they started firing some shots in the air. I ran maybe a hundred meters. Then I stopped. People were wanting to beat me. I said, *No, no, I'm not a thief, I'm an MDC member.* Then those guys came and handcuffed me. They'd left Joyous alone. She just snuck away into the crowd of people. They took me to the police station.

In one of the rooms, they started to interview me. One cop came, smiling nicely at me and said, *Ah, how are you, captain?* I kept on looking at him. Then he said, *Why are you not answering, Captain C?* I said, *I'm not Captain C. My name is Chari, but I'm not captain of anything.* Then he told me he had the phone of a man named Chinyama. In his phone, he had written my number with the name as Captain C. So this cop showed me the phone and said, *Is this not your number?* I said, *Yes, it's my number,* and he said, *So why are you refusing to admit that you are Captain C?* I said, *I don't know, maybe the owner of the phone just wrote me as Captain C but I'm only Sankoh Chari.* Then he said, *Fine, you are joking again. But you are going to start telling us the truth soon.*

They took me to another police station, driving very fast. It was now around one o'clock in the morning when I was put into another cell. I was starting to sleep when I heard my name being called. I stepped out of the cell. I was grabbed and given a clap on the face. A crack below my right eye started bleeding. I tried to see but I couldn't. I was handcuffed again, my hands behind my back, and taken out to a white Mazda B1800 pick-up truck. At the back of the Mazda was a coffin. One of them opened it. He said, what do you see? There was a dead person inside. I told him what I saw. He said, *Yes, it's one of your MDC members. He is dead and you are also dead.*

They took the corpse out and put it in the truck. Then they ordered me to go inside the coffin. They closed it and started driving. They drove and drove. Maybe forty minutes on a tar road. Then I could hear the bumpy road.

Inside that coffin, I can't tell you what I was thinking. Say you are driving and you think that you are about to have a head-on collision. Then you know that this is death. You definitely won't think anything. You won't even think of running away or whatever. You just think of facing it.

Even right now, I often don't feel like I'm alive. I don't really understand it. Even when I come across other people, I just feel like people are seeing a dead person. Up to now, I haven't had proper counseling or whatever. You look at me and I feel dead.

After some time, maybe hours, the vehicle stopped. I could hear voices. Somebody asked, *Where is that pit?*

One of them opened the coffin. I was lying, looking up. I could see only the tall trees and the stars in the sky. Then this guy started whisper-ing to me saying, *Chari, I heard you come from Mudzi. So you are my relative. I don't want you to die. Cooperate with these guys, say whatever they want, just cooperate.* I said, *It's okay, okay.* Then he called the other guys and said, *Guys, listen, Chari wants to cooperate.* I didn't know what was meant by cooperation, but still I said, *Okay, okay.* I was still inside the coffin.

So they said, *Good, if you want to cooperate, Chari, we don't want to waste time. These petrol bombings. We want you to implicate some guys you know. Okay?*

I agreed. I thought, afterward and right now as I am speaking, that it was just a survival tactic. I thought they were going to kill me. They brought me back to Harare Central. I don't know what they did with the other body, the dead person. They pulled me out of the coffin and put me in a room. One chair, one table. I was ordered to sit down on the floor, handcuffed.

A cop came in, a short man, light in complexion. And another, a tall guy with some pimples on his dark face. This one was older and had a short middle finger, shorter than his other fingers.

The short one said, *All right, Chari I've brought these papers. I want you to write the names I tell you.* I refused. For some reason I refused. Then this short cop said, *Oh you want to play with us?* They took me to another room downstairs. It was a dark. I was still handcuffed. They put a baseball stick between my legs and hands. There were two tables, and they hung me between the tables. They started beating me for maybe twenty to thirty minutes. They were beating me under the feet, on the buttocks, every-where, anywhere. Even pushing into me with the baton stick. That baton stick was terrible.

There was nothing I could do because my legs and my hands were hanging between the two tables. Then I must have collapsed. Later, I just found myself lying on my side. I said, *Can I have water to drink, because for the entire day since they arrested me I had no water.* So they said, *Okay, you want water?* They held my legs and brought me the bucket. It was full of dirty water. They put my head in that dirty water and were saying, *Drink water, drink water.*

I tried to breathe. They repeated it for three or four times. Then they took a sack and put it on my head and started beating me randomly. I don't know what was hitting me because it was dark. I screamed and said, *Let me go, I will write. You must tell me what to write because I'm confused and I don't know what to say.*

They gave me a paper. Somehow I was able to write. If you have been beaten enough, you won't feel pain anymore. The pain will run away. If you are hurt only a little bit, that's when you feel pain. The short cop told me what to write. I just wanted to finish and rest. I wrote, first, for myself, admitting that I'm the one who was behind all the petrol bombings. Then I started implicating Gabriel and the others. After that, I slept.

IT WAS ONLY A SURVIVAL TACTIC

Two weeks later I was brought before the judge to face charges. I decided to risk telling the truth because the magistrate was putting it all into the record. I knew that she probably wasn't going to listen, because she was acting under orders from Zanu-PF. Still, I felt I had to give my side. I gave all the names and descriptions of the men who were torturing me. After I finished attending the court, I found my lawyers waiting for me. So they interviewed me, and I also told them what happened while I was in the police's hands, all the torture. They said they would prepare another affidavit to challenge what I wrote to the police.

The following day I heard the guards calling my name at around seven in the morning. They said, *You are wanted at Harare Central.* The short cop started threatening me. *Are you serious? You mentioned my chef's[24] name in the court!*

So the police started interviewing me all over again. They accused me of banditry. They were saying that I had been trained in South Africa at a farm called Lalabundu in the Orange Free state. I didn't even know that

---

[24] Boss or big man.

there is a farm called Lalabundu. At that time I didn't even know there was an Orange Free State. I had never been to South Africa. This time is my first time here. But I was afraid of more beating. I was afraid they would now kill me. So as per the first arrangement, I agreed with them. I said, *Yes, I went to that place, that farm, to train as a bandit.*

The following morning they took me back to Harare Central. That's where I found Gabriel and other guys, fourteen of them. We were put into another truck and were told that we were going to court—again.

When we met we didn't talk much, because we were still heavily guarded by the police, so we just greeted each other. Again we appeared in court. They read the allegations against us. We were being accused of training in South Africa and being saboteurs, terrorists, bandits. Also, attempted murder. We had lawyers but we couldn't talk with them.

After court, we were sent back to Remand Prison. That's when I started talking to Gabriel. Gabriel told me that the other guys were saying that I'm a sell-out. But Gabriel knew me for a long time. We were working together for such a long time. Gabriel didn't say anything wrong about me.

I told Gabriel the truth, that no, it was only my survival tactic. I didn't sell out. I didn't sell anyone, I said. We can solve this issue. We can discuss it. The police forced me to implicate people.

In prison, we were living like brothers. And like with brothers, you can find some who believe you, who are comfortable with you, and others who are not comfortable, the ones who think you could sell them out. I didn't become angry. I just said, *No guys, listen, I went to court I explained exactly what happened. Because of what the police have done to me, what I said was null and void. I wrote under duress.*

Gabriel and I were inside that time for four months. We were finally granted bail. This was around the time SADC was putting pressure on Mugabe.[25] There were supposed to be talks between MDC, MDC-T,

---

[25] During the election period, the Southern African Development Community hosted a series of mediations between the Movement for Democratic Change and Zanu-PF. See the appendix on the 2008 elections.

MDC-M, and Zanu-PF.[26] So I think that is one of the things that influenced the court to grant us bail, the pressure from SADC countries. I myself was discharged from the terrorism charge. But I still, to this day, have the attempted murder charge for the bombing of the police station.

THE SCAR ON MY LEFT CHEEK

There was another conflict within MDC, a conflict over who was going to become the be MDC chairlady. One side wanted the wife of a big man in MDC. The other wanted to stay with the current chairlady.

Gabriel was lured by the big man to support his wife. For myself, I was totally against that because I was saying, *No, this thing is not a family issue. We mustn't put our relatives and friends in influential positions.* So on this, Gabriel was on one side, and I was on the other. We didn't always agree, like any family. But things began to turn violent.

I have the scar on my left cheek, see it? At an MDC rally before the March 2008 elections, someone beat me with an umbrella over this chairlady issue. Someone else hit me with a beer bottle. That day my face was covered in blood. I fought back. You know, you can see me right now, I might appear calm, but when I become angry you won't like me. I can become more violent than appears possible. If someone provokes me, I will defend myself.

So after the fight I thought, I need to address this issue. I went to Harvest House. Then I found the one who incited other youths to fight me at the rally. I said, *My friend you see this, your scar? You see what you did to me?* Before he answered I head-butted him and he fell right there in front of Harvest House. When he tried standing up, I gave him a kick.

From then on, I didn't go very much to Harvest House. I wanted to

---

[26] In 2005, the Movement for Democratic Change had split into two factions. During the period of the 2008 elections, MDC-T was lead by Morgan Tsvangirai and MDC-M was lead by Arthur Mutambara. Details of the split within the MDC can be found in the appendix section on the 2008 elections.

try to play it safe. I begin selling potatoes to make money. I would go out to the farms and buy potatoes and sell them in the city. I began telling people, *I'm no longer an MDC member*. I was doing this because I wanted to protect myself. I said, I'm now a member of Mavambo. Mavambo was a new political party which was formed by a former Zanu-PF Minister. So the word of me going to the new party spread very fast like a veld fire. But all along I have always been MDC. After the March 2008 elections, I came back to the party.

MARCH 2008 ELECTIONS

So the 2008 elections. We voted, but days went by and the government still wasn't releasing the results. You know, they held those results for almost thirty days. By that time Tendai Biti had already announced on South African television that MDC had won the election.

One day I was driving with Gabriel and we received a call. A top MDC official wanted us to mobilize people to boycott work in order to force the government to release the results.

On the day of the mass action, some people responded very well. Others were overzealous. They were burning some buses and cars and stoning the police. We wanted people to stay away from work for only that day. The next day they could go back to work. It was very successful. Within a few days, the government released the results.

Soon after the election, we received word that the police and CIO were looking for us again. They heard that Gabriel and myself were causing noises again. So we dropped out of sight again and went back to Marlborough, to that woman's place I mentioned. We couldn't go home anymore and endanger our families.

In Marlborough, they had a pub there where people used to come and have beers. While we were in hiding, Gabriel and I established our own small business, a small *braai*[27] stand. We bought chickens, roasted them,

---

[27] Barbeque.

and sold the meat to the people who came to drink beer. I remember the day the government finally released the results. Was it the 19th of April? I remember that day because we had bought two sun hats. Gabriel and I were wearing these hats like twins. We said to each other, *There's going to be more trouble.* We knew Morgan won that election outright.

A few nights later, after midnight, Gabriel and I were at our *braai* stand. We were talking with two ladies and laughing. Then another friend of ours, a guy named Wilson, started shouting, *Look, these guys are following me!* Then I saw a group of men, about twenty of them. Some of them had pistols; one of them had an AK-47. They dragged me to a Toyota Hillux, the latest model. They shoved me next to the driver. They ordered me to sit with my hands between my legs. They didn't handcuff me. They were pointing two guns on the back of my neck.

I heard Gabriel shouting. I heard him being thrown into the back of another car.

They drove like a movie. You know, the time I'm taking to talk is long compared to how quick they were. We headed north on Old Mazoe Road. We traveled at least a 140 kilometers away from Harare. Then we turned on a bumpy road and drove up up up. We reached a level point. They kicked me out of the car and blindfolded me with my shirt. There was tall grass and boulders. It was very dark. They pushed me to the ground and start beating me with a large stone. I heard Gabriel screaming now, screaming, *Maiwee! I'm dying!* Then one of them said, *Ah, if you are dying, how you can say you are dying?*[28]

I didn't cry, I just kept quiet. I pretended as if I had died or passed out. Another stone came and crushed my legs. I heard Gabriel screaming, *Froooooo!* and then silence. Then I heard another voice, the third guy screaming. I still didn't know who he was.

I kept quiet and didn't move. I thought I heard the men walking away. Now the third guy was shouting something. The men came back.

---

[28] As mentioned in the appendix section on the 2008 elections, violent and politically motivated abductions were not uncommon at this time.

The third guy went silent. I must have lifted my head. But they saw me and came back and said, *This one is still alive.* They came and crushed me again with another stone. I passed out.

Some minutes later, maybe ten or twelve minutes, I woke up. I could hear them opening doors and closing them, the engine of vehicles, then they went.

After some time I was able to stand up. I called, *Gabriel! Gabriel!*

Gabriel was a bit distant from me. He made some sound. Then he said, *Chari, I'm here my brother, these people have killed us. What about Chiedza, what is she going to do now? They've killed us.* He was talking about my daughter. Gabriel was also married and had a daughter called Tatenda, but he didn't mention his daughter, he mentioned my daughter.

I said, *Where are you?* He said, *I'm here, I can't move. I think my legs are broken,* and by that time I could hear the other guy saying, *I'm also here.* I said, *Gabriel, I'm going to get help.* I didn't know where to go and where I was going to get the power to raise myself. I looked down the mountain and saw a little bit of light. So I started moving down, slowly. If I wanted to look back up the mountain or back, I had to turn my whole body. I struggled down. At the bottom of that mountain, I reached a tar road. A signboard by the side of the road said Mutorashanga Golf Club.

So I went there and I saw a security guard. He was fast asleep. I woke him up and explained what happened to me. He quickly went to where there were other guards, three of them. They carried me to the police. There I reported what happened to me, and that I have left my friend and another man on the mountain. They took me across to the clinic that was just opposite the police station. The sister in charge came and helped me into a bed. I was telling them, *Wait, there are two people dying on the mountain. Please go and help them.* But it seemed the police didn't want to go.

The whole night I would wake up and ask the sister in charge, *Did you go and get them?* And they were saying, *No, we don't have an ambulance and the police don't have a vehicle. We will fetch them in the morning.*

Luckily around six a.m. there were some women looking for some firewood on that mountain. They came across the two guys. For some reason this time the police didn't waste time. At around seven a.m. we all were together in the clinic. Me and Gabriel and the other guy. I later got to know his name he was Bryan. They were both badly injured. Later that day the MDC office sent an ambulance for us.

At around five p.m. we were at Avenues Clinic and started receiving our treatments. That's when I was told that I had a broken right rib and Gabriel had a broken leg and one fractured leg. Bryan had a broken leg. Gabriel was transferred to Dandaro Hospital in Borrowdale. Myself and Bryan remained at Avenues Clinic.

GABRIEL, I'M GOING

You see, so many people have disappeared in Zimbabwe. We almost did but we were lucky. We were lucky more than once. We knew we couldn't keep running and that we had to leave for South Africa.

But as we were telling our families the news, Gabriel had different ideas. I can see now that Gabriel developed a negative attitude about leaving the country. He just didn't want to go. He was saying, *You know Sankoh, what if MDC wins the elections? What if these old men forget about us? So let's stay. We have got your car. We can keep on sneaking and using your car to hide ourselves.*

And then I said to him, *Ah, no Gabriel, I'm going. It isn't possible to live here right now.* I called him by his totem[29] then. His totem was Samaita Dube. I said, *No Samaita, tomorrow, I am going*, and he said, *It's fine, Mhukahuru, you go ahead and find a place for us. I will follow you in a few days to come.* Mhukahuru is my totem.

I STOPPED LAUGHING

When I came here to South Africa I had nothing. I only had a small bag

---

[29] Totems are sets of symbols and words from the natural world used for identification among Shona groups. *Samaita* translates to "zebra." *Mhukahuru* to "elephant."

with one pair of trousers and a shirt and other clothes that I was wearing and I didn't have enough time to prepare myself or to carry any paper. I went to Roodepoort in Harare and I took the bus. I paid for a ticket to Beitbridge. For security reasons, I didn't say I was going to South Africa. I simply said, *I'm going to Beitbridge.* We arrived there around eleven p.m. I talked to the bus conductor. I said, *You know what, my friend? I'm not feeling well, I want to go to South Africa, but I don't have a passport.*

Then he said, *Go to the toilet and come back and sit in the bus.* I did what he said. When I came back from the toilet, the conductor came back and gave me a passport. He said, *When they ask for passports, just hold it out. Don't open it. That's how I came here to Johannesburg, South Africa, on the bus with someone else's passport.*

Friday, the 9th of May, that's when I phoned my wife back home, telling her that I arrived safely in South Africa.

I started getting treatment at the Southern Africa Center for Torture Survivors. They helped me with my medications. They also gave me R1,000 for rent.

One day the friend I was staying with in Johannesburg received a message on his phone. The message said, *We are very sorry, brother, your friend Sankoh Chari has died.* He received the message from Zimbabwe from his sister. So I was seated together with him and he said, *Chari, look at this message.* And I read it and we started laughing. I stopped laughing. I phoned my wife. My wife's phone was not going through. I phoned another friend, an MDC colleague, and she was crying and she was only saying *Gabriel, Gabriel, Gabriel! Gabriel was found dead.*

Then I phoned back to my wife again. That's when I heard my brother Simon was also missing, that they could not find him.

A few days later, the day that Gabriel was buried, that's when I heard that my brother's body was found in the Goromonzi area. It was without a tongue and ears, and he was tied with a barbed wire.

Gabriel and my brother were driving in my car. They were on their way to Murehwa to see Gabriel's mother. Two twin cabs blocked them and shot into the car.

You know, it didn't surprise me, no. Because I had a feeling that something might happen. But I felt very guilty that these people had killed my brother for the wrong reasons. They wanted me. They thought, Gabriel and Chari are always together. Simon was short like me, but he was light in complexion.

UNFINISHED WORK

Now I just keep quiet. I'm not a part of things anymore.

Someone killed Gabriel and my own brother. That's why, let me repeat it, I often just feel like a dead person. From the day when I was put in the coffin. And things are worse now. My brother died. My best friend died. Right now I can't even help my own child, or my brother's children. Even Gabriel's child I can't help.

I'm far away from home, isolated. I'm contributing nothing to the Zimbabwean people. If only I could be re-integrated again and go back and fight for the cause, because it's unfinished work. If you go to the bible, there's a guy who dug a well. He started taking out water and drinking the water, and other people came and said, *This is our well*, and the guy said, *Okay, I'm leaving*. He went on to dig another well and started drinking water again. I still hope that soon I'm going to find another way. I'm going to try and dig another well to drink water. But right now I'm just surviving. The police officers in Zimbabwe were saying, *Chari has died, Chari has died*. It's only now that they know that Sankoh Chari is still alive.

APPENDICES

I. GLOSSARY

Tendai Biti—Finance Minister of Zimbabwe since 2009, during the rehabilitation from hyperinflation and economic disaster; **Movement for Democratic Change** member of parliament since 2000.

Wellington Chibebe—leader of the Zimbabwean Congress of Trade Unions (ZCTU) since 2001.

Biggie Chitoro—a leader of war veterans' groups during the time of the land invasions.

Philip Chiyangwa—wealthy businessman and participant in the 1990s "indigenization" program; relative of **Robert Mugabe** and former **Zanu-PF** politician.

Comrade Fatso (Samm Farai Monro)—popular Zimbabwean *toyi toyi* poet and member of the protest band Comrade Fatso and Chabvondoka, whose 2008 album *House of Hunger* was banned in the country.

Dumiso Dabengwa—former **ZIPRA** war leader, imprisoned during **Gukurahundi**, later **Zanu-PF** Home Affairs Minister; left Zanu-PF in 2008 to revive a separate **Zapu** party.

Ken Flower—first head of Rhodesia's **Central Intelligence Organization**; selected by **Robert Mugabe** to remain head of Zimbabwe's CIO during the first administration after Independence.

Geoff Foster—pediatrician and founder in 1987 of the Family AIDS Caring Trust, one of Zimbabwe's first AIDS organizations.

Border Gezi—Former **Zanu-PF** Minister for Gender, Youth and Employment from 2000, responsible for recruiting and training youth militias, the so-called **Green Bombers**; died in a car accident in 2001.

Gideon Gono—head of the Reserve Bank of Zimbabwe since 2003 and through the period of hyperinflation and economic strife; driver of Zimbabwe's economic policy.

Hopewell Gumbo—Zimbabwean activist and president of the National Students Union during the Economic Structural Adjustment Program (ESAP).

Rashiwe Guzha—a secretary in the **Central Intelligence Organization** (CIO) whose 1990 disappearance has never been explained; has become a symbol of the government's use of state intelligence forces to quell dissent; the CIO has been implicated in her abduction.

Munyaradzi Gwisai—former **Movement for Democratic Change** MP; radical voice within the MDC who attempted the move the party toward socialist policies and was expelled in 2002.

Sekai Holland—pre-Independence **Zanu** representative in Australia; founding member of the **Movement for Democratic Change**, hospitalized after being beaten in 2007; one of three ministers responsible for reconciliation and national healing in the post-2009 "unity" government.

Chenjarai Hunzvi—leader of the war veterans' farm invasions (his biography is detailed in the appendices section on war veterans and land invasions).

Learnmore Jongwe—first spokesman for the **Movement for Democratic Change**; in 2002, he was arrested and admitted to murdering his wife.

Talent Mabika—MDC activist burned to death along with **Morgan Tsvangirai's** campaign manager, **Tichaona Chiminya**, when their vehicle was stopped at gunpoint by **CIO** and **Zanu-PF** agents preceding the 2000 elections.

Lovemore Madhuku—chairman and founding member of the National Constitutional Assembly (NCA).

Betty Makoni—advocate against sexual abuse and founding director of the Girl Child Network (GCN) in 1998.

Simba Makoni—senior **Zanu-PF** official and former Finance Minister; broke with the party to challenge **Robert Mugabe** as an independent candidate for president in 2008.

Lovemore Matombo—president of the **Zimbabwe Congress of Trade Unions (ZCTU)**.

Emmerson Mnangagwa—influential former head of the **CIO** and member of the securocrat **Joint Operations Command (JOC)**.

Jason Moyo—**Zapu** leader credited with forming **ZIPRA**, assassinated in 1977; a schoolmate of John's (see John's narrative).

Jonathan Moyo—critic of **Zanu-PF** as a professor of political science during the 1980s and '90s; Zanu-PF Minister of Information from 2000 to 2005; later an independent candidate in the 2005 parliamentary elections.

Robert Mugabe—President of Zimbabwe; elected as prime minister in the 1980 elections after becoming a liberation hero in Zimbabwe's successful independence war; his leadership has been marked by accusation of large-scale human rights violations.

Arthur Mutambara—leader of a break-away faction of the **Movement for Democratic Change**; Deputy Prime Minister of Zimbabwe under the 2009 power-sharing government; former University of Zimbabwe student union president and Rhodes scholar.

Bishop Abel Muzorewa—United Methodist Church bishop; prime minister of short-lived "Zimbabwe-Rhodesia" (1979); former leader of the United African National Congress liberation movement.

Archbishop Pius Ncube—human rights advocate; critic of **Robert Mugabe**; former Catholic Archbishop of Bulawayo.

Welshman Ncube—lawyer and politician; broke away from the **Movement for Democratic Change** in 2005 to found MDC-M, which would be led by Arthur Mutambara the following year; MDC-M minister.

Joshua Nkomo—founder and early leader of **Zapu**; challenged **Robert Mugabe** in the 1980 presidential elections; died in 1999.

Cecil Rhodes—led British colonization of Northern and Southern Rhodesia (today's Zambia and Zimbabwe) under an 1889 charter to the British South African Company; founder of De Beers diamond company (British South African Company).

Perence Shiri—Air Vice Marshal, member of the **Joint Operations Command**, commander of the **Fifth Brigade** during **Gukurahundi**; target of a failed assassination attempt in 2008.

Job Sikhala—founding member of the **Movement for Democratic Change**; joined MDC-M when the party split in 2005; attempted to found his own MDC faction in 2010.

Ian Smith—prime minister of Southern Rhodesia and then Rhodesia from 1964 to 1980, proclaimed Unilateral Declaration of Independence from Britain in 1965.

Lord Arthur Christopher Soames—The British governor charged with supervising Zimbabwe's 1980 election.

Edgar Tekere—**Zanla** commander who helped **Robert Mugabe** take control of **Zanu-PF**; expelled from Zanu-PF in 1988 after criticizing corruption and opposing Mugabe's plans to make Zimbabwe a one-party state; went on to found short-lived Zimbabwe Unity Movement (ZUM).

Gift Tandare—**Movement for Democratic Change** activist killed by police during 2007 political demonstrations; his death became a driving force for opposition politics.

Josiah Tongogara—**Zanla** leader during the liberation war; died in a car accident under suspicious circumstances in 1979 on the eve of Independence.

Morgan Tsvangirai—**Movement for Democratic Change** leader and prime minister of Zimbabwe from 2009; worked as a nickel miner and union leader after dropping out of high school, eventually led the **ZCTU** and became the first chairman of the **MDC**.

Bishop Paul Verryn—longtime minister of Johannesburg's Central Methodist Church, a haven for many Zimbabwean migrants; in 2010, he was suspended from the church despite widespread support.

Organizations and Events

Central Intelligence Organization (CIO)—the most powerful arm of Zimbabwe's security services; formed by the Rhodesian government in the late 1960s and continued by **Robert Mugabe** after Independence.

The *Daily News*—influential independent (non-government) daily Zimbabwe newspaper banned in 2003; the bombing of their printing plant in 2001 attracted international media attention.

The **Fifth Brigade**—a group of largely Shona government soldiers sent to Matabeleland to quell dissent, who had been trained by the North Korean military; their campaign became known as **Gukurahundi** and is estimated to have caused 20,000 civilian deaths.

The "**Green Bombers**"—a **Zanu-PF** youth militia notorious for anti-opposition violence especially during elections, named for the color of their military-style fatigues; the Zanu-PF government has claimed that its National Youth Service Program, in which the **Green Bombers** train, aims to promote good citizenship and community service.

Gukurahundi—an armed campaign by the national army, in particular the dreaded **Fifth Brigade**, against demobilized fighters from the predominantly Ndebele-speaking armed wing of **Zapu**, the political party led by Joshua Nkomo—and then, more widely, against the people of the two Matabeleland Provinces (North and South) and the Midlands. The actual number of people who died is contested, though many experts place their estimates at 20,000, with more raped, maimed, or injured. The violence ended after **Zanu** and Zapu reached a unity agreement on December 22, 1987, and merged the two parties to form one party known as **Zanu-PF**. (The two parties had contested the first democratic elections in 1980 together, as the Patriotic Front.)

Joint Operations Command (JOC)—A high-level council of military, security, and intelligence leaders, which **Robert Mugabe** reportedly used to enforce the law to the political advantage of **Zanu-PF**. This group was formally disbanded and replaced by the unity government's National Security Council, but the international press and investigations by international organizations chronicled frequent clandestine meetings even after 2008. (For more details, see the appendix section on the 2008 elections.)

Movement for Democratic Change (MDC)—Zimbabwe's first national oppositional political party; founded in September 1999 out of a coalition of unions, student groups, and civil society organizations, including the **National Constitutional Assembly** (see timeline); split in 2005 into factions led by **Morgan Tsvangirai** (MDC-T) and Arthur Mutambara (MDC-M).

National Constitutional Assembly (NCA)—A coalition of civil society groups formed in 1997 to advocate for a new constitution.

Police Internal Security Intelligence (PISI)—a division within the Ministry of Home Affairs, resembling the **Central Intelligence Organization**; it is often difficult for experts to determine which organization is responsible for abductions and detentions.

Women of Zimbabwe Arise (WOZA)—founded in 2003 as a women's civic movement to empower and lobby for female leadership and gender freedoms; in 2010, claims 75,000 female and male members.

Zimbabwe African National Union (Zanu/Zanla)—nationalist/guerilla liberation organization and political party formed by splitting from **Zapu**, citing a desire for immediate armed confrontation over international intervention; led by **Robert Mugabe**, Herbert Chitepo, and Ndabaningi Sithole; the Zimbabwe African National Liberation Army (Zanla) is its military wing.

Zimbabwe African National Union, Patriotic Front (Zanu-PF)—the ruling and dominant party for most of independent Zimbabwe's history, formed by the alliance of **Zanu** and **Zapu** in 1987; led by **Robert Mugabe**.

Zimbabwe African People's Union (Zapu/ZIPRA)—nationalist/guerilla liberation organization and political party founded by **Joshua Nkomo** in 1961; the Zimbabwe People's Revolutionary Army (ZIPRA) is its military wing.

Zimbabwe Congress of Trade Unions (ZCTU)—an activist umbrella organization for unions; responsible for organizing strikes and protests led by **Morgan Tsvangirai** from 1989 to 1999.

Zimbabwe National Army (ZNA)—created at independence from the Rhodesian Army, **Zanla**, and **ZIPRA**.

II. TIMELINE

1000 (approximate)—Centralized states begin to emerge among the Shona people, the largest group of inhabitants between the Zambezi and Limpopo Rivers, who build a city called Zimbabwe or Great Zimbabwe.

1300 (approximate)—Competition begins between Shona states looking to secure trade with Arab and, eventually, Portuguese merchants.

1822—Mzilikazi, a Southern African king, begins the northward journey that will end with him and his followers settling in what he named kwaBulawayo; along the way, his growing group becomes known by the name Matabele, and comes to incorporate many of the Ndebele people.

1889—Queen Victoria of England grants Cecil Rhodes's British South Africa Company a royal charter to colonize the land that becomes Southern Rhodesia (and is now known as Zimbabwe).

1896–1897—Ndebele and Shona stage a revolt—now known as the "first *chimurenga*"— against British occupying forces.

1923—Southern Rhodesia, its charter expired and its bid for incorporation into South Africa voted down by referendum, establishes itself as a self-governing colony with its own legislative assembly.

1953—Southern Rhodesia forms the Central African Federation with Northern Rhodesia (today known as Zambia) and Nyasaland (today known as Malawi).

1961—Robert Mugabe and Joshua Nkomo found the Zimbabwe African People's Union (Zapu) less than a week after Nkomo's nationalist National Democratic Party (NDP) is banned among civil unrest; Zapu is banned the following year.

1963—British government breaks up the Central African Federation, granting independence to Northern Rhodesia and Nyasaland; Southern Rhodesia remains a British colony.

—Ndabiningi Sithole founds the Zimbabwe African National Union (Zanu), breaking away from Zapu with the support of Herbert Chitepo, Enos Nkala, Robert Mugabe, and others; Zanu denounces Joshua Nkomo and promises a confrontational stance.

1964—Zanu and Zapu are both banned, and their leadership is detained; the parties continue to exist in exile.

1965—Ian Smith makes a Unilateral Declaration of Independence from the British government, renames the country Rhodesia.

1972—Guerrilla violence and politics intensify in response to the arrival in Zimbabwe of the Pearce Commission, an attempt to reallow political activity toward the discussion of Rhodesian/British constitutional agreements; many experts mark this date as the start of liberation war in full.

1976—Zanu and Zapu form a military alliance, called the Patriotic Front (PF).

1978—Under pressure from international economic sanctions and South African political pressure, Ian Smith reaches an "internal settlement" with Bishop Abel Muzorewa; the war continues as nationalists reject Muzorewa and Smith's "Zimbabwe-Rhodesia."

1979—Britain convenes a peace conference in London, where the Lancaster House Agreement ending the war is signed by representatives of the British Government, the Patriotic Front, Zapu, Zanu, and Zimbabwe-Rhodesia; the agreement promises whites twenty of the one hundred seats in the newly independent nation's Parliament.

1980—More political realignment for the Independence elections; Zanu-PF's Robert Mugabe becomes prime minister and his party gains a parliamentary majority, while Joshua Nkomo and PF-Zapu maintain a regional stronghold in Matabeleland.

1982—Mugabe ejects Nkomo from his cabinet.

1982–87—During the largely secret Gukurahundi campaign, Mugabe sends the Fifth Brigade to overpower dissent in the mostly Ndebele Matabeleland, resulting in an estimated twenty thousand civilian deaths; this would not be widely reported until 1997.

—Toward the end of 1987, the Lancaster House Accords expire and the constitution is amended to discontinue reserved parliamentary seats for whites.

—In December 1987, Gukurahundi ends when Zanu-PF and PF-Zapu sign the Unity Accord, PF-Zapu folds into the reshaped Zanu-PF; the Accord grants amnesty not only to political dissidents but to various criminals if they surrender in the following six months.

1990—Zimbabwe's Economic Structural Adjustment Program (ESAP) is launched (details in the appendix on Zimbabwe's economic decline).

1997—National Constitutional Assembly (NCA), a collection of civic society groups such as unions and student groups, is founded.

—Government misuse of war veterans' funds becomes a public scandal; Mugabe responds with unbudgeted payout (see appendix section on war veterans).

—ESAP ends in massive capital flight; Zimbabwean currency loses 74 percent of its value in a single day.

—Morgan Tsvangirai's Zimbabwe Congress of Trade Unions (ZCTU) leads a widely successful strike, Zimbabwe's first general strike in over fifty years.

1998—Economic problems continue, riots and strikes spread across the country.

—Mugabe sends the military to assist the Congolese government in a civil war in the Democratic Republic of Congo.

1999—Led by Morgan Tsvangirai, the Movement for Democratic Change (MDC) forms.

—Joshua Nkomo dies.

2000—Farm invasions begin (see appendix section on land invasions).

—The MDC secures its first major victory, leading a successful opposition to a constitutional referendum proposed by Mugabe.

2001—Finance Minister Simba Makoni announces that foreign reserves have run out, publicly acknowledging the economic crisis.

2002—Parliament passes the Public Order and Security Act (POSA) and the Access to Information and Protection of Privacy Act (AIPPA), limiting media freedom and freedom of expression.

—Mugabe reelected; presidential elections become the subject of increased international criticism, leading to Zimbabwe's suspension from the Commonwealth of Nations (formerly known as the British Commonwealth).

2003—Large general strike occurs; anti-opposition violence and arrests follow.

2005—Tens of thousands of urban shanties and street stalls destroyed in Operation Murambatsvina; vendors beaten and arrested; the UN estimates 700,000 people are newly homeless.

—MDC splits into two factions—MDC-T, led by Morgan Tsvangirai, and MDC-M, led by Arthur Mutambara.

2007—Morgan Tsvangirai hospitalized after arrest and beating; images of his injuries add momentum to his 2008 presidential campaign (see the appendix section on the 2008 elections).

2008—Zimbabwe holds countrywide elections for president, parliament, and local offices; after much turmoil, Mugabe and Tsvangirai sign a power-sharing agreement (detailed in the appendix section on the 2008 elections).

—Xenophobic violence erupts in South Africa (detailed in appendix section on Zimbabweans in South Africa).

2009—Government allows official use of foreign currencies to combat hyperinflation (see the appendix section on Zimbabwe's economic decline).

—Tsvangirai is sworn in as prime minister.

—Susan Tsvangirai, Morgan's wife, dies in a car crash amid wide suspicion of foul play.

2010—New law requires foreign-owned business to sell majority stake to locals.

—Official diamond sales resume and black market sales continue amid controversy and suspicion of large-scale human rights abuses in the newly discovered Marange diamond fields; a Mugabe confidant calls the discovery "Zanu-PF's salvation."

III. ZIMBABWEANS IN SOUTH AFRICA

Migration out of Zimbabwe can be a measure of the country's internal problems, and since 2000 it has reached unprecedented numbers. Zimbabwean citizens have been displaced from their homes by two large forces. The first, politically motivated evictions by Zanu-PF and its allies, targets farms, rural homes, urban housing, factories, offices, schools, and churches. During the same period, deep economic troubles throughout the country forced some Zimbabweans to move in search of food, money, work, or safety. Middle-class professionals and others who can afford airfare left for industrialized countries, largely the United Kingdom, but those who couldn't are often unable to find a sustainable livelihood even if they relocate domestically. The Internal Displacement Monitoring Center, an international body that works with the UN, noted in 2008 that in terms of humanitarian need, "it is sometimes difficult to distinguish between IDPs [internally displaced persons] and the general population in Zimbabwe." Many Zimbabweans look for asylum across the Limpopo River in South Africa—the first large group to seek political and economic haven in the country that, not too long ago, had been well known for producing its own asylum seekers.

Since most of these border crossings are undocumented, determining the total number of migrants is imprecise, and requires indirect calculations. Human Rights Watch acknowledged a general understanding that Zimbabwe-to-South-Africa emigration increased during 2005, the year of Operation Murambatsvina, and continued to grow large enough that just the number of deportations from South Africa *back into Zimbabwe* exceeded eighty thousand in 2006 and doubled in 2007. One 2008 estimate counted 3 million Zimbabwean citizens living in South Africa—nearly a quarter of Zimbabwe's population, and a scale of emigration unprecedented outside of war zones.

Some Zimbabweans travel to South Africa legally as students, skilled laborers, academics, and agricultural or mine workers, but many arrive undocumented for seasonal farm work or to stay and seek asylum. Crossing the Limpopo River is possible over dry patches for most of the year, but during the rainy season—especially around Christmas, when traffic is heavy with Zimbabweans returning home to visit family and then back to jobs in South Africa—a number of migrants drown, leaving human remains on its banks. Additionally, border crossers risk robbery, assault, rape, and occasionally murder by *magumaguma* (loosely translated: people who seek to make a living through dubious means), who were unknown at the border in 2001, but reported on the Zimbabwean side by 2004 and on both sides by 2008. In recent years, the transient population of the South African border town of Musina has swelled with Zimbabweans waiting to move further south while taking exploitative jobs scouring for scrap metal in shut-down copper mines or cutting wood in exchange for food. One exchange rate had two or three wheelbarrows of cut wood for a single plate of *sadza*.

Zimbabwean migrants to South Africa can't be reduced to only one group. The Northern Limpopo region, just beyond the river from Zimbabwe, contains commercial farms that have employed a migratory Zimbabwean population for decades, but since

2000 the number, geographic origins within Zimbabwe, and social circumstances of Zimbabwean farm workers there have changed. Some workers seek farm labor because of friends or relatives already working on farms, others are out of money, starving, or had their belongings stolen on their trip across the border and find that the farms present the first jobs in the border zone; some are trafficked against their will. All are attracted by the purchasing power of South African currency in Zimbabwe. Most are seasonal pickers or packshed workers who work the picking season, April to September, then return to Zimbabwe or move to another part of South Africa.

Until the late 1990s, South African state officials made an exception for this area, allowing farm owners to hire Zimbabwean workers without requiring state permits. This practice ended as conditions in Zimbabwe began to generate more migrants and South Africa deregulated and stopped subsidies to its commercial farms, making the accessible and disposable labor force attractive to farm owners facing heightened competition. A 2007 estimate had 70-85 percent of the workers on these farms originating from Zimbabwe, and increased deportation raids have targeted even those farm workers with valid identification. As the world economy soured toward the end of the decade, Zimbabweans who worked the farms for less than the South African minimum wage bore the resentment of South African nationals worried that the farm workers' actions had eliminated full-wage jobs rightfully belonging to nationals.

For the more permanent emigrants, the most pressing need is finding accommodation. Some can settle with relatives or friends, but many arrive without arrangements: Johannesburg's Central Methodist Church is able to crowd in over one thousand people, who sleep on every available surface. Most Zimbabweans in South Africa find support in communities of their countrymen, living in small shacks or rooms and taking turns sleeping in four-hour shifts. Deportation raids, however, are a constant problem. After police detained 350 people from a raid in Johannesburg in early 2008, the judge presiding over the South African court granting their release described the treatment of the detainees as being worse than during the days of apartheid. In March 2009, South African authorities expelled thousands of Zimbabweans from the Musina showground field where tens of thousands had applied for asylum since mid-2008. When many of the expelled arrived in Johannesburg, businesses in the Central Business District sued the city and its Central Methodist Church, complaining that the crowded and unhygienic environment was hurting business, and erected a metal gate preventing migrants from sleeping on church grounds.

The provision in the South African Constitution providing the right to health for "everyone" in the country has been tested in recent years, and the country's asylum system is stretched thin; though the Department of Health has reaffirmed the right of asylum seekers to the same public healthcare available to South African citizens, documented and undocumented migrants have been frequently denied access. Filling the gaps often falls to international aid: since December 2007, Doctors Without Borders has expanded its South African presence to provide medical care to Zimbabweans in Musina and central Johannesburg, and the Catholic Church in Musina's Nancefield township has provided monthly food relief since early 2008. The migrant population has suffered recent outbreaks of tuberculosis and cholera, in addition to sharing the regional problem of HIV, and recent migrants—fleeing unofficial conscription into Zanu-PF or political violence—come to South Africa with anxiety and, in the description of a Methodist bishop in Johannesburg who tries to find them places to stay, "derangement."

The South African government, which has never before had to deal with such heavy immigration, characterized undocumented migrant Zimbabweans until 2009 strictly as voluntary "economic migrants," not "refugees"—without this latter term's claim to protection and assistance that South African and international law gives to those seeking asylum and fleeing a war or humanitarian crisis. As recently as 2006, even those Zimbabweans with asylum-seeker permits reported being told, when stopped by police, to pay a bribe so that their papers would not be destroyed. Some of the Zimbabweans who come to South Africa under a legitimate work permit avoid the government's crossing point, fearing excessive lineups and corrupt officials, and then face the same dangers that an official permit is supposed to help them avoid. South Africa's Department of Home Affairs largely keeps to a narrow interpretation of its refugee laws, one that limits asylum to people fleeing individual persecution, not groups or even individuals in flight from public events, and researchers who have observed the processing of asylum requests report numerous irregularities and requests made of asylum seekers that violate national and international law. Through 2007, South Africa had recognized only 2 percent of Zimbabwean asylum claims, and there are still no legal instruments to recognize the many Zimbabweans who qualify for refugee status but choose not to apply for asylum due to a need to cross the border repeatedly and support family members at home. Health and aid organizations have attempted to step in: since 2008, offices for UNHCR Refugee Reception and a Labor Migration Center run by the International Organization for Migration have joined Lawyers for Human Rights in the border zone.

The government's focus on detainment and deportation has been so great that the United Nations High Commission for Refugees found that over a forty-day period during the Zimbabwean election violence in the summer of 2008, a period when the UNHCR had requested a deportation freeze, South Africa deported 17,000 Zimbabweans and granted asylum to only 500 of the 35,000 who formally applied. Migrants who find themselves deported back to Zimbabwe are released upon repatriation, as authorities there lack the capacity to hold deportees. Once released, many create what migration scholars call the "revolving door," as they make their way back toward the border. Some migrants have been observed returning on foot within an hour of being dismissed, and others have been able to minimize their time away from a job in Johannesburg by phoning their taxi driver from detainment in South Africa and relaying the date on which they will be sent back to Zimbabwean authorities at the border.

Zimbabweans in South Africa also have to face regular xenophobia, which can sometimes turn violent. Xenophobic incidents have occurred sporadically in South Africa in the post-apartheid period, but the most notable outbreak occurred in May 2008. Looting and destruction of foreign-owned homes, property, and businesses spread across South Africa and resulted in the deaths of more than sixty migrants—though not all from Zimbabwe—injuries to more than 600, and the displacement of between 40,000 and 80,000 people within South Africa. South African authorities subsequently arrested 1,384 suspects.

Residents of many areas affected by the May 2008 violence often blamed the attacks on the failure of migration control, and calls to tighten the South African side of the South Africa/Zimbabwe border have been repeated since. Today, one kilometer from the bank of the Limpopo River sits a three-line barbed-wire fence, which can be charged with electricity. The border is patrolled by police, South African military and governmental agencies, and at least one private security agency. Despite this, a human smuggling industry operates daily, and many African migrants heading to South Africa illegally from countries other than Zimbabwe choose to cross at this border.

In April 2009, under pressure from NGOs and health organizations, outgoing Home Affairs Minister Nosiviwe Mapisa-Nqakula announced a moratorium on deportations and a special dispensation permit allowing migrants without documentation to stay for six months. The next month, her department announced a ninety-day entrance visa waiver—but only for Zimbabweans who have passports—eligibility for a twelve-month special dispensation permit, and a moratorium on deportations. The special arrangement ends in December 2010.

IV. HIV/AIDS

Although HIV/AIDS is a medical condition, its impact—particularly in Zimbabwe—arises as strongly from politics and economics as it does from biology. The relocations of Operation Murambatsvina caused many Zimbabweans to lose home-based care or consistent access to their daily antiretroviral (ARV) therapy. In places where patients are able to access their ARV drugs, many have stopped in the midst of food shortages, claiming that the drugs are too painful to take on an empty stomach—and although interviews by humanitarian groups have found that many of the patients affected by such events were eventually able to resume treatment, even short-term disruptions of antiretroviral therapy have been shown to contribute to developing a resistance to ARV medication. Researchers at the University of Zimbabwe, concerned that HIV/AIDS had cut into the country's workforce and diverted national investment, found it responsible for weakening national economic growth by 13.3 percent in the decade from 1994 to 2003, and international reaction to the political violence and human rights record of the Mugabe government resulted in withdrawn aid from foreign governments and humanitarian organizations. The medical journal *The Lancet* reported that thousands of medical professionals have left their jobs or the country, looking for other work in the face of national inflation that had reduced the salary of a government doctor to less than US$1 a month by the end of 2008. Douglas Gwatidzo, chairman of the Zimbabwe Doctors for Human rights, told the journal that this left only one doctor for every 12,000 people.

Further, government policies that restrict or eliminate informal trading and attacks on the informal economy, which employed an estimated three times as many Zimbabweans as the formal economy before Operation Murambatsvina, have cut into the ability of many people living with HIV/AIDS to earn a livelihood, and have increased incidents of high-risk "transactional sex." Though the government of Zimbabwe has created a number of free medical care programs, they are irregularly funded, and often require extensive documentation for enrollment—pay slips and income tax returns that may be difficult to obtain for Zimbabweans who work in the informal economy, or for wives and husbands who don't live together. Humanitarian-aid workers have documented what they call an "arbitrary" application of the fee exemptions created to bring these programs within reach for those who could not otherwise afford them. HIV/AIDS organizations and the U.S. Department of State have found irregularities in the spending of aid funding, and journalists reported that some HIV medication intended for the public was being sent instead to HIV-positive Zanu-PF officials. Workers distributing condoms during election periods in Harare have reported harassment and attacks by police, Zanu-PF officials, and youth militia, who accused them of working for the political opposition.

Once discovered in Zimbabwe, HIV/AIDS spread quickly, but now seems to have leveled off and even decreased, thanks to large decreases in mother-to-child transmission and changes in behavior after the introduction of education and awareness programs. By 1990, five years after the nation's first case had been reported, antenatal clinics estimated HIV prevalence in 10 percent of the population. By 2003, when Zimbabwe's government made its first official assessment, almost one in four Zimbabweans' was found to be infected, and life expectancy for all Zimbabweans—infected or not—had fallen by fifteen years. The following year, 75 percent of hospital bed occupancy was HIV-related. In 2009, despite a nationwide drop to as low as 13.7 percent (which is still high by international standards), almost 230,000 people in urgent need of antiretroviral therapy (including over 20,000 children) do not receive it.

In these conditions, a large portion of HIV/AIDS treatment has fallen to humanitarian aid groups. In Bulawayo, the 3,000 children registered in Doctors Without Borders' (MSF) program make up the highest concentration of HIV-positive children in any of the organization's programs worldwide. At the end of 2007, nearly one-tenth of all Zimbabweans receiving antiretroviral treatment did so through MSF.

But a powerful stigma against those with HIV/AIDS still exists. In 2008, MSF Pediatrics Counselor Christopher Dube reported that many HIV-positive parents keep their status secret, and if they learn that their children have been born with the disease, may try to hide that fact from them. Children who learn of the disease by overhearing whispers understand it as something to be ashamed of, and in places where there is little available treatment, testing can seem pointless. "Why have you tested me?" one patient whose home was demolished in Operation Murambatsvina and could not afford medication asked her doctor, as reported to the BBC. "You have just put me on a death sentence because I'm scared now because I know I am HIV positive. If you test me, it was to give me tablets."

V. POLITICAL VIOLENCE, THE WAR VETERANS, AND LAND INVASIONS

The farm invasions of the early 2000s produced, in the description of Oxford's Jocelyn Alexander, "a strange spectacle: a government effectively unraveling its own state with great vigor, and operating outside it through often fairly autonomous forces at district and provincial levels, led by veterans and Zanu-PF." The war-veteran-led occupations and invasions of Zimbabwe's commercial farms marked perhaps the largest political realignment since the nation had thrown off British colonialism two decades earlier. While Zanu-PF looked to buttress its waning power with support from an increasingly powerful group of liberation-war veterans, democratic opposition from a constellation of loosely related farmers, students, unionists, and other Zimbabweans in different corners of the country found common cause in the Movement for Democratic Change (MDC). The war veterans, in what many understood as an act of retribution against initial MDC success and a deterrent against future opposition, began leading takeovers of the nation's largely white-owned commercial farms. The invasions operated with the support of Mugabe's Zanu-PF, becoming most intense during election time. Though agriculture was the sector most directly affected by the newfound influence of the war veterans, veteran- and party-led changes restructured Zimbabwe's army, police, court systems, and economy. Most significantly, these actions demonstrated a takeover of local decision-making bodies in the interest of the central government, and how small the difference had become between party and state.

The Independence war had been won by two Zimbabwean guerrilla armies, which sometimes continued to spar with one another, and did not unite until the formation of the Zimbabwean National Liberation War Veterans Association in 1989. "Ex-combatants" became "war veterans," and through the association they spent much of the next decade lobbying for compensation for their services and sacrifices during the war.

Of the 60,000 or so men and women who had been members of the two armies in 1980, only 20,000 became part of the national post-Independence military. Many of the rest had lived in poverty since the end of the war, unable to find jobs and lacking education in part because they had spent their school years training and in combat. They watched as payouts from the government's official war victims' disability fund found their way into the hands of senior government ministers and Mercedes-driving party officials— Robert Mugabe's brother, in one example, received $70,000 after being assessed with ulcers and a scar on his knee.

In the 1990s, a powerful assessor for the fund, Chenjerai "Hitler" Hunzvi, began organizing veteran demonstrations for pensions and other benefits on Harare's streets while simultaneously directing veterans' compensation to the political elite. War veterans openly heckled Mugabe while he delivered a Heroes' Day speech, assaulted Zanu-PF headquarters, and threatened senior party officials until some literally ran for safety. Hunzvi and his demonstrators, many of whom were plainly too young to have served in the liberation war, caused public problems for Mugabe and for a government that had already begun to struggle. When the misuse of veterans' funds became a public scandal in 1997, Mugabe deflected political pressure with a one-time payment for veterans followed by monthly checks, free medical care and education, and land. The decision was made in haste; none of these had been budgeted for.

The actions of veterans in the War Veterans Association quickly became less about proper compensation for work done in the past than about the politics of the present. Hunzvi, the most visible of all war veterans demonstrating against the government, had himself not served in combat. For much of the war, he lived in Poland, where he trained as a doctor and married. His wife, who eventually left him, wrote a memoir entitled *White Slave* and remembered Hunzvi as an "unfaithful, vain sadist" who beat her. Yet in Zimbabwe, Hunzvi moved the veterans to the center of Zimbabwean politics, presenting a potentially powerful constituency as the Mugabe government attempted to recover from declining aid and a shrinking national economy that had reduced the party's political base, as well as an air of threat if the veterans' demands were not met.

Zimbabwean society began to split around the issue of war veterans. Some authentic veterans refused the payouts, and were unwilling to accept the implication of support for Zanu-PF that payouts presented. Trade unionists attacked the veterans' newfound centrality, arguing that all Zimbabweans had paid a high price during the war, and people who had been detained by nationalists or supported guerillas on the battlefield—such as the communal farmers who fed them and suffered attacks by the Rhodesian military—threatened party leaders with knowledge of misuses of war violence. Many veterans who took payouts became economically and socially isolated from their civilian neighbors, and found refreshed bonds with old comrades, especially as veterans' associations required former guerillas to tell stories of their training, fighting areas, and battles, as well as to recall their war names (such as, for Hunzvi, "Hitler") before receiving payment. They formed local associations, traveled to meetings throughout the country, and interacted with their old commanders and the veterans' associations' new leadership, many of whom owed their authority to their political connections and had been placed in their positions by politicians looking for ways to bolster the fading power of their party.

Along with the payouts, Zanu-PF needed to offer something persuasive to maintain its rural constituency, and land was one of the only commodities it had left. In 1997, it used long-dormant government powers aimed at post-Independence land redistribution to mark over 1,400 large-scale farms for acquisition—the first time such decisions had been made by national party leaders rather than less-centralized state bureaucracies. At the same time, it amplified rhetoric designating white farmers as colonists who refused to forfeit land inherited from the inequities of a racist colonial history. In fact, many of the white farmers working at the time had purchased their land after Independence, but as a group had been highly critical of the ruling party.

Much of this attempt at land reform stalled in legal battles, but a larger political conflict had arisen: the white commercial farmers, black small landholders, workers, students, and businessmen who contested the 1997 land redistributions suddenly found themselves with a shared interest, and went on to form the Movement for Democratic Change (MDC) in 1999. With land a central political issue, political opposition emerged from across Zimbabwe and changed the geography of post-Independence politics: from all over Zimbabwe, the MDC formed the first truly national opposition party.

Open invasions of many of these commercial farms began soon after the MDC's first victory. A Zanu-PF supported constitutional referendum was voted down in an open election in February 2000, and by early March the independent press began to report the involvement of government's Central Intelligence Organization (CIO) and Zanu-PF headquarters in directing veterans to specific farms—largely those whose farmers had contested the government's claim to them—and make allegations of party-supplied food, trucks, and logistical support. Zanu-PF delivered funds to the war veterans to "campaign" for the party, and lists of specific farms to occupy.

Land invasions intensified around and after a close parliamentary election that June. Though Zanu-PF won the election overall—campaigning with the slogan "Land is the Economy; the Economy is Land"—it lost in all of Zimbabwe's major towns, and entire regions of Matabeleland, the Manicaland, and the Midlands. (Notably, these would be the main areas to see violent displacement in the following decade.) After June 2000, the groups of occupiers grew larger. War veterans maintained leadership roles, but began to direct larger numbers of invaders drawn from party youth and residents of the poorer urban and rural areas where War Veterans Association had strengthened its influence since 1989. There was an attraction to *jambanja* (loosely: invasion; can also be used to refer to disorder or lawlessness) in a country whose economy and public institutions were slowly falling apart, and some new recruits assumed that occupying a farm meant automatic wealth. The government soon announced an accelerated "Fast Track" land reform program to redistribute the wealth of the country's farms more evenly across its population, though with little planning or attention to infrastructure, support, or budgeting. This would eventually result in the displacement of almost all white commercial farmers. Human Rights Watch detailed one of the first farmer deaths due to invasion violence, Martin Olds:

> ...*the farm of Martin Olds, in Nyamandlovu, near Bulawayo, Matabeleland, was invaded by more than one hundred Zanu-PF militia members, led by war veterans. According to a spokesperson for Zanu-PF, Olds opened fire, hitting five of the invaders with shotgun pellets, who then fired back. Neighboring farmers, who came to the scene after Olds radioed for help indicating he had been shot, but could not gain access, insist that Olds was defending his house as the intruders attempted to break into it. Police arrived at the house while the gunfight was ongoing but did not intervene. When the house was set alight, Olds was forced outside, and was shot twice in the head at close range. The intruders then left the farm, not seeking to occupy it. In July 2000, Olds' widow fled Zimbabwe and applied for asylum in the U.K. In March 2001, Olds' mother, Gloria Olds, was shot dead on the same farm, which she had refused to leave.*

It was not uncommon for farms, like Olds', to be invaded but not occupied: Human Rights Watch also reported that settlers were instructed not to build permanent shelters on invaded land, and that groups were moving from farm to farm shortly after invading. What little organization directed the farm invasions seemed aimed at disruption more than land redistribution—veteran leaders and Zanu-PF militia based themselves on farms while locating alleged supporters of the political opposition in nearby areas and executing intimidation campaigns. Some occupiers were "pushed onto" commercial farms, or paid when they were reluctant to move. "They're just being dumped onto the land," a white commercial farmer and MDC activist, whose land near Bulawayo had been occupied, told *The New Yorker* in 2002. "They're victims, in their own way, as much as we are."

Even the timing of the invasions indicated that redistributing sustainable farms had not been a high priority. "From the point of view of someone interested in farming, this was the worst time of year to occupy land," Jocelyn Alexander has written. "It was harvest season and no productive use of the land could be made for months to come. Many of the land-hungry were, in the period between the [February] referendum and the [June] election, limited in their capacity to sustain occupations without support. Those with jobs or crops to harvest could not easily remain on the farms for months. Those without jobs could not remain on the farms without support in the form of at least food."

Before the "Fast Track" land reform began, commercial farming had been a central part of the Zimbabwean economy, and some of the most robust in Southern Africa. Its economic support extended past agriculture alone: 40 percent of Zimbabwe's foreign exchange earnings came from agricultural products, and it supplied 60 percent of the manufacturing sector. The 4,500 white-owned farms employed as many as 350,000 full-time farm workers, and around a quarter-million seasonal or causal workers. Including their dependents, this work supported nearly 20 percent of Zimbabwe's population through wages alone. By the start of 2003, only 100,000 farm workers remained employed. In the same period, production of maize—a Zimbabwean staple food—declined by 90 percent, wheat by more than half, soybeans by nearly 80 percent, and tobacco by more than two-thirds. Though a drought had helped push production downward after 2001, the agricultural decline has been found to have begun in 2000, coinciding with the start of farm invasions and land reform, and measures of agricultural production and food reserves soon fell past the levels caused by earlier droughts. Commercial agriculture largely vanished—before 1997, an average of 1,600 tractors were sold each year; in 2002 the number of tractors sold was eight. By 2008, all but 400 of the 4,500 farms had new ownership; most were destroyed. The country's white population, numbering 200,000 in 1980, shrank through emigration to South Africa, Nigeria, Zambia, the U.K., Australia, New Zealand, Canada, and the U.S. to one-tenth of that.

Between 2000 and the presidential election in 2002, fast track land reform expanded into what war veterans and Zanu-PF called the "third *chimurenga*." This framed the farm invasions in a specific narrative of Zimbabwean history. The first two *chimurengas* were nationalist uprisings against a white, colonial enemy: the first, failed, uprisings of the 1890s and the successful liberation wars of the 1970s. Both also centered on land. If the farm invasions were to be the third *chimurenga*, the invading veterans would be the liberators of the land, freeing it from the grasp of white domination and international financial institutions trying to use their allegedly neocolonial and imperial arguments of democracy and civil rights to deny Zimbabweans a rightful cultural and material heritage, and a relationship to the land as it should be. In this narrative, Mugabe and

Zanu-PF could then cast themselves as responding to popular pressure for land reform—from party-supporting communal farmers and the veterans of its war of liberation—as they moved to take control of local government institutions and attack political dissent.

The night before the 2002 presidential election, Zanu-PF militias beat more than a dozen MDC polling agents, in an attempt to send a message to polling agents throughout the country. Many rural polling stations were situated in areas of heavy Zanu-PF militia activity, and on election day close to half of the rural polling stations operated without the MDC polling agents who were supposed to defend the party's interest in fair voting practices. In the run-up to the election, MDC supporters were assaulted for offenses including "wearing an MDC shirt," "servicing an MDC candidate's vehicle," or "aiding an MDC supporter"—which in at least one case meant helping someone whom the militia had beaten get to the hospital—as well as selling MDC membership cards or trying to register a list of MDC polling agents. Voter turnout in MDC strongholds was low, and there was wide accusation of vote rigging. The International Crisis Group reported that every Zimbabwean civil society organization established to support or assess the electoral process judged it as unfree and unfair, as did the governments of United States, the United Kingdom, Germany, Norway, Sweden, Australia, New Zealand, and Canada.

Anti-MDC political violence continued after the election: state broadcasting began playing a "Chave Chimurenga" ("war has begun") song in August 2002, as part of a wide "Hondo ye Minda" ("war in the fields") propaganda campaign. By the next March this song was withdrawn, but replaced in party ideology with explanations that Zimbabwe's troubles were the result of exaggerated "sanctions" instigated by the British. But Zanu-PF began to experience some internal divisions from members who wanted a more orderly and legal process and, more significantly, began to find the war veterans—a group that sometimes had its own interests—less useful than the more pliable youth militias or the official military and police forces that had become used to carrying out political violence. (Some veterans, of course, had become members of the police.) Some experts surmised that youth militias and the war veterans had begun to compete for political patronage, and fought police and army members for control of food distribution networks as food insecurity increased. By the end of 2002, the war veterans' influence had waned. The year before, Chenjerai Hunzvi had died, seemingly of AIDS and malaria.

During the time of their influence, however, Zimbabwe had become a party-state. Local arms of government came under direct or indirect party control, land ministries with technocratic experts no longer made land distribution decisions, judges were threatened or ignored and replaced, new laws were written to legalize state action after the fact, the police recruited veterans and party youth and worked with a political interest, the army acted less and less like a professional force, and new institutions—such as land committees—were created to circumvent the existing laws. These committees, in addition to organizing invasions, shut down rural councils and schools and chased elected representatives out of the middle levels of Zimbabwean government. Invasions also broke up local communities, closing or limiting access to schools, clinics, and clean water. (Teachers were a particularly popular target for war veterans.) Wildlife poaching grew out of control. But the sector most affected, of course, was agriculture. As the output of small-

and medium-scale farming failed to meet anticipations, exports dropped, unemployment rose, other agriculture-reliant industries continued to contract, and Zimbabwe entered a period of hunger and national food shortages.

When the land invasions began in 2000—twenty years after Independence—white Zimbabweans still controlled most of the country's wealth, though they were less than 1 percent of its population. Those 4,500 farms had accounted for between 50 and 70 percent of the country's arable land. The correction of this imbalance through land reform had been a central issue of Zimbabwean politics and life since the end of colonialism; part of the farm invasions' power to amass support and participation came from a very real and widespread desire for land. This partially explains how Mugabe was able to use it not only to catapult his campaign but to reshape Zimbabwean politics. But clearly his solution had left pretty much everyone far worse off. Philip Gourevitch, reporting from Zimbabwe in 2002, wrote

...looking back, many Zimbabweans will tell you that if Mugabe had stepped down, as many in his party had urged him to do, at the time of the last Presidential elections, in 1996, he would probably be remembered forgivingly, as he likes to imagine himself, as a hero of liberation, and an eminent African statesman—if not a Nelson Mandela, whose all-eclipsing nobility Mugabe bitterly resents. He would certainly not rank among the infamous dictators for whom he has expressed admiration over the years.

Writing a couple of years later, Zimbabwean economist Rob Davies put it more starkly: "What we are seeing in Zimbabwe at present...is the destruction of the future by the rhetoric of redress for the past."

VI. ECONOMIC DECLINE

Most experts explain Zimbabwe's economy through three major periods since Independence: the "socialist" or "welfarist," state-directed model of the 1980s; the globalized, international-finance development model of most of the 1990s; and the decline that has occurred throughout the political and humanitarian crises since the turn of the century. Though this short history appears to contain suggestions from many different corners of economic thought, what has struck a number of analysts is the way in which these varied developmental models have been put in the service a much more singular force: creating a national, post-colonial economy without, in an observation written by Horace Campbell and supported by a number of other experts, "fundamentally transforming the colonial economic relations."

This would be an economy in which the vast majority of the people do not own productive resources, but "rent" them from a privileged few. One "in which the ruling party created incentives for trading goods...as virtually the only way to survive," according to Brian Raftopoulos, a civic activist and a director at Solidarity Peace Trust. "The rewards for long-term investment in production were miniscule compared to the rapid profits of buying cheap and selling dear." In this view, the various economic policies since Independence can be understood not as part of an economy that sustains itself and creates growth, but—according to economist Rob Davies—as part of "a process of acquisition of private wealth" for a very small group. For Davies, "it would be wrong to interpret this as a part of a process of creating a new 'capitalist' class, since what has been accumulated is not capital." Rather than accumulating economic value, which can then be reinvested and self-sustaining, "it has been destroyed."

Today, analysts disagree on when Zimbabwe's "apparently endless economic downturn" began—with the land invasions in 2000, with the international flight from Zimbabwe currency markets following the war veteran payout in 1997, with the onset of the Economic Structural Adjustment Program in 1991, with the end of colonialism in the 1980s, with a steep fall in gross domestic product in 1974—because the bulk of analyses aimed at finding a starting point for the decline of Zimbabwe's economy quickly become veiled arguments about Zimbabwean politics. Without a doubt the two are interrelated, but a maintaining clear focus in economic analysis remains important: according to political economist Patrick Bond, one of many who has tackled this question, political analyses are "certainly welcomed," but "while the specific form of the current crisis is obviously very much based upon President Mugabe's desperation to hold on to power at all costs, there is also a much deeper problem that transcends the rise of the new Zimbabwe elite."

After Independence, Zimbabwe experienced an economic boom, but a number of the circumstances that ended colonization and fueled the economy prevented the new government from achieving fundamental and structural economic changes. Part of the Lancaster House agreement, which ended the liberation war in 1979, reserved a number of seats in Parliament for whites and prevented the forced redistribution of any land which the owner did not wish to sell. While these provisions may have prevented an immediate capital flight, they effectively slowed the country's transition out of colonialism as white farmers hesitated to hand over the privileges inherited from colonial times. "Issues around the radical restructuring of the legacy of economic inequality were effectively put on hold" for a decade, research specialist and author James Muzondidya has explained, until the Lancaster House provisions expired.

Social welfare, nonetheless, was able to improve drastically for much of the population. The government improved or established sanitation in rural areas, and built roads, clinics, and schools. By 1988, 84 percent of the population had access to safe drinking water—an improvement that earned Zimbabwe's government praise from the World Health Organization and UNICEF. Infant mortality and crude death rates dropped, while life expectancy and adult literacy increased. In the first decade after Independence, the number of primary and secondary schools had risen by 80 percent; from 1979 to 1985, enrollment in primary schools rose from 82,000 to almost 2.25 million, and enrollment in secondary schools rose from 66,000 to just below 500,000. From Independence until 1985, more children went to primary school in Zimbabwe than had during the 90 years of white minority rule of Southern Rhodesia.

Most of these improvements, however, were less radical than they first seemed. Many of the gains were financed through loans from international organizations or foreign governments, and a large part of the Zimbabwean economy was literally owned by foreign companies, as many of the most robust industries had been set up and run in Zimbabwe by multinational corporations based elsewhere. Many of these enterprises offered those in power, or those connected to power, positions that bestowed them with great wealth—this provided an incentive to keep economic relations as they were while it minimized any appearance of foreign dominance.

Further, government attempts to develop a black middle class and to "Africanize" public service distributed economic gains unevenly to a new elite, with no significant narrowing of income and wealth inequality. One estimate tracked the bulk of resources and two-thirds of the national income during the 1980s to only 3 percent of the population, made up mostly of white farmers and a small black bourgeoisie. Small businesses and the black middle class, meanwhile, found difficulty entering large sectors of the economy and securing loans from white- and foreign-owned banks. In 1989, the *Financial Times* reported that 97 percent of bank loans went to white-owned businesses. Nonetheless, there was relatively little popular pressure to correct these lingering inequalities in a time of vastly improved social services and the appearance of economic security.

As that first decade wore on, droughts, weakening trade positions, high interest rates, and high oil prices forced the government to be convinced by international financial institutions to abandon some of its social policies and focus more on servicing government debt. By 1987, Finance and Economic Minister Bernard Chidzero conceded that there would be long-term problems in sustaining the initial strategy for Zimbabwe's development—though at least one economist suggests that this should be interpreted as a recognition that the Zimbabwean elite began to see the limits of using the state to acquire personal wealth drawing near. The type of global "structural adjustment" program the government soon entered, in other cases, almost always coincided with the fall of a political regime.

With socialism, after 1989, as no longer a legitimate alternative, the Zimbabwean government introduced the Economic Structural Adjustment Program (ESAP) in 1991, working with the International Monetary Fund and the World Bank. After a severe drought that year decreased Zimbabwe's chances of achieving many of its ESAP development goals, the International Monetary Fund took much stronger control.

At the start of ESAP, two of the Zimbabwean government's three highest expenditures had been education and health care. These were two of the first government services to be reduced under ESAP, and the progress made by health and education services quickly eroded. During the stress of the drought, the IMF imposed user fees for primary education and rural health clinics. Primary-school dropout rates increased—especially for girls and especially when school fees were introduced—and a 1993 UNICEF survey noted that twice as many women were dying during childbirth as had before 1990, and fewer people were visiting hospitals and clinics, citing cost, at the time when HIV/AIDS was becoming a national pandemic. In 1991, average economic growth declined from 4 percent to 0.9 percent. By 1998–1999, when growth "recovered" to only 2.9 percent, many economists began calling the 1990s Zimbabwe's "lost decade."

ESAP incentivized Zimbabwe to produce for the global economy over regional or national ones, even when drought and food security became major concerns. It centered growth around Zimbabwe's large commercial farms, which began planning crops for distant export where before they had grown crops for the region. Cotton, tobacco, paprika, game meat, flowers, and ostrich replaced maize, sorghum, and groundnuts. Smaller, communal farms attempted to make up production of these staple crops, but they were hit hardest by drought and lacked many of the resources needed to overcome climate challenges. Zimbabwean manufacturers also looked outward, often becoming traders who found importation and resale more profitable than local production had been—a strategy that may work for individual actors but, on the whole, moves direct control over production outside the country. Manufacture, as a sector of the economy, contracted by 40 percent between 1992 and 1996.

Worse still, ESAP allowed global demand to determine agricultural production and small-farm subsidies in developing nations, while large-scale consumers—notably the United States and the European Union—typically have the economic strength to maintain protectionist policies. Their decreased demand for products produced in Zimbabwe may decrease or change what Zimbabwe's large farms will produce, and leave little or no surplus when unforeseen conditions—such as drought—reduce the domestic food supply. In the early 1990s, Zimbabwe's trade deficit skyrocketed.

In general, the 1990s marked a high point of international development's use of the ideology of neoliberal globalization, which undergirded the development of Zimbabwe. This, loosely, is a set of ideas organized by the claim that market forces, combined with appropriate banking and finance practices, allocate resources better than directed planning—a school of thought later recognized even by its practitioners as not always in the best long-term interest of the regions ostensibly being "developed," especially regions emerging out of a situation of conflict. A Zimbabwean financial journalist called World Bank statements on ESAP's progress "the devotion of a faith unmoved by facts," and the

United Nations Conference on Trade and Development, in 2000, found that the needs of local political history and economies, such as the communal farms in rural Zimbabwe, will come into conflict with the assumptions of globalization. "Sub-Saharan Africa," it reported, "suffers from structural handicaps that are impossible to remove or reduce through the standard policy reform programs...some ingredients of reforms have actually aggravated constraints on the growth of smallholder production." Even the World Bank, commenting on the reductions in Zimbabwe's social services, eventually conceded that "budget cutting appears to have been an end in itself." Under ESAP, Zimbabwe's exports increased, but its economic health declined.

Understandably, ESAP became extremely unpopular. Struggling farmers and rural communities saw fertile pastureland set aside for products destined to head overseas, and government land reserves sold to foreign tourist firms. Food prices increased as real wages declined; Harare experienced food and protest riots in 1993 and 1995. Increased unemployment raised pressure on rural land and natural resources to be productive, as distressed urban workers sent their families to stay at their rural homes, sometimes returning with them. Laborers, including civil servants, went on strike repeatedly, causing politicians to worry about their legitimacy and the legitimacy of the party. (There were other indications that the party was growing more desperate: in 1998 they began sending soldiers to fight in a civil war in the Democratic Republic of Congo on behalf of its government, allegedly for access to resources and new market opportunities for the Zimbabwean elite. Aaron, in his narrative, describes combat there.) Trade unions became more powerful and more confrontational, vocal civic groups formed, and student protests increased—an alignment that would eventually lead to the formation of the Movement for Democratic Change. According to Patrick Bond, "the failure of ESAP to redress the inequalities inherent in the Zimbabwean economy means that the majority of the people cannot not take advantage of the opportunities that are offered."

In theory, neoliberal globalization was supposed to create a "flow" of resources and capital across the world, an almost-perfectly-efficient market. In practice, as anthropologist Blair Rutherford describes,

> ...forms of international investment and projects into Africa largely {took} place in the form of enclaves (e.g. particular mining operations or wildlife conservancies), with great emphasis on securing their boundaries against the surrounding African locales and peoples.... The "global" does not "flow," thereby connecting and watering contiguous spaces; it hops instead, efficiently connecting the enclaved points in the network while excluding (with equal efficiency) the spaces that lie between the points.

Those with access to political favor or easy credit, however—those able to enter the "enclaves"—captured great benefits. What Rob Davies called "the rise of an indigenous speculative...rentier...class" had been created. Well-connected businesspeople enjoyed newly imported luxury goods and utilized the cheaper labor provided by deregulation, access to move money out of the country, and lower expenditures as the real value of wages declined. Commercial farmers also did well in this economy, though they (and their shareholders) took a larger portion of the profits compared to their farmworkers than they had in the 1980s—a 1998 IMF report noted that they "gained almost all the share [of the GDP] that wage earners lost." Their wealth set them apart from the majority of Zimbabweans, undoubtedly adding to any resentment based on their position in the narratives of Zimbabwean nationalism and helping them become visible targets for the land invasions to come.

Experts date Zimbabwe's definitive move out of ESAP very specifically: November 14, 1997. Attempting to recover from a stock market crash two months earlier, Mugabe had raised his rhetoric on the topic of land redistribution, began preparations to send soldiers to the conflict in the Democratic Republic of Congo, and made unbudgeted payouts to veterans of the independence war. International investors fled, causing the Zimbabwean dollar to lose 74 percent of its value in a four-hour period. Massive inflation began and city dwellers rioted over price increases; the government responded with measures including a price freeze on staple foods and tariffs on luxury imports. With the reintroduction of such strict, central economic policy, and with foreign debt now virtually unpayable, Zimbabwe's experiment with the global marketplace had largely ended.

This period marked a turning point for the Zanu-PF government and for Mugabe, who rediscovered his nationalism and began to explain Zimbabwe's economic problems as the result of victimization by the imperialist West. He justified his recent policy decisions, in this telling, as a fight against the ghosts of colonialism. At times, he blamed "detractors" for causing shortages "every time the country comes out of elections," and accused the U.S. and U.K. governments of controlling weather patterns to cause drought. He generally declined to recognize that Zimbabwe's deregulatory policies and social-service cuts had been put in place by a succession of three orthodox finance ministers and two governors of the Reserve Bank, or comment on the government's near relentlessness in searching for international investors in commercial agriculture. Without money from Western donors, Mugabe and Zanu-PF left many of the "imperialist" structures in place, courting investment instead from Libya, Malaysia, and China.

As international divestment and limited sanctions caused constant shortages of foreign currency, the government often addressed debt by simply printing more money. Inflation became hyperinflation and grew out of control, and a robust black market developed, with—again—advantages and opportunities for profit going to those with connections to power, particularly the few who could access foreign exchange. Bernard, in his narrative, shows just how messy, in practice, this could be.

The black market rate of the Zimbabwean dollar began to deviate greatly from the official rate with the start of fast-track land reform in 2000. The government, however, maintained an official rate of Z$55 to US$1 for more than two years, while unofficial street rates hit the hundreds and even thousands. This hurt exporters hardest, who sold their goods overseas at official foreign currency rates, but could only buy raw materials at domestic prices set by the black market, and so had to do so at much higher real prices than proceeds from their international sales supported. However, the rate difference worked to the great advantage of government officials and beneficiaries of political patronage, who could find great personal wealth on the reverse side of these same economic mechanisms.

As described in a 2003 report by the International Crisis Group:

> *Those so connected are usually first in line at the Reserve Bank of Zimbabwe to convert their Zimbabwe dollars into hard currency at the official rate. For example, Z$55 million converts to only US$36,000 at the more realistic black market rate. But if the Z$55 million is changed by the Reserve Bank at the official rate it comes to US$1 million. Such exchanges allowed fortunes to be amassed in foreign currency by a few, while the economy was increasingly impoverished.*

In 2003, the government readjusted the official rate to 800:1. By this time, many "connected" Zimbabweans had, through fast-track reform and land invasions, become owners of the export-reliant commercial farms, or secured business loans and bought largely devalued industrial companies (some refused to repay these loans, finding it more profitable to wait for inflation to reduce the real value of their debt). The International Crisis Group referred to these arrangements, so heavily reliant on patronage, as a "mafia economy" (the same term Bernard used in his narrative).

Hyperinflation and currency overvaluation continued out of control, despite numerous government attempts at intervention throughout the decade. In March 2008 the U.S. dollar traded for 25 million Zimbabwean dollars; two months later, it traded for one billion. Business planning became virtually impossible. Jon Lee Anderson, reporting from Zimbabwe for *The New Yorker*, noted food prices tripling overnight and salaries almost immediately made worthless. Pension funds, as well, essentially disappeared—one reporter talked to a sixty-year-old Zimbabwean who tried to collect his Z$75-trillion pension fund and received three U.S. cents. Banks set withdrawal limits that reached as low as one U.S. dollar per day, so as not to run out of cash—lines could reach 1,000 people by the early morning—while supermarkets sold half-liter water bottles for close to US$19. By May 2006, the country's smallest bill (the $500 note) became known to be more cost effective as toilet paper—which was selling at the time for $417 per single square—than as money, and a sign warning migrants not to flush "zim dollars" down the toilet hung in the bathroom at South African Emigration, Beitbridge.

The shortage of foreign currency also created widespread bartering, but information on fair exchange rates was difficult to find in areas far from city centers. One report found evidence of urban butchers using this lack of information to their advantage, sending trucks into rural areas to "extort" cattle from villagers desperate for even very small amounts of maize. In various rural exchanges, a single chicken could equal the value of: a pair of track shoes, a bar of soap, two bars of soap, five kilograms of maize, six kilograms of maize, ten kilograms of maize, two kilograms of maize seed, five kilograms of maize seed, a call on a mobile phone, or a visit to a clinic. Chickens have also been used as bus fare and to pay school fees. Experts described the situation as having "turned just about everyone without access to real currency into an informal trader."

The Reserve Bank of Zimbabwe stopped releasing official inflation statistics in July 2008, and economists largely stopped measuring inflation after they found it to be 6.5 quindecillion novemdecillion percent—65 followed by 107 zeroes—in December 2008.

At that point, prices doubled every 24.7 hours. Even before inflation reached such levels, Human Rights Watch had claimed that "Zimbabwe's entire economy is in a decline so severe that the average Zimbabwean is worse off in 2003 than in 1980 at Independence."

In a way, Operation Murambatsvina—the government displacement of hundreds of thousands of urban Zimbabweans from informal housing and the disruption of informal urban economies in 2005–2006—was an attempt to rein in black and parallel markets that traded in foreign currency. Other attempts at violent state-directed crackdown had largely failed, but Zimbabwe subsequently made more successful attempts to re-enter the world economy. In January 2009, the unity government indefinitely suspended the Zimbabwean dollar and instead sanctioned a number of foreign currencies, which mirrored what had already been happening in practice. Thousands of doctors, teachers, and civil servants returned to work as ministries began to pay salaries in U.S. dollars, and staple foods returned to market shelves. The IMF provided a US$510 million loan to the unity government in September 2009, on the condition that part of the money be used to repay older IMF loans on which Zimbabwe had defaulted, and still owed. In 2009, inflation fell to 6 percent.

VII. THE 2008 ELECTIONS

In 2008, Zimbabwe held presidential, parliamentary, and local elections together for the first time. The results dealt a severe blow to Zanu-PF and to Robert Mugabe—who received fewer votes for president than MDC's Morgan Tsvangirai, though exactly how many will most likely never be known. Through the runoff that followed, Tsvangirai and the MDC earned unprecedented control within the institutions of state, but the "unity government" that resulted faces major challenges that it has yet to overcome. As Zimbabwe continues the complex transition toward multi-party democracy, its future may be determined by the growing divisions within each party, and within government institutions, as much as by the opposition of Tsvangirai's MDC to Mugabe's Zanu-PF.

Perhaps the most influential of these internal divisions is the one that has divided the MDC into two factions. Since its founding as an umbrella institution for a number of civic and political groups in the late 1990s, the MDC has never enjoyed a very stable unity. In the early 2000s, Zimbabwean geographic and ethnic tensions exacerbated these divisions: rumors circulated that a largely Ndebele group of lawyers and academics planned to replace Tsvangirai, the MDC chairman and a Shona, with a Ndebele chairman. (Shona is Zimbabwe's majority ethnic group, and the Ndebele its largest minority.) Members of Tsvangirai's personal security team attacked suspected plotters, to much controversy, and Tsvangirai was forced to expel almost thirty MDC members amid questions about his leadership. Disagreements about participation in the 2005 senate elections also proved fractious, with party leaders unable to reach consensus on whether participation in elections and in a government with Mugabe at its head would mean a fatal compromise of MDC goals.

By the end of 2005, the MDC had split into two factions: Tsvangirai's majority MDC-T and the newer MDC-M, led since 2006 by Arthur Mutambara. Tsvangirai remained popular, but MDC-T suffered from reports of youth violence, lack of accountability, and patronage. These resulted from the faction's mostly unsuccessful attempts to create structures outside of the main MDC organs that could work around Zanu-PF surveillance, provide food assistance, and help rural Zimbabweans avoid political repression during a time of land invasions, food insecurity, and displacement. The young participants in this parallel MDC, trying to work around Zanu-PF, reported to a small handful of MDC leaders and sometimes fought repression with violence—vices that resembled Zanu-PF governance to many citizens. MDC-T and MDC-M were unable to unite before Zimbabwe went to the polls in 2008. The state press emphasized the split, publicizing Mutambara's rallies in the run-up to the election.

In early 2007, civic mobilization and state violence both escalated, culminating in the beating and arrest of more than fifty activists in the notorious police raid on Highfield on March 11. (Sankoh witnessed the raid, and describes his memory of it in his narrative.) Though Mugabe had recently banned political rallies and demonstrations in Harare, a coalition of political and civil-society organizations called the Save Zimbabwe Campaign planned a "prayer meeting" at the Zimbabwe Grounds in Highfield, a Harare suburb, for this day. Police arrived before the meeting was to start, and prevented it with tear gas, water cannons, bullets, batons, and rifle beatings. When Morgan Tsvangirai drove there to attend the meeting, he found the area cordoned off and closed down on presidential orders. Later, informed that many MDC activists and civic leaders had been arrested and were being held in town, he drove to Machipisa police station, where upon arrival he was reportedly pulled from his car, arrested, and had his head slammed against the station wall. Once inside, his beating continued; he lost consciousness three times, only to be revived with cold water and further violence. When television footage of his swollen face, taken after he left the hospital, emerged in the press—along with the information that he had a fractured skull and enough blood loss to require transfusions, and that a bodyguard who had suffered beatings with him died from his injuries—the crackdown in Highfield became international news. "The combination of the beating, and the physical and moral courage he showed, won him the sympathy of the nation," one of Tsvangirai's advisers told the press. The body of the television cameraman, Edward Chikombo, was discovered within a few days.

Zimbabwe's politics had become a regional problem. The countries of the Southern African Development Community (SADC) convened an "Extra-Ordinary" summit at the end of the month to address Zimbabwe's crisis, mediate talks between its political parties, and create conditions for free and fair elections in 2008. Yet Mugabe barely attempted a public justification that might paint his government as interested in democracy or the rule of law. Some government ministers attempted to justify the events as rightful state action enforcing the ban on protests, but Mugabe held a public rally to commend the use of force and warn Tsvangirai and the MDC that there would be more to come. "I told the police to beat him a lot," he explained. "He and his MDC must stop their terrorist activities. We are saying to him, 'Stop it now or you will regret it.'" When asked about Tsvangirai at the SADC summit, he claimed, "I told them he was beaten but he asked for it."

Closer to the March 2008 elections, internal divisions within Zanu-PF began to surface: it became clear that some members had made plans for succession after Mugabe. Fearing sabotage, Mugabe has steadily aligned himself with the party's military or "securocrat" wing, and since 2007 had placed military allies in committees that supervise cabinet and senior government officials, extending party division. The February before the elections, Zanu-PF's Simba Makoni announced his own, independent, candidacy for president, after the SADC had been unable to convince Mugabe to retire and hand Makoni control of the party and, ostensibly, of the country. This marked the first-ever open challenge to Mugabe from within his party.

Makoni was quickly expelled from Zanu-PF and labeled a traitor, but his claims that his former party was unable to relieve the country's poverty and that its own money printing had fueled hyperinflation—claims from a senior Zanu-PF figure that the sources of poverty were not Britain or targeted sanctions, as Mugabe had consistently asserted—were incredibly destabilizing.

While Makoni attempted to pick off factions within Zanu-PF, deteriorating economic and food conditions eroded the party's rural voter base. Mugabe's land reform, by 2008, was recognized as a failure, and the party found itself unable to hand out food and seed to Zanu-PF party cardholders as it had at previous elections, since national food insecurity meant the supply was too low for even the government to have a meaningful surplus. Mugabe's gifts of tractors and farming tools, in exchange for votes, went to the well-connected elite, who by now controlled much of the land. "Is that the meaning of independence," some Zimbabweans reportedly retorted, "that these people must now eat for us?" Mugabe fell into talking about the liberation war, which meant less and less to voters too young to have lived through it and looking for solutions to the problems they knew.

At the polls in late March, Zanu-PF lost its parliamentary majority for the first time since Independence. But the results were extremely slow to trickle out. The Zimbabwe Electoral Commission's (ZEC) first private results, given to the Zanu-PF Politburo the day after the polls closed, reportedly had Tsvangirai winning 58 percent of the presidential vote, Mugabe 27 percent, and Makoni 15. Mugabe is said to have responded by ordering the ZEC to declare him elected, with 53 percent of the vote, and to reduce Makoni's share to 5 percent in retribution for his "treachery." But by this point he had clearly lost the power to execute such pronouncements.

The ZEC resisted, arguing that such massive manipulation would be too obvious, and the "securocrat" army, police, and intelligence leaders worried that the backlash to such manipulation would leave the country ungovernable. Thabo Mbeki, the President of South Africa and the SADC emissary tasked with overseeing the elections, suggested—he had been in near-constant communication by this time—"adjusting" the results to bring Tsvangirai under 50 percent, increasing Mugabe's result to 41 percent, and deflating Makoni to 10–12. If this was to be done, an electoral rule requiring the winner to receive over 50 percent of the vote would necessitate a runoff election, which, Mbeki suggested, would allow Mugabe to honorably withdraw and Zanu-PF, with security forces heavily involved in the runoff, to throw its support behind Makoni. Reportedly, Zanu-PF leadership accepted this idea, but Mugabe refused.

According to sources, a moderate wing of the party, led by its two vice presidents, privately called for Mugabe to negotiate a settlement and step down, while an opposing faction pushed Mugabe to refuse anything short of victory. Securocrats assured Mugabe that they could deliver it, or that they could deliver a coup, more immediately, if Mugabe proved too hesitant. By May 14, former military commander Dumsio Dabengwa had told the International Crisis Group that "the country is now being run by military junta."

The election results appeared to have caught Zanu-PF completely off-guard, and the party projected an indecisiveness Zimbabwean citizens had never before seen. After two days without official announcements, state-run television began broadcasting, slowly, parliamentary results: the winners of three or four constituencies would be announced every few hours, with regularly scheduled programming in between. At this time, an independent Zimbabwean monitoring group released projections that showed Tsvangirai receiving 49.4 percent of the vote against Mugabe's 41.8 percent.

After two more days, MDC declared victory in both the parliamentary and presidential elections, and the ZEC had reportedly announced privately to Mugabe that he had failed to win the presidential election. Reports began to circulate that the government's Joint Operations Command (JOC), composed of the leaders of Zanu-PF security and intelligence forces, were advising Mugabe to concede, and that MDC leadership was in back-channel negotiations with Zanu-PF army leaders to guarantee the latter immunity from prosecution under a new government—though, looking back, some experts see this as a disingenuous strategy by Zanu-PF to create time for internal decisions and forestall the MDC from organizing mass demonstrations. While some JOC leaders were reportedly prepared, under certain conditions, to accept a power-sharing agreement headed by Tsvangirai, others refused, fearing for their security and unwilling to serve a leader who had not taken part in the liberation war. But the final decision was far from clear. On April 2, four days after the polls closed, CNN reported that Mugabe was to step down that very night.

On April 3, still in the absence of official results, Zanu-PF appeared to reach its decision: the crackdown began. Police raided the MDC's Harare headquarters, taking documents and arresting and beating MDC members. Reporters from the *New York Times* and the *Sunday Telegraph* were arrested for "committing journalism" and imprisoned for four days. Hundreds of "war veterans" brought violence to city streets. The SADC, in an effort to prevent cheating, had enforced a law during the election requiring all votes to be counted at the polling station and the results photographed and publicly posted. While this undoubtedly played a powerful role in preventing an outright election theft, it also provided a target list of villages that had voted MDC, useful to Zanu-PF when it began its Operation Makavhoterapapi ("Where did you put your cross?" or "Where did you put your X?").

Besides targeting those who had voted "wrongly," Operation Makavhoterapapi also targeted election observers, polling officials, ZEC officials, and anyone who had a role in a local MDC victory—or could have a role in a future one. A new wave of farm invasions began, with Zanu-PF attempting somewhat to hide its role in the violence through a smokescreen of war veterans and youth militias. In May and June, "bases" were set up in Harare—home to MDC's urban stronghold—reaching even the wealthiest suburbs. At the bases, all-night *pungwes*—guerilla mobilization meetings common during the liberation war—were held, where slogans were sung, MDC supporters were forced to burn their party regalia, and "sell-outs" were beaten. A number of abducted Zimbabweans reported beatings and torture, including mutilation, at the bases, and others reported (like Sankoh and Gabriel, in Sankoh's narrative) being beaten or tortured in the hills or the countryside until they were left for dead.

A number of MDC politicians were murdered with their families, and bodies of abducted activists began to appear on farms; their funerals became public, political events. Tsvangirai went into hiding, spending much of his time out of the country. Entire villages and smaller towns underwent forced conversions or "re-education," with alleged MDC supporters beaten publicly. Zanu-PF or its allies blocked access to villages targeted for violence, and warned hospitals to treat victims only under the threat of retaliation. Human Rights Watch called it the worst election violence in Zimbabwe's history.

Responses to the violence exposed another fissure that stood in Mugabe's way, between the broadly "anti-colonial" and the "pro-Western" heads of regional states. While some would not speak out against Mugabe and the election-related violence, the lack of regional unity was apparent by April, when Zimbabwean newspapers became captivated by the refusal of dockworkers in Durban, South Africa, to unload a Chinese merchant vessel carrying thousands of tons of arms and ammunition headed for Zimbabwe—some of it undoubtedly to be used to suppress political opposition. The chairman of the SADC publicly called for states in the region to bar the ship, and human rights activists, unions, and church groups acted to keep the weapons from Zimbabwe. The ship next tried to dock in Namibia, but civil leaders and unions pressured the usually Mugabe-friendly government there to send it back out to sea. It was also refused in Mozambique. After several weeks, Zanu-PF announced that it had received the arms, unloaded in Angola—which claimed to allow the boat to dock only to unload other cargo—then shipped by train to the Democratic Republic of Congo, and loaded on military supply flights to Harare.

Official results of the presidential election were announced on May 2. Five weeks had passed without an elected president, legally appointed cabinet, or assembly of parliament. Tsvangirai was given 47.9 percent of the vote, Mugabe 43.2 percent, and Makoni 8.3 (with the rest given to a fourth candidate; Mutambara had supported Makoni). Two weeks later, the runoff was announced for June 27, Tsvangirai having already stated that he would participate. During May and June, however, he wavered, at times demanding certain conditions to ensure a fair election, at others saying he would not take part—weighing an election that looked increasingly unwinnable against violence targeting his supporters—and MDC officials continued to pursue the possibility of a coalition government.

Zanu-PF suppression continued. In late May, the party issued one directive prohibiting CARE International, an aid agency, from distributing food aid in Masvingo—claiming that CARE was using food to support the MDC—and another placing all food distribution in rural areas under the command of a government ministry. On June 4, the government suspended all local and international aid and humanitarian agencies entirely. The UN, Western governments, and aid agencies soon expressed concern about the suspensions and about food insecurity, amid reports of "devastating" food shortages in rural Zimbabwe. The Zanu-PF suspension also prevented aid workers from entering rural areas and villages, where violence could be carried out without international witnesses.

In an effort to further isolate some areas, militias ordered rural residents to remove satellite television receivers from their homes, and assaulted suburbanites seen holding copies of non-state newspapers. A newspaper delivery truck near Masvingo, containing 60,000 copies of *The Zimbabwean*, was hijacked and set aflame, its drivers beaten. Despite increases in import duties and surcharges for foreign papers, however, papers like *The Zimbabwean* (which is printed in South Africa) sold in record-setting numbers.

On June 22, only five days before the scheduled runoff, Tsvangirai pulled out of the election for good, saying that the violence had made a free and fair election impossible. The ZEC ruled that the election would occur nonetheless. When Mugabe declared himself the winner, he failed to receive the support, or even the silence, that he had been used to from Zimbabwe's neighboring states. The SADC condemned the election and recommended a continued mediation, while the African Union and other multi-nation groups released public comments on the election's lack of credibility. "Even ten years ago, what Mugabe has done would be a non-event," explained David Coltart, an MDC member of parliament who would be an eventual minister of education. "Now a significant and increasing number of African leaders are embarrassed, even angry, about his behavior."

The SADC resumed its dialogue with Zimbabwean political leaders, aiming toward a unity government. In late July, Zanu-PF and the two MDC factions signed a memorandum of understanding, which provided an outline for a dialogue that would lead to an agreement for a new government. But talks quickly unraveled, with Zanu-PF violating some of the agreed-upon terms and hoping to contain Tsvangirai with a ceremonial position in the new government; violence continued. By August, Zimbabwean hospitals had run out of crutches, having to import hundreds more. On August 29, the government softened its earlier restrictions on aid organizations, but humanitarian agencies, including those of the UN, abandoned attempts to deliver food to rural areas after facing local resistance by war veterans, soldiers, intelligence agents, and local government outposts.

By September, massive economic problems, international pressure, and a spreading cholera outbreak brought Mugabe back to the negotiating table. Some MDC members, such as eventual finance minister Tendai Biti, argued against a power-sharing deal, on the grounds that Tsvangirai had clearly won in March and should form a new government without Mugabe, or mobilize support to force Mugabe's resignation. Despite this, MDC-T reached a deal with MDC-M and Zanu-PF to sign a Global Political Agreement (GPA) that September, and formed a transitional power-sharing government in February 2009. Mugabe would remain president, Tsvangirai would become prime minister, and Mutambara would become deputy prime minister.

Despite near-constant tension, the power-sharing government has made significant accomplishments since 2009: civil servants who had left the government began working again, hospitals and schools reopened, legislation changing the national currency slowed inflation and filled stores with goods once again, human rights abuses declined, and a cholera epidemic has been brought under control. But the transition to a democratic government has been slow, and frequently undermined—at its worst, the MDC has disengaged from government in protest.

In violation of the GPA, Mugabe claimed the most powerful government ministries for Zanu-PF, unilaterally appointed permanent Zanu-PF secretaries even to ministries that MDC formally headed, and has appropriated the functions of some MDC-led ministries to others controlled by Zanu-PF. Tsvangirai has been prevented from chairing sessions of cabinet that the president could not attend, a responsibility of the prime minister by law, and Zanu-PF obstructionism combined with MDC inexperience stalled the passage of laws made to diminish Zanu-PF control of state institutions. In the new government's first year, its security council met just once, though the old-guard JOC reportedly continued to hold weekly meetings without MDC-T attendance. Additionally, the police began targeting MDC legislators for arrest, in what has been understood as an attempt to clear away the MDC's small parliamentary majority.

It is these last challenges, in the security sector, that have experts most worried. The 2008 elections indebted Mugabe to a small cadre of securocrats who have become disproportionately powerful. A successful transition could cost them the wealth and assets they gained from farm invasions or, more recently, from Chinese government loans to the military and the private sale of diamonds from the Marange fields. It could also bring about international prosecutions for human rights violations. Analysts from Human Rights Watch, reporting on the methods of violence and repression securocrats use to protect these privileges, describe them as "effectively running a parallel government."

Some MDC-T activists and legislators fear that a securocrat-run military coup would follow an outright MDC election victory or the death of Mugabe, who is eighty-six years old and has consistently blocked attempts at security reform. The issue was too sensitive to be addressed during the SADC political mediations that brought about the GPA, but has become an item on the schedule of discussions to come. The time left to construct a solution, however, may be limited: increasing Zanu-PF factionalization in the transitional government indicates that the party would not remain united after Mugabe leaves government, while rank-and-file soldiers, who have begun to disobey orders and rioted in 2008 in response to cash shortages—some were later executed as punishment—largely exhibit approval of the economic benefits of power-sharing. Officers, in fear of possible mutiny, have restricted the distribution of weapons to much of the military.

Since 2008, the institutions that won the liberation war and have controlled independent Zimbabwe seem to be slowly breaking apart. The fault lines could foreshadow what a future Zimbabwean politics might look like, and how history will see Zimbabwe today. Tsvangirai, reflecting on Zimbabwean history and Mugabe's place in it, described his feelings in 2008 as "divided." "He is, on the one hand, the man who liberated our country from the white colonialists, and he is also the man who has murdered and repressed in a dictatorial manner. I say: he is the founding father of Zimbabwe, and the problem we have is to save the positive side of his contribution to this country, and to let history judge his negative contributions." The political struggles in Zimbabwe today are largely a debate not over how to put the country's inherited institutions back together, but one of tearing those positive contributions from the negative ones: the fight is about where, not if, they are going to break.

SOURCES

AIDS-Free World. "Electing to Rape: Sexual Terror in Mugabe's Zimbabwe." Myriad Editions: Dec 2009.

Alexander, Jocelyn. "'Squatters,' Veterans and the State in Zimbabwe." In *Zimbabwe's Unfinished Business: Rethinking Land, State and Nation in the Context of Crisis*, edited by Amanda Hammar, Brian Raftopoulos, and Stig Jensen, 83–117. Harare: Weaver Press, 2003.

———. "Zimbabwe Since 1997: Land & the Legacies of War," in *Turning Points in Africa Democracy*, edited by Abdul Raufu Mustapha and Lindsay Whitfield, 185–201. Rochester: James Currey, 2009.

Alexander, Jocelyn and JoAnn McGregor. "Veterans, Violence, and Nationalism in Zimbabwe." In *States of Violence: Politics, Youth, and Memory in Contemporary Africa,* edited by Edna G. Bay and Donald L. Donham, 215–236. Charlottesville: University of Virginia Press, 2006.

Alexander, Jocelyn and Blessing-Miles Tendi. "A Tale of Two Elections: Zimbabwe at the Polls in 2008." *Concerned African Scholars Bulletin* No. 80 (Winter 2008): Special Issue on Zimbabwe (II). Dec 13, 2008. http://concernedafricascholars.org/a-tale-of-two-elections [accessed June 10, 2010].

Amnesty International. "Zimbabwe: Time for Accountability." 2008.

Anderson, Jon Lee. "The Destroyer: Robert Mugabe and the destruction of Zimbabwe." *The New Yorker*. Oct 27, 2008. http://www.newyorker.com/reporting/2008/10/27/081027fa_fact_anderson?currentPage=all

Ansell, Amy E. "Operation 'Final Solution': Intimidation and Violence Against White Farmers in Post-Election Zimbabwe." *Concerned African Scholars Bulletin No. 79: Special Issue on Zimbabwe Crisis.* June 25, 2008. http://concernedafricascholars.org/operation-final-solution [accessed May 27, 2010].

BBC News. "Zimbabwe Voices: Mary." May 17, 2006. http://news.bbc.co.uk/2/hi/africa/4989930.stm [accessed May 5, 2010].

Bond, Patrick. "Competing Explanations of Zimbabwe's Long Economic Crisis." *Safundi: The Journal of South African and American Studies*, Vol. 8, No. 2 (April 2007): 149–181.

Bond, Patrick and Masimba Manyanya. *Zimbabwe's Plunge: Exhausted Nationalism, Neoliberalism, and the Struggle for Social Justice.* Trenton: Africa World Press, 2002.

Campbell, Horace. "The Zimbabwean Working Peoples: Between a Political Rock and an Economic Hard Place." *Concerned African Scholars Bulletin* No. 80. (Winter 2008): Special Issue on Zimbabwe (II). Dec 13, 2008. http://concernedafricascholars.org/the-zimbabwean-working-peoples [accessed June 7, 2010].

Catholic Commission for Justice and Peace in Zimbabwe and The Legal Resources Foundation. "Breaking the Silence, Building True Peace: A Report Into the Disturbances in Matabeleland and the Midlands, 1980–1988." 1997.

Chitiyo, George and Morgan Chitiyo. "The Impact of the HIV/AIDS and Economic Crises on Orphans and Other Vulnerable Children in Zimbabwe." *Childhood Education.* Vol. 85, No. 6 (Aug 15, 2009): 347–351.

Davies, Rob. "Memories of Underdevelopment: A Personal Interpretation of Zimbabwe's Economic Decline." In *Zimbabwe: Injustice and Political Reconciliation,* edited by Brian Raftopoulos and Tyrone Savage, 19–42. Cape Town: Institute for Justice and Reconciliation, 2004.

Doctors Without Borders. "FIELD NEWS: South Africa: MSF Provides Health Care to Zimbabwean Migrants." April 11, 2008.

——— "Month in Focus, February 2010: Haiti and Zimbabwe." Feb 23, 2010. http://www.msf.org/msfinternational/invoke.cfm?objectid=FA4A280B-15C5-F00A-25BA55B23C39BFAC&component=toolkit.article&method=full_html [accessed May 5, 2010].

——— "PRESS RELEASE: Forced Closure of Refugee Area Further Endangers Zimbabweans in South Africa." March 4, 2009. http://doctorswithoutborders.org/press/release.cfm?id=3450&cat=press-release.

——— "SPECIAL REPORT: No Refuge, Access Denied: Medical and Humanitarian Needs of Zimbabweans in South Africa." June 2, 2009. http://doctorswithoutborders.org/publications/article.cfm?id=3646&cat=special-report.

——— "Top Ten Humanitarian Crises of 2008: Health Crisis Sweeps Zimbabwe as Violence and Economic Collapse Spread." http://www.doctorswithoutborders.org/publications/topten/2008/story.cfm?id=3234 [accessed May 1, 2010].

Forced Migration Studies Progamme. "Report on Human Smuggling Across the South Africa/Zimbabwe Border." March 2009.

Forced Migration Studies Progamme and The Musina Legal Advice Office. "Special Report: Fact or Fiction? Zimbabwean Cross-Border Migration into South Africa." Sept 4, 2007.

Gourevitch, Philip. "Hanging On. *The New Yorker.* April 9, 2007. http://www.newyorker.com/talk/comment/2007/04/09/070409taco_talk_gourevitch [accessed June 25 2010].

——— "Struggles." *The New Yorker.* June 9, 2008. http://www.newyorker.com/talk/comment/2008/06/09/080609taco_talk_gourevitch#ixzz0eLgtRb3c.

——— "Wasteland." *The New Yorker.* June 3, 2002. http://www.newyorker.com/archive/2002/06/03/020603fa_fact1 [accessed May 25, 2010].

Hammar, Amanda. "In the name of sovereignty: Displacement and state-making in post-independence Zimbabwe." *Journal of Contemporary African Studies* 26:4 (2008): 417–434.

——— "Reflections on Displacement in Zimbabwe." *Concerned African Scholars Bulletin No. 80* (Winter 2008): Special Issue on Zimbabwe (II). http://concernedafricascholars.org/reflections-on-displacement-in-zimbabwe [accessed May 27, 2010].

Hammar, Amanda and Brian Raftopoulos. "Zimbabwe's Unfinished Business: Rethinking Land, State and Nation." In *Zimbabwe's Unfinished Business: Rethinking Land, State and Nation in the Context of Crisis*, edited by Amanda Hammar, Brian Raftopoulos, and Stig Jensen, 1–47. Harare: Weaver Press, 2003.

Hammar, Amanda, Stig Jenson, and Brian Raftopoulos. *Zimbabwe's Unfinished Business: Rethinking Land, State, and Nation in the Context of Crisis*. Harare: Weaver Press, 2003.

Hammer, Joshua. "Dictator Mugabe Makes a Comeback." *The New York Review of Books*. Oct 22, 2009. http://www.nybooks.com/articles/archives/2009/oct/22/dictator-mugabe-makes-a-comeback/?pagination=false [accessed June 8 2010].

——— "Letter from Zimbabwe: Big Man." *The New Yorker*. June 26, 2008.

——— "The Reign of Thuggery." *The New York Review of Books*. June 26, 2008. http://www.nybooks.com/articles/archives/2008/jun/26/the-reign-of-thuggery/?pagination=false [accessed June 25 2010].

——— "Scandal in Africa." *The New York Review of Books*. August 14, 2008. http://www.nybooks.com/articles/archives/2008/aug/14/scandal-in-africa/?pagination=false [accessed June 26, 2010].

Harvey, Charles. "The Limited Impact of Financial Sector Reforms in Zimbabwe." Institute of Development Studies: IDS Working Paper 36 (1996).

Human Rights Watch. "All Over Again: Human Rights Abuses and Flawed Electoral Conditions in Zimbabwe's Coming General Elections." Vol. 20, no. 2(A). March 2008.

——— "Bashing Dissent: Escalating Violence and State Repression in Zimbabwe." Vol. 19, No. 6(A). May 2007.

——— "'Bullets For Each of You': State-Sponsored Violence Since Zimbabwe's March 29 Elections." June 2008.

——— "False Dawn: The Zimbabwe Power-Sharing Government's Failure to Deliver Human Rights Improvements." August 2009.

——— "Fast Track Land Reform in Zimbabwe." Vol. 14, No. 1(A). March 2002.

——— "Neighbors in Need: Zimbabweans Seeking Refuge in South Africa." June 2008.

——— "No Bright Future: Government Failures, Human Rights Abuses and Squandered Progress in the Fight against AIDS in Zimbabwe." Vol. 18, No. 5(A). July 2006.

———— "No Healing Here: Violence, Discrimination, and Barriers to Health for Migrants in South Africa." Dec 2009.

———— "Not Eligible: The Politicization of Food in Zimbabwe." Vol. 15, No. 17(A). Oct 2003.

———— "'Our Hands Are Tied': Erosion of the Rule of Law in Zimbabwe." November 2008.

———— "Sleight of Hand: Repression of the Media and the Illusion of Reform in Zimbabwe." April 2010.

———— "'They Beat Me Like a Dog': Political Persecution of Opposition Activists and Supporters in Zimbabwe." August 2008.

International Crisis Group. "Ending Zimbabwe's Nightmare: A Possible Way Forward." Africa Briefing No. 56. December 16, 2008.

———— "Negotiating Zimbabwe's Transition." Africa Briefing No. 51. May 21, 2008.

———— "Zimbabwe: An End to the Stalemate?" Africa Report No. 122. March 5, 2007.

———— "Zimbabwe at the Crossroads: Transition or Conflict?" Africa Report No. 41. March 22, 2002.

———— "Zimbabwe: Danger and Opportunity." Africa Report No. 60. March 10, 2003.

———— "Zimbabwe: Engaging the Inclusive Government." Africa Briefing No. 59. April 20, 2009.

———— "Zimbabwe: Political and Security Challenges to the Transition." Africa Briefing No. 70. March 3, 2010.

———— "Zimbabwe: The Politics of National Liberation and International Division." Africa Report No. 52. Oct 17, 2002.

———— "Zimbabwe: Prospects From a Flawed Election." Africa Report No. 138. March 20, 2008.

International Organization for Migration. "IOM Labour Migration Centre Opens in Beitbridge." Aug 28, 2009. http://www.iom.int/jahia/Jahia/media/press-briefing-notes/pbnAF/cache/offonce?entryId=26035.

IRIN. "South Africa: Reintegrating Zimbabweans is a hard sell." Dec 3, 2009. http://www.irinnews.org/Report.aspx?ReportId=87312.

———— "Southern Africa: Zimbabweans test the definition of refugee." Dec 15, 2009. http://www.irinnews.org/Report.aspx?ReportId=87434.

———— "Zimbabwe: An Economy Running on Chickens." Dec 22, 2009. http://www.irinnews.org/Report.aspx?ReportId=87523 [accessed June 8, 2010].

————"Zimbabwe: Inflation at 6.5 Quindecillion Novemdecillion Percent." Jan 21, 2009. http://www.irinnews.org/Report.aspx?ReportId=82500 [accessed June 8, 2010].

Johnson, R.W. "Where Do We Go From Here?" *London Review of Books* Vol 30, No. 9. May 8, 2008.

Kaiser Family Foundation. "Global Challenges: HIV/AIDS Has Significantly Weakened Zimbabwe's Economy, Study Finds." June 19, 2006. http://www.kaisernetwork.org/daily_reports/rep_index.cfm?DR_ID=37969 [accessed May 4, 2010].

Kriger, Norma. "Can Elections End Mugabe's Dictatorship?" *Concerned African Scholars Bulletin* No. 79 (Spring 2008): Special Issue on Zimbabwe Crisis. June 2008. http://concernedafricascholars.org/bulletin/79/kriger [accessed June 23 2010].

————"Waiting for Power-Sharing: A False Promise?" *Concerned African Scholars Bulletin* No. 80 (Winter 2008): Special Issue on Zimbabwe (II). December 13, 2008. http://concernedafricascholars.org/waiting-for-power-sharing [accessed June 26, 2010].

McGregor, JoAnn. "The Politics of Disruption: War Veterans and the Local State in Zimbabwe." *African Affairs*. Vol. 101, No. 402 (2002): 9–37.

Meldrum, Andrew. "Zimbabwe's health-care system struggles on." *The Lancet*. Vol. 371 (March 29, 2008): 1059–1060.

Moyo, Bhekinkosi. "Zimbabwe Violence reminiscent of Gukurahundi massacres." *Mail & Guardian Online* (South Africa). June 16, 2008. http://www.thoughtleader.co.za/bhekinkosimoyo/2008/06/16/zimbabwe-violence-reminiscent-of-gukurahundi-massacres-believe-me-you-don%E2%80%99t-want-to-go-there%E2%80%80%A6/ [accessed Aug 13, 2010].

Muñoz, Sònia. "Zimbabwe's Export Performance: The Impact of the Parallel Market and Governance Factors." IMF Working Paper. January 2006.

Muzondidya, James. "From Buoyancy to Crisis, 1980–1997." In *Becoming Zimbabwe: A History from the Pre-Colonial Period to 2008* edited by Brian Raftopoulos and Alois Mlambo, 167–200. Harare: Weaver Press, 2009.

————"Survival Strategies Among Zimbabwean Migrants in South Africa." Conference paper, June 2008.

Office of the United Nations High Commissioner for Refugees (UNHCR). Border officials work overtime to help Zimbabwean asylum seekers. Nov 5, 2008. http://www.unhcr.org/4911c9b62.html.

Phimister, Ian and Brian Raftopoulos. "Mugabe, Mbeki and the Politics of Anti-Imperialism." *Review of African Political Economy*. Vol. 31, No. 101: An African Scramble? (Sept, 2004): 385–400.

Polzer, Tara. "Regularizing Zimbabwean Migration to South Africa." University of

Witwatersrand, Forced Migration Studies Program. May 2009.

Raftopoulos, Brian. "The Crisis in Zimbabwe, 1998–2008," in *Becoming Zimbabwe: A History from the Pre-Colonial Period to 2008* edited by Brian Raftopoulos and Alois Mlambo, 201–232. Harare: Weaver Press, 2009.

————— "Reflections on Opposition Politics in Zimbabwe: The Politics of the Movement for Democratic Change (MDC)," in *Zimbabwe in Crisis: The International Response and the Space of Silence*, edited by Ranka Primorac and Stephen Chan, 125–152. London: Routledge, 2007.

Raftopoulos, Brian and Ian Phimister. "Zimbabwe Now: The Political Economy of Crisis and Coercion." *Historical Materialism*, Vol. 12, No. 4 (2004), Pp. 355-382.

Rhodes, Tom. "Bad to Worse in Zimbabwe." The Committee to Protect Journalists. June 23, 2008.

Rutherford, Blair. "An Unsettled Belonging: Zimbabwean farm workers in Limpopo Province, South Africa." *Journal of Contemporary African Studies* 26:4 (Oct 2008): 401–415.

————— "Zimbabwean Land Redistribution!: Globalization and Neoliberal Narratives and Transnational Connections," in *Neoliberalism and Globalizatin in Africa: Contestations on the Embattled Continent*, edited by Joseph Mensah, 203–220. New York: Palgrave Macmillan, 2008.

————— "Zimbabweans Living in the South African Border-Zone: Negotiating, Suffering, and Surviving." *Concerned African Scholars Bulletin No. 80: Special Issue on Zimbabwe (II)*. Winter 2008.

Rutherford, Blair and Lincoln Addison. "Zimbabwean Farm Workers in Northern South Africa." *Review of African Political Economy* 34:114 (2007).

Sachikonye, Lloyd M. "The Situation of Farm Workers after Land Reform in Zimbabwe." Farm Community Trust of Zimbabwe. March 2003.

————— "Structural Adjustment, State and Organized Labor in Zimbabwe," in *Social Change and Economic Reform in Africa*, edited by Peter Gibbon, 244–269. Uppsala: Nordiska Afrikainstitutet, The Scandinavian Institute of African Studies, 1993.

Scarnecchia, Timothy. "Editorial: In the Shadow of Gukurahundi." *Concerned African Citizen Bulletin* No. 80 (Winter 2008): Special Issue on Zimbabwe (II). December 13, 2008. http://concernedafricascholars.org/in-the-shadow-of-gukurahundi [accessed June 25, 2010].

Scarnecchia, Timothy and Wendy Urban-Mead. "ACAS Bulletin 80: Special Issue on Zimbabwe 2." *ACAS Bulletin*. No 80: Special Issue on Zimbabwe II (Winter 2008). http://concernedafricascholars.org/bulletin/80 [accessed June 8 2010].

Smith, David. "IMF Provides $510M Loan For Zimbabwe Amid Worries That Mugabe

Will Grab Funds." *The Guardian.* Sept 4, 2009. http://www.guardian.co.uk/world/2009/sep/04/zimbabwe-imf-loan-mdc-mugabe [accessed June 8, 2010].

Solidarity Peace Trust. "A Difficult Dialogue: Zimbabwe-South African Economic Relations Since 2000." Oct 23, 2007.

———— "Desperately Seeking Sanity: What Prospects For a New Beginning in Zimbabwe?" July 29, 2008.

———— "Destructive Engagement: Violence, Mediation and Politics in Zimbabwe." July 10, 2007.

———— "'Gone to Egoli': Economic Survival Strategies in Matabeleland." June 30, 2009.

———— "No War in Zimbabwe: An Account of the Exodus of a Nation's People." Nov 2004.

———— "Subverting Justice: The Role of the Judiciary in Denying the Will of the Zimbabwean Electorate Since 2000." March 2005.

The Southern African Migration Project. "The Perfect Storm: The Realities of Xenophobia in Contemporary South Africa." 2008.

Stavropoulou, Jòanna. "Listening to HIV+ Kids in Zimbabwe." *MSF Field News.* Oct 24, 2008. http://www.doctorswithoutborders.org/news/article.cfm?id=3155 [accessed May 5, 2010].

Teslik, Lee Hudson. "Zimbabwe's Economic Implosion." Council on Foreign Relations— Analysis Brief. Sept. 18, 2007. http://www.cfr.org/publication/14215/zimbabwes_economic_implosion.html?breadcrumb=/region/publication_list%3Fid%3D158%26page%3D2 [accessed June 8, 2010].

Thompson, Carol. "Globalizing Land and Food in Zimbabwe: Implications for Southern Africa." *African Studies Quarterly* Vol. 7, No. 2&3 (2003). http://www.africa.ufl.edu/asq/v7/v7i2a10.htm [accessed June 7, 2010].

Todd, Charles, Sunanda Ray, Farai Madzimbamuto, and David Sanders. "What is the way forward for health in Zimbabwe?" *The Lancet.* Vol. 375 (February 13, 2010): 606–609.

UNAIDS. "Evidence for HIV Decline in Zimbabwe: A Comprehensive Review of the Epidemiological Data." November 2005.

United Kingdom Border Agency Country of Origin Information Service. "Country of Origin Information Report: Zimbabwe." Dec 23, 2009.

United Nations Office for the Coordination of Humanitarian Affairs (OCHA). "Zimbabwe 2010 Consolidated Appeal."

United States Department of State. "2008 Human Rights Report: Zimbabwe." Feb 25, 2009. http://www.state.gov/g/drl/rls/hrrpt/2008/af/119032.htm [accessed May 5, 2010].

———— *Trafficking in Persons Report 2009 - Zimbabwe*, June 16, 2009, available at: http://www.unhcr.org/refworld/docid/4a42147f1a.html [accessed February 2, 2010].

World Health Organization. "World Health Statistics 2009." 2009.

Zimbabwe Human Rights NGO Forum and The Justice for Agriculture Trust in Zimbabwe. "Adding insult to injury: A Preliminary Report on Human Rights Violations on Commercial Farms, 2000 to 2005." June 2007.

Zimbabwe Reporter [staff]. "How to Stop Anti-Zim Xenophobic Attacks After World Cup." May 21, 2010. http://zimbabwereporter.com/morenews/1022.html [Accessed June 5, 2010].

The *Zimbabwean* [staff]. "Bill Watch 22/2010 – 8th June [Parliament to Meet then Adjourn for Constitution Outreach]." June 8, 2010. http://www.thezimbabwean.co.uk/index. php?option=com_content&view=article&id=31682:bill-watch-222010-8th-june-parliament-to-meet-then-adjourn-forconstitution-outreach&catid=52&Itemid=32 [accessed June 26, 2010].

The VOICE OF WITNESS SERIES

Voice of Witness is a nonprofit book series, published by McSweeney's, that empowers those most closely affected by contemporary social injustice. Using oral history as a foundation, the series depicts human rights crises in the United States and around the world. There are currently five books in the series, including:

SURVIVING JUSTICE
America's Wrongfully Convicted and Exonerated
Edited by Lola Vollen and Dave Eggers   Foreword by Scott Turow

These oral histories prove that the problem of wrongful conviction is far-reaching and very real. Through a series of all-too-common circumstances— eyewitness misidentification, inept defense lawyers, coercive interrogation—the lives of these men and women of all different backgrounds were irreversibly disrupted. In *Surviving Justice: America's Wrongfully Convicted and Exonerated*, thirteen exonerees describe their experiences—the events that led to their convictions, their years in prison, and the process of adjusting to their new lives outside.

ISBN: 978-1-934781-25-8   469 pages   Paperback

VOICES FROM THE STORM
The People of New Orleans on Hurricane Katrina and Its Aftermath
Edited by Chris Ying and Lola Vollen

The second book in the McSweeney's Voice of Witness series, *Voices from the Storm* is a chronological account of the worst natural disaster in modern American history. Thirteen New Orleanians describe the days leading up to Hurricane Katrina, the storm itself, and the harrowing confusion of the days and months afterward. Their stories weave and intersect, ultimately creating an eye-opening portrait of courage in the face of terror, and of hope amidst nearly complete devastation.

ISBN: 978-1-932416-68-8   320 pages   Paperback

UNDERGROUND AMERICA
Narratives of Undocumented Lives
Edited by Peter Orner   Foreword by Luis Alberto Urrea

They arrive from around the world for countless reasons. Many come simply to make a living. Others are fleeing persecution in their native countries. But by living and working in the U.S. without legal status, millions of immigrants risk deportation and imprisonment. They are living underground, with little protection from exploitation at the hands of human smugglers, employers, or law enforcement. *Underground America* presents the remarkable oral histories of men and women struggling to carve a life for themselves in the U.S.

ISBN: 978-1-934781-15-9   379 pages   Hardcover and paperback

OUT OF EXILE
The Abducted and Displaced People of Sudan
Edited by Craig Walzer
Additional interviews and an introduction by Dave Eggers
and Valentino Achak Deng

Millions of people have fled from conflicts and persecution in all parts of Sudan, and many thousands more have been enslaved as human spoils of war. In this book, refugees and abductees recount their escapes from the wars in Darfur and South Sudan, from political and religious persecution, and from abduction by militias. They tell of life before the war, and of the hope that they might someday find peace again.

ISBN: 978-1-934781-13-5   465 pages   Hardcover and paperback

Thanks to the generosity and assistance of many donors and volunteers, Voice of Witness is currently at work collecting oral histories for a variety of new projects around the world. For more information about the series, or to find out how you can help or donate to the cause, visit the Voice of Witness website:

VOICEOFWITNESS.ORG

ACKNOWLEDGEMENTS

Thank you: Jordan Bass, Adam Krefman, Juliet Litman, mimi lok, Brian McMullen, Andrea Mudd, Juliana Sloane, Chris Ying.

We acknowledge the generous support of the Multi-Agency Grants Initiative (MAGI): the Humanist Institute for Co-operation with Developing Countries (HIVOS), Atlantic Philanthropies, Uthando, and the Ford Foundation. We would also like to thank the San Francisco State Creative Writing Program, and the University of Montana Creative Program.

While many people have given generous assistance, the editors take full responsibility for the contents of this collection. A great many of the individuals we would like to thank must remain anonymous. We are extremely grateful to them and to: Sagal Abshir, Tom Barbash, heeten bhagat, Themba Butao, Stephanie Charters, Bev Clark, Colleen Crawford Cousins, Katie Crouch, Phoebe Orner Crouch, Colleen Dawson, Shari Eppel, Shereen Essof, Azola Goqwana, Deena Hurwitz, Dan Jawitz, David Krause, Shelley, Hugh Lewin, Alex Magaisa, Patience Mandishona, Betty Makoni, Jacob Matakanye (Musina Legal Advice Office), Jaykumar Menon, Canaan Mhlanga, Nakai, Yogesh Nathoo and Ross Parsons, Farai and Ramai, Bridget and Lunhar Pickering, Rhoda and Dan Pierce, David Krause, Emilia Potenza and Lael Bethlehem, Robert Preskill, "Themba and Pamela," Tony, Bev and Kate Reeler, Cathy Rose, Sarah Rowe, Jane Shepherd, Irene Staunton and Murray McCartney, Tom Barbash, Lesley Ruda, Sally-Jean Shackleton (Women'sNet), Gabriel Shumba, Sabelo Sibanda, Martha Tholanah, C.T., Nkhumi Tshivhase, Emily Wellman, Lawyers for Human Rights.

Although the information contained in the section introductions, the footnotes, the glossary, and the appendices has all been fact-checked to the best of our ability, please be aware that the situation in Zimbabwe and among the diaspora changes very quickly. As for Zimbabwe's history and politics, much of it, like all history and politics, is often subject to individual interpretation. Any and all errors are the responsibility of the editors and not those who graciously assisted the making of this book.

About THE EDITORS

PETER ORNER is the author of *The Second Coming of Mavala Shikongo*—
a novel set in Namibia and a finalist for the *Los Angeles Times* Book Award—
and *Esther Stories*, finalist for the PEN/Hemingway Award. He is also the
editor of *Underground America*, an oral history of undocumented people living in the U.S. also published by McSweeney's and Voice of Witness. A
2006 Guggenheim Fellow, Orner is an associate professor at San Francisco
State University.

Born in Zambia and raised in Zimbabwe, ANNIE HOLMES is a doc-
umentary filmmaker who has worked extensively in television and film
for many years. She has also published short fiction widely, both in the
U.S. and Africa, as well as a memoir about Zimbabwean independence
entitled *Good Red*. Holmes currently directs communications for an international feminist network.